THE HEROIC LEGEND OF
ARSLAN

STORY BY
YOSHIKI TANAKA

MANGA BY
HIROMU ARAKAWA

3

THE HEROIC LEGEND OF ARSLAN

TABLE OF CONTENTS

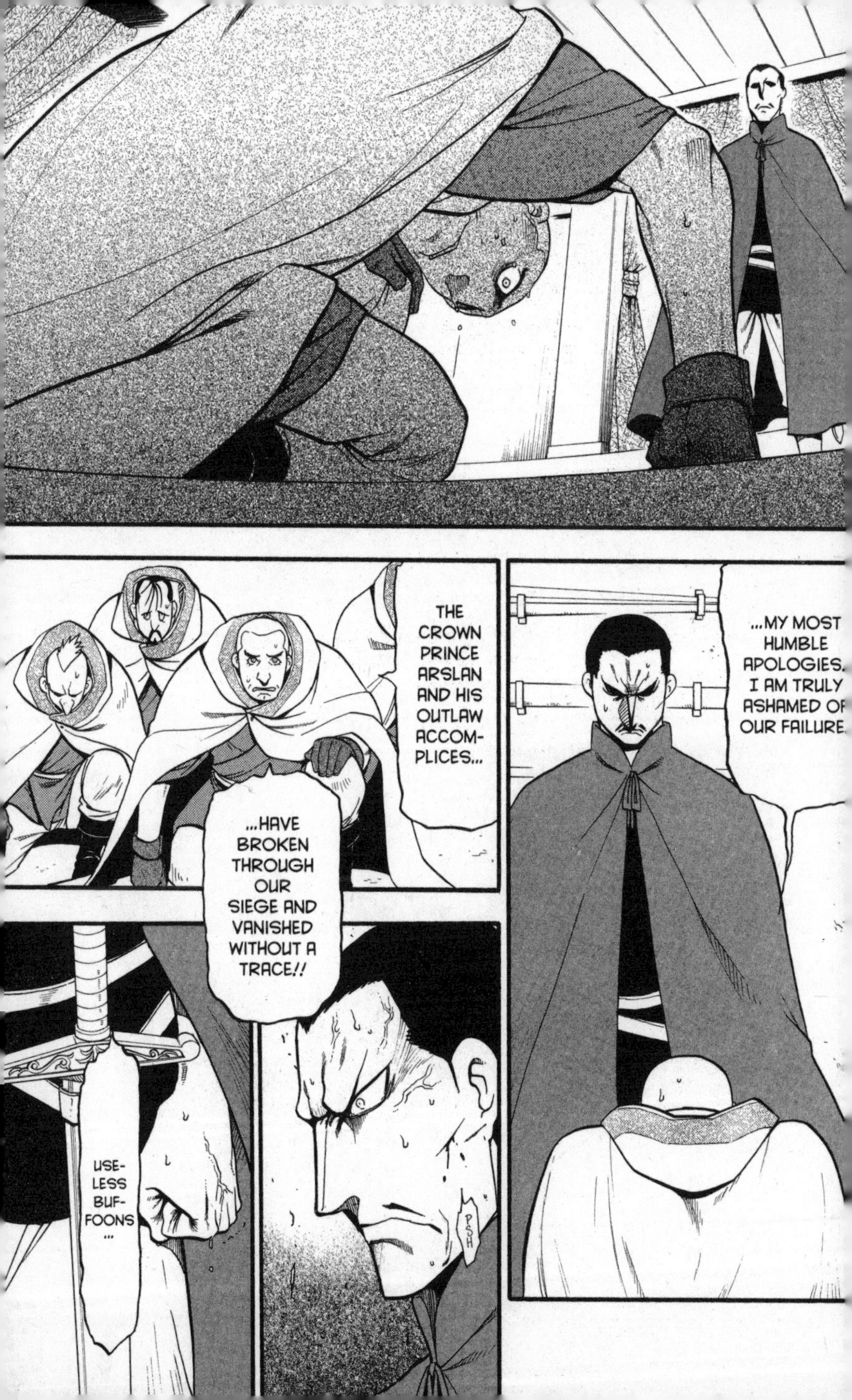
...MY MOST HUMBLE APOLOGIES. I AM TRULY ASHAMED OF OUR FAILURE.
THE CROWN PRINCE ARSLAN AND HIS OUTLAW ACCOMPLICES...
...HAVE BROKEN THROUGH OUR SIEGE AND VANISHED WITHOUT A TRACE!!
PSH
USE-LESS BUF-FOONS...

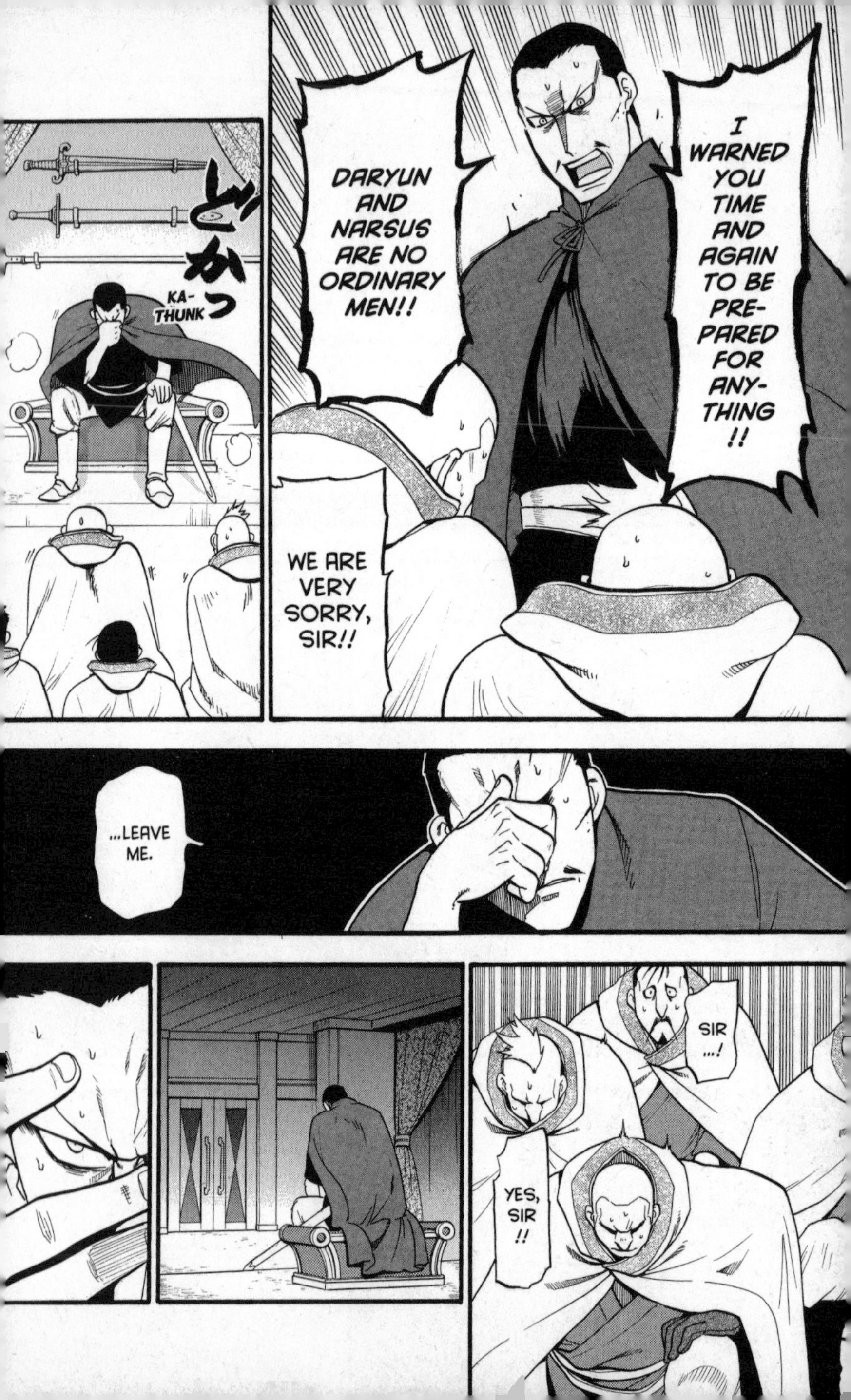
I WARNED YOU TIME AND AGAIN TO BE PRE-PARED FOR ANY-THING!!
DARYUN AND NARSUS ARE NO ORDINARY MEN!!
WE ARE VERY SORRY, SIR!!
どかっ
KA-THUNK
...LEAVE ME.
SIR ...!
YES, SIR!!

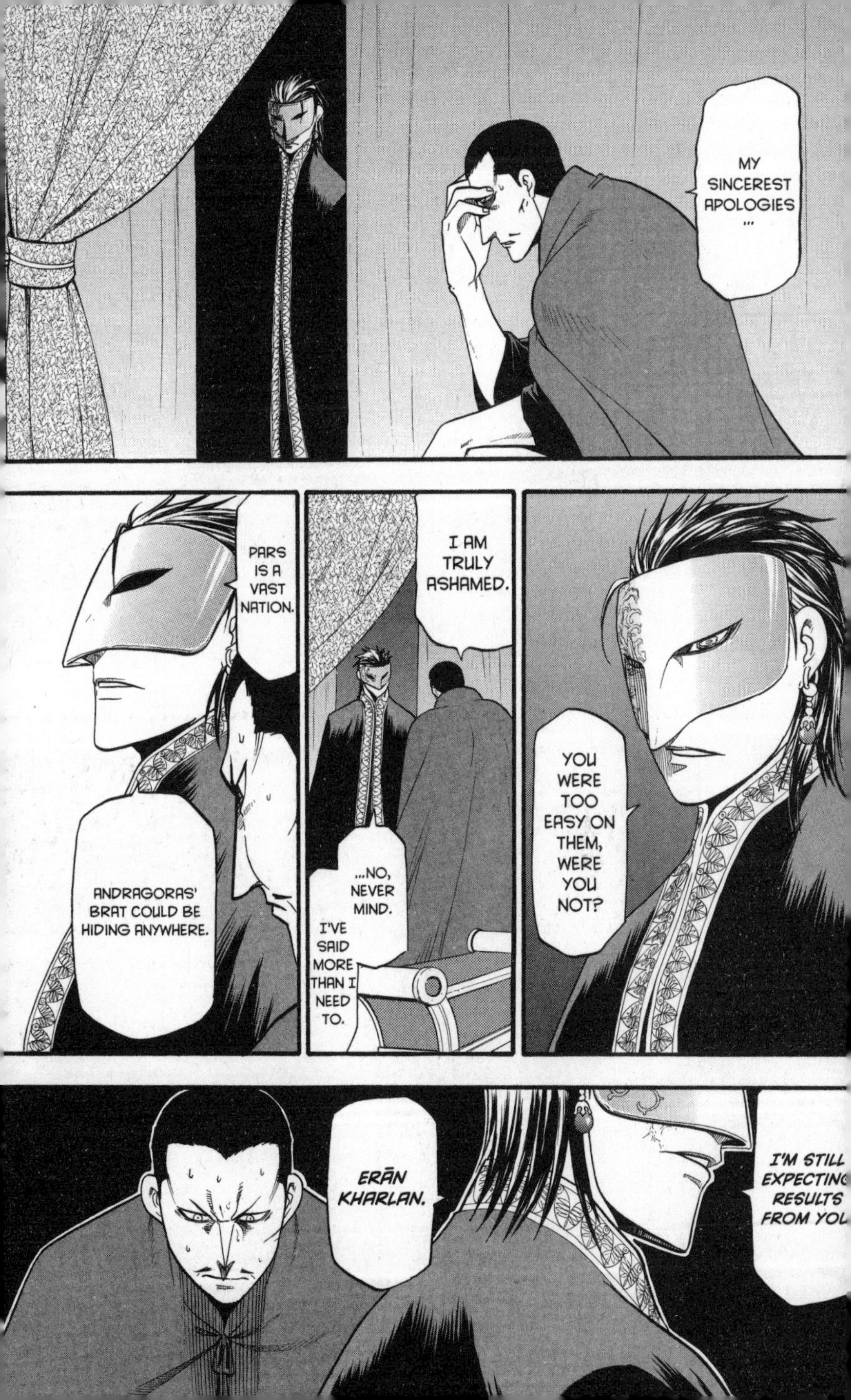
MY SINCEREST APOLOGIES ...
YOU WERE TOO EASY ON THEM, WERE YOU NOT?
I AM TRULY ASHAMED.
...NO, NEVER MIND.
I'VE SAID MORE THAN I NEED TO.
PARS IS A VAST NATION.
ANDRAGORAS' BRAT COULD BE HIDING ANYWHERE.
I'M STILL EXPECTING RESULTS FROM YOU
ERĀN KHARLAN.

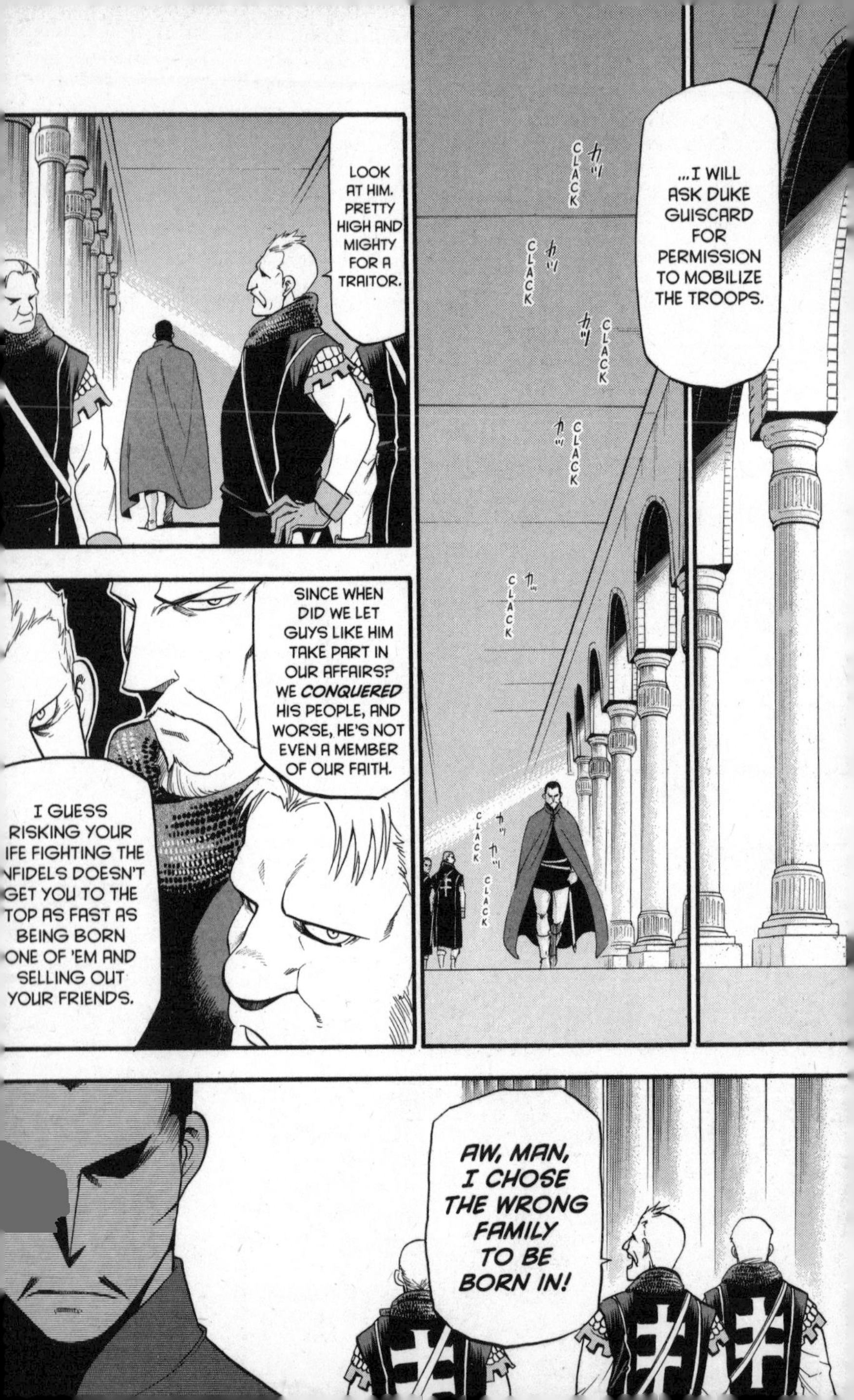

...I WILL ASK DUKE GUISCARD FOR PERMISSION TO MOBILIZE THE TROOPS.
カッ CLACK
カッ CLACK
カッ CLACK
カッ CLACK
カッ CLACK
カッ CLACK
カッ CLACK
LOOK AT HIM. PRETTY HIGH AND MIGHTY FOR A TRAITOR.
SINCE WHEN DID WE LET GUYS LIKE HIM TAKE PART IN OUR AFFAIRS? WE *CONQUERED* HIS PEOPLE, AND WORSE, HE'S NOT EVEN A MEMBER OF OUR FAITH.
I GUESS RISKING YOUR IFE FIGHTING THE NFIDELS DOESN'T GET YOU TO THE TOP AS FAST AS BEING BORN ONE OF 'EM AND SELLING OUT YOUR FRIENDS.
AW, MAN, I CHOSE THE WRONG FAMILY TO BE BORN IN!

CHAPTER 11: KHARLAN GOES TO BATTLE

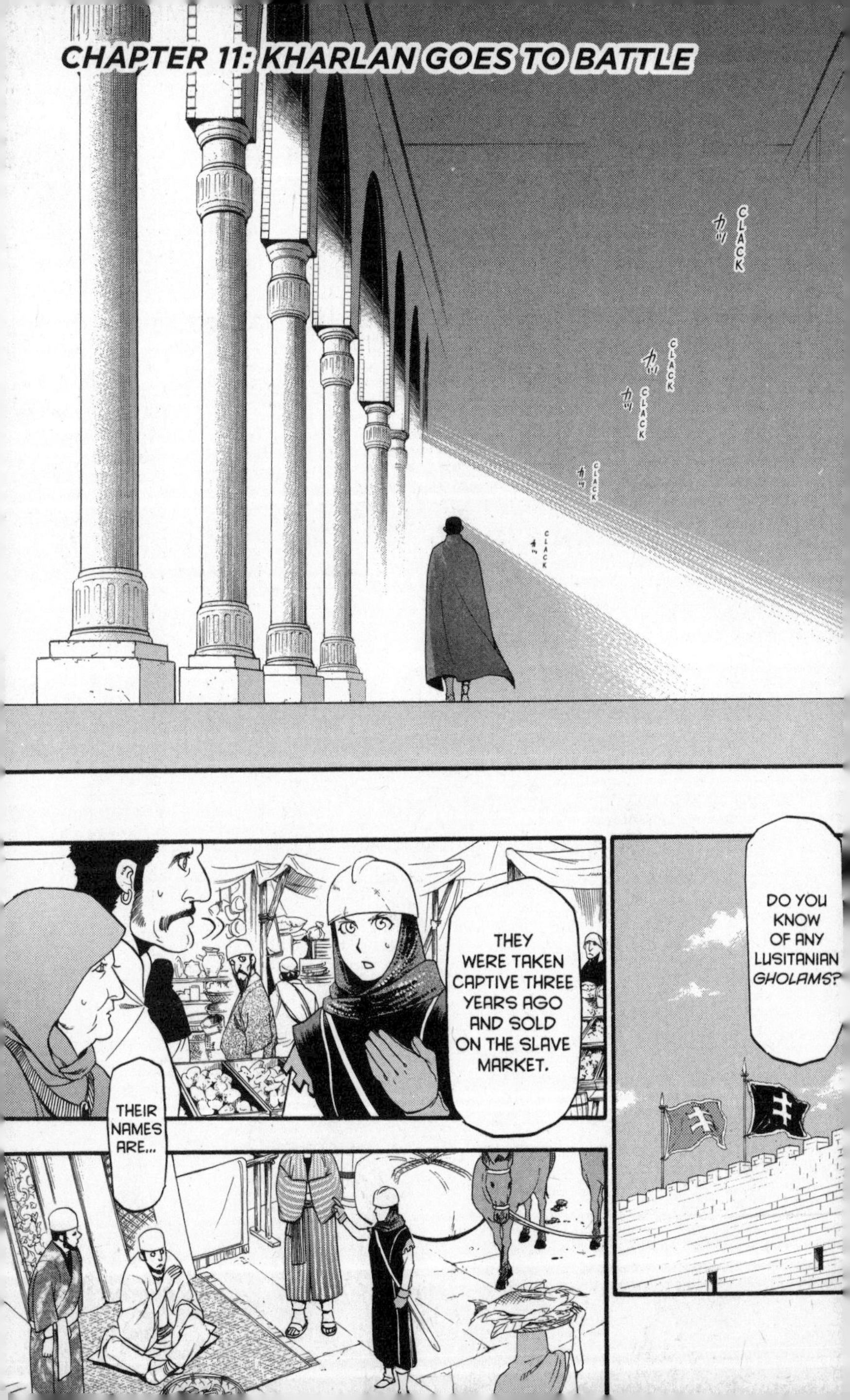
CLACK
CLACK
CLACK
CLACK
CLACK
DO YOU KNOW OF ANY LUSITANIAN *GHOLAMS*?
THEY WERE TAKEN CAPTIVE THREE YEARS AGO AND SOLD ON THE SLAVE MARKET.
THEIR NAMES ARE...

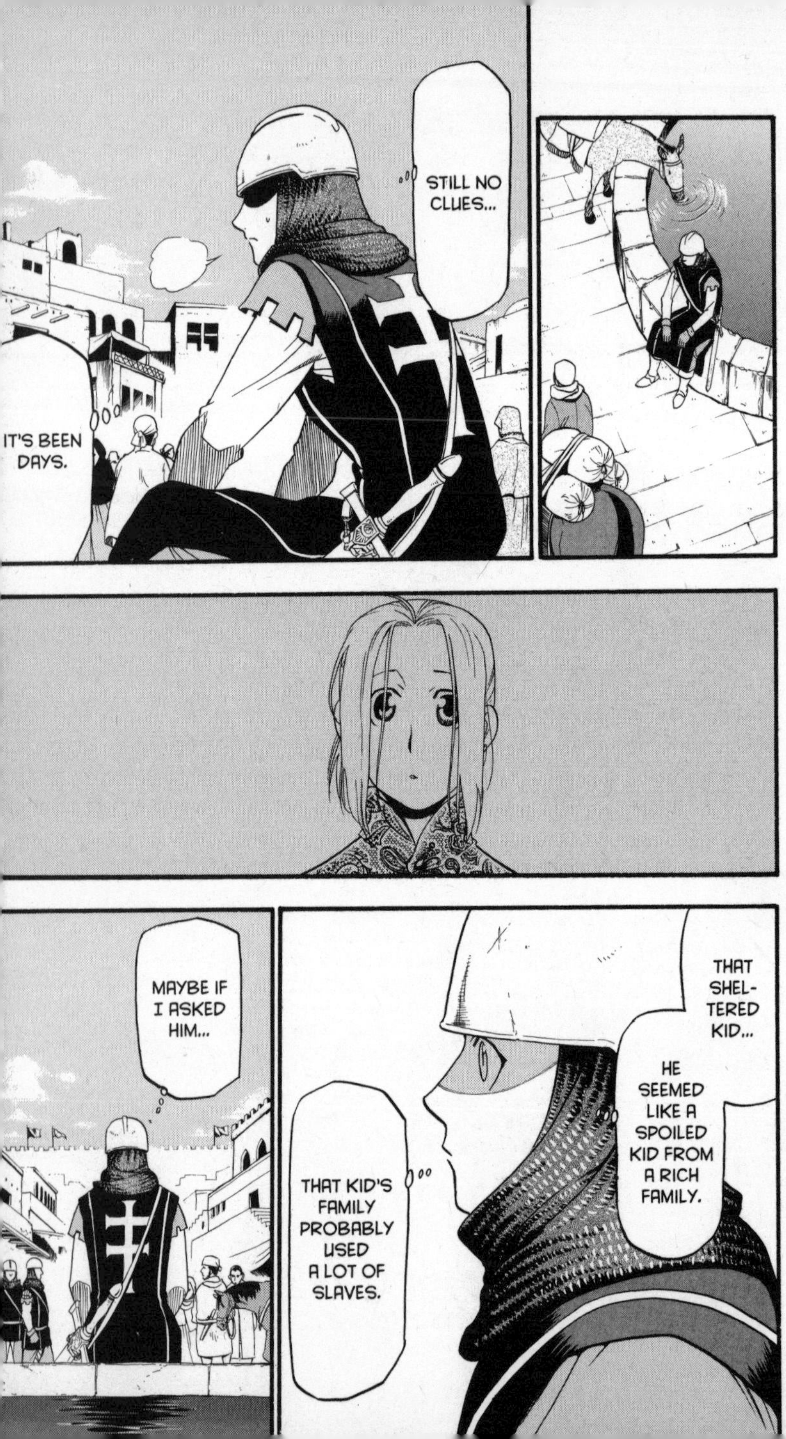
STILL NO CLUES...
IT'S BEEN DAYS.
THAT SHEL-TERED KID...
HE SEEMED LIKE A SPOILED KID FROM A RICH FAMILY.
THAT KID'S FAMILY PROBABLY USED A LOT OF SLAVES.
MAYBE IF I ASKED HIM...

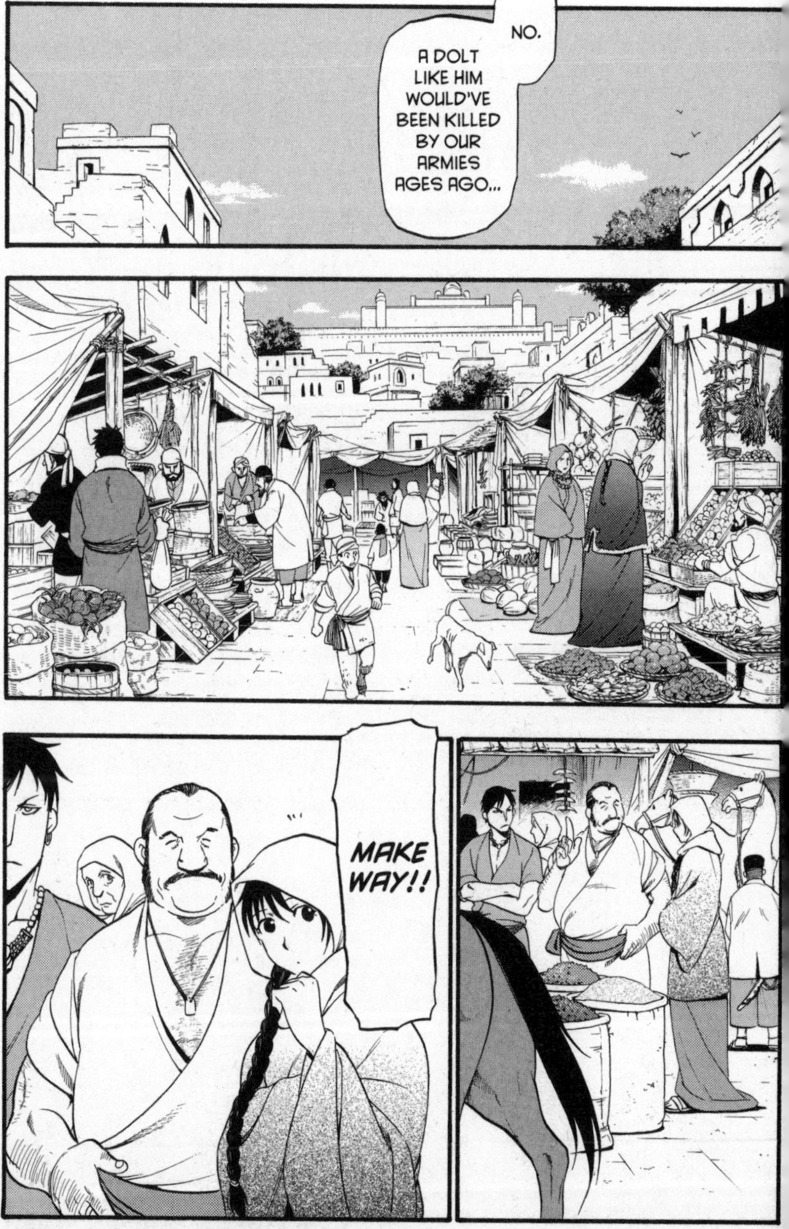
NO.
A DOLT LIKE HIM WOULD'VE BEEN KILLED BY OUR ARMIES AGES AGO...
MAKE WAY!!

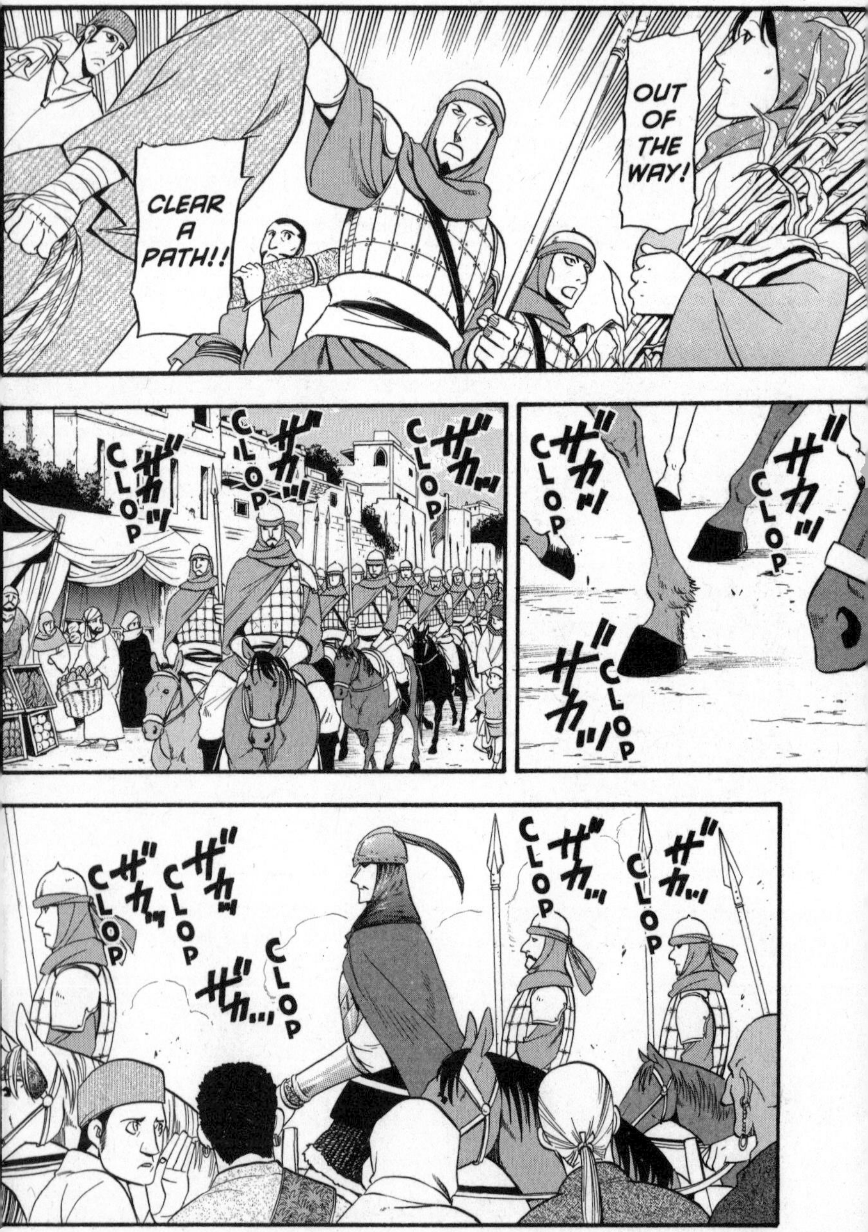
OUT OF THE WAY!
CLEAR A PATH!!
ザカッ
CLOP
ザカッ
CLOP
ザカッ
CLOP
ザカッ
CLOP
ザカッ
CLOP
ザカッ
CLOP
ザカッ
CLOP
ザカッ
CLOP
ザカッ
CLOP
ザカッ
CLOP
ザカッ
CLOP

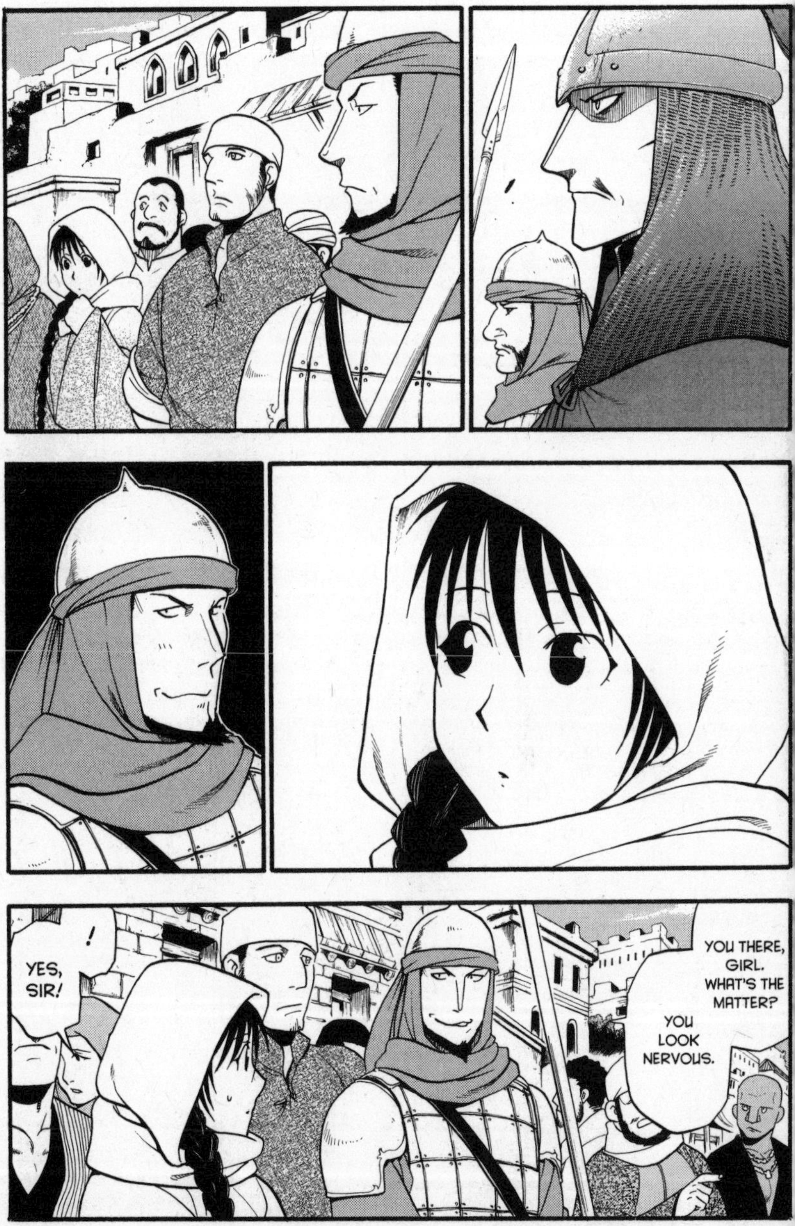
YOU THERE, GIRL. WHAT'S THE MATTER?
YOU LOOK NERVOUS.
!
YES, SIR!

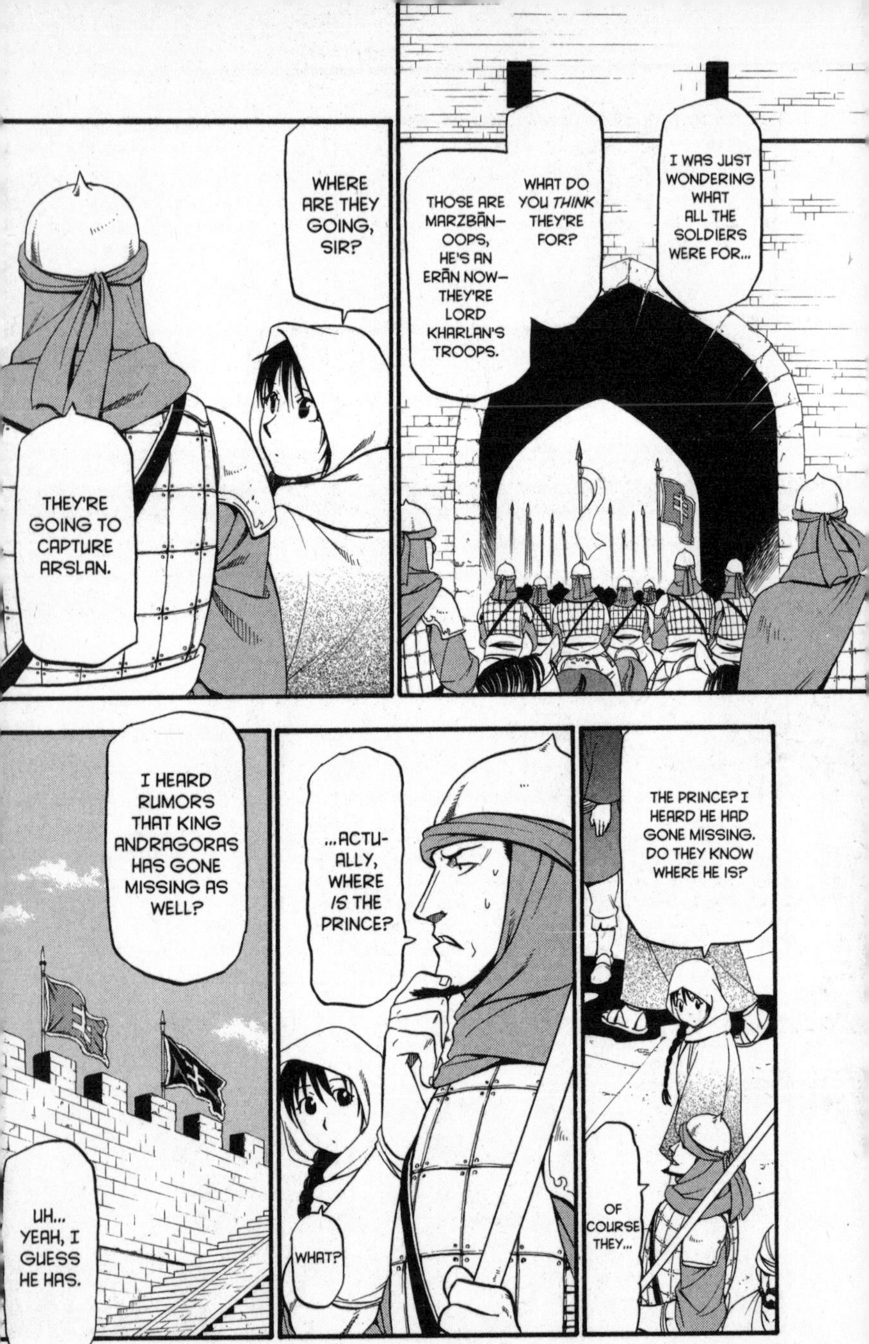
I WAS JUST WONDERING WHAT ALL THE SOLDIERS WERE FOR...
WHAT DO YOU *THINK* THEY'RE FOR?
THOSE ARE MARZBĀN—OOPS, HE'S AN ERĀN NOW—THEY'RE LORD KHARLAN'S TROOPS.
WHERE ARE THEY GOING, SIR?
THEY'RE GOING TO CAPTURE ARSLAN.
THE PRINCE? I HEARD HE HAD GONE MISSING. DO THEY KNOW WHERE HE IS?
OF COURSE THEY...
...ACTU-ALLY, WHERE *IS* THE PRINCE?
WHAT?
I HEARD RUMORS THAT KING ANDRAGORAS HAS GONE MISSING AS WELL?
UH... YEAH, I GUESS HE HAS.

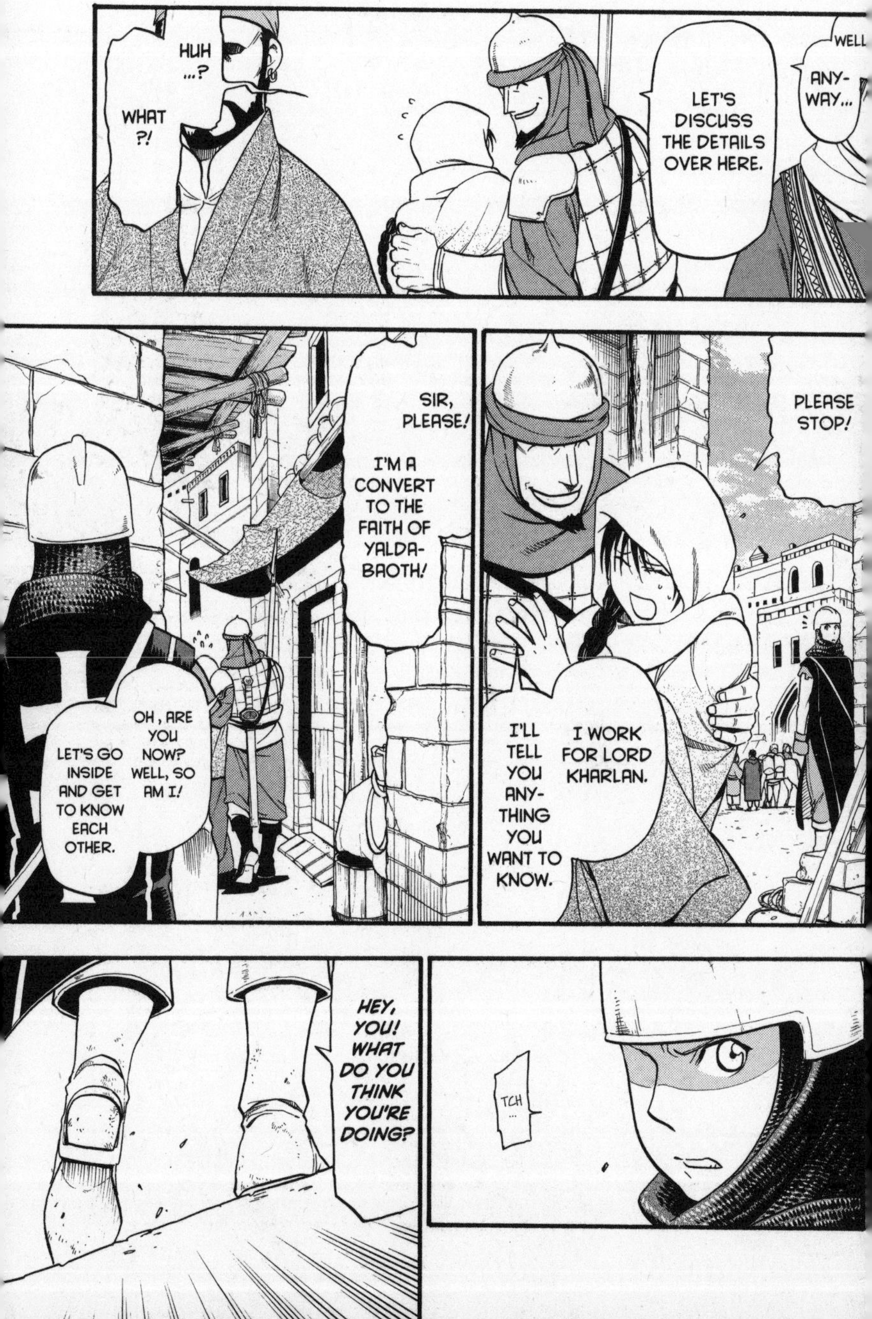
WELL ANYWAY...
LET'S DISCUSS THE DETAILS OVER HERE.
HUH ...?
WHAT ?!
PLEASE STOP!
I WORK FOR LORD KHARLAN.
I'LL TELL YOU ANYTHING YOU WANT TO KNOW.
SIR, PLEASE!
I'M A CONVERT TO THE FAITH OF YALDABAOTH!
OH, ARE YOU NOW? WELL, SO AM I!
LET'S GO INSIDE AND GET TO KNOW EACH OTHER.
TCH ...
HEY, YOU! WHAT DO YOU THINK YOU'RE DOING?

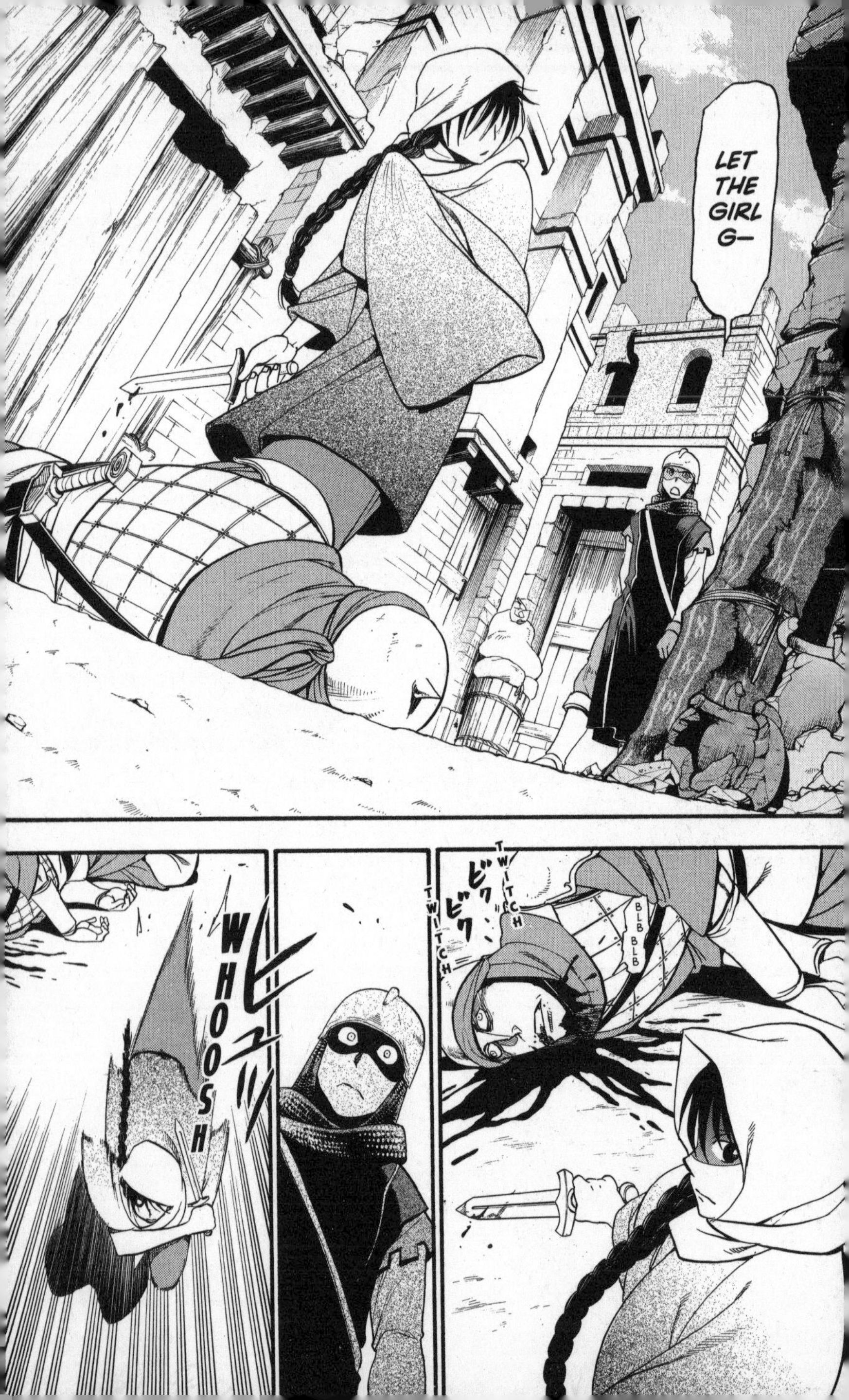
LET THE GIRL G—
TWITCH
ビク
ビク
TWITCH
BLB BLB
WHOOOSH

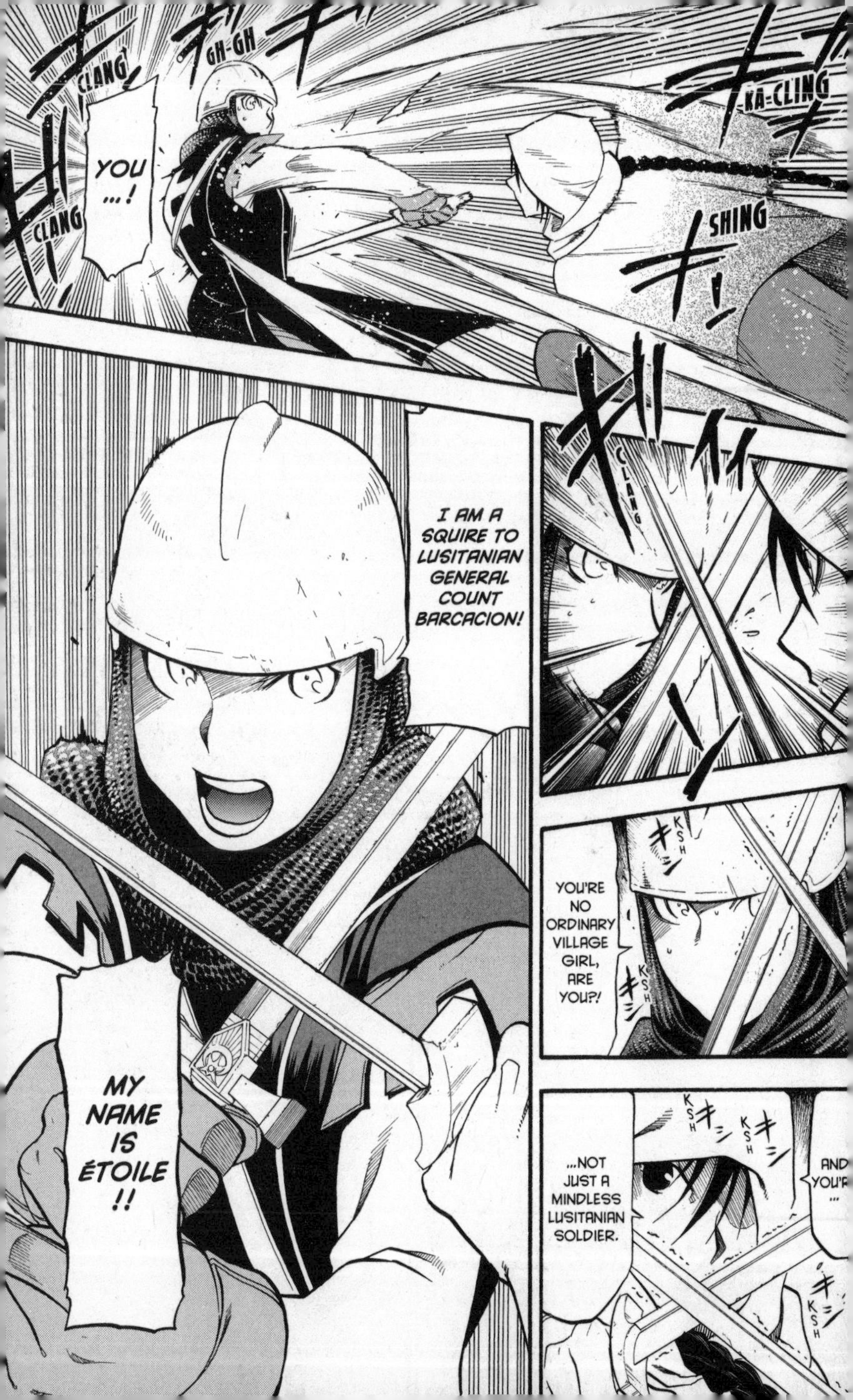
KA-CLING
SHING
GH-GH
CLANG
YOU ...!
CLANG
CLANG
KSH
YOU'RE NO ORDINARY VILLAGE GIRL, ARE YOU?!
KSH
KSH
KSH
AND YOU'R ...
...NOT JUST A MINDLESS LUSITANIAN SOLDIER.
KSH
I AM A SQUIRE TO LUSITANIAN GENERAL COUNT BARCACION!
MY NAME IS ÉTOILE !!

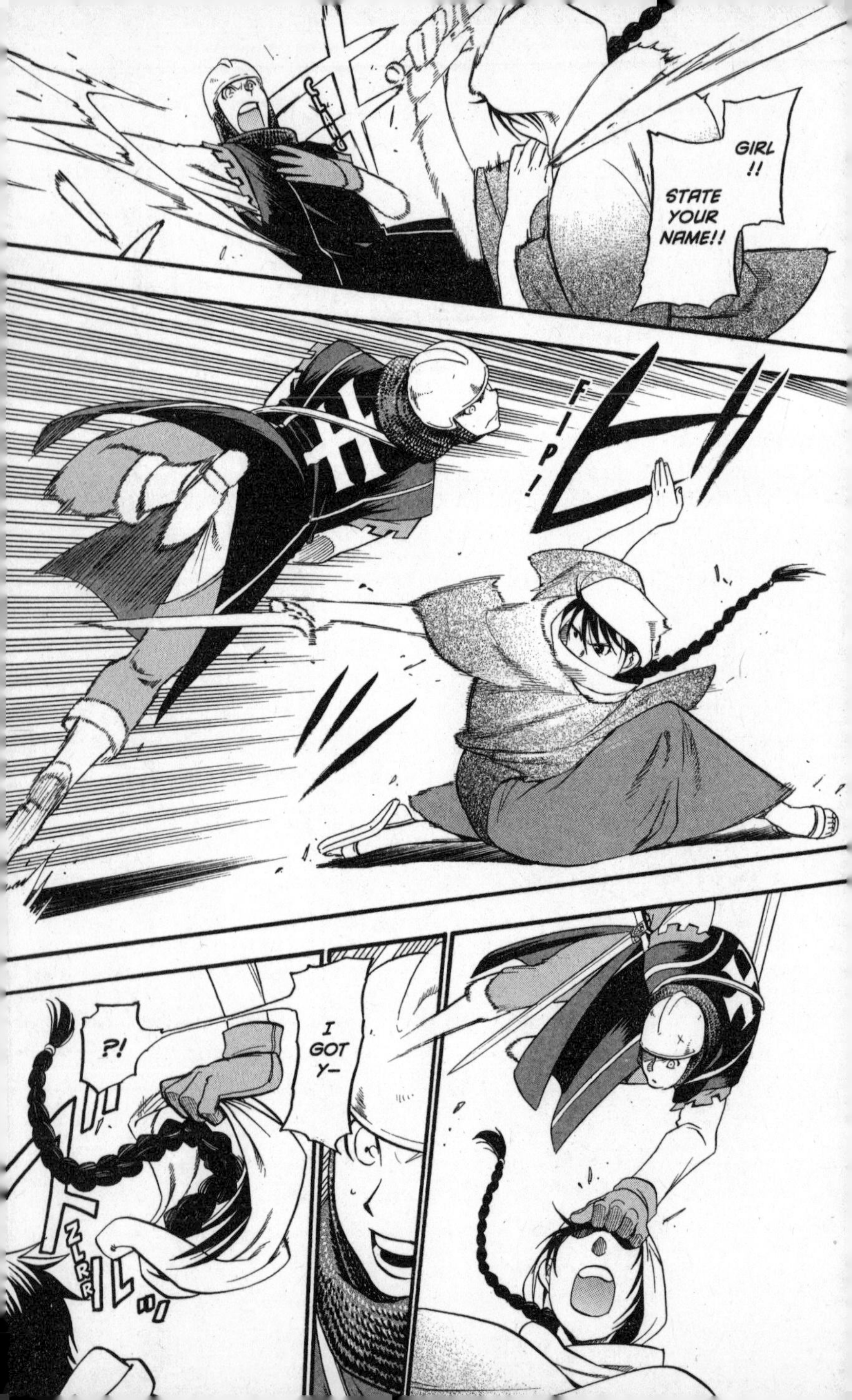
GIRL !!
STATE YOUR NAME!!
FLIP!
I GOT Y—
?!
ZLRR

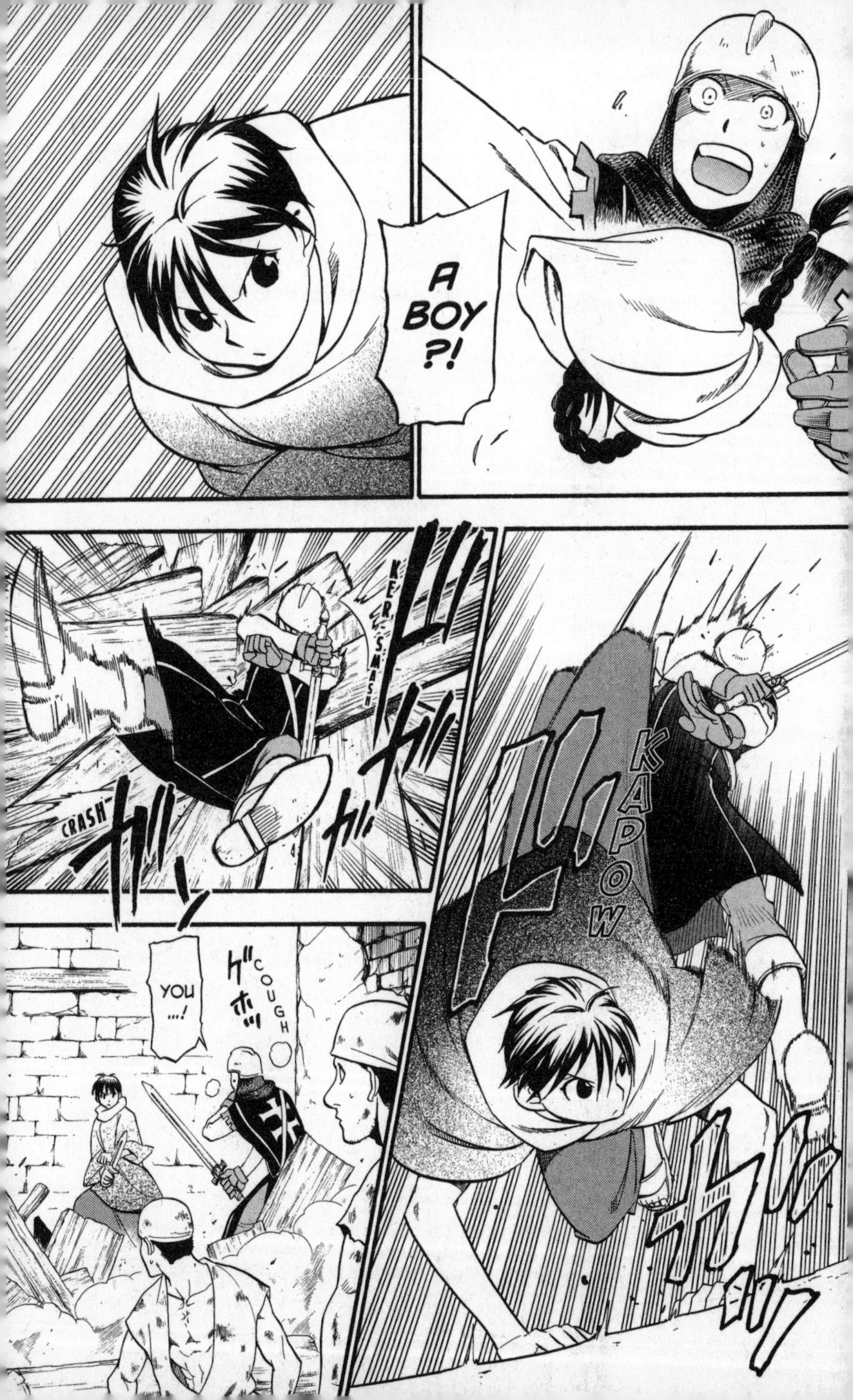
A BOY?!
KAPOW
KER-SMASH
CRASH
YOU...!
COUGH

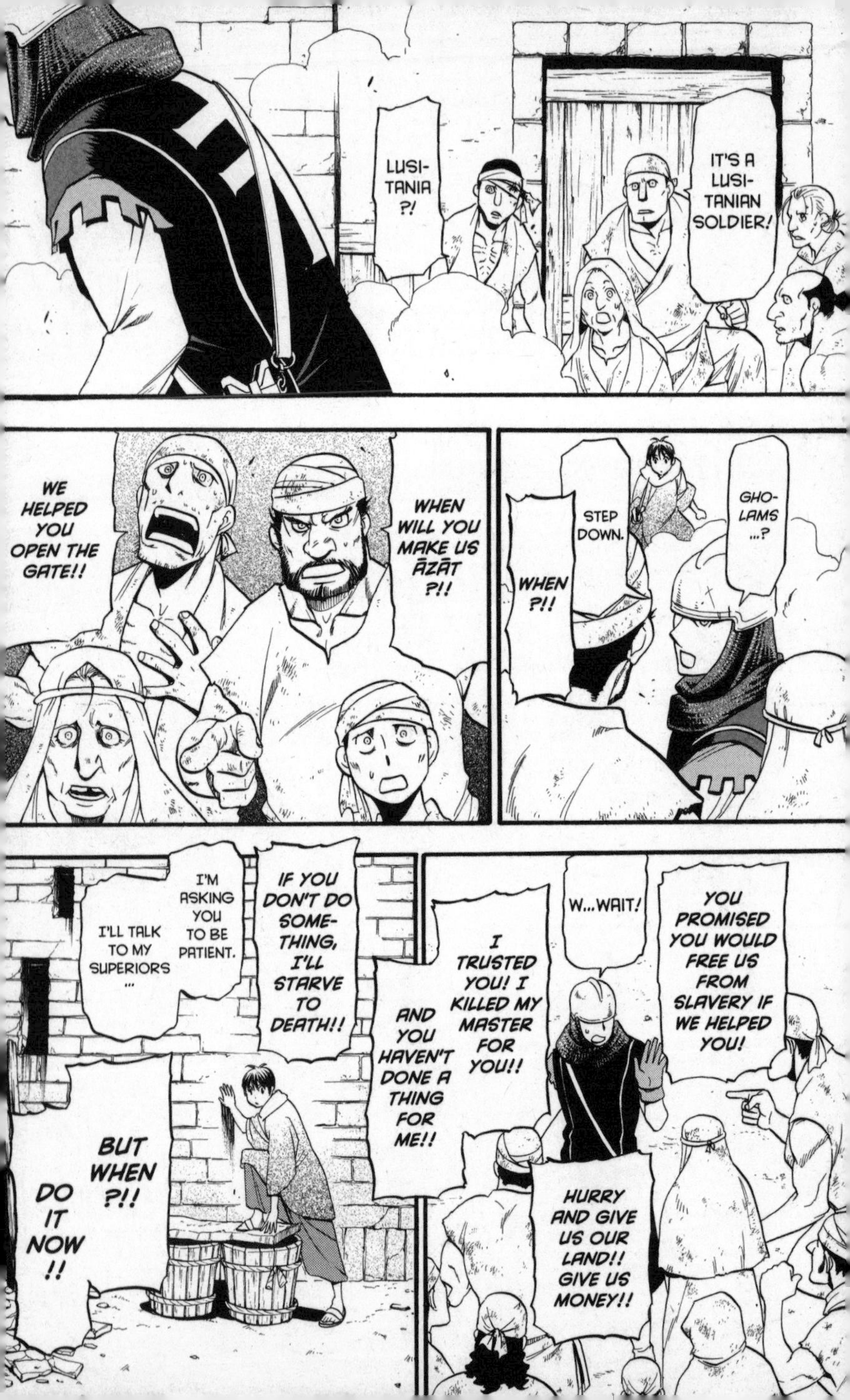
IT'S A LUSITANIAN SOLDIER!
LUSITANIA?!
GHOLAMS...?
STEP DOWN.
WHEN?!!
WHEN WILL YOU MAKE US ĀZĀT?!!
WE HELPED YOU OPEN THE GATE!!
YOU PROMISED YOU WOULD FREE US FROM SLAVERY IF WE HELPED YOU!
W...WAIT!
I TRUSTED YOU! I KILLED MY MASTER FOR YOU!!
AND YOU HAVEN'T DONE A THING FOR ME!!
HURRY AND GIVE US OUR LAND!! GIVE US MONEY!!
IF YOU DON'T DO SOMETHING, I'LL STARVE TO DEATH!!
I'M ASKING YOU TO BE PATIENT.
I'LL TALK TO MY SUPERIORS...
BUT WHEN?!!
DO IT NOW!!

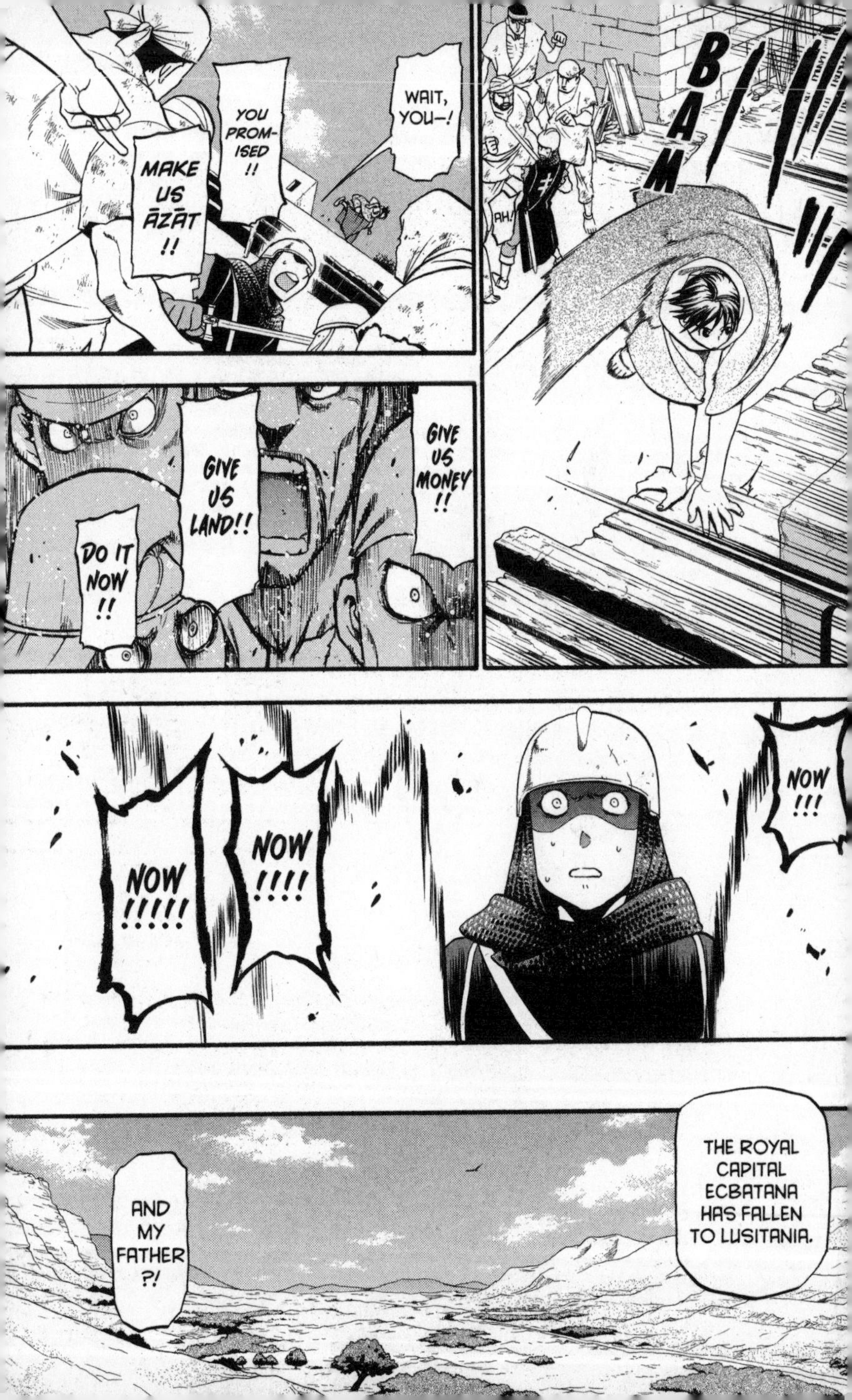
BAM
AH!
WAIT, YOU–!
YOU PROMISED !!
MAKE US ĀZĀT !!
GIVE US MONEY !!
GIVE US LAND!!
DO IT NOW !!
NOW !!!
NOW !!!!
NOW !!!!!
THE ROYAL CAPITAL ECBATANA HAS FALLEN TO LUSITANIA.
AND MY FATHER ?!

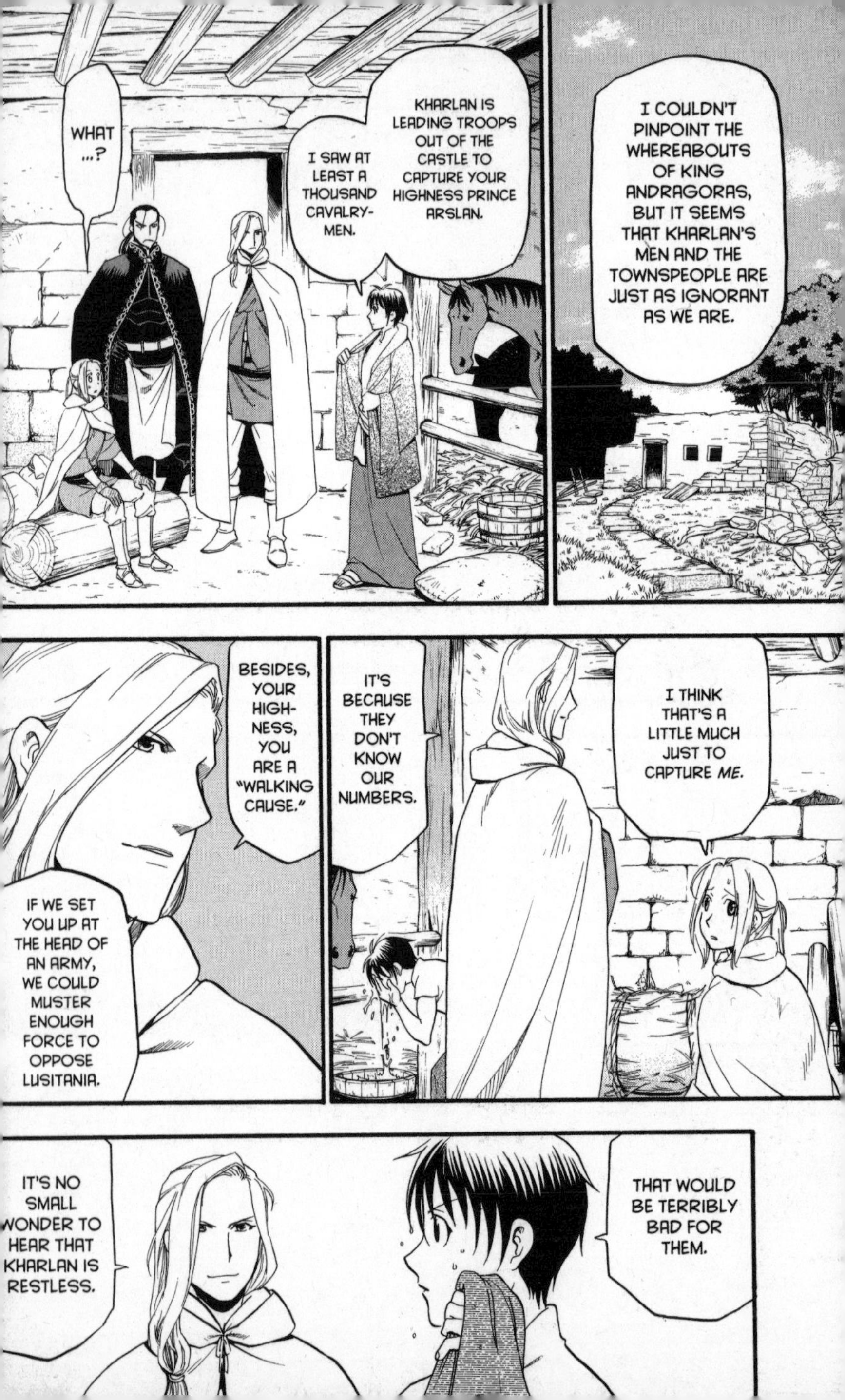
I COULDN'T PINPOINT THE WHEREABOUTS OF KING ANDRAGORAS, BUT IT SEEMS THAT KHARLAN'S MEN AND THE TOWNSPEOPLE ARE JUST AS IGNORANT AS WE ARE.
KHARLAN IS LEADING TROOPS OUT OF THE CASTLE TO CAPTURE YOUR HIGHNESS PRINCE ARSLAN.
I SAW AT LEAST A THOUSAND CAVALRY-MEN.
WHAT ...?
I THINK THAT'S A LITTLE MUCH JUST TO CAPTURE *ME.*
IT'S BECAUSE THEY DON'T KNOW OUR NUMBERS.
BESIDES, YOUR HIGH-NESS, YOU ARE A "WALKING CAUSE."
IF WE SET YOU UP AT THE HEAD OF AN ARMY, WE COULD MUSTER ENOUGH FORCE TO OPPOSE LUSITANIA.
THAT WOULD BE TERRIBLY BAD FOR THEM.
IT'S NO SMALL WONDER TO HEAR THAT KHARLAN IS RESTLESS.

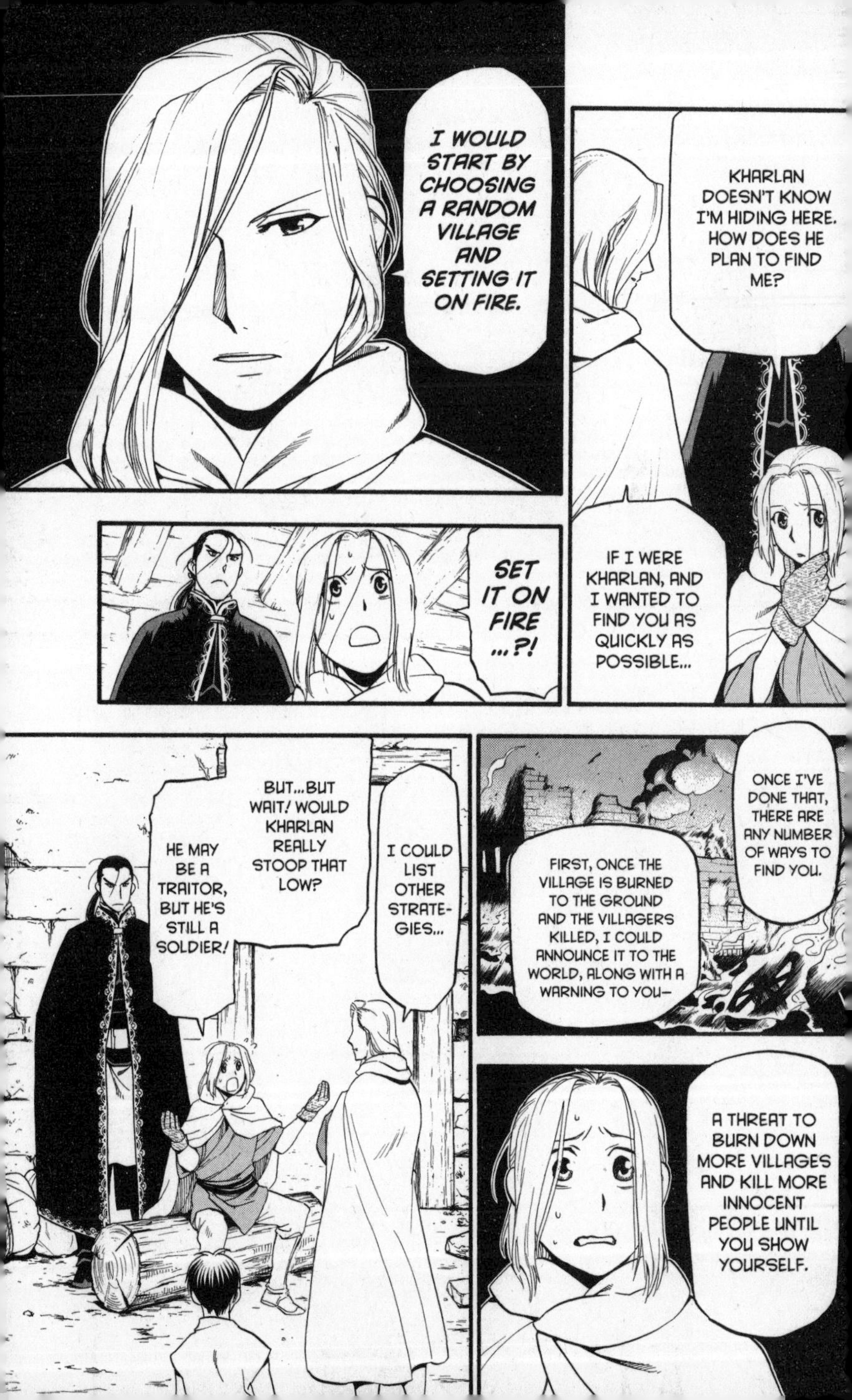
KHARLAN DOESN'T KNOW I'M HIDING HERE. HOW DOES HE PLAN TO FIND ME?
IF I WERE KHARLAN, AND I WANTED TO FIND YOU AS QUICKLY AS POSSIBLE...
I WOULD START BY CHOOSING A RANDOM VILLAGE AND SETTING IT ON FIRE.
SET IT ON FIRE ...?!
ONCE I'VE DONE THAT, THERE ARE ANY NUMBER OF WAYS TO FIND YOU.
FIRST, ONCE THE VILLAGE IS BURNED TO THE GROUND AND THE VILLAGERS KILLED, I COULD ANNOUNCE IT TO THE WORLD, ALONG WITH A WARNING TO YOU—
A THREAT TO BURN DOWN MORE VILLAGES AND KILL MORE INNOCENT PEOPLE UNTIL YOU SHOW YOURSELF.
I COULD LIST OTHER STRATE-GIES...
BUT...BUT WAIT! WOULD KHARLAN REALLY STOOP THAT LOW?
HE MAY BE A TRAITOR, BUT HE'S STILL A SOLDIER!

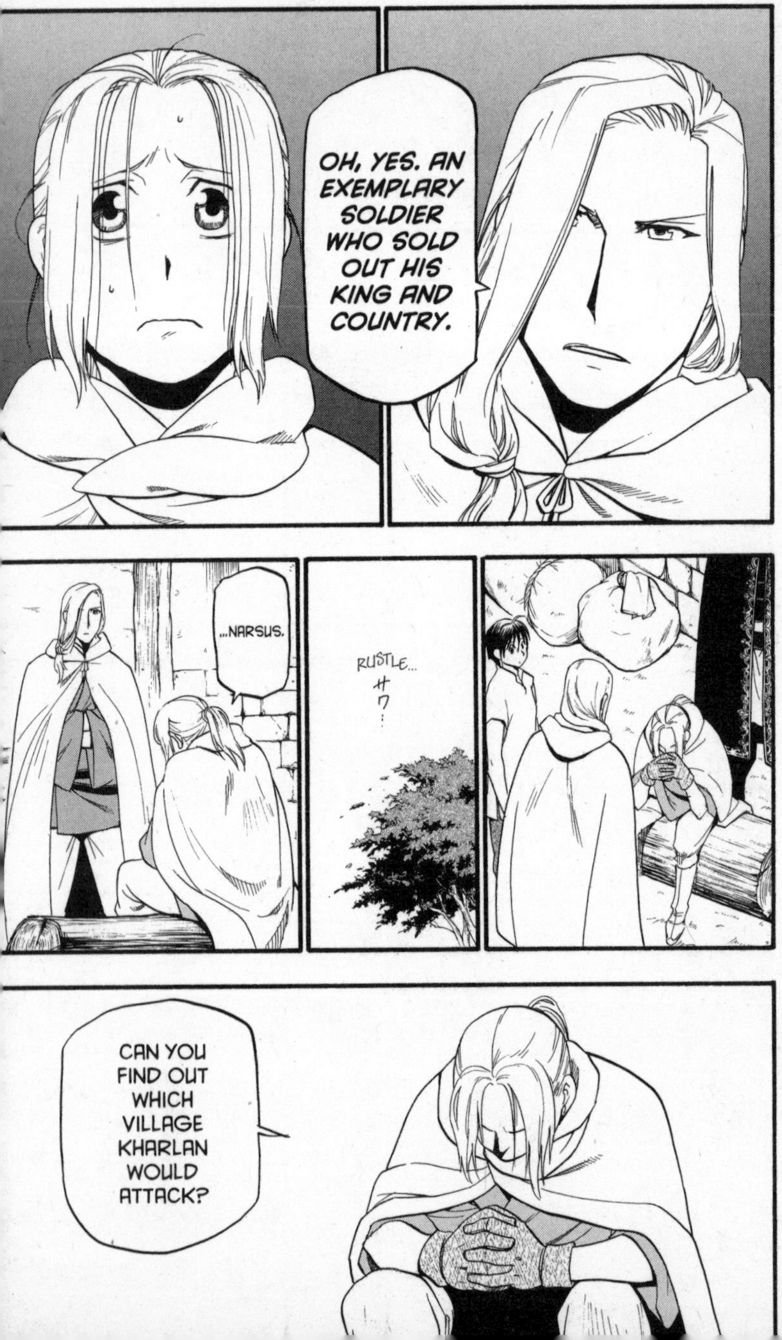
OH, YES. AN EXEMPLARY SOLDIER WHO SOLD OUT HIS KING AND COUNTRY.
RUSTLE...
サワ…
...NARSUS.
CAN YOU FIND OUT WHICH VILLAGE KHARLAN WOULD ATTACK?

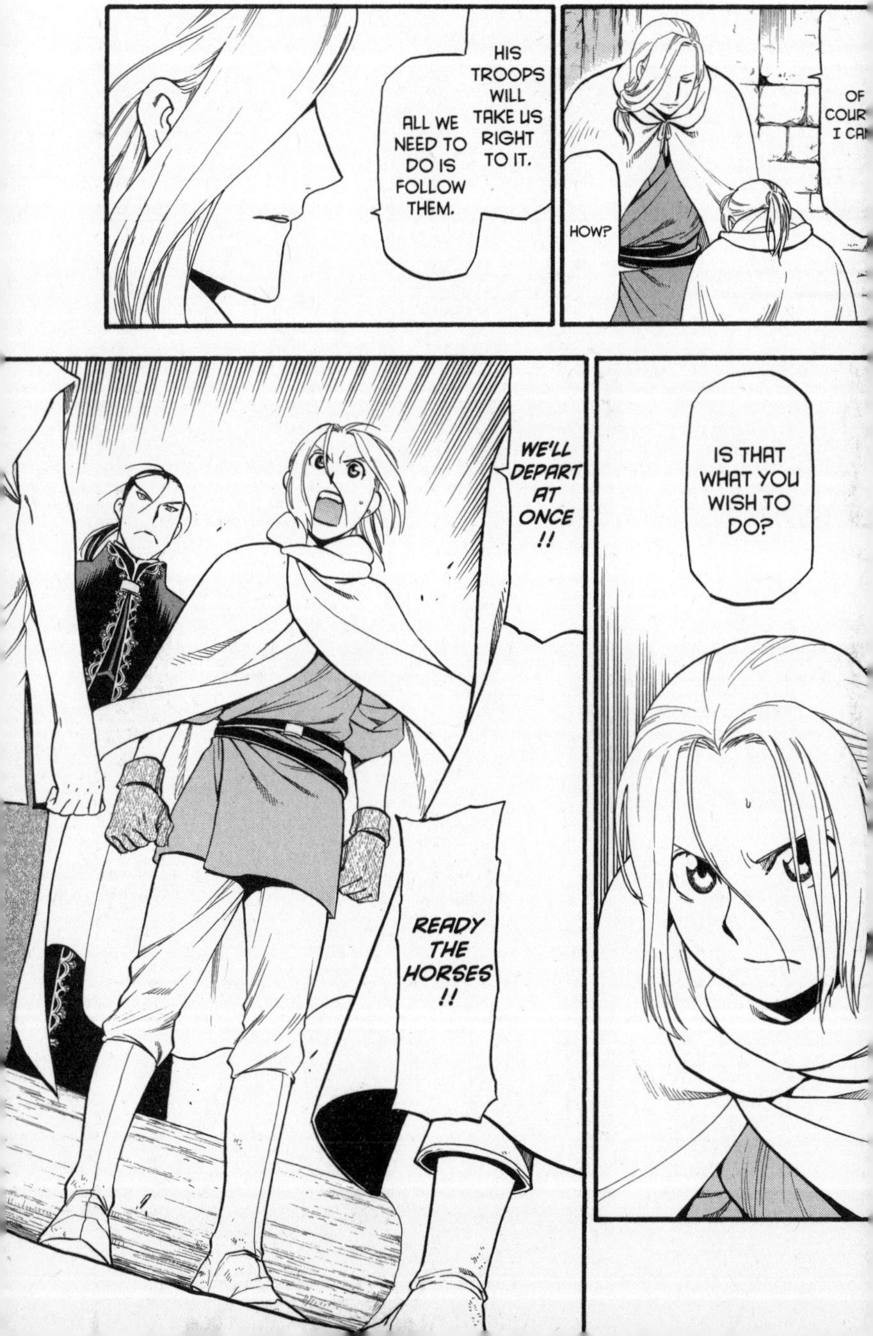
OF COUR I CA
HOW?
HIS TROOPS WILL TAKE US RIGHT TO IT.
ALL WE NEED TO DO IS FOLLOW THEM.
IS THAT WHAT YOU WISH TO DO?
WE'LL DEPART AT ONCE!!
READY THE HORSES!!

THE HEROIC LEGEND OF
ARSLAN

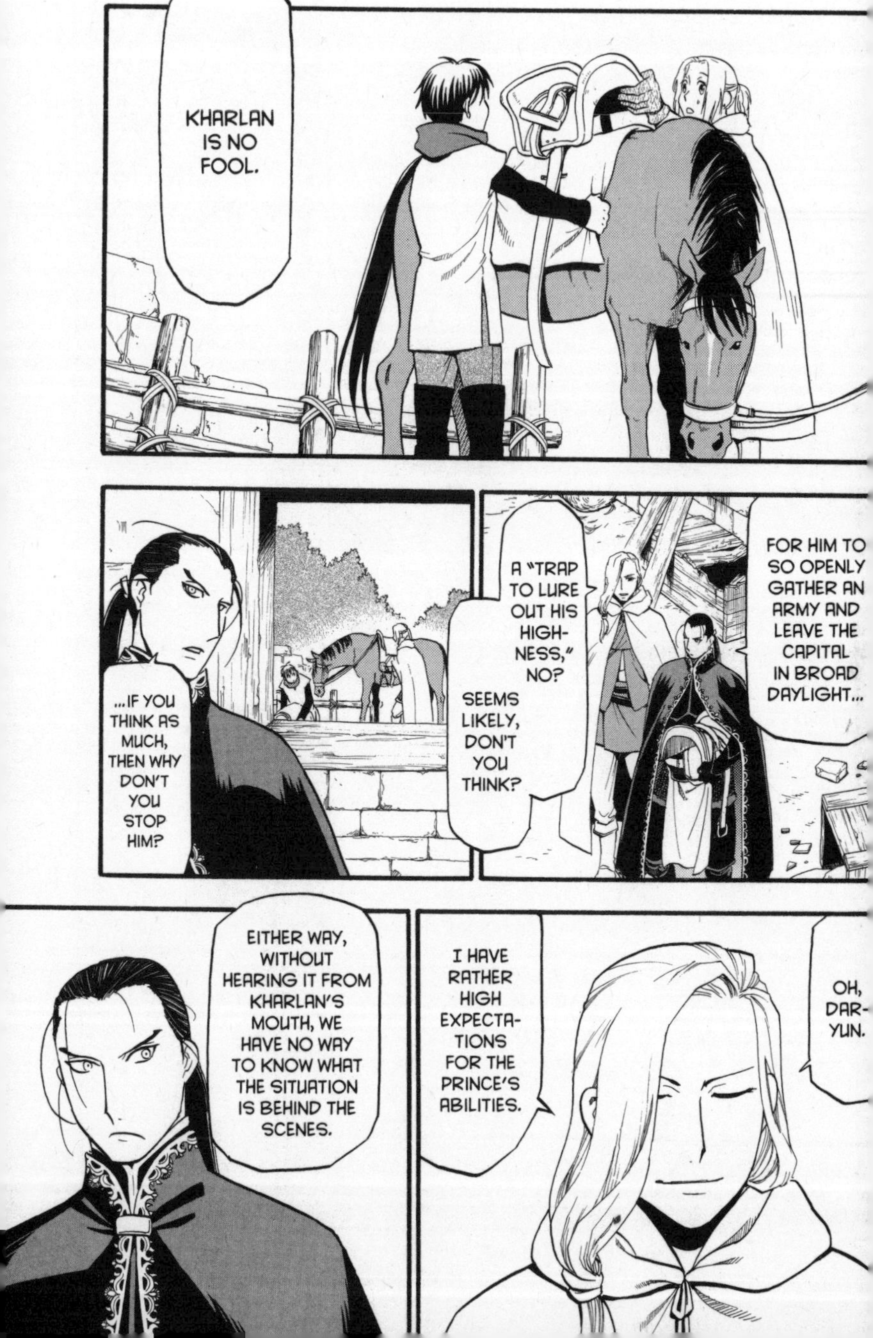
KHARLAN IS NO FOOL.
FOR HIM TO SO OPENLY GATHER AN ARMY AND LEAVE THE CAPITAL IN BROAD DAYLIGHT...
A "TRAP TO LURE OUT HIS HIGHNESS," NO?
SEEMS LIKELY, DON'T YOU THINK?
...IF YOU THINK AS MUCH, THEN WHY DON'T YOU STOP HIM?
OH, DARYUN.
I HAVE RATHER HIGH EXPECTATIONS FOR THE PRINCE'S ABILITIES.
EITHER WAY, WITHOUT HEARING IT FROM KHARLAN'S MOUTH, WE HAVE NO WAY TO KNOW WHAT THE SITUATION IS BEHIND THE SCENES.

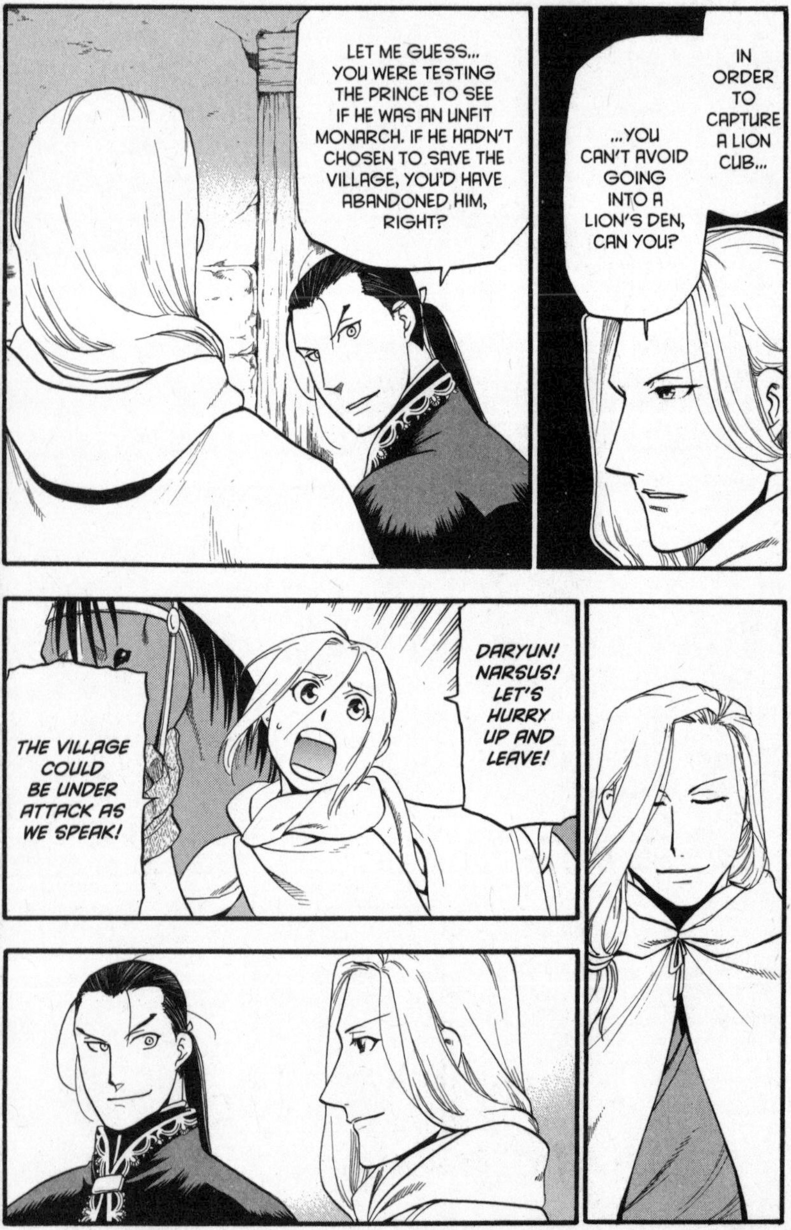
IN ORDER TO CAPTURE A LION CUB...
...YOU CAN'T AVOID GOING INTO A LION'S DEN, CAN YOU?
LET ME GUESS... YOU WERE TESTING THE PRINCE TO SEE IF HE WAS AN UNFIT MONARCH. IF HE HADN'T CHOSEN TO SAVE THE VILLAGE, YOU'D HAVE ABANDONED HIM, RIGHT?
DARYUN! NARSUS! LET'S HURRY UP AND LEAVE!
THE VILLAGE COULD BE UNDER ATTACK AS WE SPEAK!

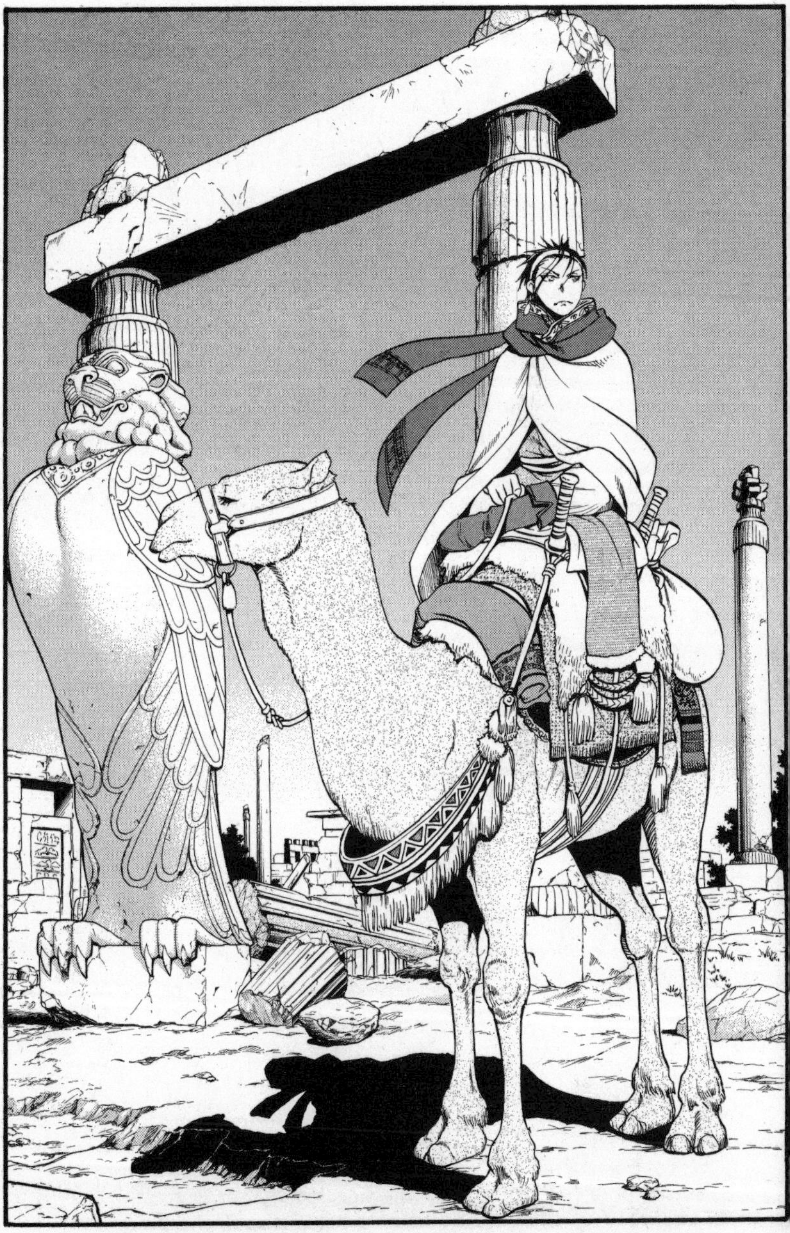

Chapter Twelve: A Peerless Beauty

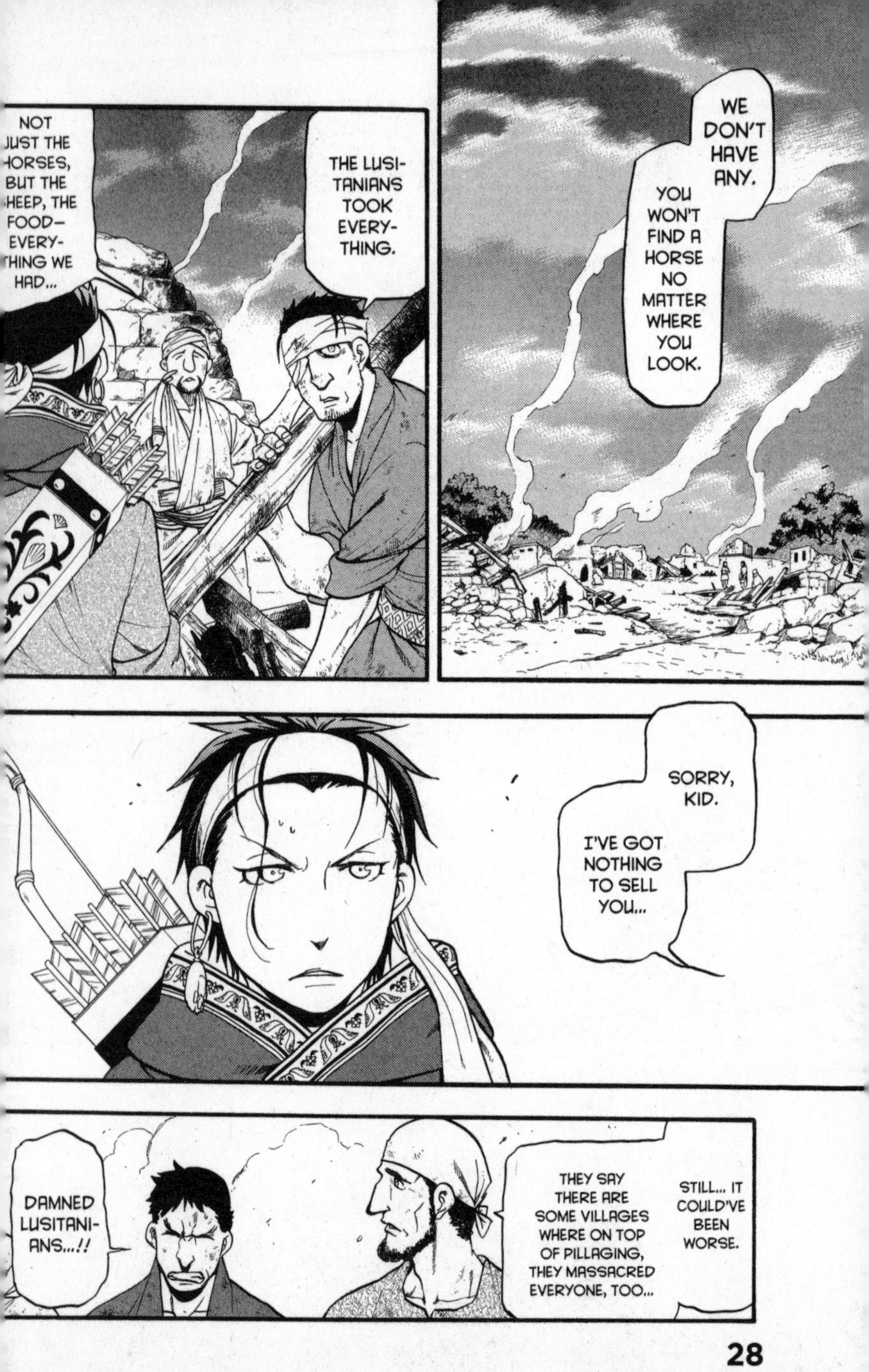

WE DON'T HAVE ANY.
YOU WON'T FIND A HORSE NO MATTER WHERE YOU LOOK.
THE LUSI-TANIANS TOOK EVERY-THING.
NOT JUST THE HORSES, BUT THE SHEEP, THE FOOD—EVERY-THING WE HAD...
SORRY, KID.
I'VE GOT NOTHING TO SELL YOU...
STILL... IT COULD'VE BEEN WORSE.
THEY SAY THERE ARE SOME VILLAGES WHERE ON TOP OF PILLAGING, THEY MASSACRED EVERYONE, TOO...
DAMNED LUSITANI-ANS...!!

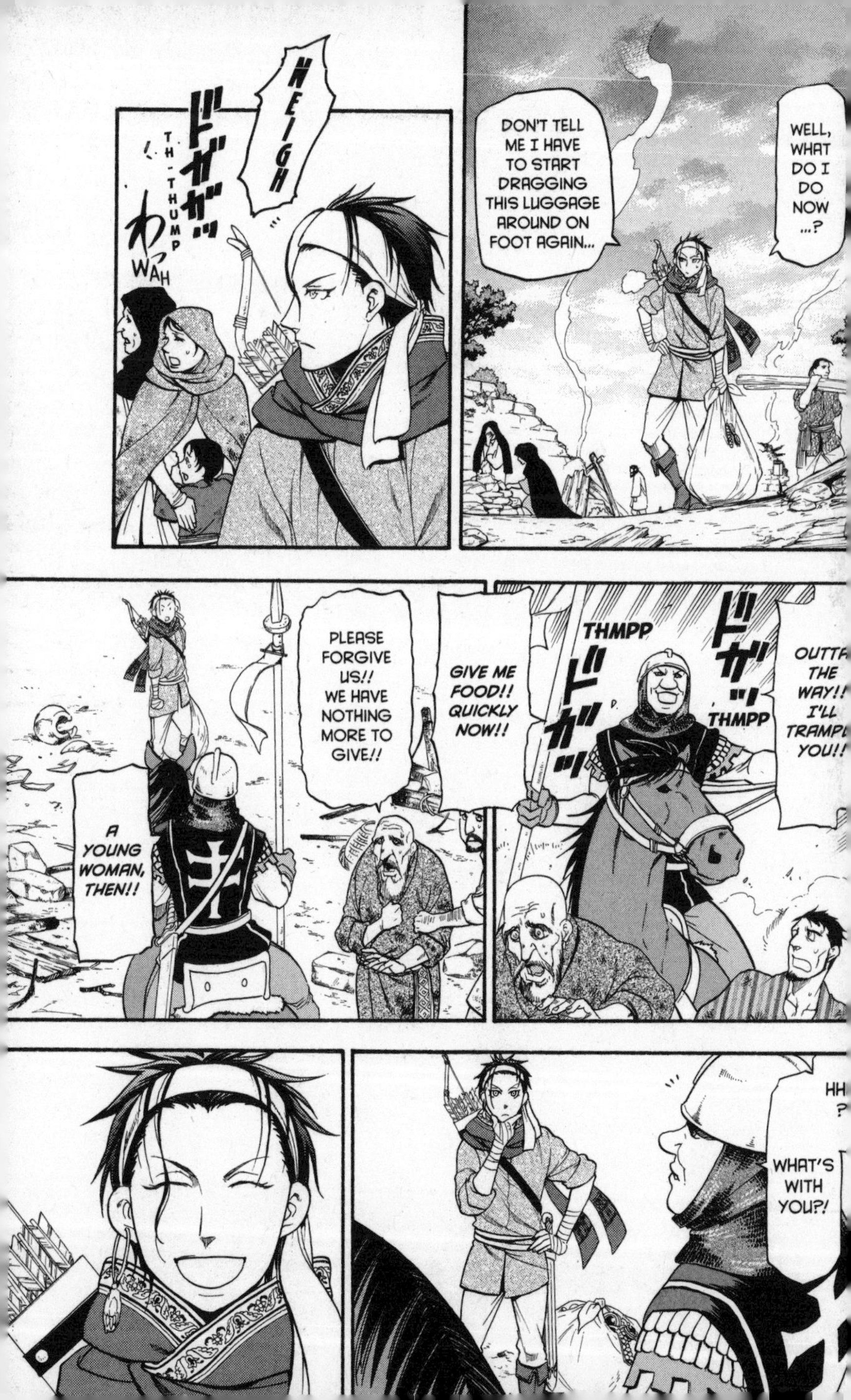
WELL, WHAT DO I DO NOW ...?
DON'T TELL ME I HAVE TO START DRAGGING THIS LUGGAGE AROUND ON FOOT AGAIN...
NEIGH
ドガガッ
TH-THUMP
わっ
WAH
ドガッ
THMPP
OUTTA THE WAY!! I'LL TRAMPL YOU!!
ドガッ
THMPP
GIVE ME FOOD!! QUICKLY NOW!!
PLEASE FORGIVE US!! WE HAVE NOTHING MORE TO GIVE!!
A YOUNG WOMAN, THEN!!
HH ?
WHAT'S WITH YOU?!

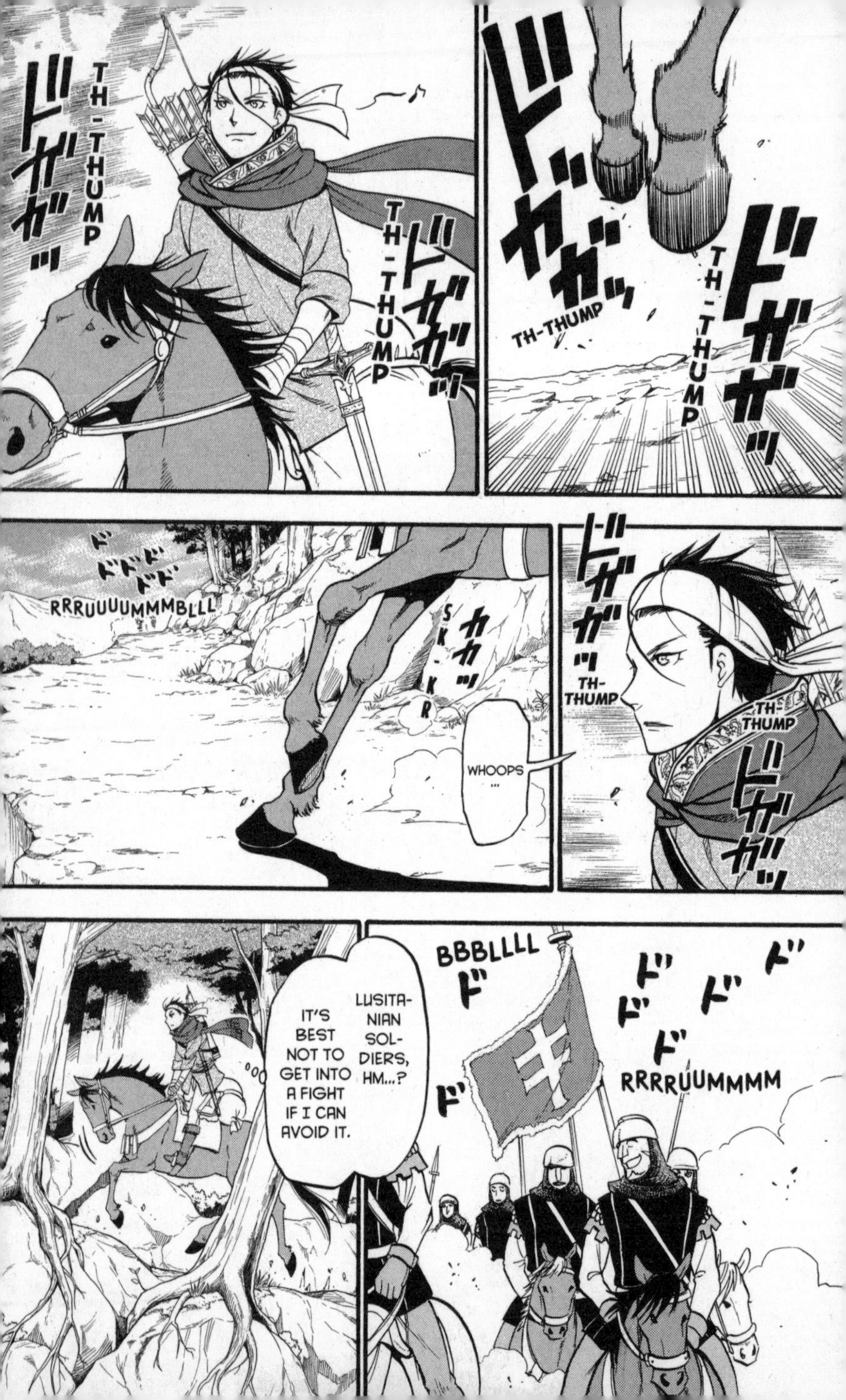
TH-THUMP
TH-THUMP
TH-THUMP
TH-THUMP
TH-THUMP
TH-THUMP
WHOOPS...
SK-KR
RRRUUUUMMMBLLL
BBBLLLL
RRRRUUMMMM
LUSITANIAN SOLDIERS, HM...?
IT'S BEST NOT TO GET INTO A FIGHT IF I CAN AVOID IT.

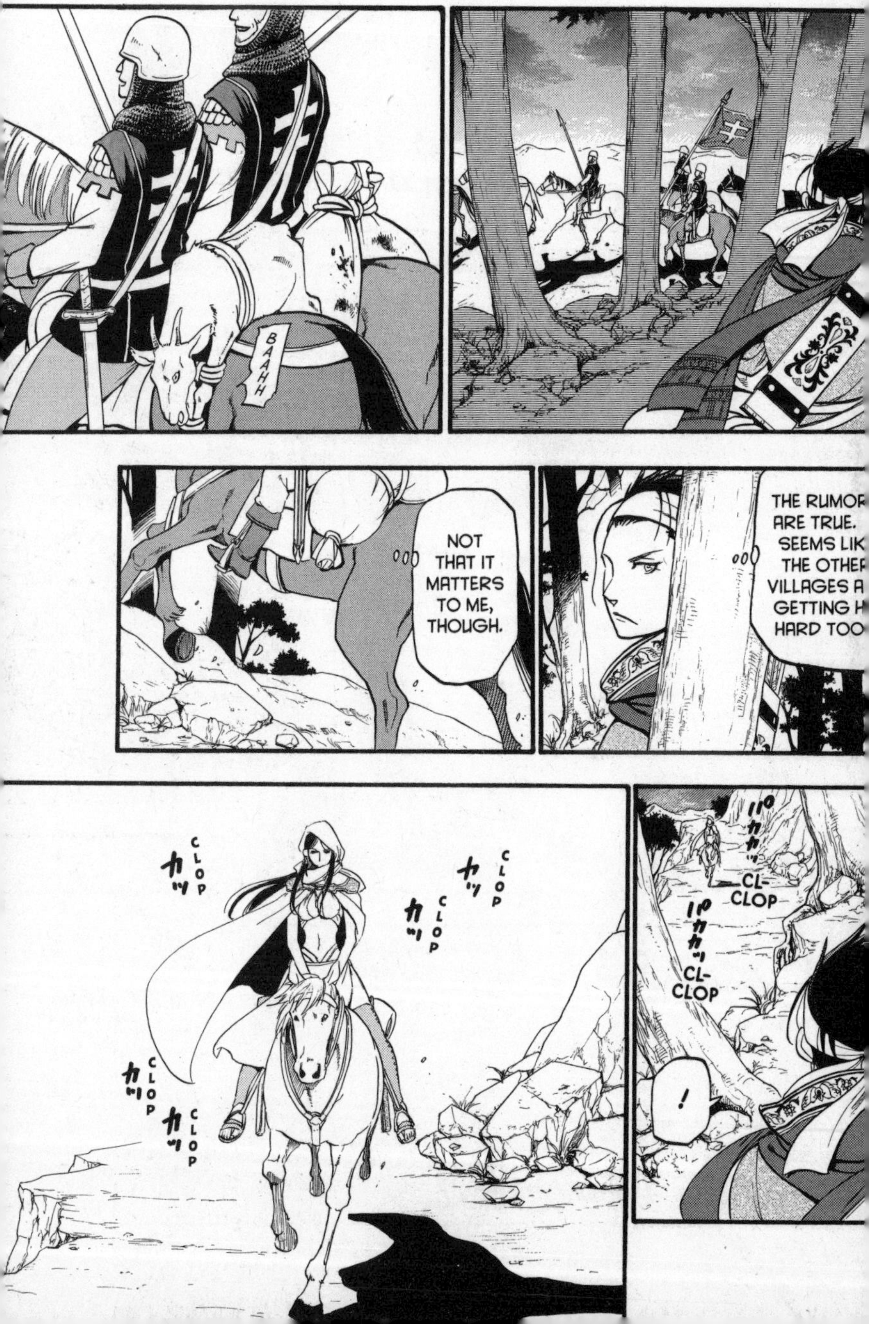
BAAHH
THE RUMOR ARE TRUE. SEEMS LIK THE OTHER VILLAGES A GETTING H HARD TOO
NOT THAT IT MATTERS TO ME, THOUGH.
パカカッ CL-CLOP
パカカッ CL-CLOP
!
カッ CLOP
カッ CLOP
カッ CLOP
カッ CLOP
カッ CLOP

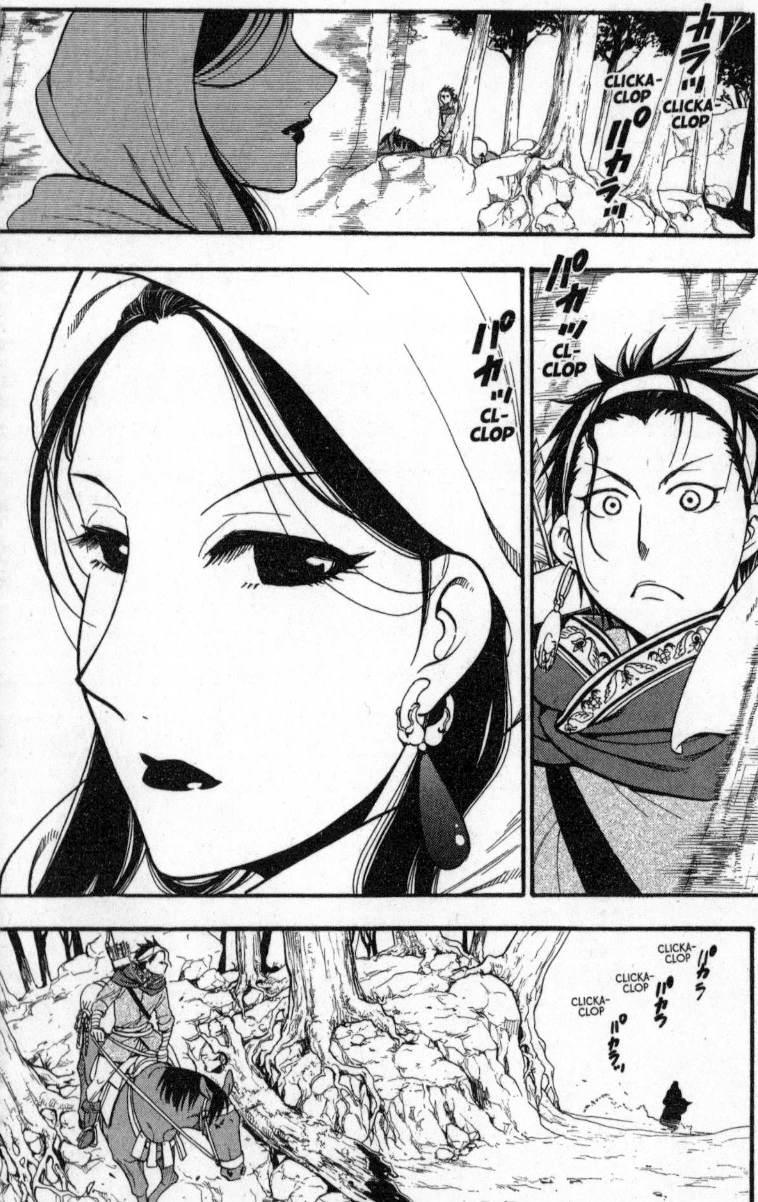
パカラッ
CLICKA-CLOP
パカラッ
CLICKA-CLOP
パカッ
CL-CLOP
パカッ
CL-CLOP
パカラ
CLICKA-CLOP
パカラ
CLICKA-CLOP
パカラッ
CLICKA-CLOP

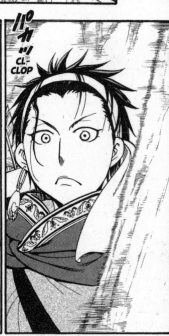

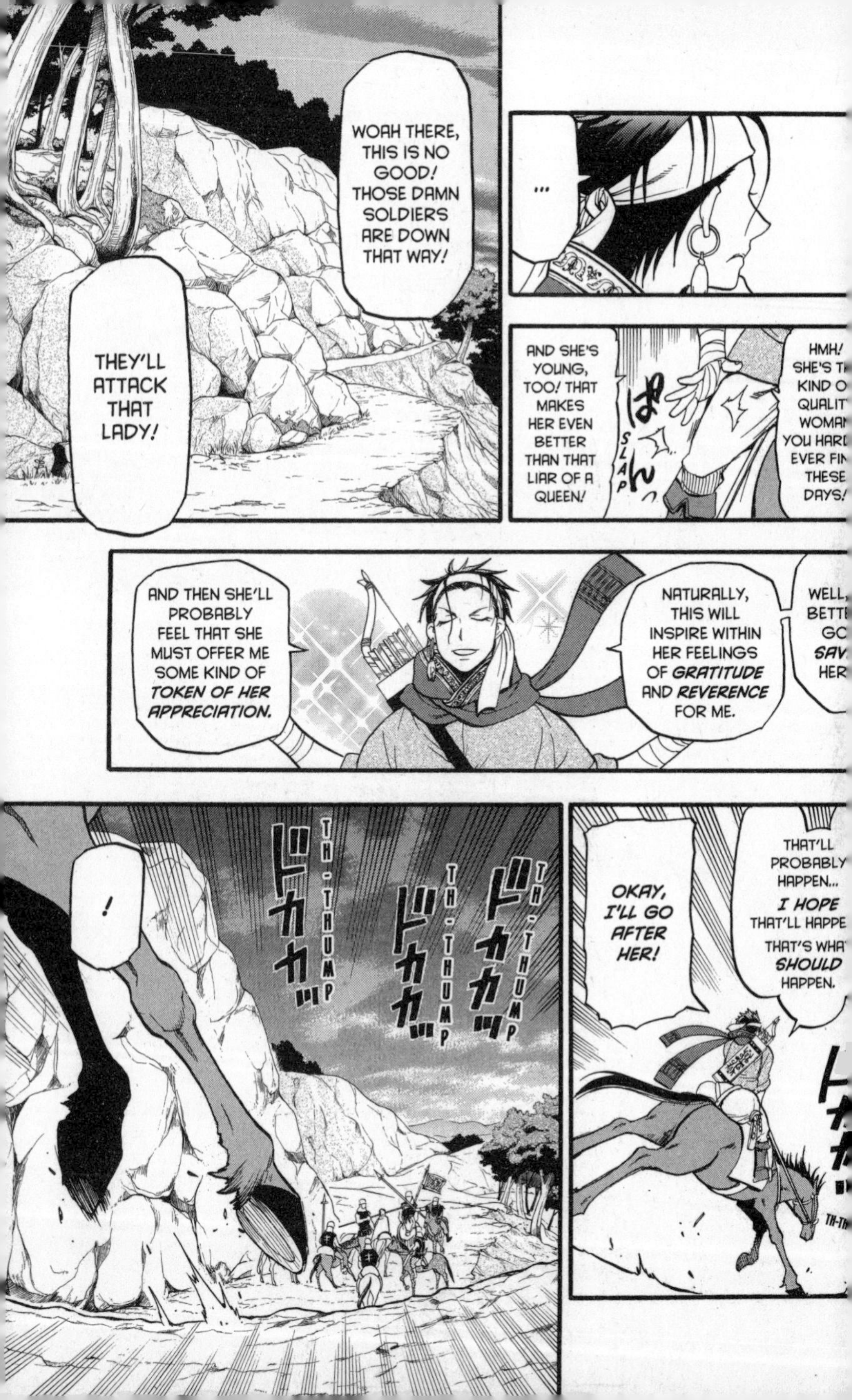
...
HMH! SHE'S T KIND O QUALIT WOMAN YOU HARD EVER FIN THESE DAYS!
SLAP
AND SHE'S YOUNG, TOO! THAT MAKES HER EVEN BETTER THAN THAT LIAR OF A QUEEN!
WOAH THERE, THIS IS NO GOOD! THOSE DAMN SOLDIERS ARE DOWN THAT WAY!
THEY'LL ATTACK THAT LADY!
WELL, BETTE GO SAV HER
NATURALLY, THIS WILL INSPIRE WITHIN HER FEELINGS OF GRATITUDE AND REVERENCE FOR ME.
AND THEN SHE'LL PROBABLY FEEL THAT SHE MUST OFFER ME SOME KIND OF TOKEN OF HER APPRECIATION.
THAT'LL PROBABLY HAPPEN... I HOPE THAT'LL HAPPE THAT'S WHA SHOULD HAPPEN.
OKAY, I'LL GO AFTER HER!
TH-TH
TH-THUMP
TH-THUMP
TH-THUMP
!

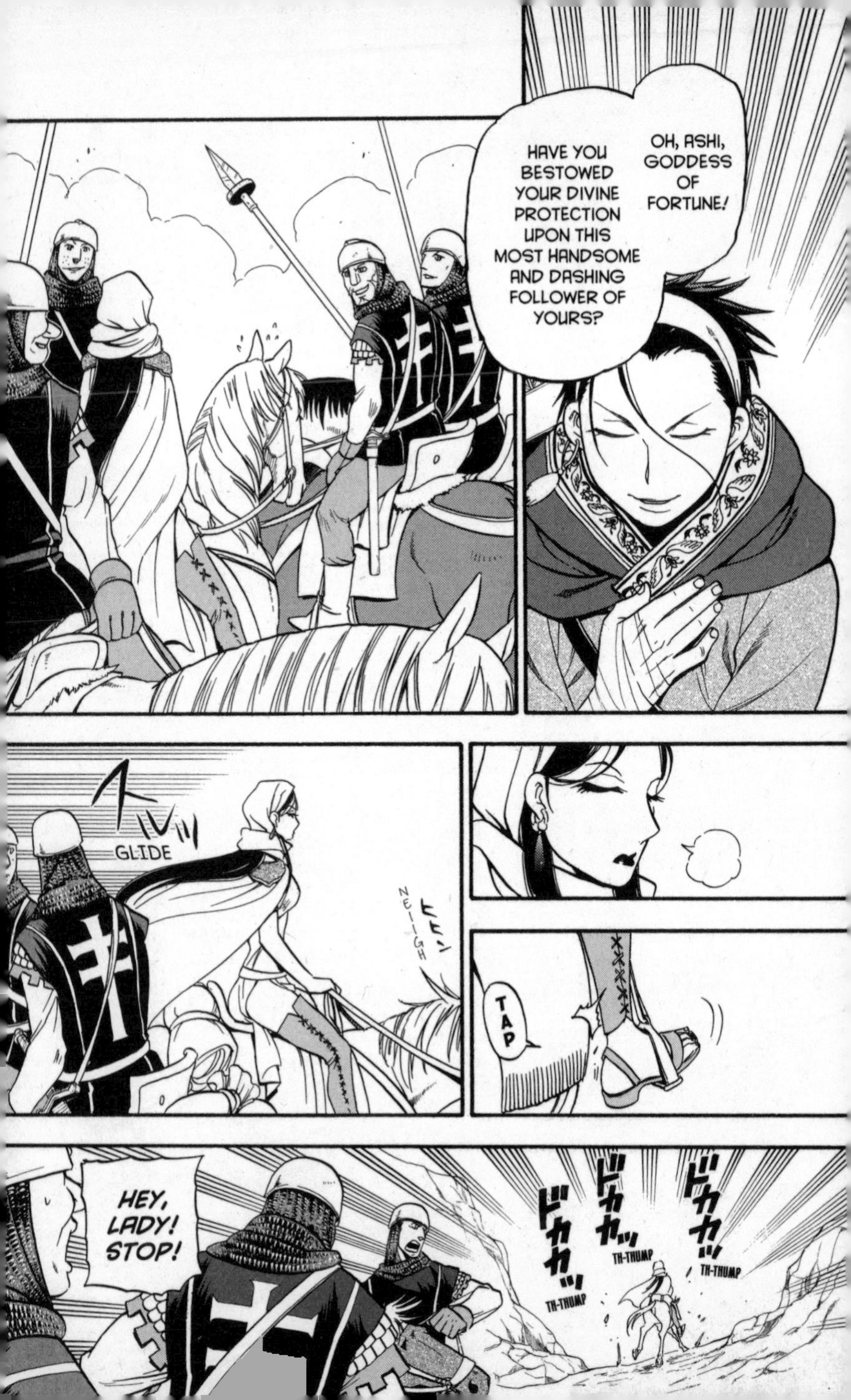
OH, ASHI, GODDESS OF FORTUNE!
HAVE YOU BESTOWED YOUR DIVINE PROTECTION UPON THIS MOST HANDSOME AND DASHING FOLLOWER OF YOURS?
TAP
GLIDE
NEIGH
TH-THUMP
TH-THUMP
TH-THUMP
HEY, LADY! STOP!

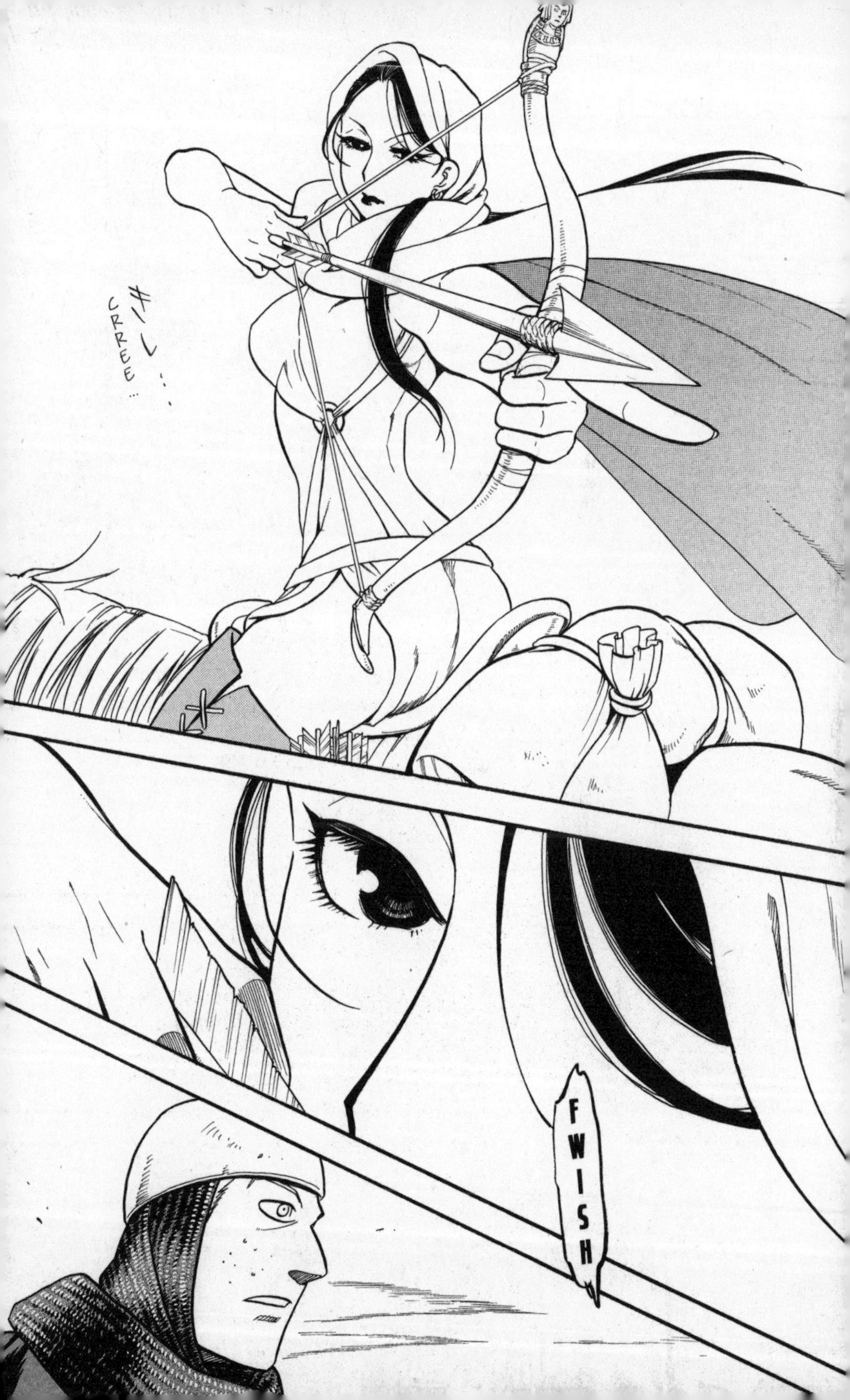
ギル…
CRREE…
FWISH

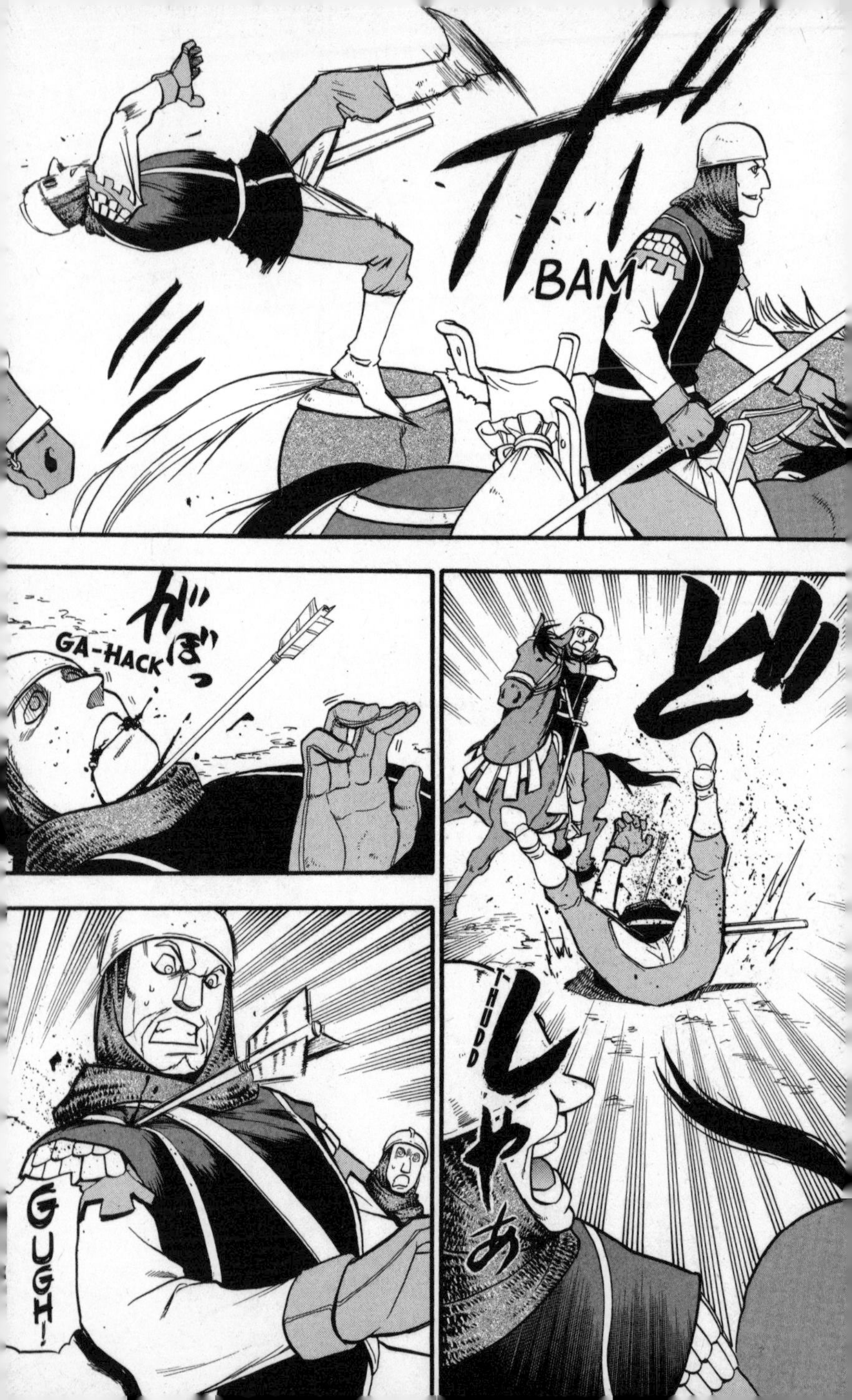
BAM
どしゃあ
THUDD
がぼっ
GA-HACK
GUGH!

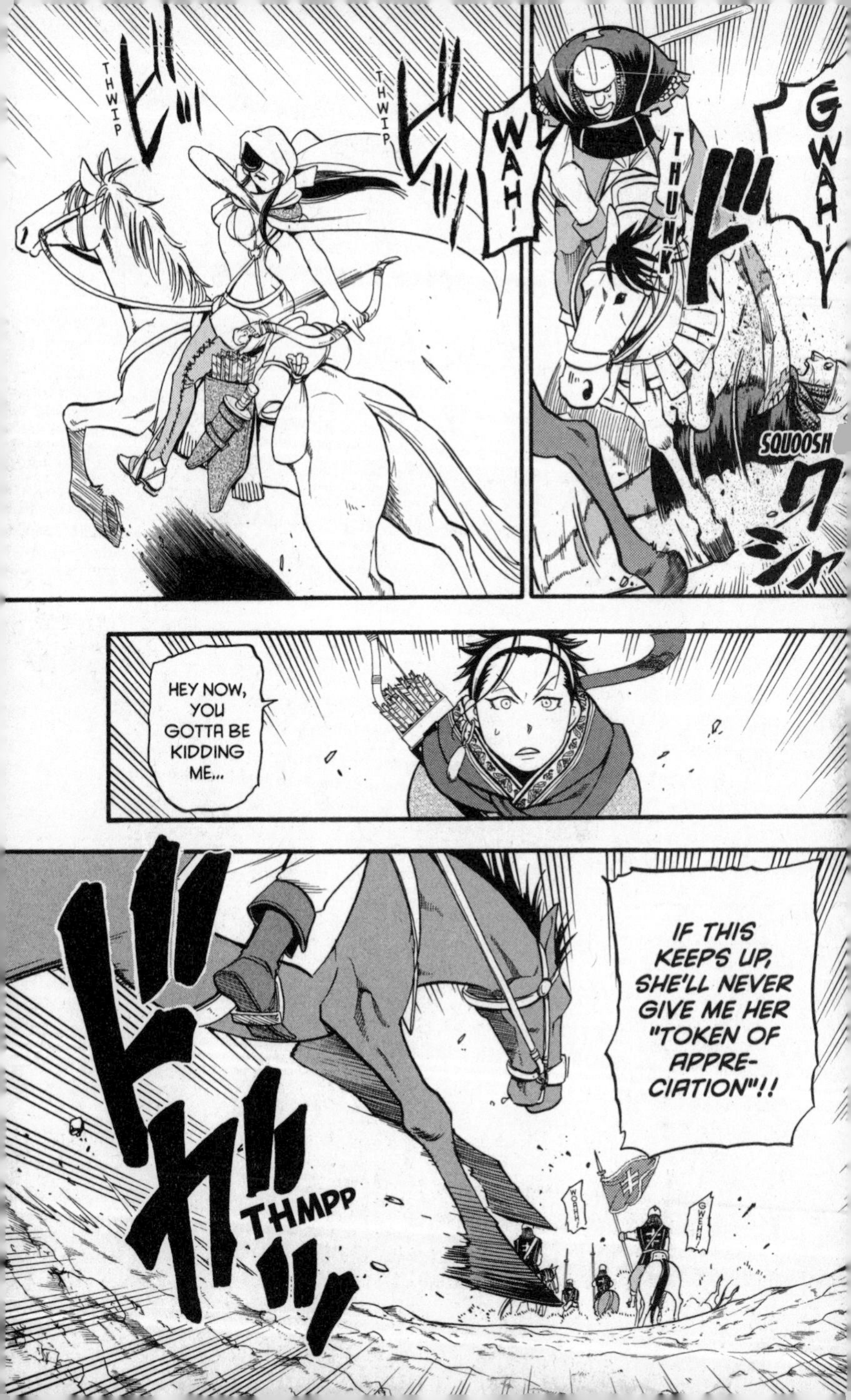

WAH!
THUNK
GWAH!
SQUOOSH
THWIP
THWIP
HEY NOW, YOU GOTTA BE KIDDING ME...
IF THIS KEEPS UP, SHE'LL NEVER GIVE ME HER "TOKEN OF APPRE-CIATION"!!
GWEH!
WOAH!
THMPP

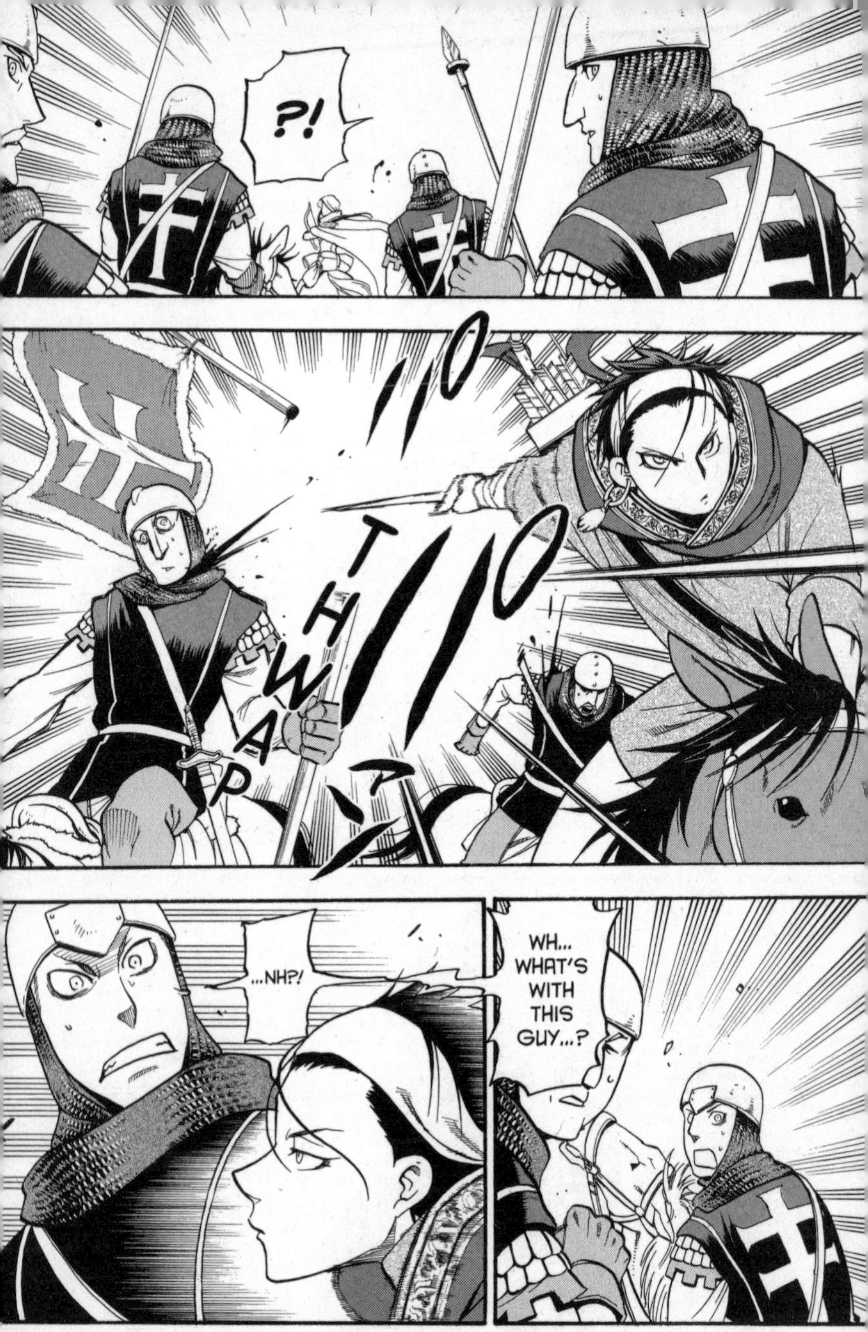
?!
THWAP
WH... WHAT'S WITH THIS GUY...?
...NH?!

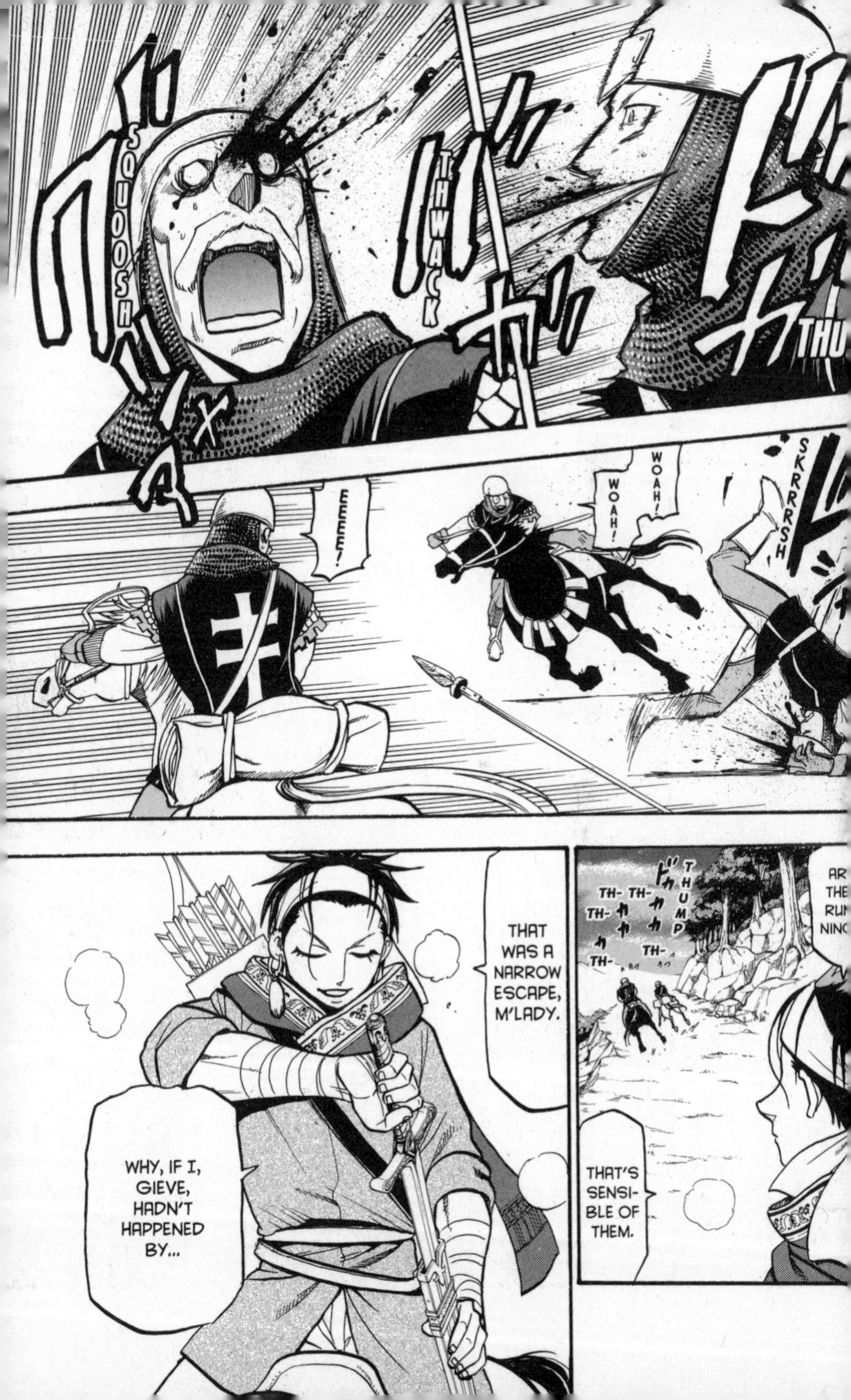
THU
THWACK
SQUOOSH
SKRRRSH
WOAH! WOAH!
EEEEE!
AR THE RUN NING
THUMP
TH- TH- TH- TH- TH-
THAT'S SENSIBLE OF THEM.
THAT WAS A NARROW ESCAPE, M'LADY.
WHY, IF I, GIEVE, HADN'T HAPPENED BY...

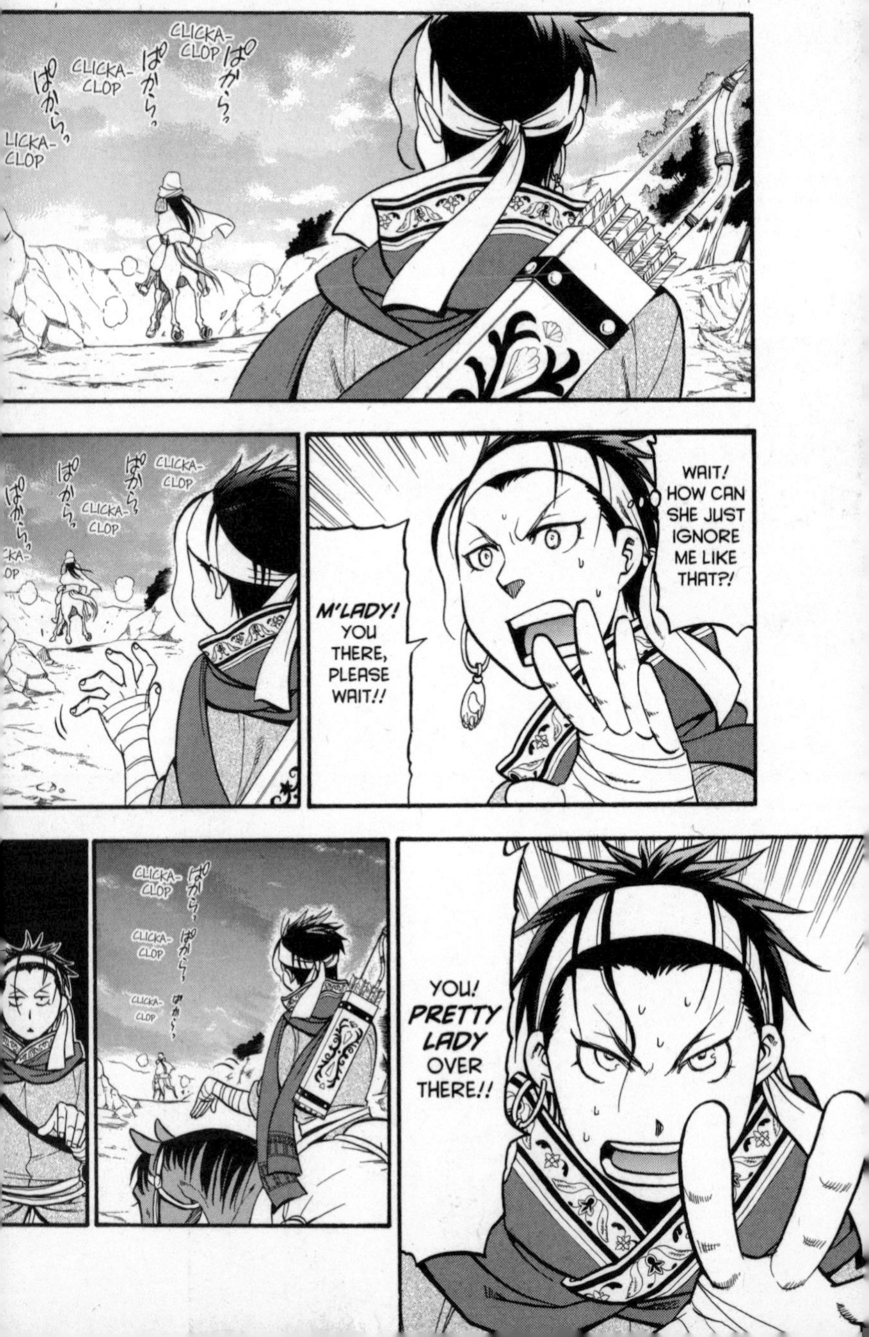
CLICKA-CLOP
ぱからっ
CLICKA-CLOP
ぱからっ
LICKA-CLOP
ぱからっ
WAIT! HOW CAN SHE JUST IGNORE ME LIKE THAT?!
M'LADY! YOU THERE, PLEASE WAIT!!
CLICKA-CLOP
ぱからっ
CLICKA-CLOP
ぱからっ
ぱからっ
YOU! PRETTY LADY OVER THERE!!
CLICKA-CLOP
ぱからっ
CLICKA-CLOP
ぱからっ
CLICKA-CLOP
ぱからっ

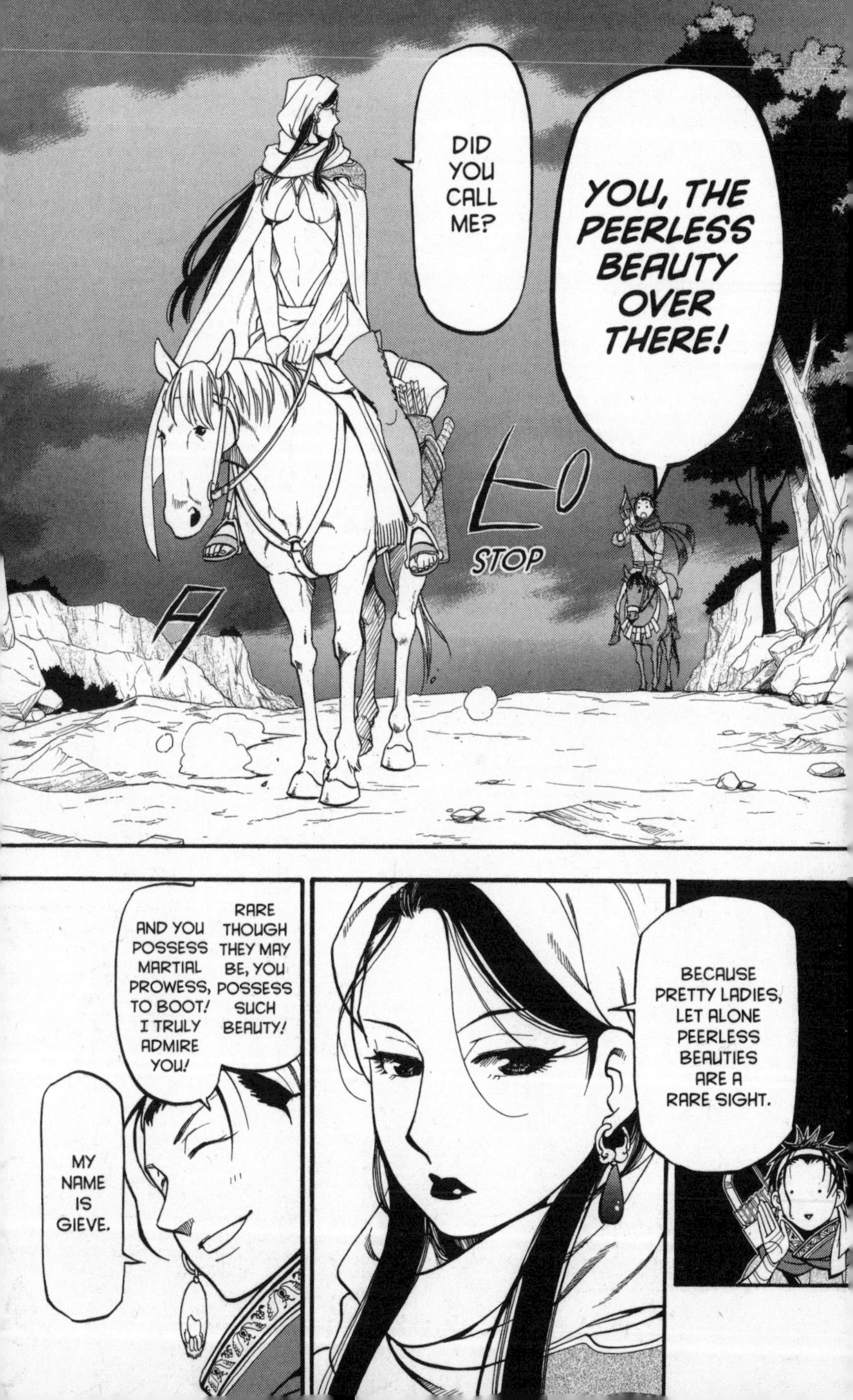
YOU, THE PEERLESS BEAUTY OVER THERE!
DID YOU CALL ME?
STOP
BECAUSE PRETTY LADIES, LET ALONE PEERLESS BEAUTIES ARE A RARE SIGHT.
RARE THOUGH THEY MAY BE, YOU POSSESS SUCH BEAUTY!
AND YOU POSSESS MARTIAL PROWESS, TO BOOT! I TRULY ADMIRE YOU!
MY NAME IS GIEVE.

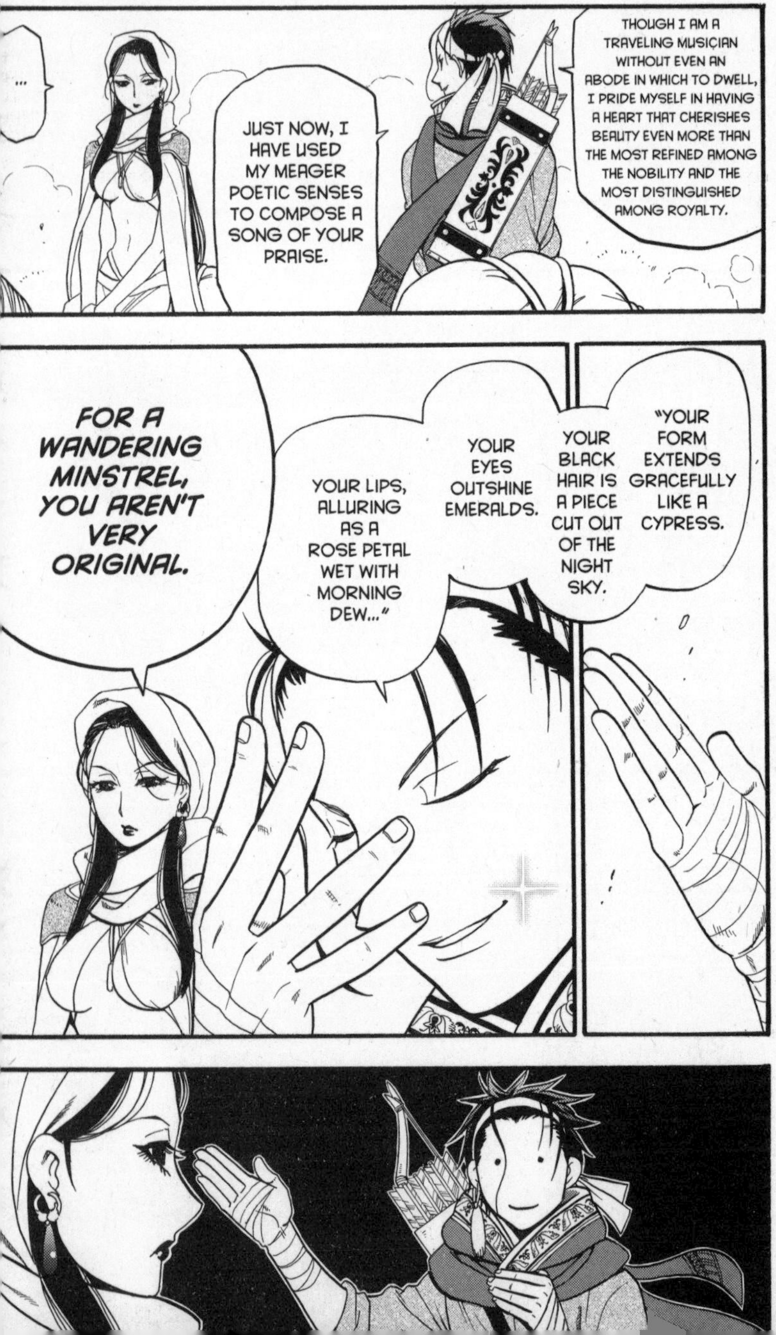
THOUGH I AM A TRAVELING MUSICIAN WITHOUT EVEN AN ABODE IN WHICH TO DWELL, I PRIDE MYSELF IN HAVING A HEART THAT CHERISHES BEAUTY EVEN MORE THAN THE MOST REFINED AMONG THE NOBILITY AND THE MOST DISTINGUISHED AMONG ROYALTY.
JUST NOW, I HAVE USED MY MEAGER POETIC SENSES TO COMPOSE A SONG OF YOUR PRAISE.
...
"YOUR FORM EXTENDS GRACEFULLY LIKE A CYPRESS.
YOUR BLACK HAIR IS A PIECE CUT OUT OF THE NIGHT SKY.
YOUR EYES OUTSHINE EMERALDS.
YOUR LIPS, ALLURING AS A ROSE PETAL WET WITH MORNING DEW..."
FOR A WANDERING MINSTREL, YOU AREN'T VERY ORIGINAL.

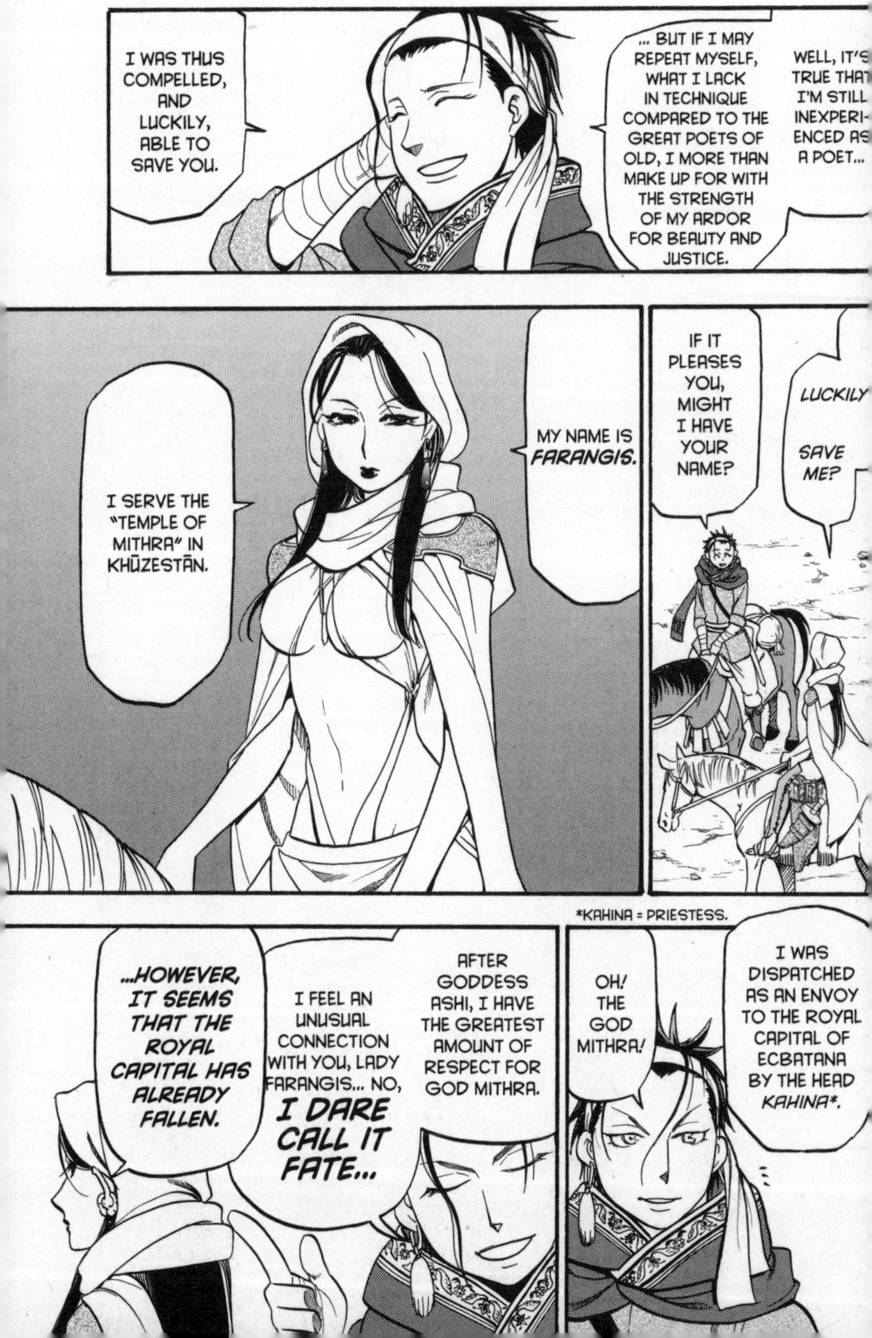
WELL, IT'S TRUE THAT I'M STILL INEXPERIENCED AS A POET...
... BUT IF I MAY REPEAT MYSELF, WHAT I LACK IN TECHNIQUE COMPARED TO THE GREAT POETS OF OLD, I MORE THAN MAKE UP FOR WITH THE STRENGTH OF MY ARDOR FOR BEAUTY AND JUSTICE.
I WAS THUS COMPELLED, AND LUCKILY, ABLE TO SAVE YOU.
LUCKILY SAVE ME?
IF IT PLEASES YOU, MIGHT I HAVE YOUR NAME?
MY NAME IS *FARANGIS.*
I SERVE THE "TEMPLE OF MITHRA" IN KHŪZESTĀN.
I WAS DISPATCHED AS AN ENVOY TO THE ROYAL CAPITAL OF ECBATANA BY THE HEAD *KAHINA**.
OH! THE GOD MITHRA!
AFTER GODDESS ASHI, I HAVE THE GREATEST AMOUNT OF RESPECT FOR GOD MITHRA.
I FEEL AN UNUSUAL CONNECTION WITH YOU, LADY FARANGIS... NO, ***I DARE CALL IT FATE...***
...HOWEVER, IT SEEMS THAT THE ROYAL CAPITAL HAS ALREADY FALLEN.

*KAHINA = PRIESTESS.

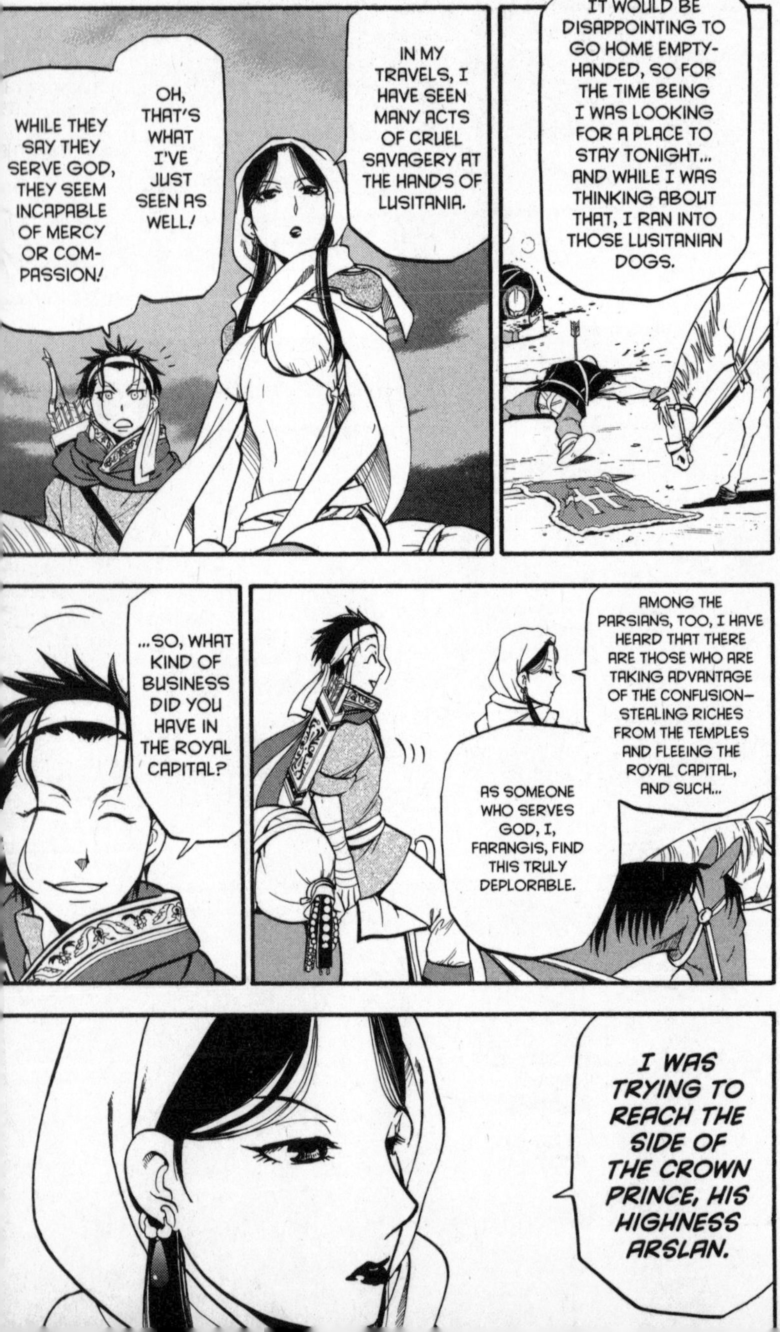
IT WOULD BE DISAPPOINTING TO GO HOME EMPTY-HANDED, SO FOR THE TIME BEING I WAS LOOKING FOR A PLACE TO STAY TONIGHT... AND WHILE I WAS THINKING ABOUT THAT, I RAN INTO THOSE LUSITANIAN DOGS.
IN MY TRAVELS, I HAVE SEEN MANY ACTS OF CRUEL SAVAGERY AT THE HANDS OF LUSITANIA.
OH, THAT'S WHAT I'VE JUST SEEN AS WELL!
WHILE THEY SAY THEY SERVE GOD, THEY SEEM INCAPABLE OF MERCY OR COM-PASSION!
AMONG THE PARSIANS, TOO, I HAVE HEARD THAT THERE ARE THOSE WHO ARE TAKING ADVANTAGE OF THE CONFUSION—STEALING RICHES FROM THE TEMPLES AND FLEEING THE ROYAL CAPITAL, AND SUCH...
AS SOMEONE WHO SERVES GOD, I, FARANGIS, FIND THIS TRULY DEPLORABLE.
...SO, WHAT KIND OF BUSINESS DID YOU HAVE IN THE ROYAL CAPITAL?
I WAS TRYING TO REACH THE SIDE OF THE CROWN PRINCE, HIS HIGHNESS ARSLAN.

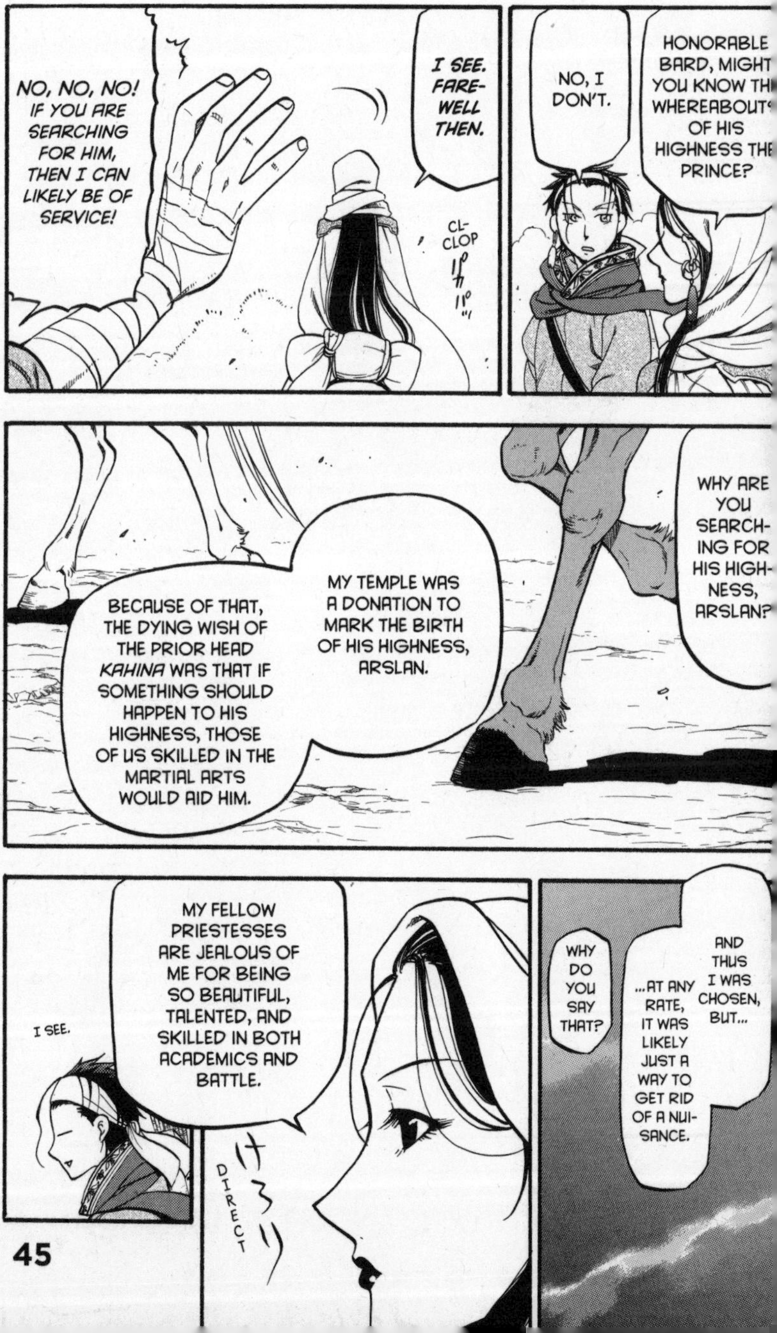
HONORABLE BARD, MIGHT YOU KNOW THE WHEREABOUTS OF HIS HIGHNESS THE PRINCE?
NO, I DON'T.
I SEE. FARE-WELL THEN.
CL-CLOP
NO, NO, NO! IF YOU ARE SEARCHING FOR HIM, THEN I CAN LIKELY BE OF SERVICE!
WHY ARE YOU SEARCH-ING FOR HIS HIGH-NESS, ARSLAN?
MY TEMPLE WAS A DONATION TO MARK THE BIRTH OF HIS HIGHNESS, ARSLAN.
BECAUSE OF THAT, THE DYING WISH OF THE PRIOR HEAD *KAHINA* WAS THAT IF SOMETHING SHOULD HAPPEN TO HIS HIGHNESS, THOSE OF US SKILLED IN THE MARTIAL ARTS WOULD AID HIM.
AND THUS I WAS CHOSEN, BUT...
...AT ANY RATE, IT WAS LIKELY JUST A WAY TO GET RID OF A NUI-SANCE.
WHY DO YOU SAY THAT?
MY FELLOW PRIESTESSES ARE JEALOUS OF ME FOR BEING SO BEAUTIFUL, TALENTED, AND SKILLED IN BOTH ACADEMICS AND BATTLE.
I SEE.
DIRECT

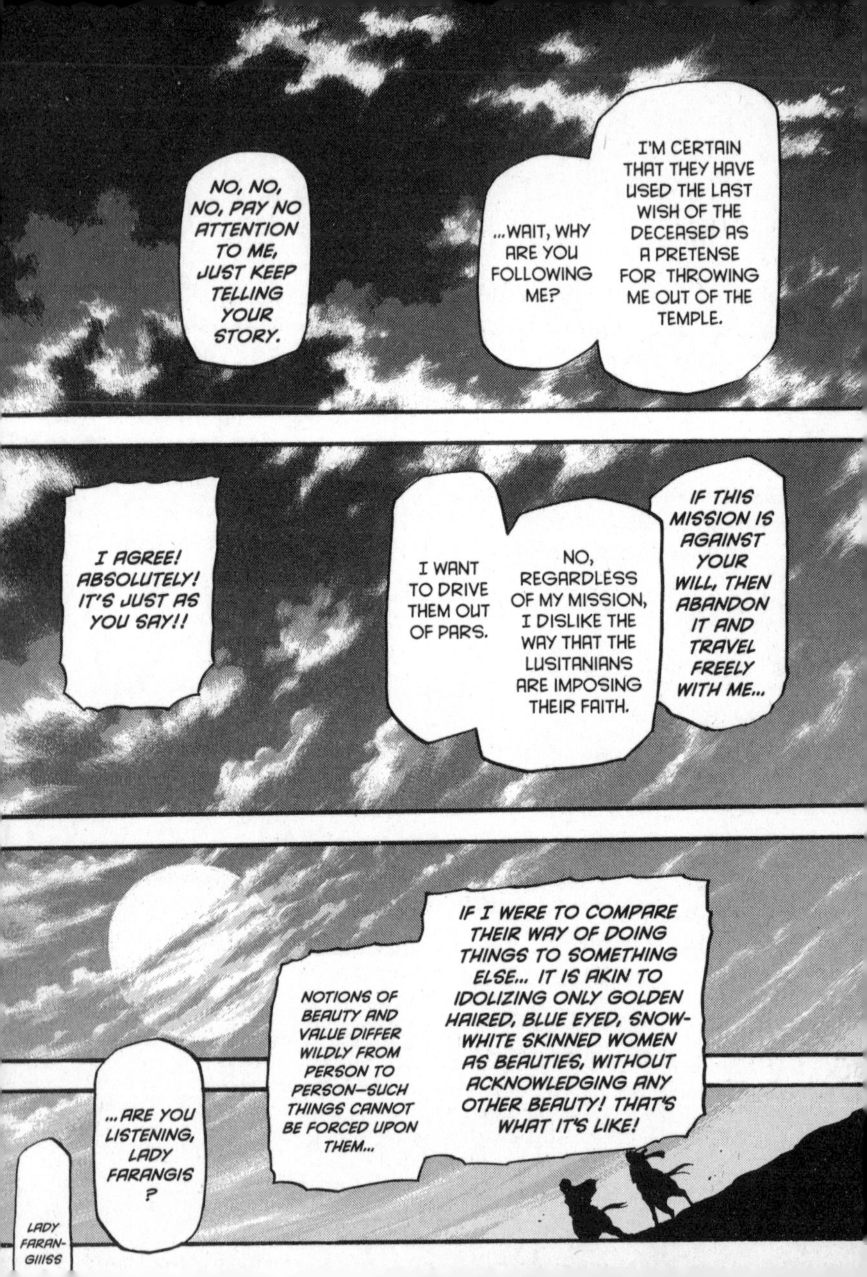
I'M CERTAIN THAT THEY HAVE USED THE LAST WISH OF THE DECEASED AS A PRETENSE FOR THROWING ME OUT OF THE TEMPLE.
...WAIT, WHY ARE YOU FOLLOWING ME?
NO, NO, NO, PAY NO ATTENTION TO ME, JUST KEEP TELLING YOUR STORY.
IF THIS MISSION IS AGAINST YOUR WILL, THEN ABANDON IT AND TRAVEL FREELY WITH ME...
NO, REGARDLESS OF MY MISSION, I DISLIKE THE WAY THAT THE LUSITANIANS ARE IMPOSING THEIR FAITH.
I WANT TO DRIVE THEM OUT OF PARS.
I AGREE! ABSOLUTELY! IT'S JUST AS YOU SAY!!
IF I WERE TO COMPARE THEIR WAY OF DOING THINGS TO SOMETHING ELSE... IT IS AKIN TO IDOLIZING ONLY GOLDEN HAIRED, BLUE EYED, SNOW-WHITE SKINNED WOMEN AS BEAUTIES, WITHOUT ACKNOWLEDGING ANY OTHER BEAUTY! THAT'S WHAT IT'S LIKE!
NOTIONS OF BEAUTY AND VALUE DIFFER WILDLY FROM PERSON TO PERSON—SUCH THINGS CANNOT BE FORCED UPON THEM...
...ARE YOU LISTENING, LADY FARANGIS ?
LADY FARAN-GIIISS

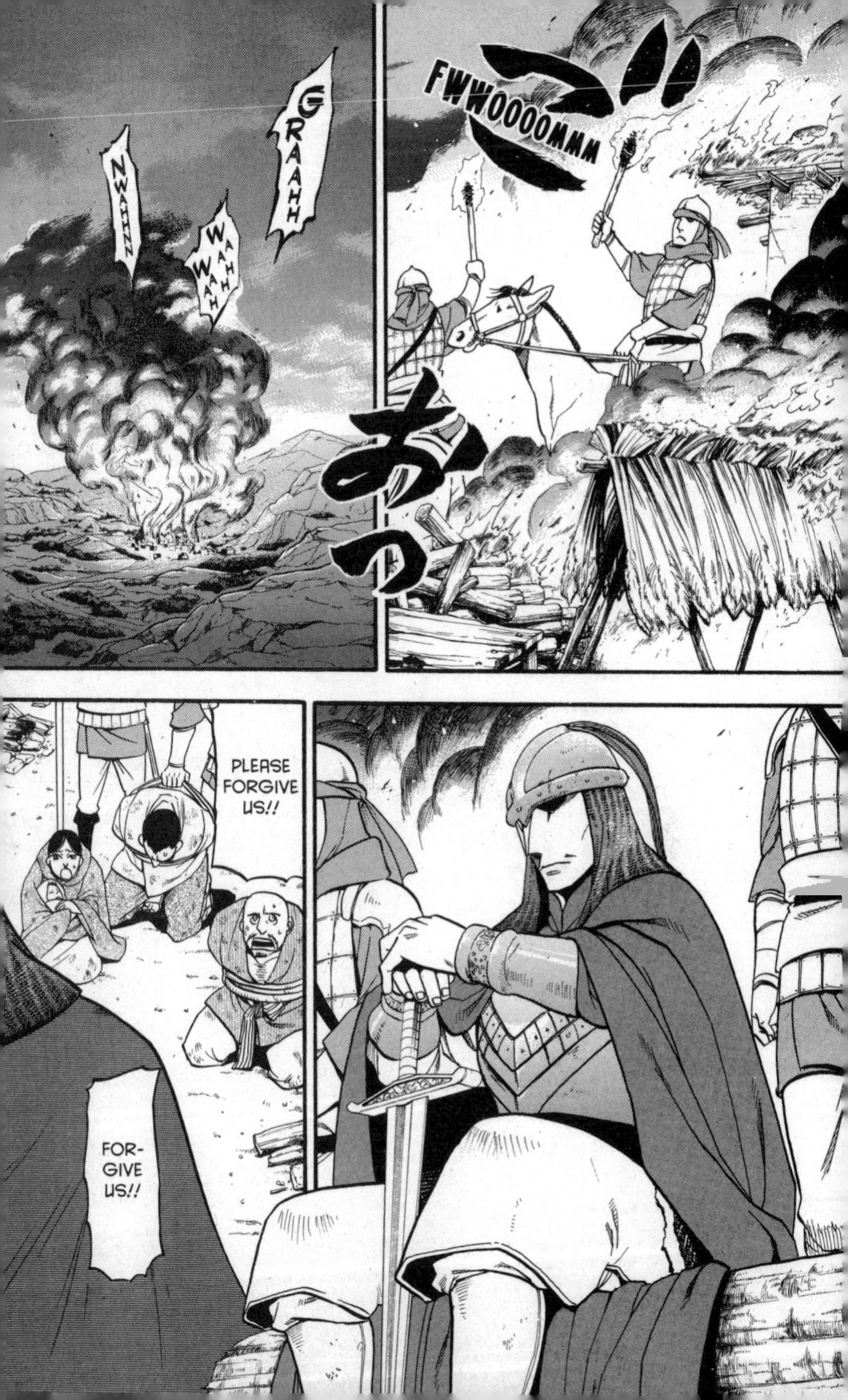
FWWOOOOMMM
あつ
GRAAAHH
NWAHHNN
WAH WAH WAH
PLEASE FORGIVE US!!
FOR-GIVE US!!

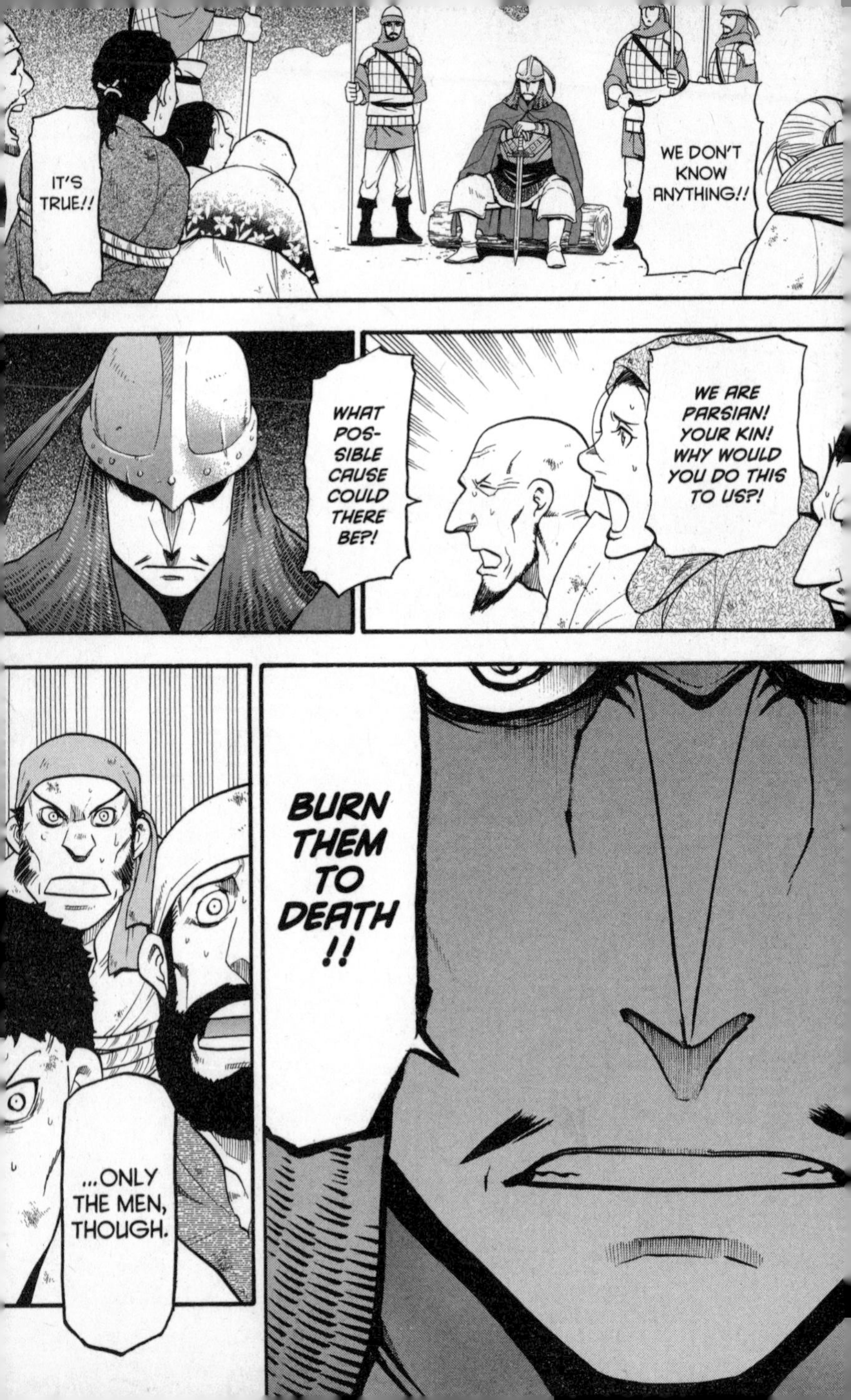
WE DON'T KNOW ANYTHING!!
IT'S TRUE!!
WE ARE PARSIAN! YOUR KIN! WHY WOULD YOU DO THIS TO US?!
WHAT POS-SIBLE CAUSE COULD THERE BE?!
BURN THEM TO DEATH!!
...ONLY THE MEN, THOUGH.

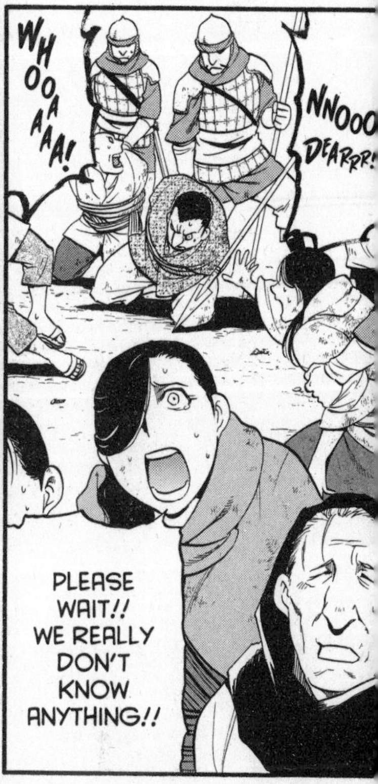
NNOOO DEARRR!
WHOOAAAA!
PLEASE WAIT!! WE REALLY DON'T KNOW ANYTHING!!

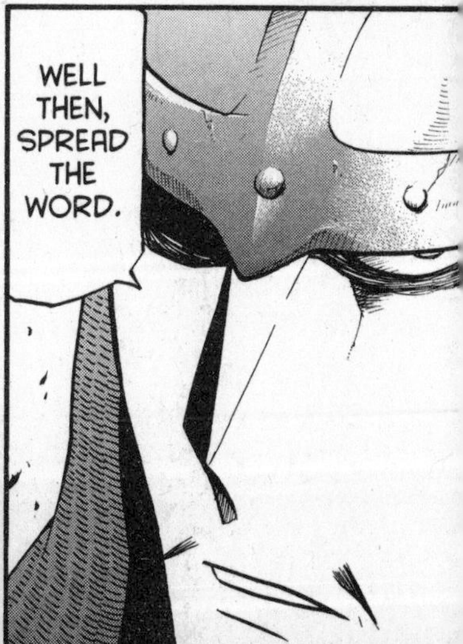
WELL THEN, SPREAD THE WORD.

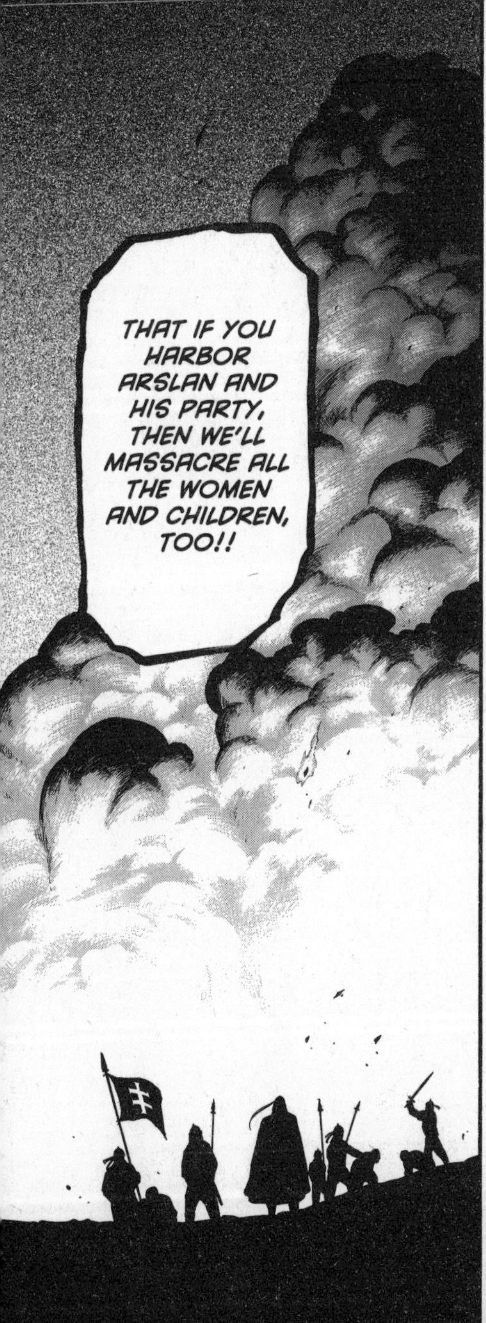
THAT IF YOU HARBOR ARSLAN AND HIS PARTY, THEN WE'LL MASSACRE ALL THE WOMEN AND CHILDREN, TOO!!

THE HEROIC LEGEND OF
ARSLAN

Chapter Thirteen: The Traitor Hero

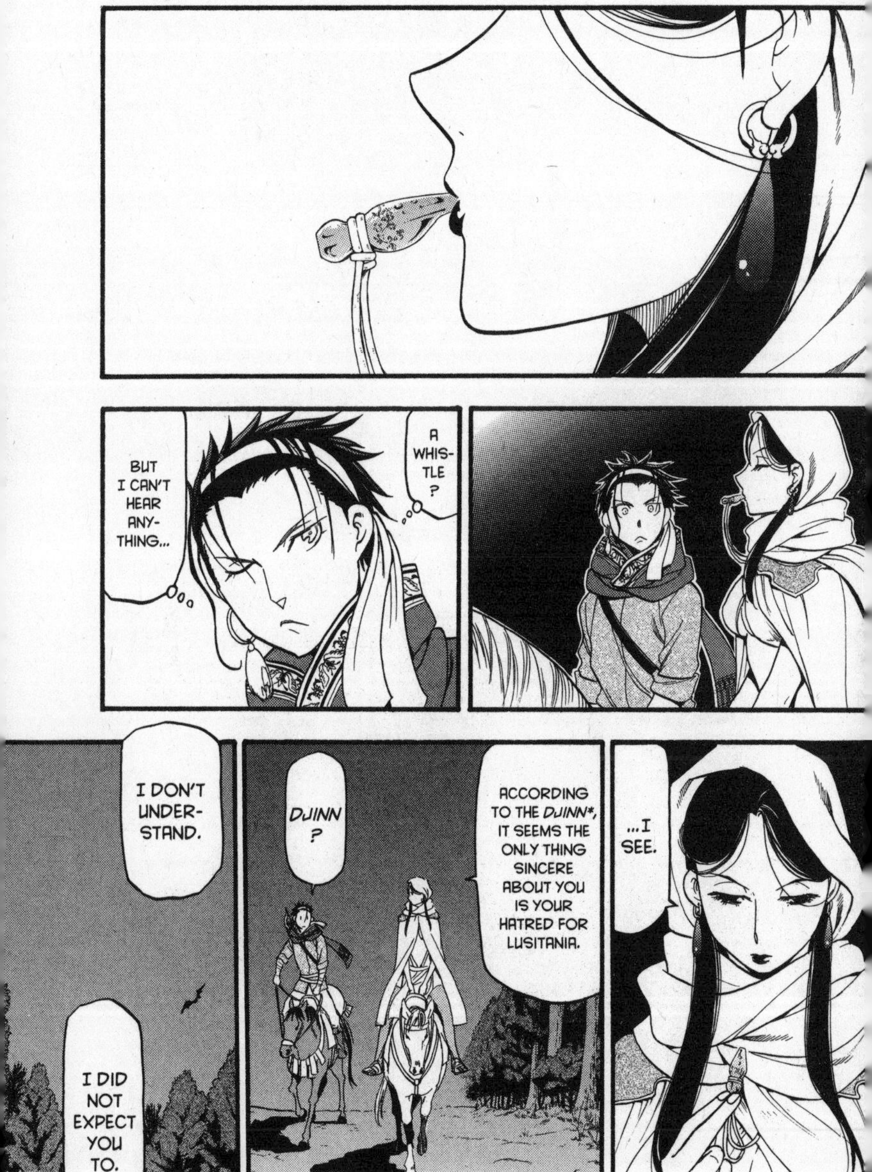
A WHISTLE?
BUT I CAN'T HEAR ANYTHING...
...I SEE.
ACCORDING TO THE *DJINN**, IT SEEMS THE ONLY THING SINCERE ABOUT YOU IS YOUR HATRED FOR LUSITANIA.
DJINN?
I DON'T UNDERSTAND.
I DID NOT EXPECT YOU TO.

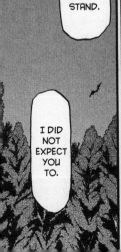

*DJINN: (SOMETIMES CALLED GENIES IN ENGLISH) ARE SUPERNATURAL SPIRITS APPEARING IN NEAR-EASTERN MYTHOLOGY. THEY'RE OFTEN DESCRIBED AS NATURAL CREATURES MADE OF PURE FIRE THAT LIVE IN A WORLD UNSEEN TO MOST HUMANS.

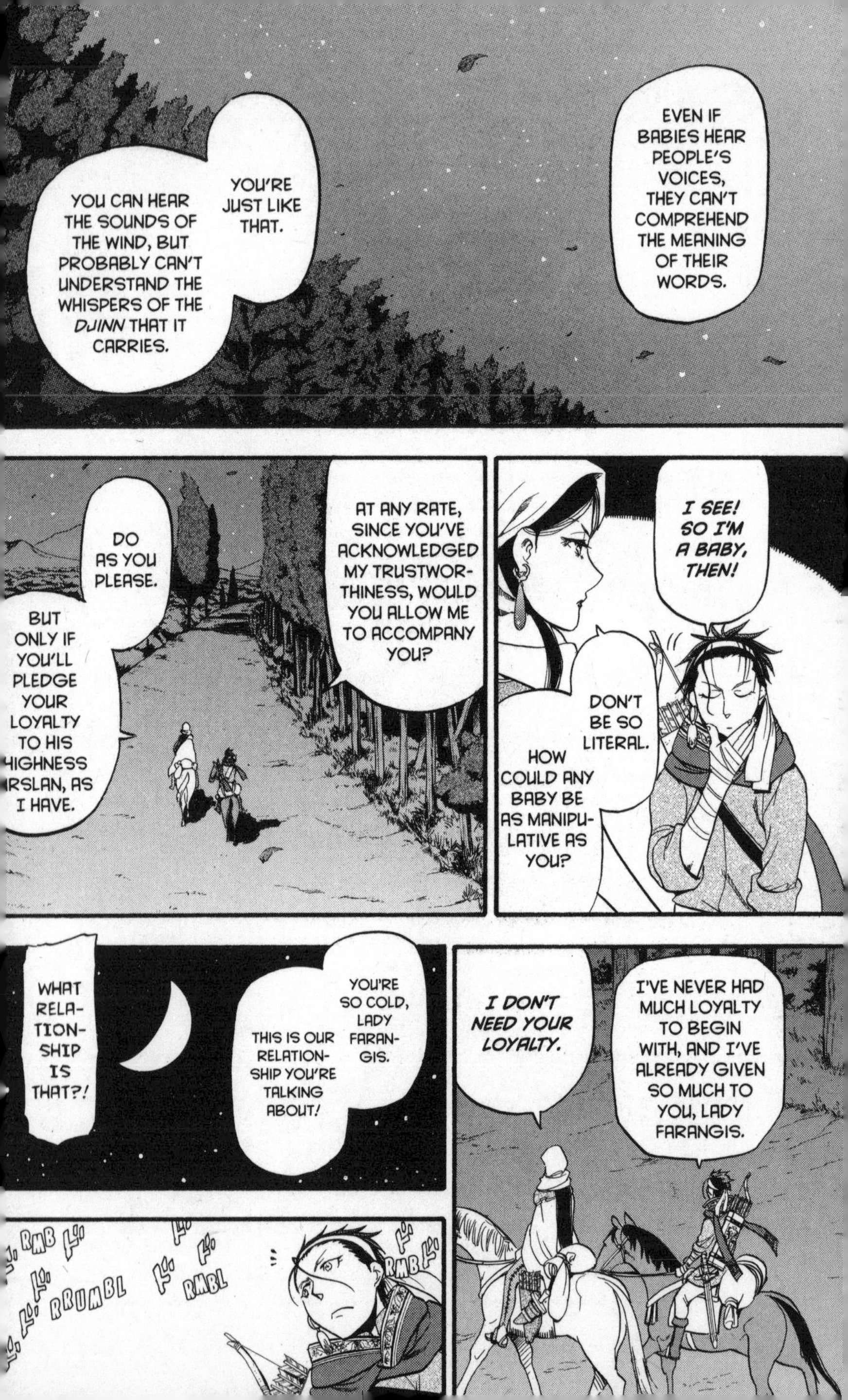
EVEN IF BABIES HEAR PEOPLE'S VOICES, THEY CAN'T COMPREHEND THE MEANING OF THEIR WORDS.
YOU'RE JUST LIKE THAT.
YOU CAN HEAR THE SOUNDS OF THE WIND, BUT PROBABLY CAN'T UNDERSTAND THE WHISPERS OF THE *DJINN* THAT IT CARRIES.
I SEE! SO I'M A BABY, THEN!
DON'T BE SO LITERAL.
HOW COULD ANY BABY BE AS MANIPULATIVE AS YOU?
AT ANY RATE, SINCE YOU'VE ACKNOWLEDGED MY TRUSTWORTHINESS, WOULD YOU ALLOW ME TO ACCOMPANY YOU?
DO AS YOU PLEASE.
BUT ONLY IF YOU'LL PLEDGE YOUR LOYALTY TO HIS HIGHNESS RSLAN, AS I HAVE.
I'VE NEVER HAD MUCH LOYALTY TO BEGIN WITH, AND I'VE ALREADY GIVEN SO MUCH TO YOU, LADY FARANGIS.
I DON'T NEED YOUR LOYALTY.
YOU'RE SO COLD, LADY FARANGIS.
THIS IS OUR RELATIONSHIP YOU'RE TALKING ABOUT!
WHAT RELATIONSHIP IS THAT?!
RMB
RMBL
RRUMBL
RMB

RRUMMBL

RMBL

RRUMMMBBLLL

RMBL

I DON'T THINK SO.

PAR-
SIAN
SOL-
DIERS
...

53

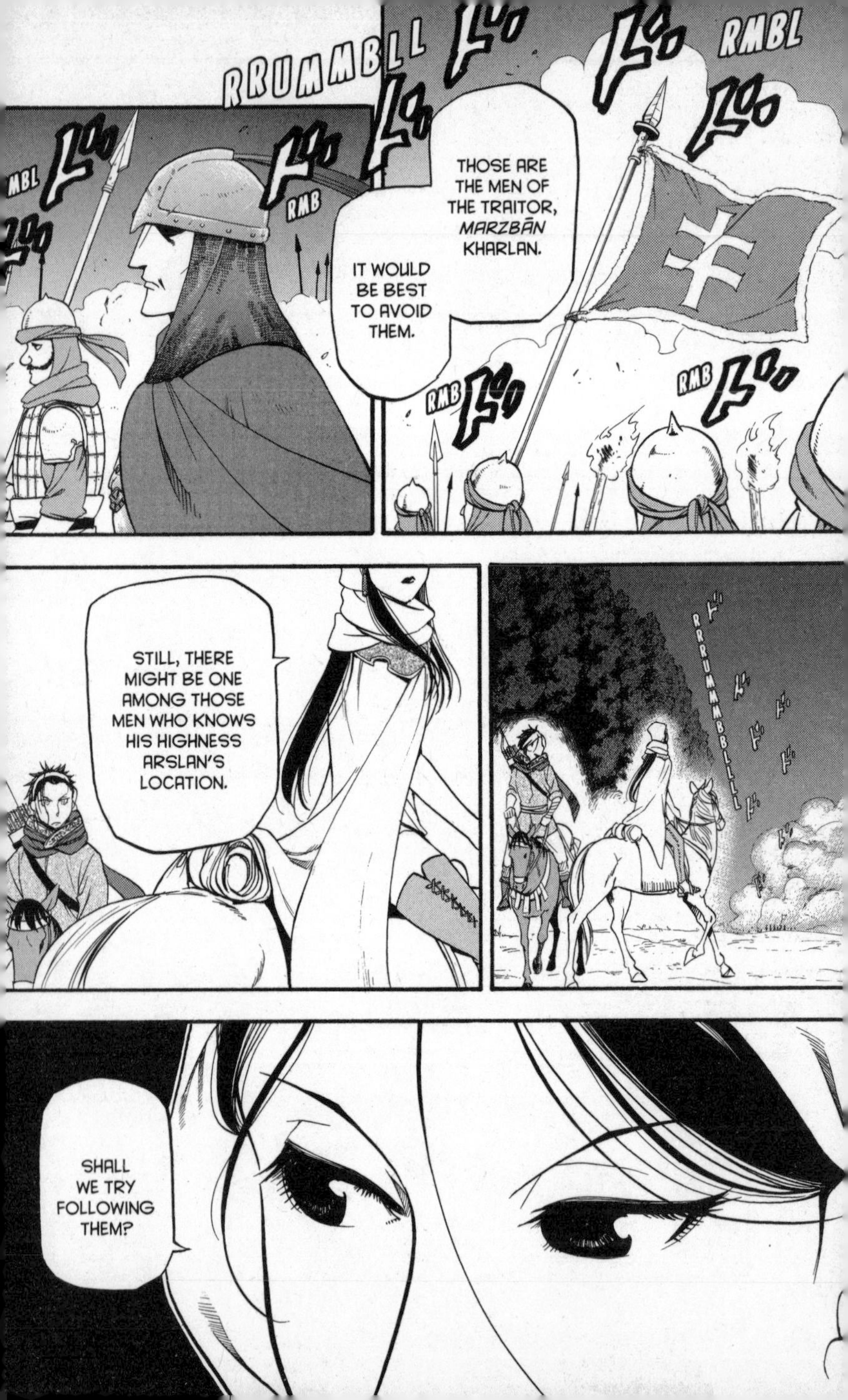
RMBL
RRUMMBLL
THOSE ARE THE MEN OF THE TRAITOR, *MARZBĀN* KHARLAN.
RMB
RMB
IT WOULD BE BEST TO AVOID THEM.
RMB
MBL
RRRUMMMBBLLLL
STILL, THERE MIGHT BE ONE AMONG THOSE MEN WHO KNOWS HIS HIGHNESS ARSLAN'S LOCATION.
SHALL WE TRY FOLLOWING THEM?

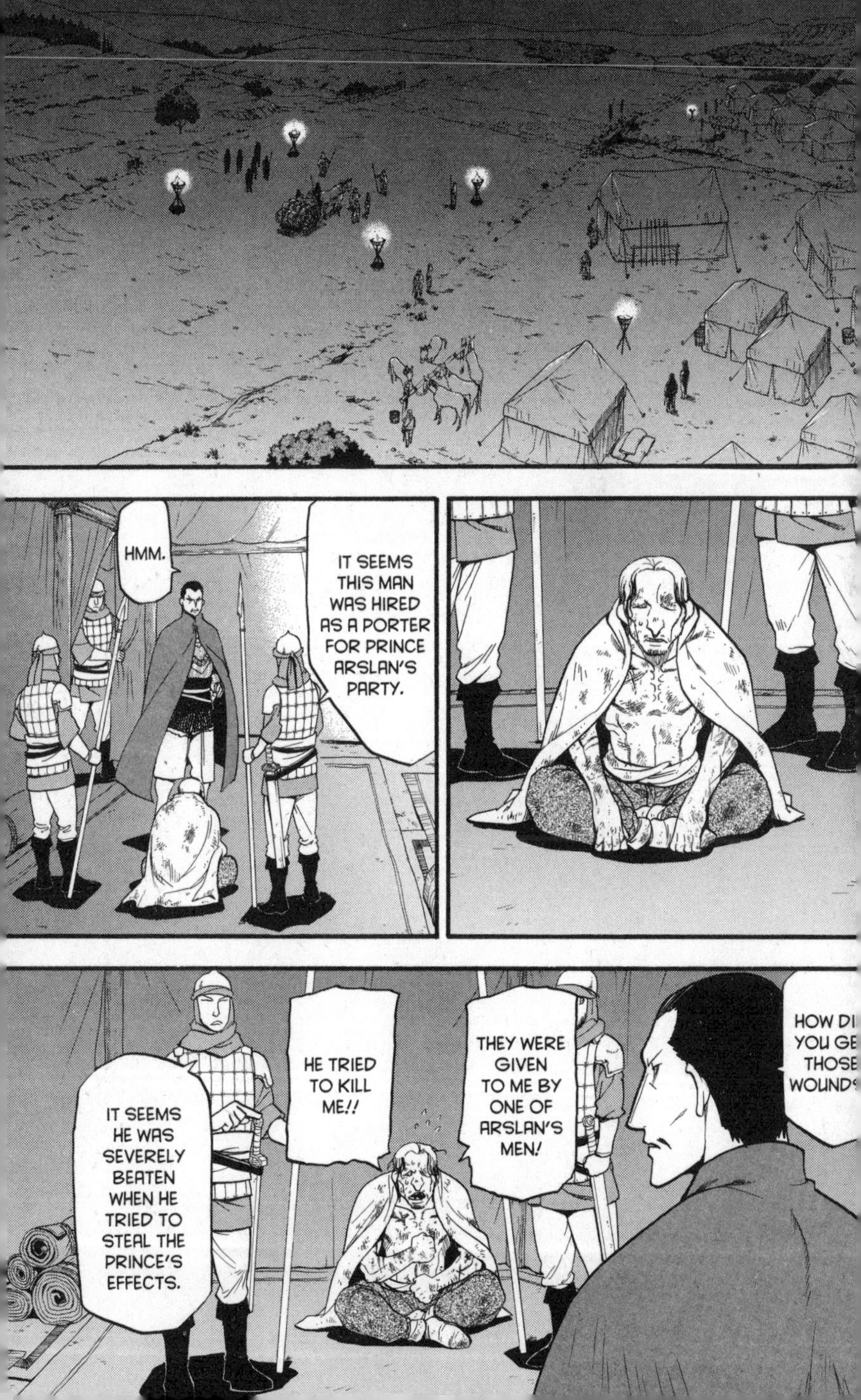
IT SEEMS THIS MAN WAS HIRED AS A PORTER FOR PRINCE ARSLAN'S PARTY.
HMM.
HOW DI YOU GE THOSE WOUNDS
THEY WERE GIVEN TO ME BY ONE OF ARSLAN'S MEN!
HE TRIED TO KILL ME!!
IT SEEMS HE WAS SEVERELY BEATEN WHEN HE TRIED TO STEAL THE PRINCE'S EFFECTS.

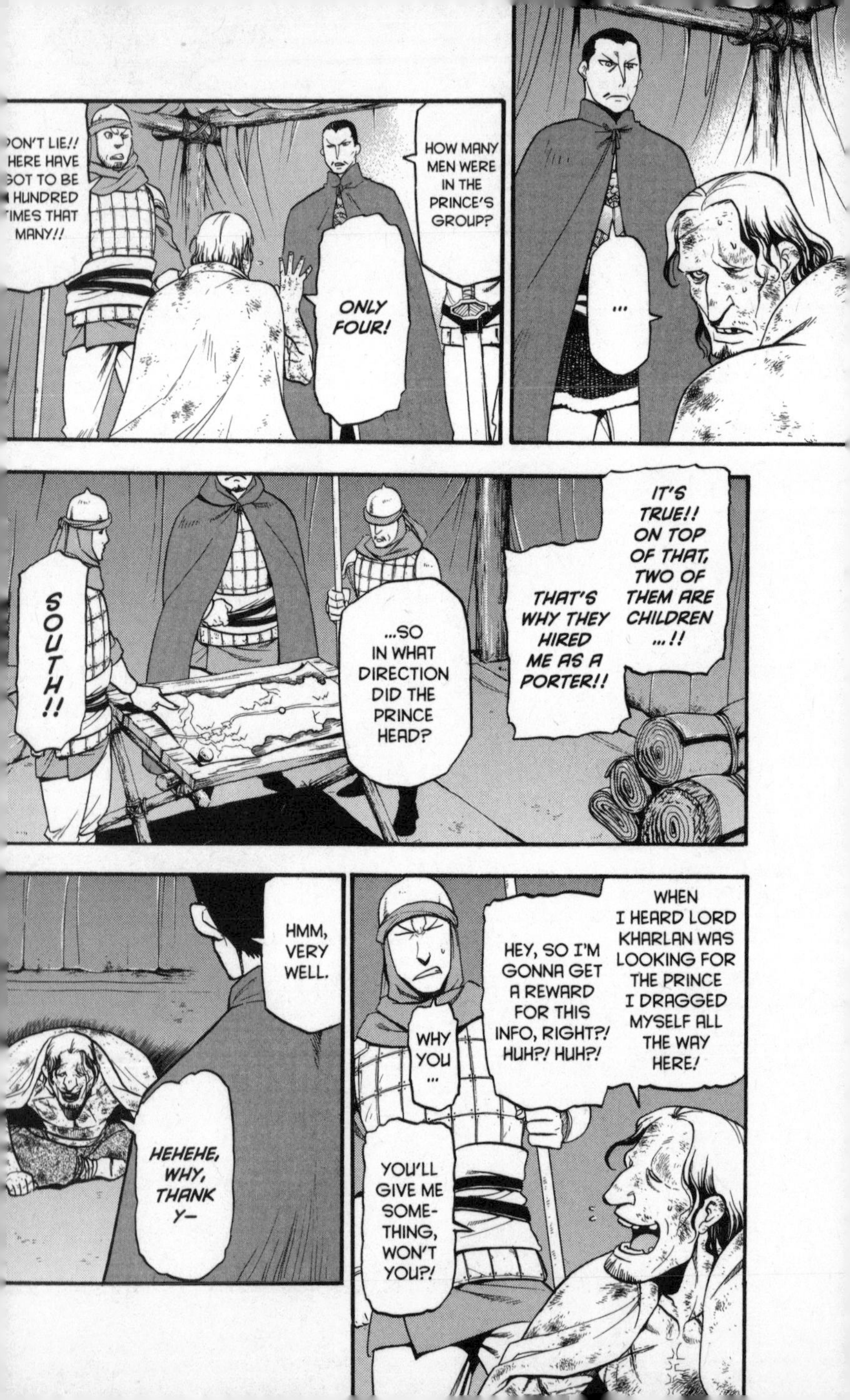
...
HOW MANY MEN WERE IN THE PRINCE'S GROUP?
ONLY FOUR!
DON'T LIE!! HERE HAVE GOT TO BE HUNDRED TIMES THAT MANY!!
IT'S TRUE!! ON TOP OF THAT, TWO OF THEM ARE CHILDREN ...!!
THAT'S WHY THEY HIRED ME AS A PORTER!!
...SO IN WHAT DIRECTION DID THE PRINCE HEAD?
SOUTH!!
WHEN I HEARD LORD KHARLAN WAS LOOKING FOR THE PRINCE I DRAGGED MYSELF ALL THE WAY HERE!
HEY, SO I'M GONNA GET A REWARD FOR THIS INFO, RIGHT?! HUH?! HUH?!
WHY YOU ...
YOU'LL GIVE ME SOMETHING, WON'T YOU?!
HMM, VERY WELL.
HEHEHE, WHY, THANK Y—

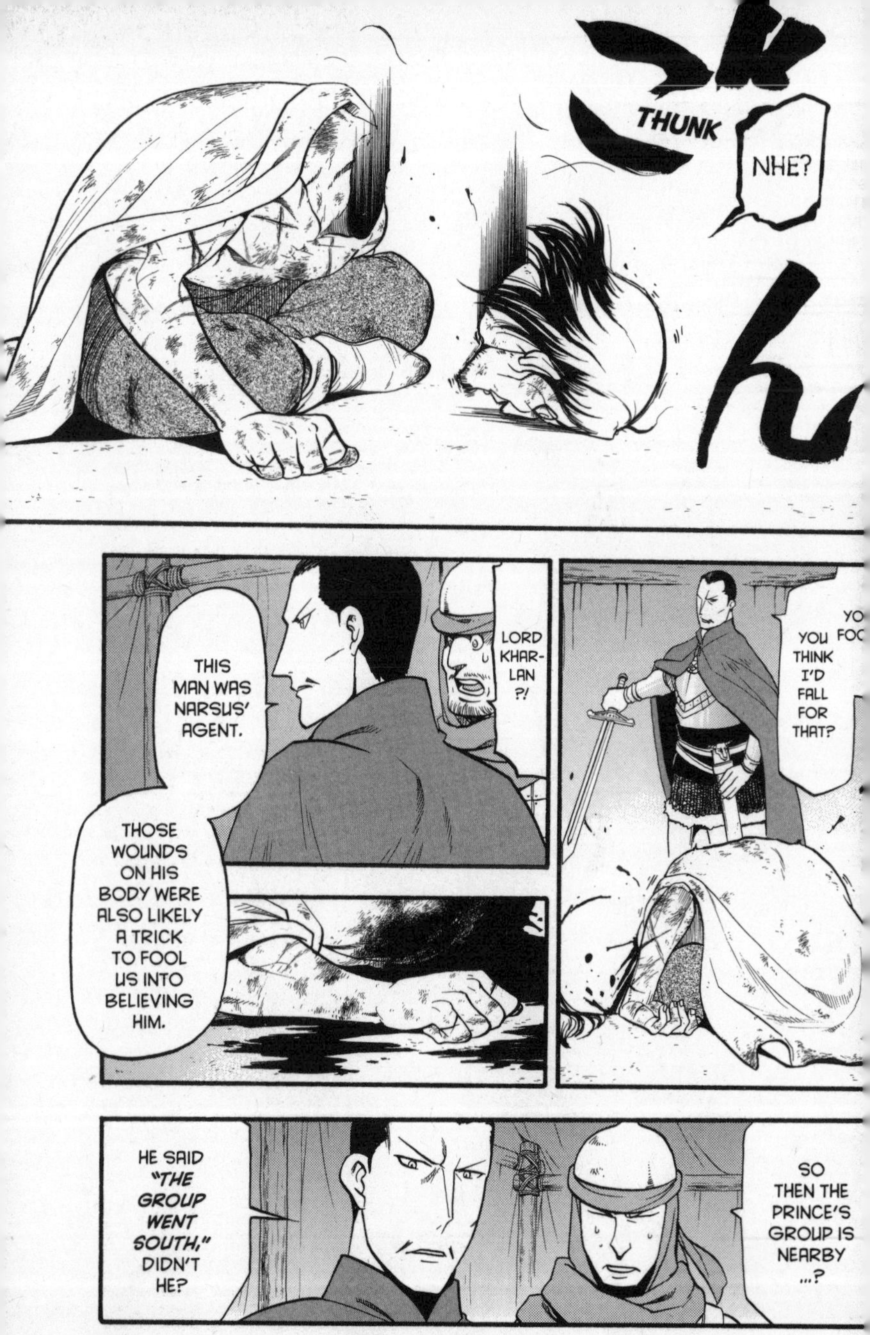
THUNK
NHE?
YOU THINK I'D FALL FOR THAT?
LORD KHARLAN?!
THIS MAN WAS NARSUS' AGENT.
THOSE WOUNDS ON HIS BODY WERE ALSO LIKELY A TRICK TO FOOL US INTO BELIEVING HIM.
SO THEN THE PRINCE'S GROUP IS NEARBY ...?
HE SAID *"THE GROUP WENT SOUTH,"* DIDN'T HE?

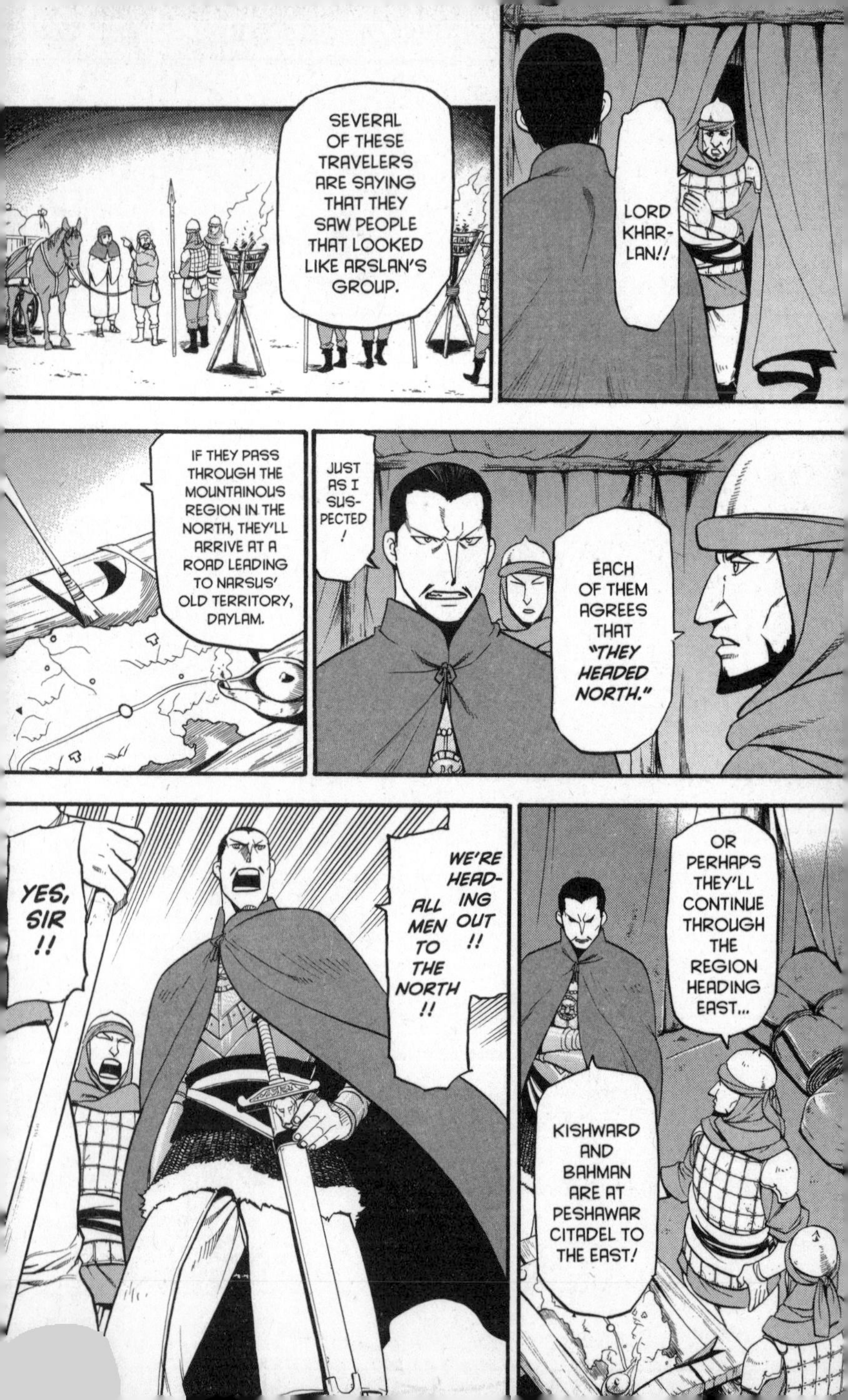
LORD KHARLAN!!
SEVERAL OF THESE TRAVELERS ARE SAYING THAT THEY SAW PEOPLE THAT LOOKED LIKE ARSLAN'S GROUP.
EACH OF THEM AGREES THAT "THEY HEADED NORTH."
JUST AS I SUSPECTED!
IF THEY PASS THROUGH THE MOUNTAINOUS REGION IN THE NORTH, THEY'LL ARRIVE AT A ROAD LEADING TO NARSUS' OLD TERRITORY, DAYLAM.
OR PERHAPS THEY'LL CONTINUE THROUGH THE REGION HEADING EAST...
KISHWARD AND BAHMAN ARE AT PESHAWAR CITADEL TO THE EAST!
WE'RE HEADING OUT!!
ALL MEN TO THE NORTH!!
YES, SIR!!

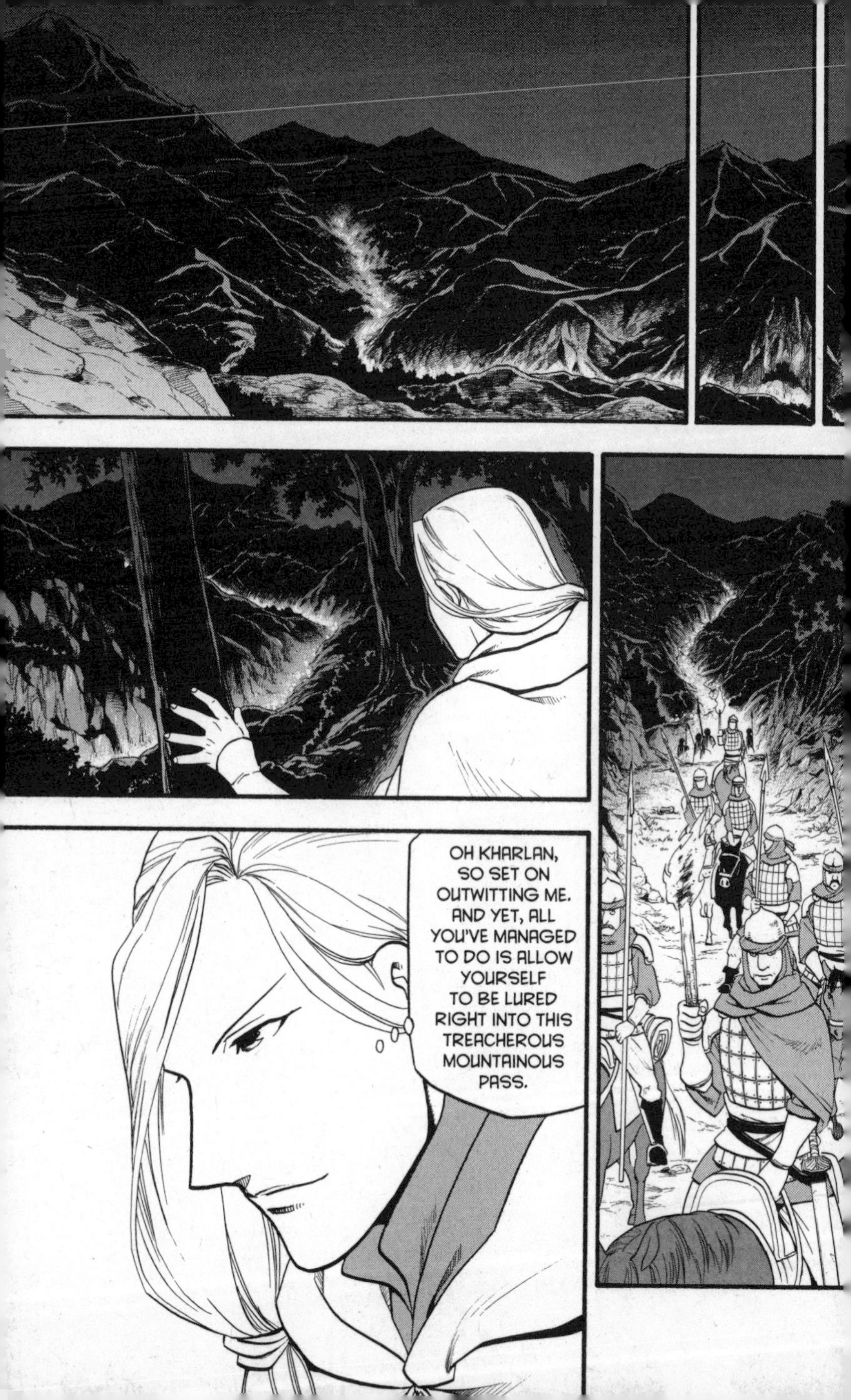
OH KHARLAN, SO SET ON OUTWITTING ME. AND YET, ALL YOU'VE MANAGED TO DO IS ALLOW YOURSELF TO BE LURED RIGHT INTO THIS TREACHEROUS MOUNTAINOUS PASS.

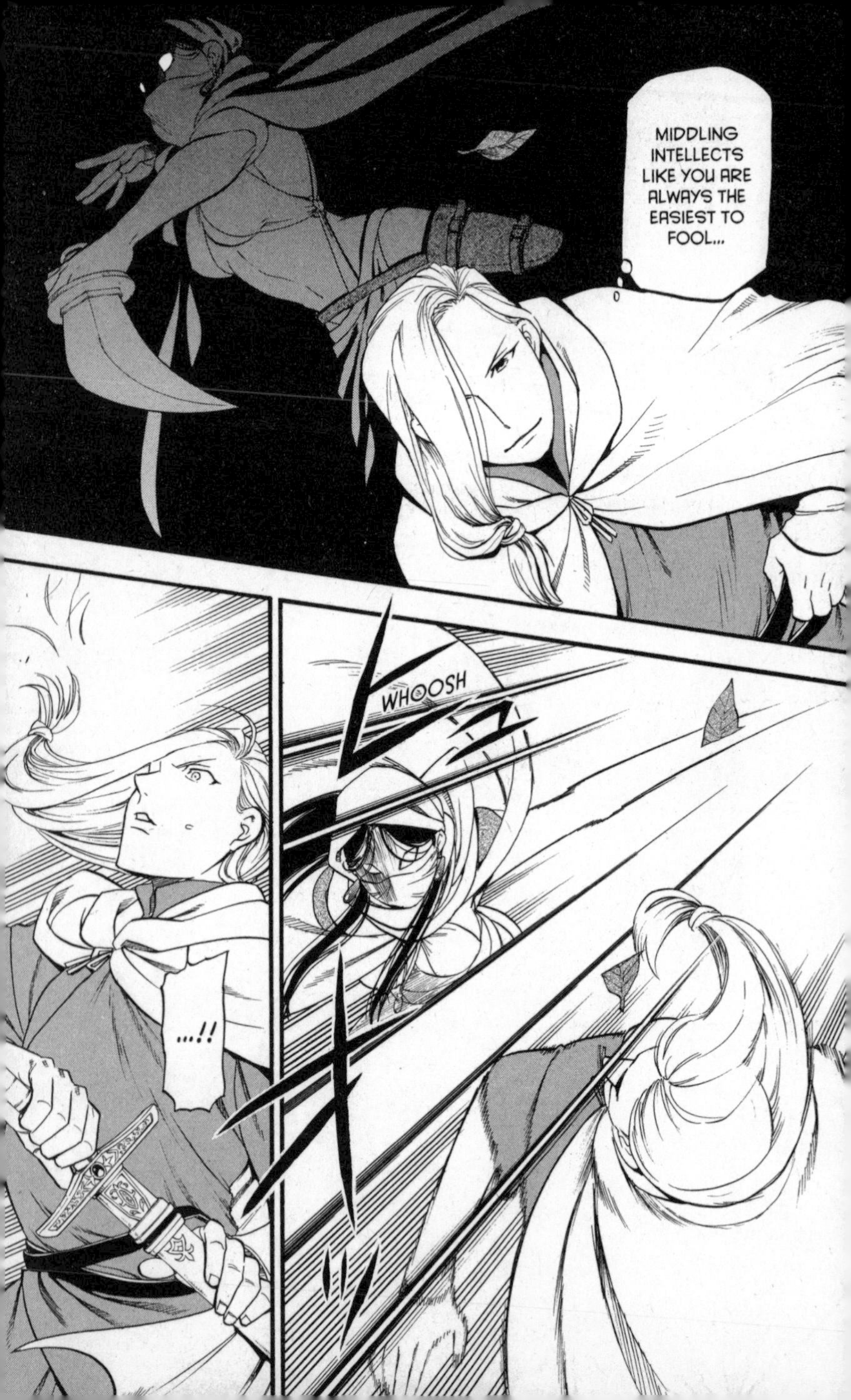
MIDDLING INTELLECTS LIKE YOU ARE ALWAYS THE EASIEST TO FOOL...
WHOOSH
...!!

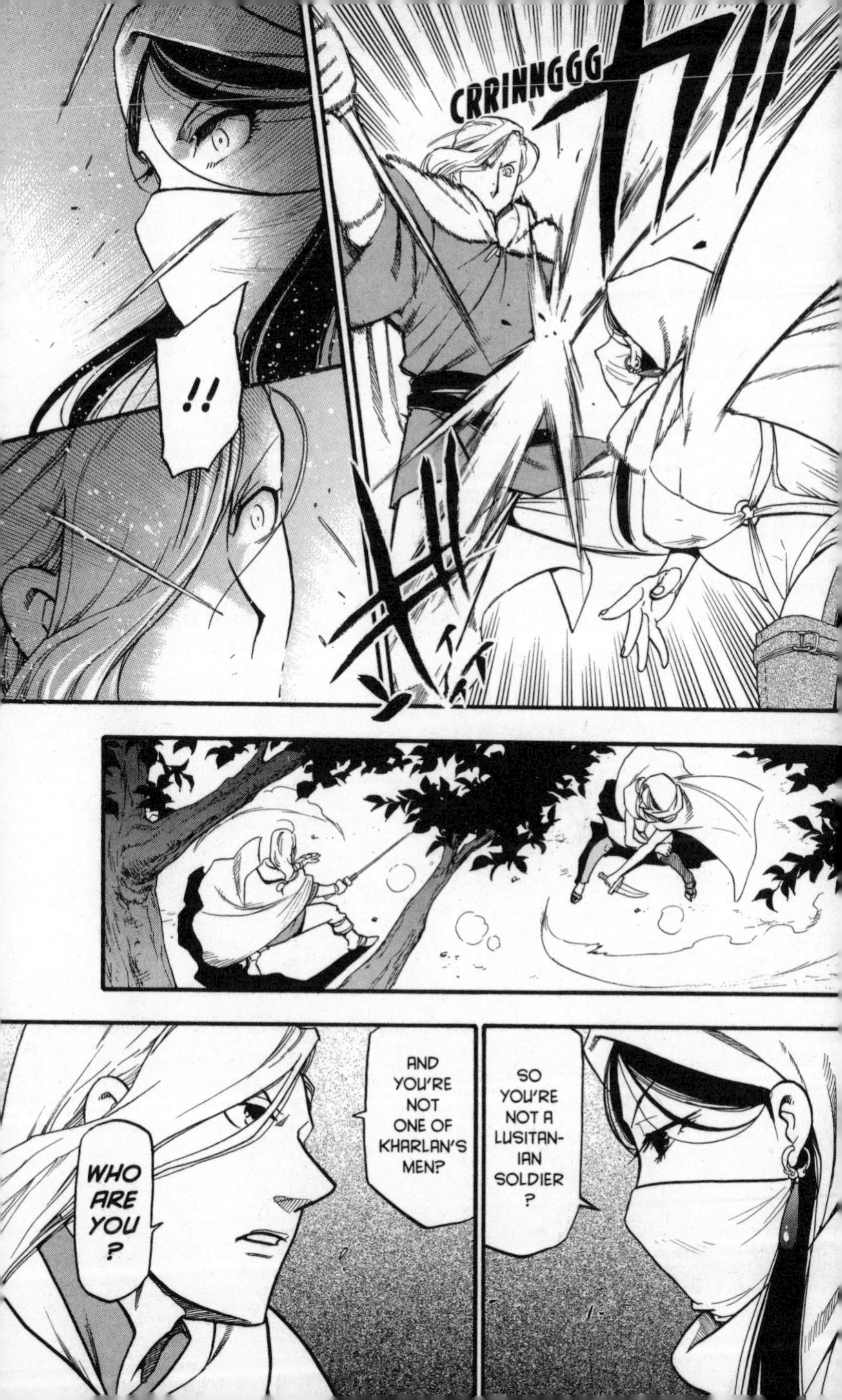
CRRINNGGG
!!
SO YOU'RE NOT A LUSITAN-IAN SOLDIER?
AND YOU'RE NOT ONE OF KHARLAN'S MEN?
WHO ARE YOU?

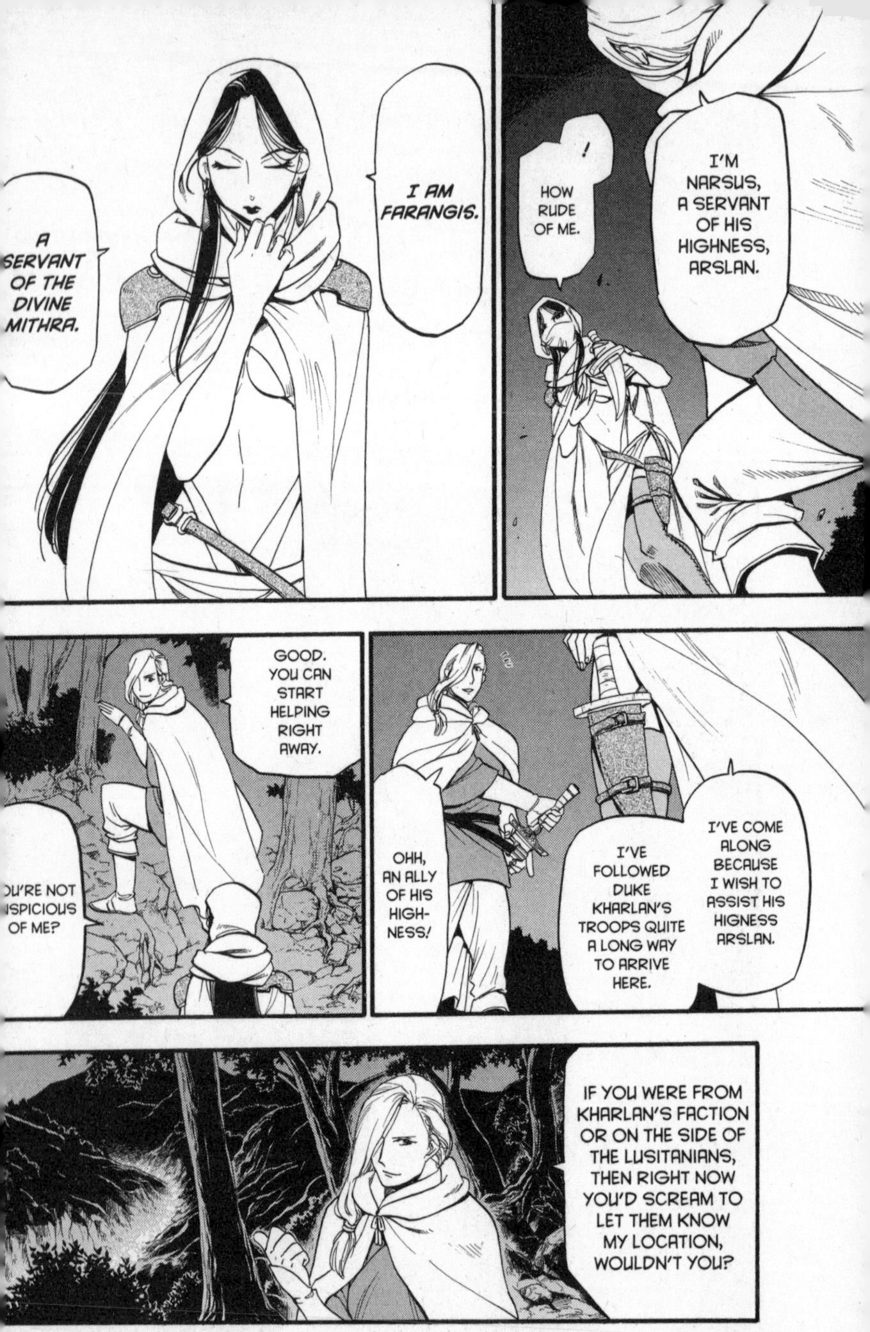
I'M NARSUS, A SERVANT OF HIS HIGHNESS, ARSLAN.
!
HOW RUDE OF ME.
I AM FARANGIS.
A SERVANT OF THE DIVINE MITHRA.
I'VE COME ALONG BECAUSE I WISH TO ASSIST HIS HIGNESS ARSLAN.
I'VE FOLLOWED DUKE KHARLAN'S TROOPS QUITE A LONG WAY TO ARRIVE HERE.
OHH, AN ALLY OF HIS HIGH-NESS!
GOOD. YOU CAN START HELPING RIGHT AWAY.
U'RE NOT SPICIOUS OF ME?
IF YOU WERE FROM KHARLAN'S FACTION OR ON THE SIDE OF THE LUSITANIANS, THEN RIGHT NOW YOU'D SCREAM TO LET THEM KNOW MY LOCATION, WOULDN'T YOU?

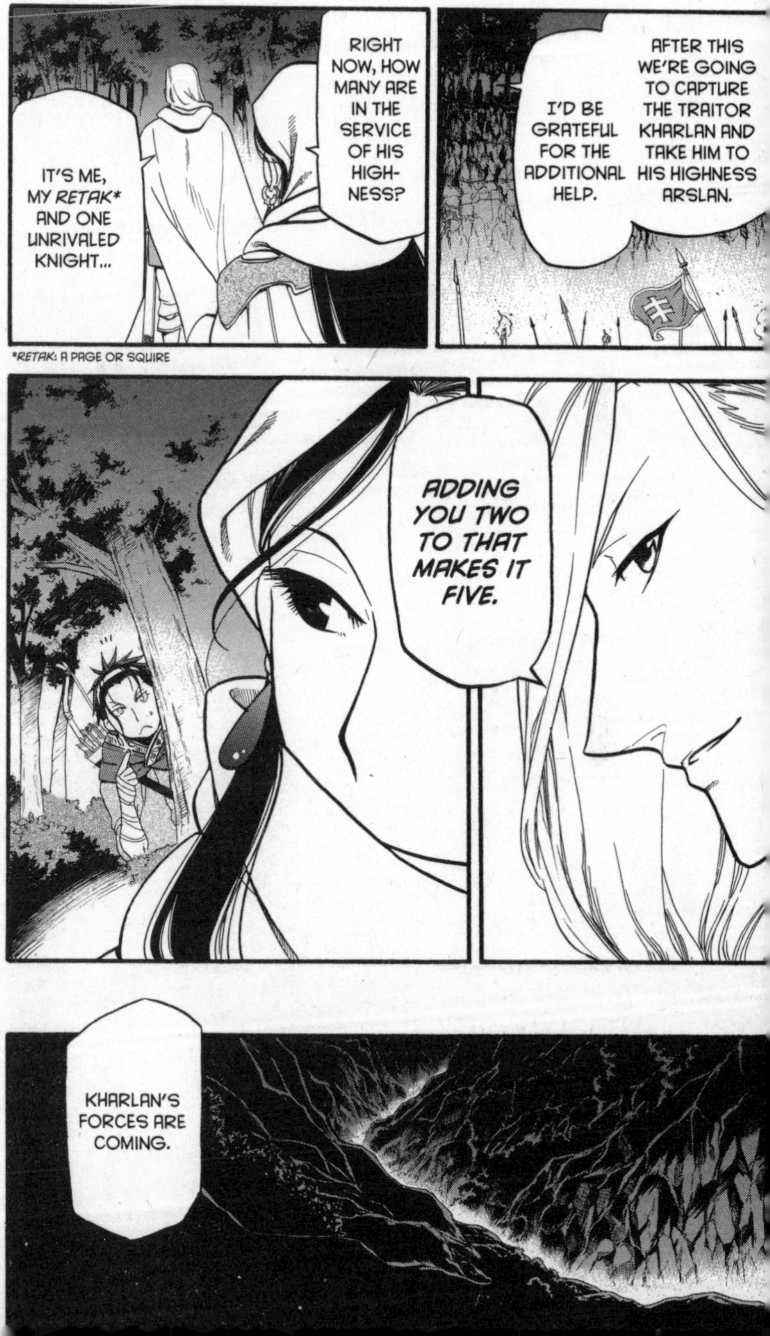
AFTER THIS WE'RE GOING TO CAPTURE THE TRAITOR KHARLAN AND TAKE HIM TO HIS HIGHNESS ARSLAN.
I'D BE GRATEFUL FOR THE ADDITIONAL HELP.
RIGHT NOW, HOW MANY ARE IN THE SERVICE OF HIS HIGHNESS?
IT'S ME, MY *RETAK** AND ONE UNRIVALED KNIGHT...
ADDING YOU TWO TO THAT MAKES IT FIVE.
KHARLAN'S FORCES ARE COMING.

**RETAK*: A PAGE OR SQUIRE

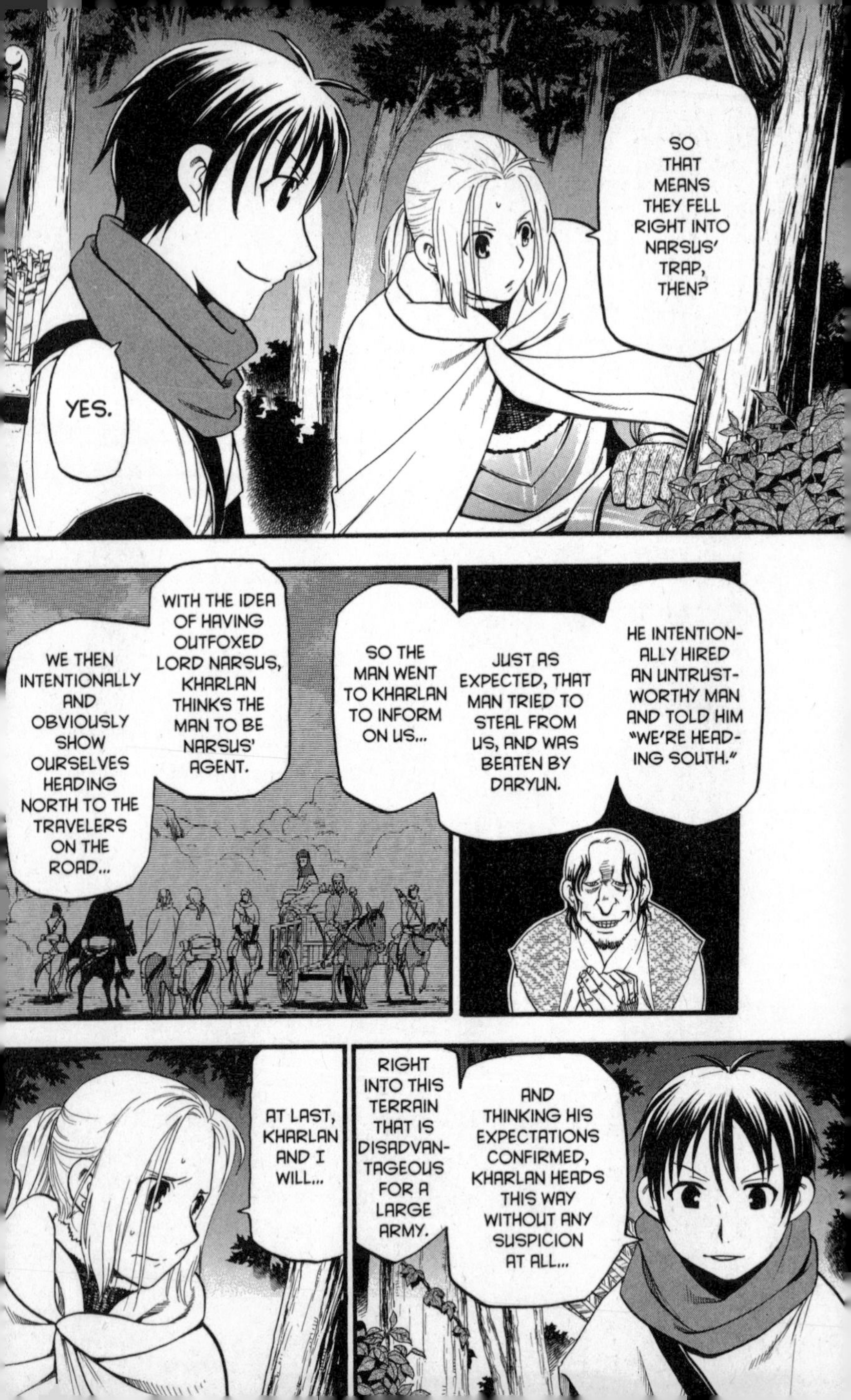
SO THAT MEANS THEY FELL RIGHT INTO NARSUS' TRAP, THEN?
YES.
HE INTENTIONALLY HIRED AN UNTRUSTWORTHY MAN AND TOLD HIM "WE'RE HEADING SOUTH."
JUST AS EXPECTED, THAT MAN TRIED TO STEAL FROM US, AND WAS BEATEN BY DARYUN.
SO THE MAN WENT TO KHARLAN TO INFORM ON US...
WITH THE IDEA OF HAVING OUTFOXED LORD NARSUS, KHARLAN THINKS THE MAN TO BE NARSUS' AGENT.
WE THEN INTENTIONALLY AND OBVIOUSLY SHOW OURSELVES HEADING NORTH TO THE TRAVELERS ON THE ROAD...
AND THINKING HIS EXPECTATIONS CONFIRMED, KHARLAN HEADS THIS WAY WITHOUT ANY SUSPICION AT ALL...
RIGHT INTO THIS TERRAIN THAT IS DISADVANTAGEOUS FOR A LARGE ARMY.
AT LAST, KHARLAN AND I WILL...

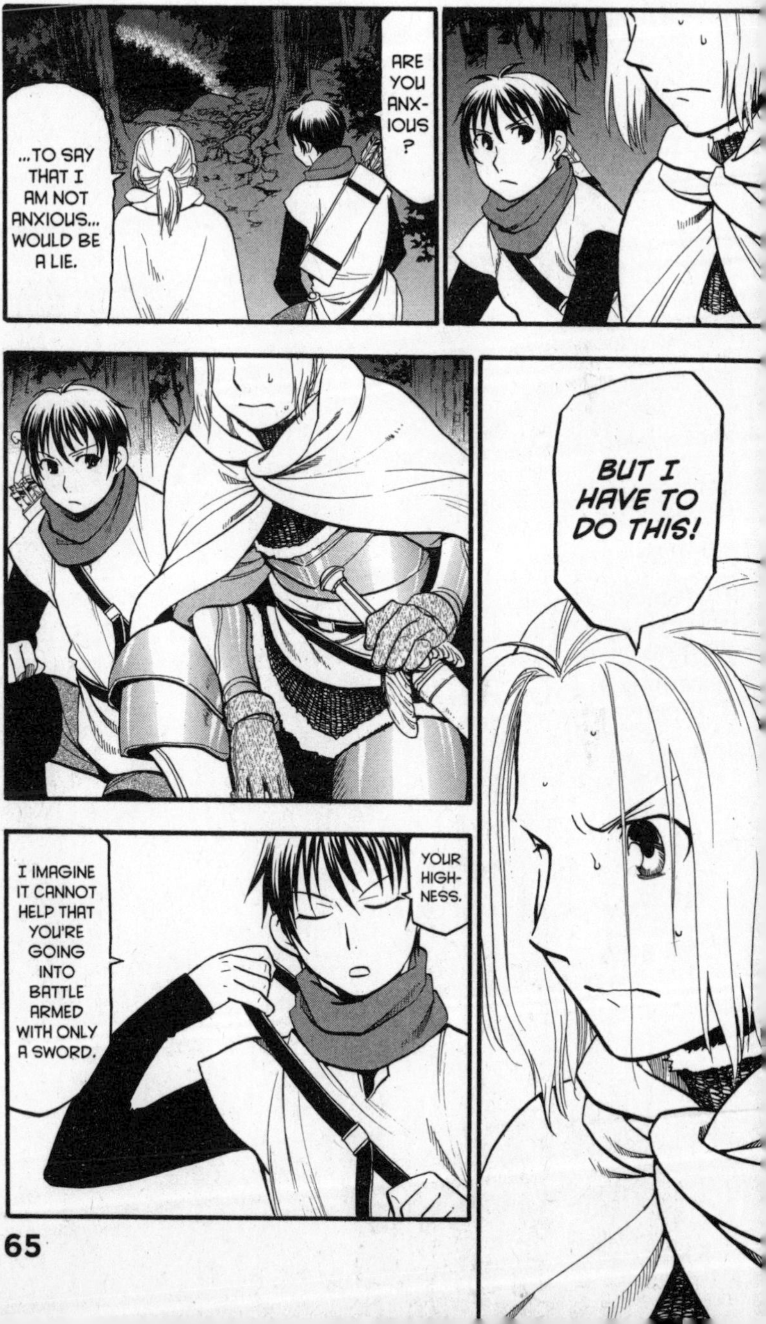
ARE YOU ANXIOUS?
...TO SAY THAT I AM NOT ANXIOUS... WOULD BE A LIE.
BUT I HAVE TO DO THIS!
YOUR HIGHNESS.
I IMAGINE IT CANNOT HELP THAT YOU'RE GOING INTO BATTLE ARMED WITH ONLY A SWORD.

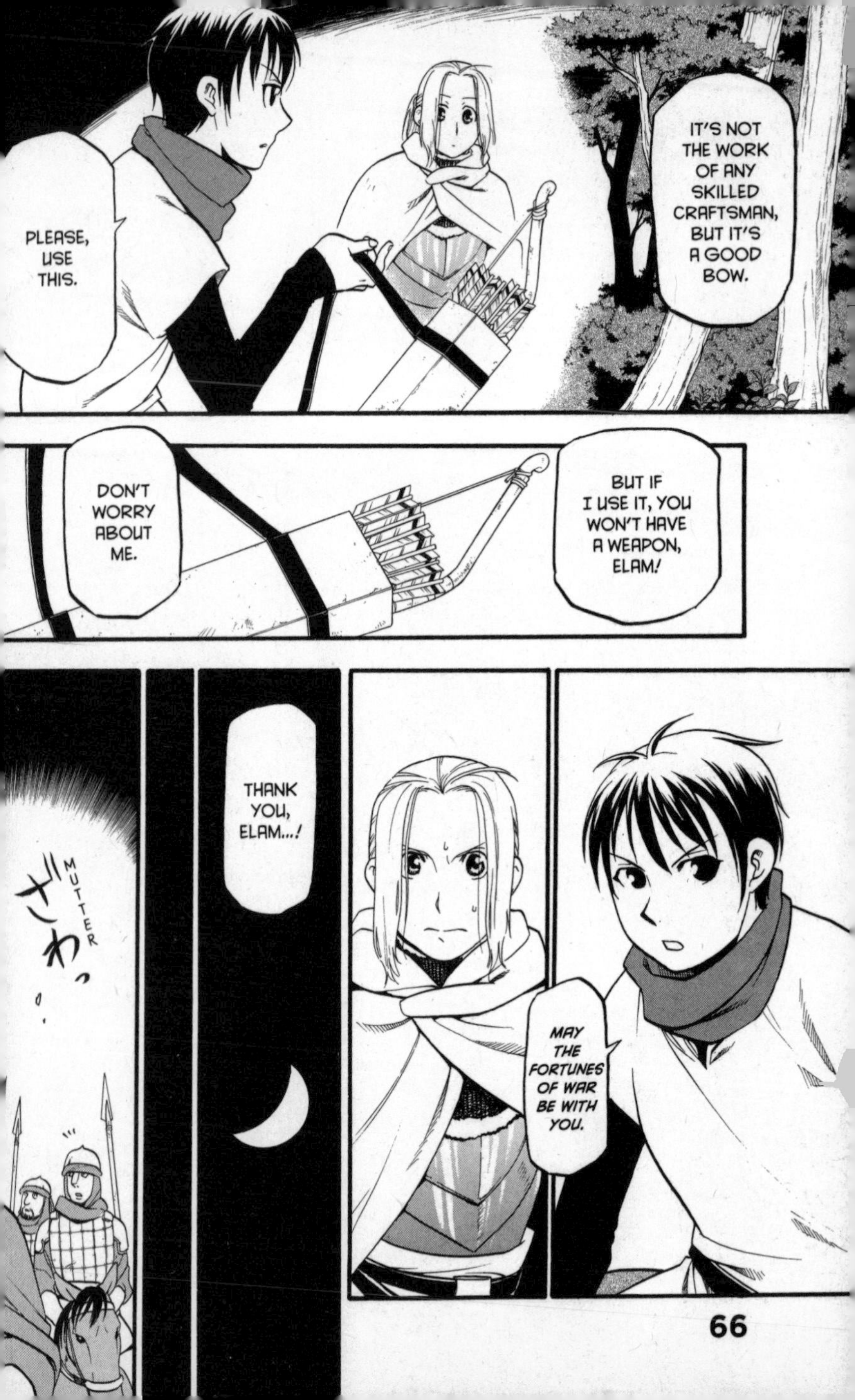
IT'S NOT THE WORK OF ANY SKILLED CRAFTSMAN, BUT IT'S A GOOD BOW.
PLEASE, USE THIS.
BUT IF I USE IT, YOU WON'T HAVE A WEAPON, ELAM!
DON'T WORRY ABOUT ME.
MAY THE FORTUNES OF WAR BE WITH YOU.
THANK YOU, ELAM...!
ざわっ
MUTTER

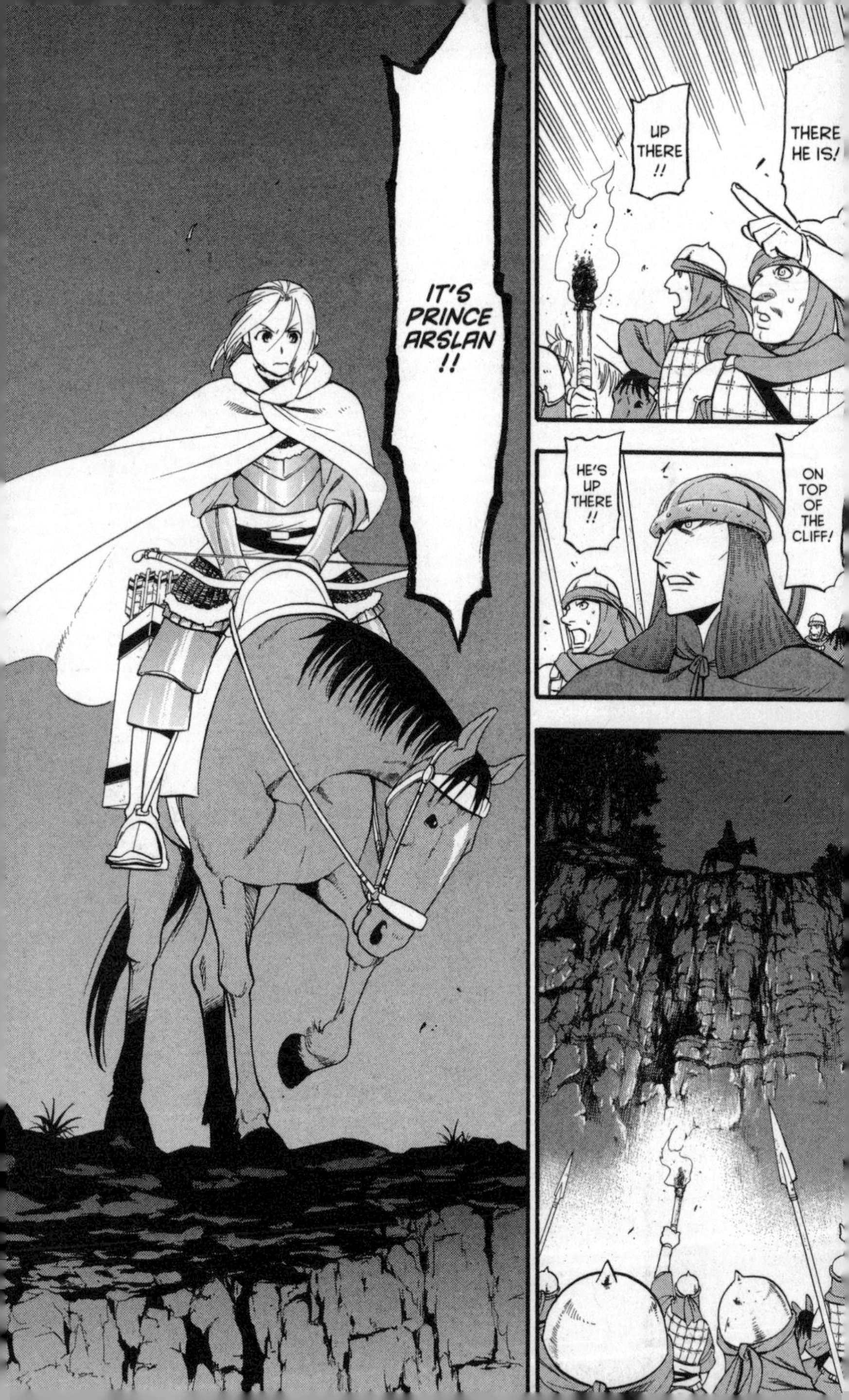
THERE HE IS!
UP THERE !!
ON TOP OF THE CLIFF!
HE'S UP THERE !!
IT'S PRINCE ARSLAN !!

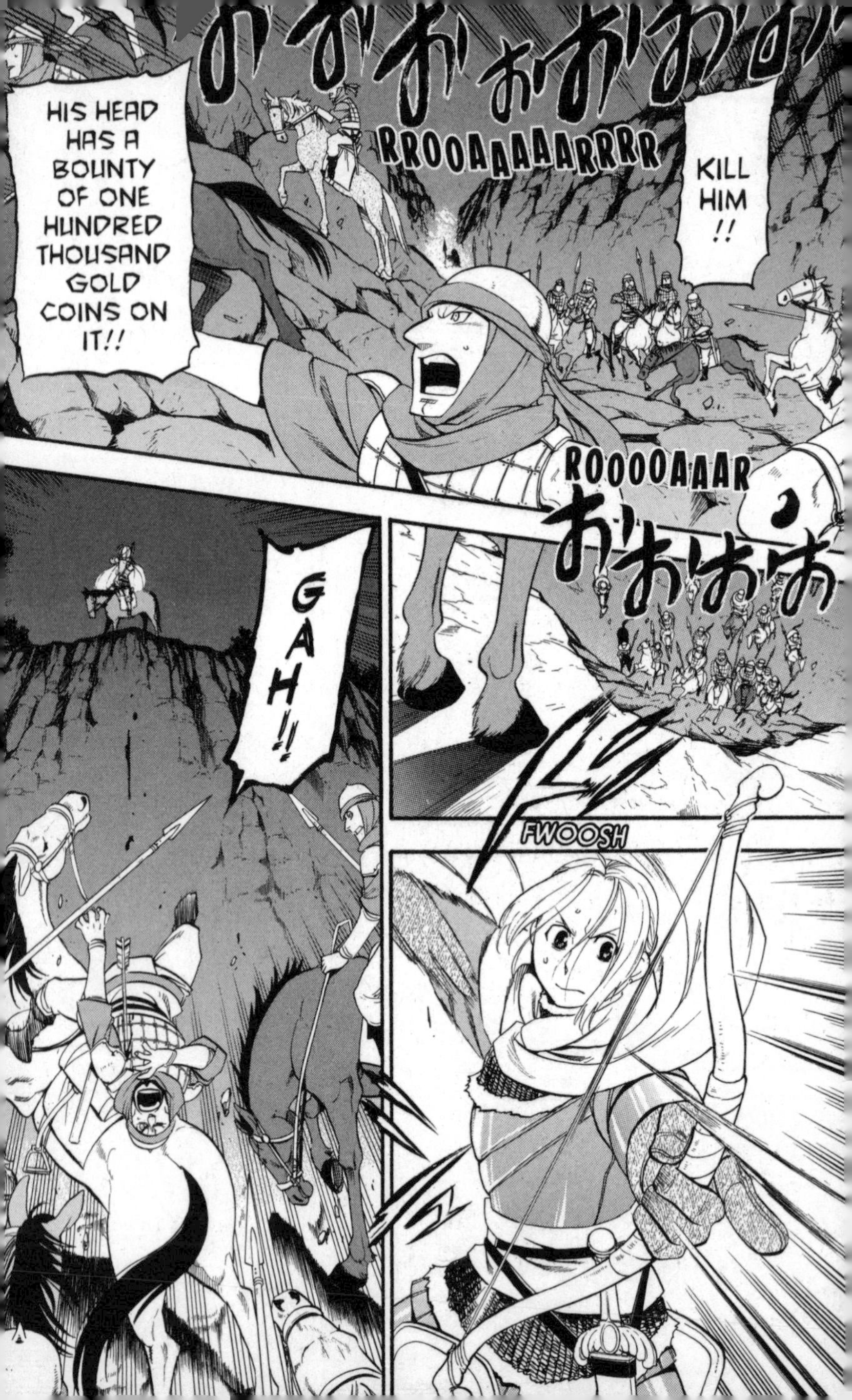
RROOAAAAARRRR
KILL HIM!!
HIS HEAD HAS A BOUNTY OF ONE HUNDRED THOUSAND GOLD COINS ON IT!!
ROOOOAAAR
FWOOSH
GAH!!!

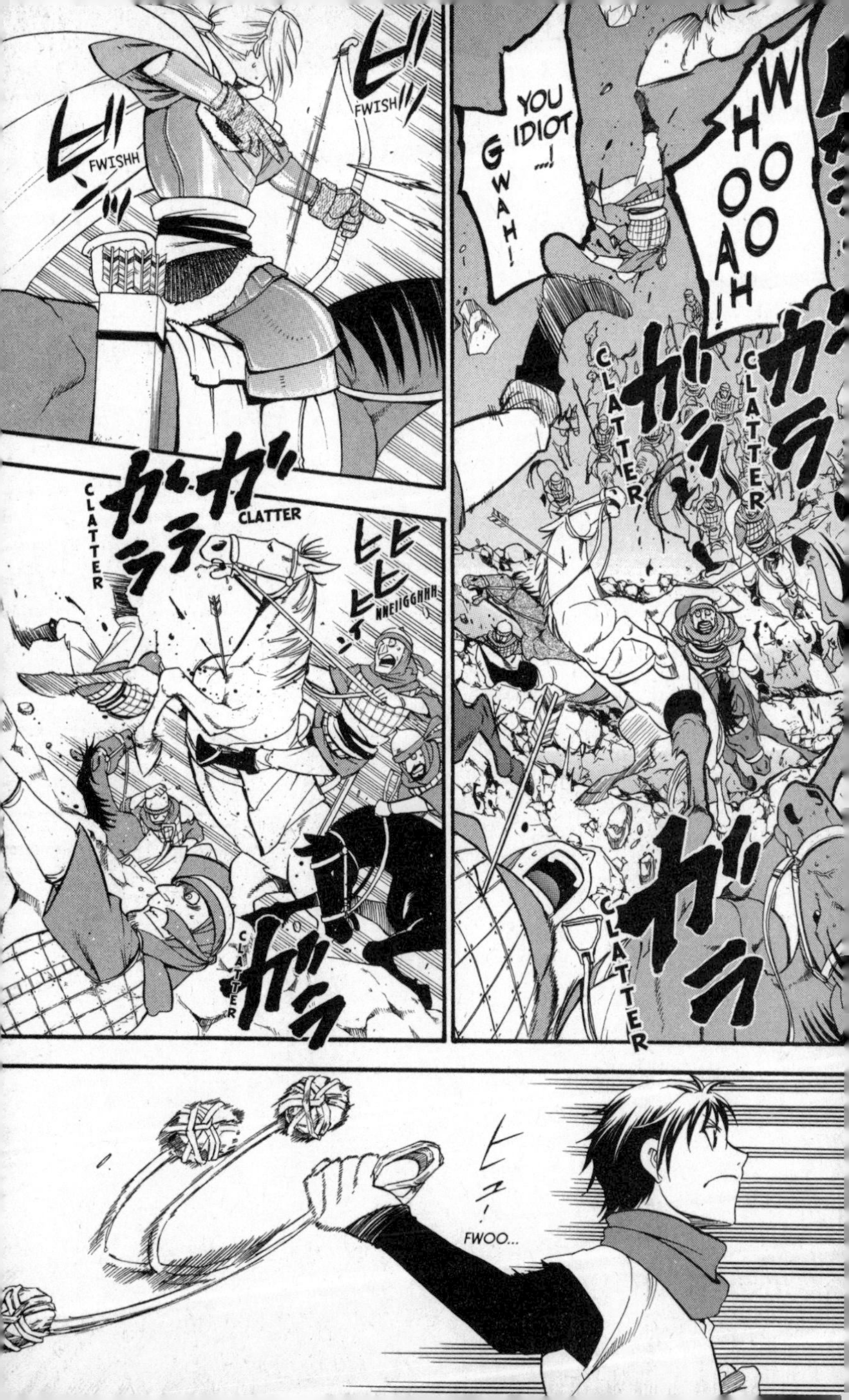

WHOOOOAH!
YOU IDIOT ...!
GWAH!
CLATTER
CLATTER
CLATTER
FWISH
FWISHH
CLATTER
CLATTER
NNEIIGGHHH
CLATTER
FWOO...

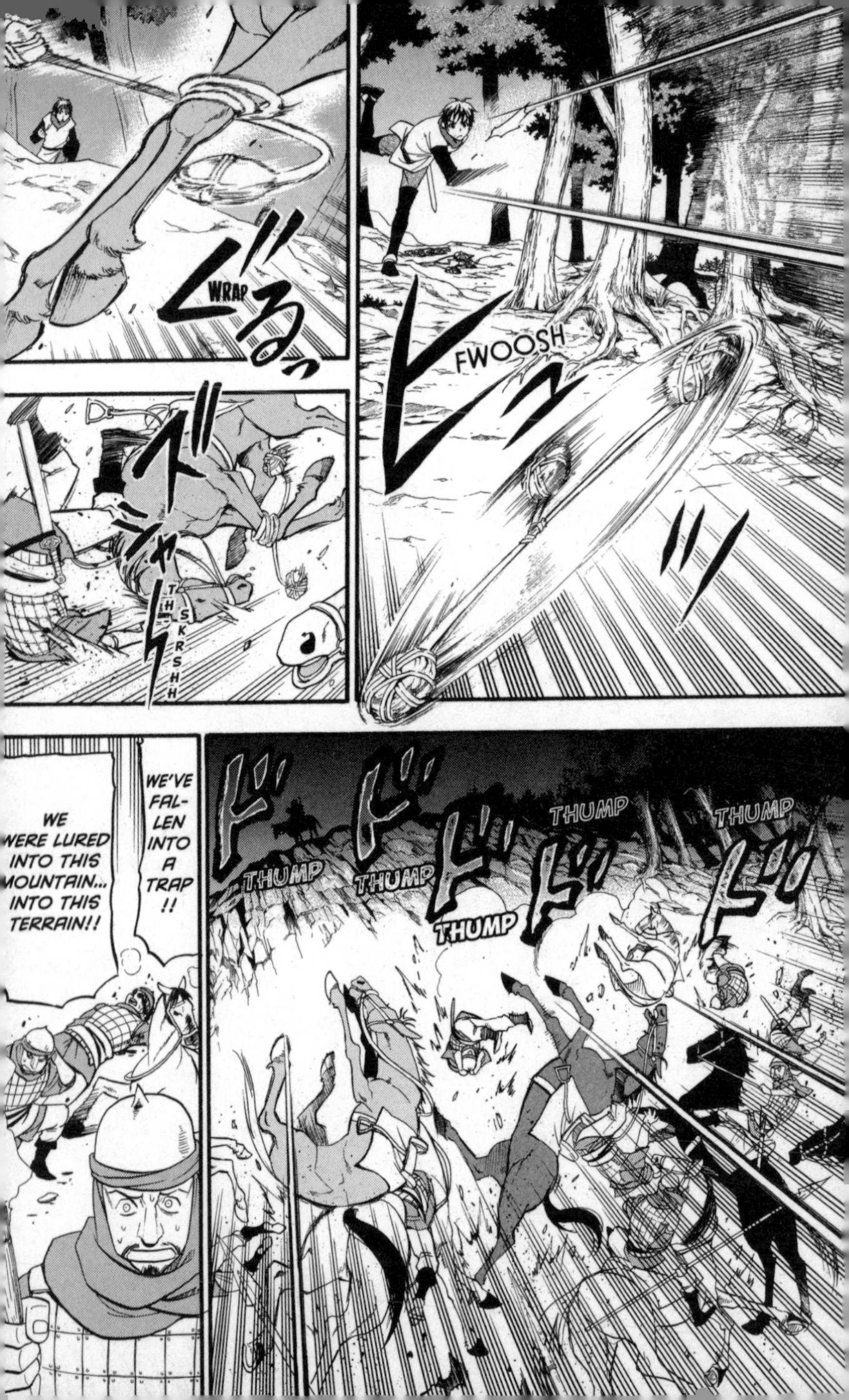
FWOOSH
WRAP
THSKRSHH
THUMP
THUMP
THUMP
THUMP
THUMP
THUMP
WE'VE FALLEN INTO A TRAP!!
WE WERE LURED INTO THIS MOUNTAIN... INTO THIS TERRAIN!!

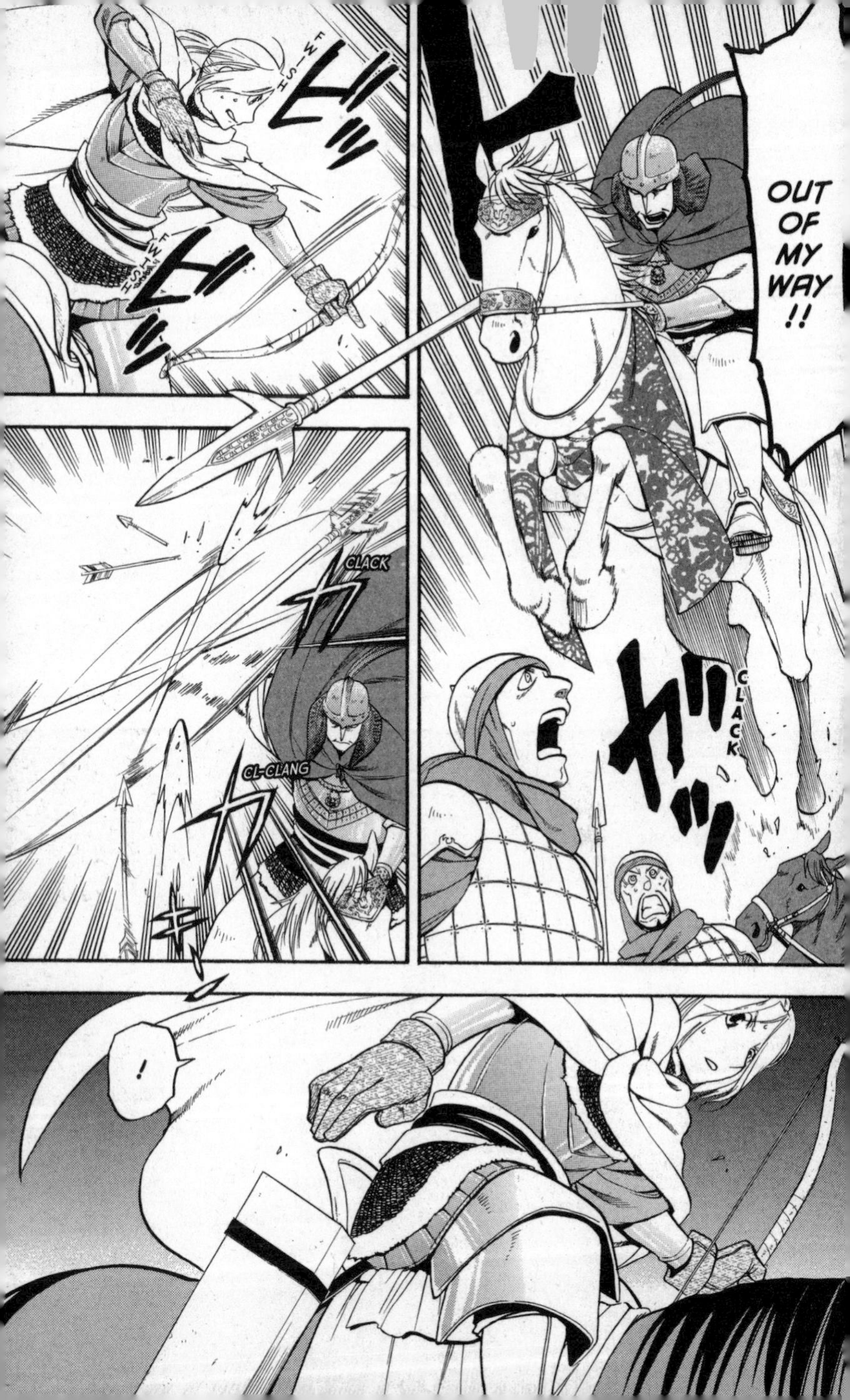
OUT OF MY WAY!!
CLACK
CLACK
FWI-SH
FWISH
CLACK
CL-CLANG
!

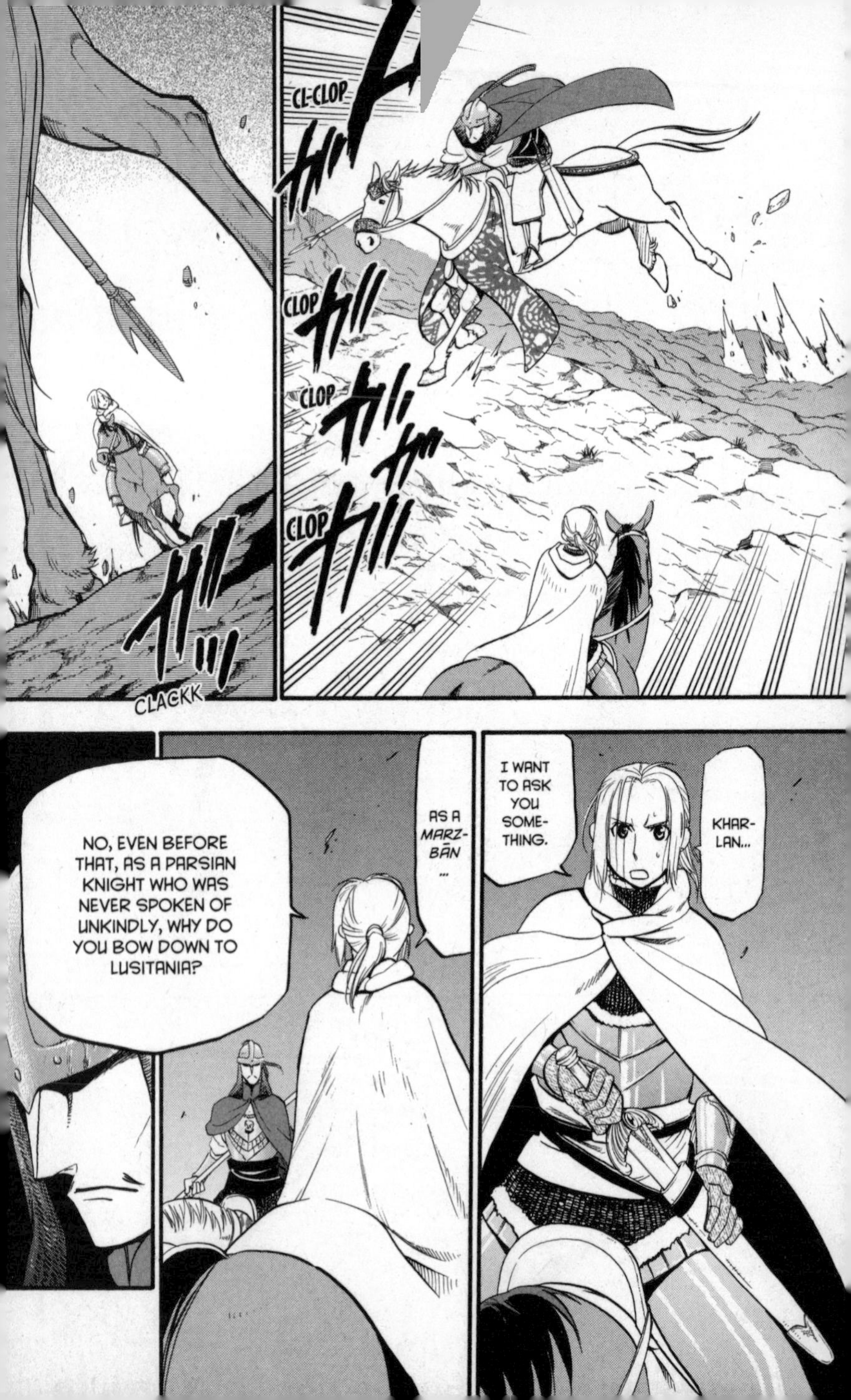
CL-CLOP
CLOP
CLOP
CLOP
CLACKK
KHAR-LAN...
I WANT TO ASK YOU SOME-THING.
AS A MARZ-BĀN ...
NO, EVEN BEFORE THAT, AS A PARSIAN KNIGHT WHO WAS NEVER SPOKEN OF UNKINDLY, WHY DO YOU BOW DOWN TO LUSITANIA?

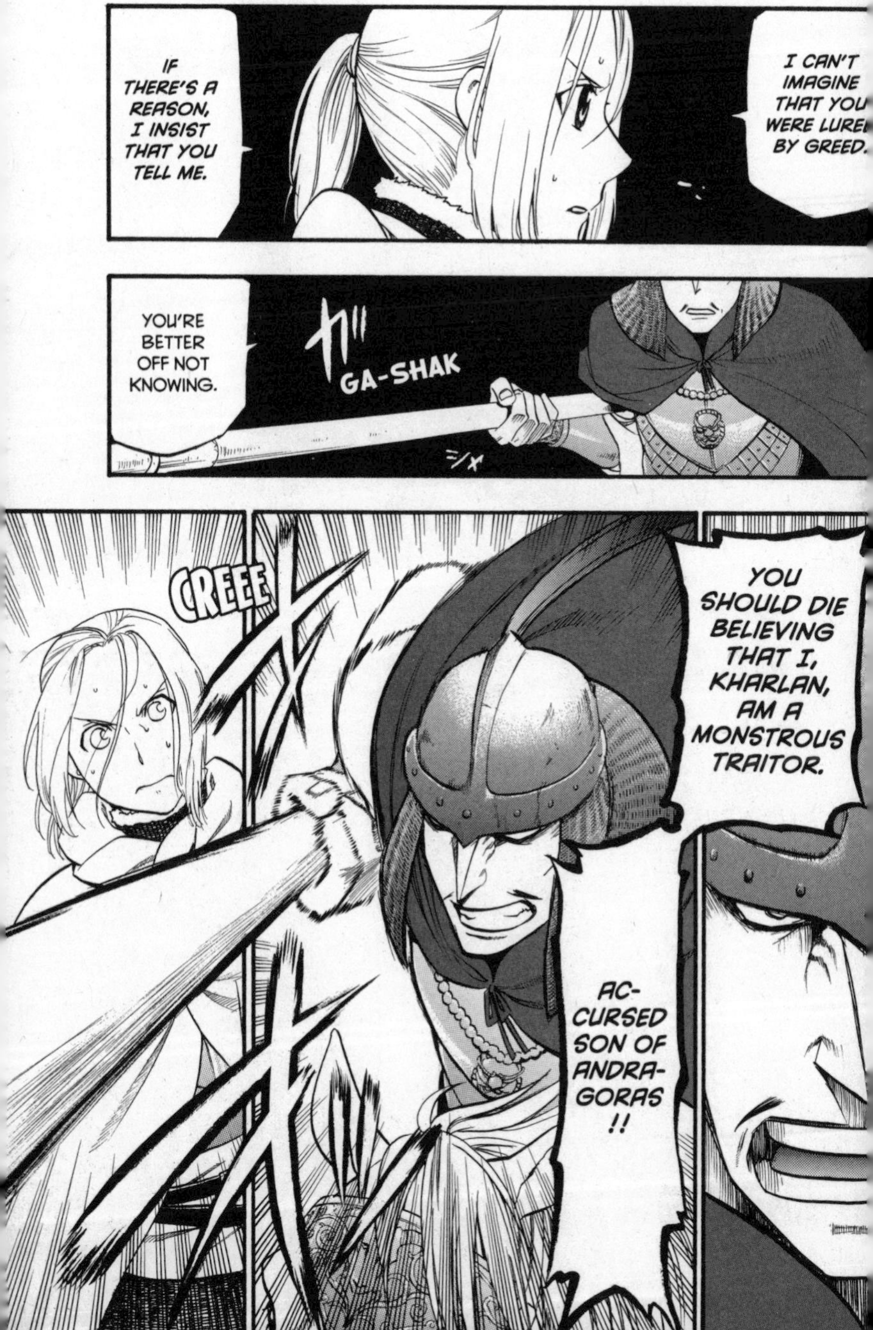
I CAN'T IMAGINE THAT YOU WERE LURED BY GREED.
IF THERE'S A REASON, I INSIST THAT YOU TELL ME.
YOU'RE BETTER OFF NOT KNOWING.
GA-SHAK
YOU SHOULD DIE BELIEVING THAT I, KHARLAN, AM A MONSTROUS TRAITOR.
AC-CURSED SON OF ANDRA-GORAS!!
CREEE

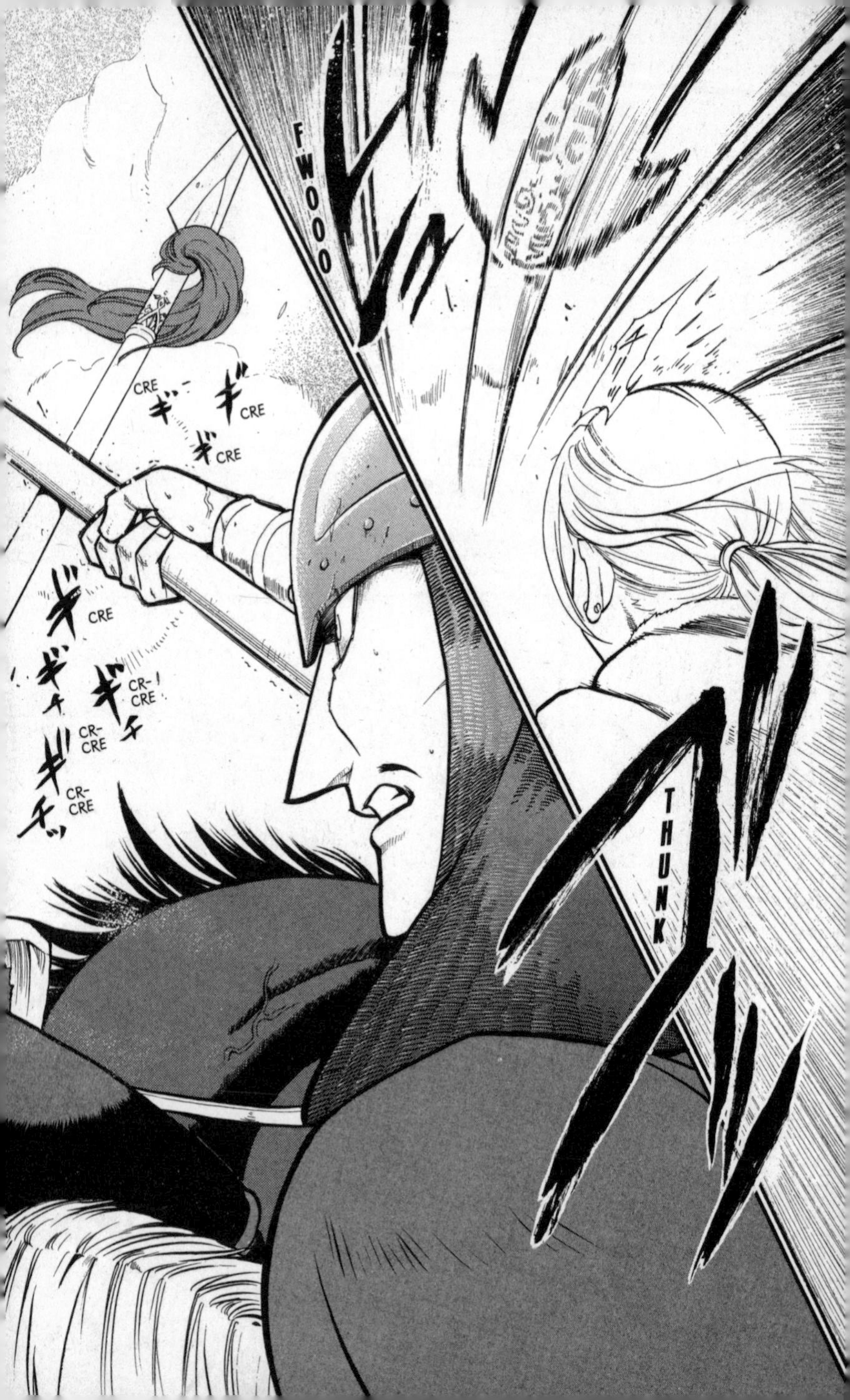
FWOOO
THUNK
CRE
CRE
CRE
CRE
CR-CRE
CR-CRE
CR-CRE

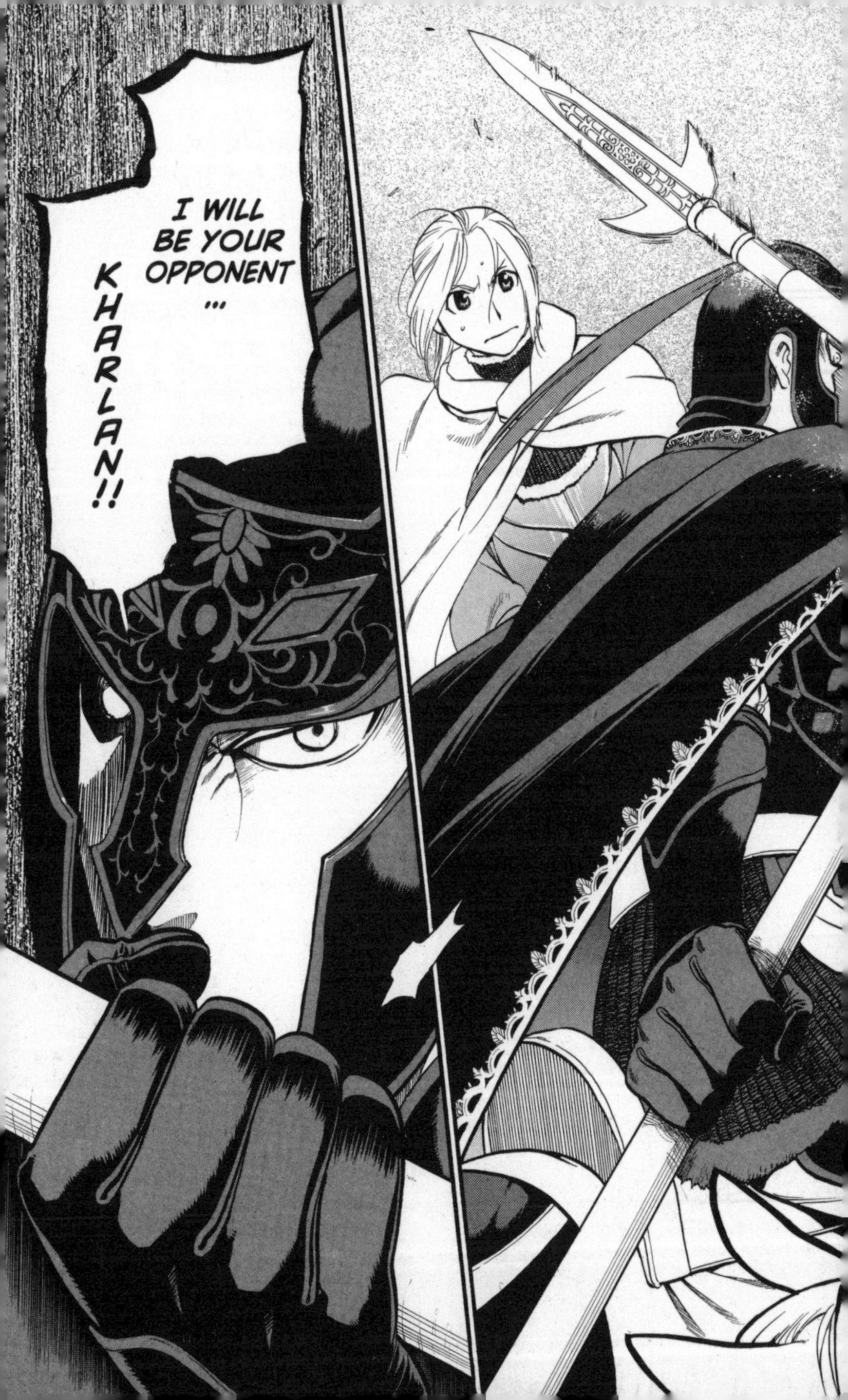
I WILL BE YOUR OPPONENT ...
KHARLAN!!

THE HEROIC LEGEND OF
ARSLAN

Chapter Fourteen: The King's Whereabout.

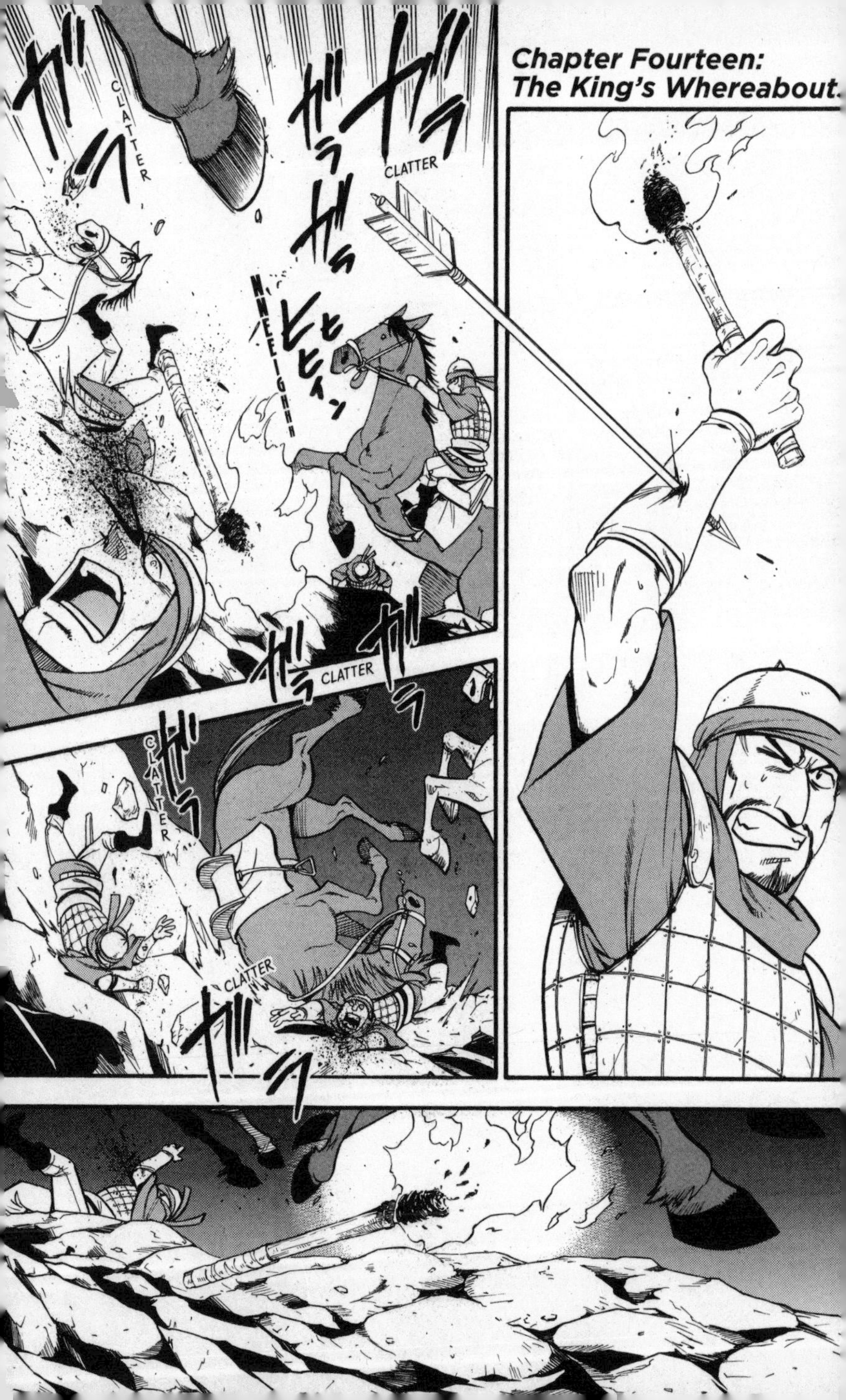

ガラ
CLATTER
ガラ
CLATTER
ガラ
ガラ
ヒヒィン
NNEEIGHHH
ガラ
CLATTER
ガラ
ガラ
CLATTER
ガラ
CLATTER

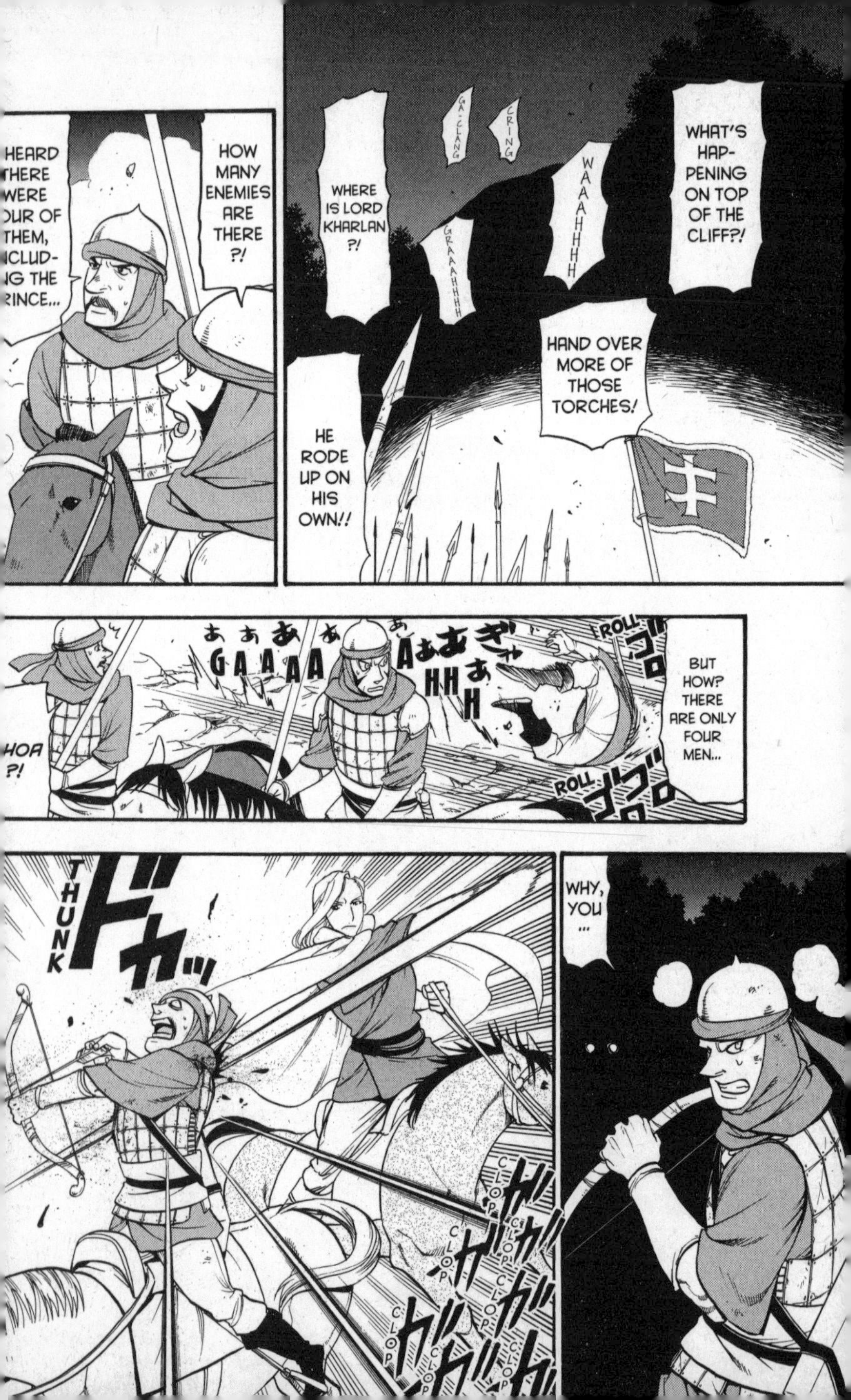
WHAT'S HAP-PENING ON TOP OF THE CLIFF?!
CRING
GA-CLANG
WAAAAHHHH
GRAAAAHHHH
WHERE IS LORD KHARLAN?!
HAND OVER MORE OF THOSE TORCHES!
HE RODE UP ON HIS OWN!!
HOW MANY ENEMIES ARE THERE?!
HEARD THERE WERE OUR OF THEM, NCLUD-NG THE RINCE...
BUT HOW? THERE ARE ONLY FOUR MEN...
ROLL
ROLL
AHHH
GAAAA
HOA?!
WHY, YOU ...
THUNK
CLOP CLOP CLOP CLOP CLOP CLOP CLOP CLOP

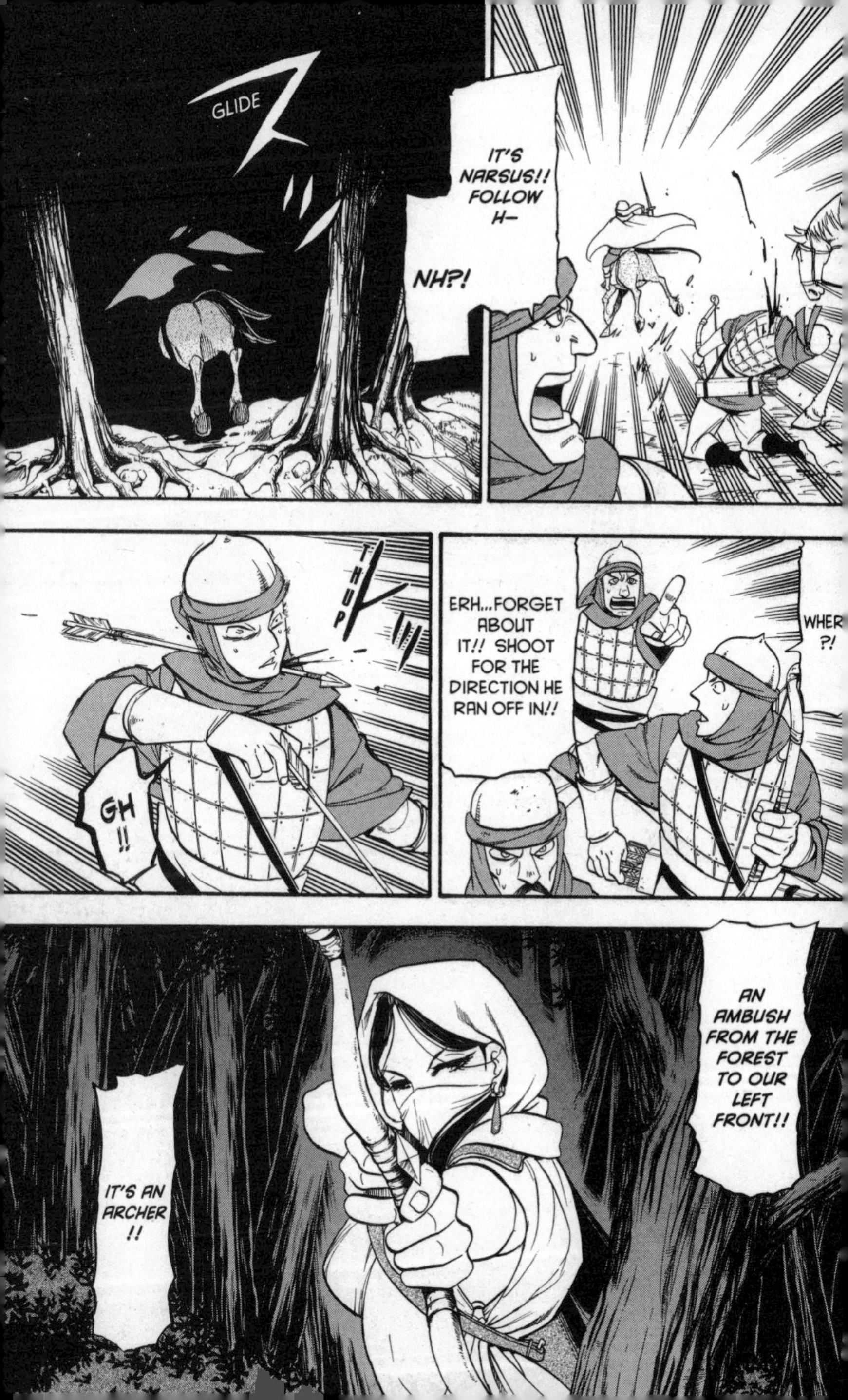
IT'S NARSUS!! FOLLOW H—
NH?!
GLIDE
WHER ?!
ERH...FORGET ABOUT IT!! SHOOT FOR THE DIRECTION HE RAN OFF IN!!
THUP
GH !!
AN AMBUSH FROM THE FOREST TO OUR LEFT FRONT!!
IT'S AN ARCHER !!

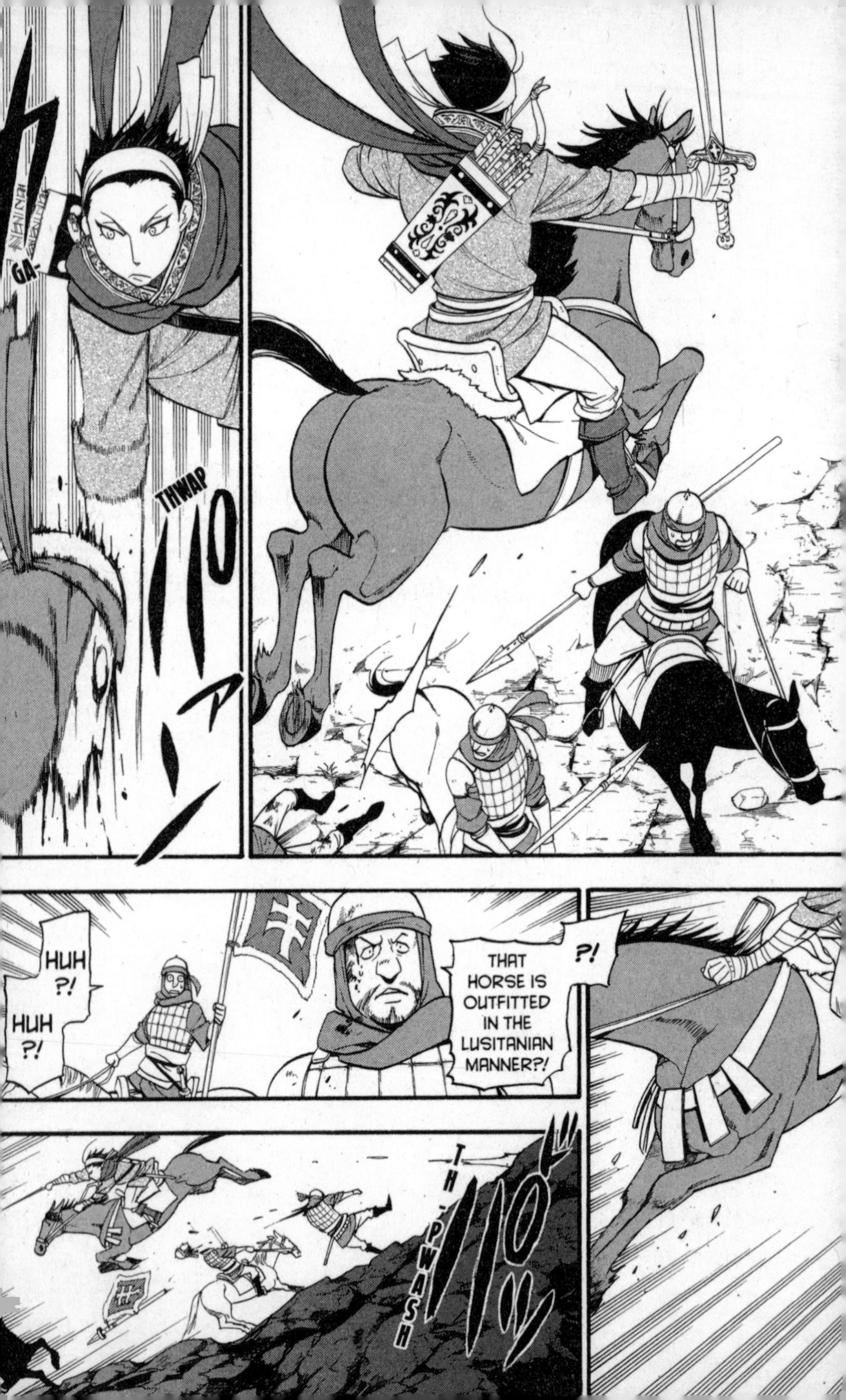
GA-
THWAP
?!
THAT HORSE IS OUTFITTED IN THE LUSITANIAN MANNER?!
HUH ?!
HUH ?!
TH-PWASH

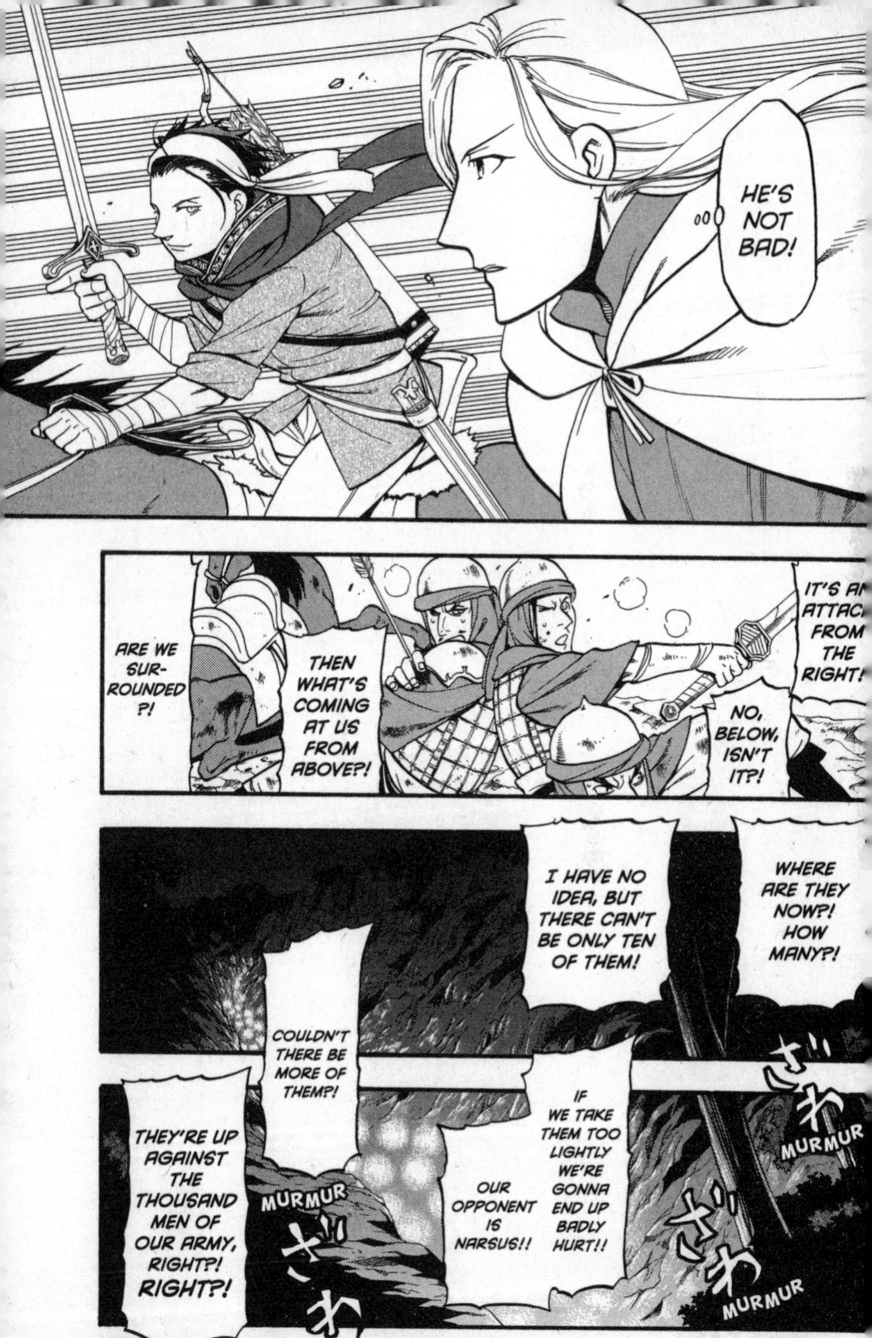
...!!
HE'S NOT BAD!
IT'S A ATTAC FROM THE RIGHT!
NO, BELOW, ISN'T IT?!
THEN WHAT'S COMING AT US FROM ABOVE?!
ARE WE SURROUNDED?!
WHERE ARE THEY NOW?! HOW MANY?!
I HAVE NO IDEA, BUT THERE CAN'T BE ONLY TEN OF THEM!
COULDN'T THERE BE MORE OF THEM?!
ざわ
MURMUR
ざわ
MURMUR
IF WE TAKE THEM TOO LIGHTLY WE'RE GONNA END UP BADLY HURT!!
OUR OPPONENT IS NARSUS!!
THEY'RE UP AGAINST THE THOUSAND MEN OF OUR ARMY, RIGHT?! RIGHT?!
MURMUR
ざわ

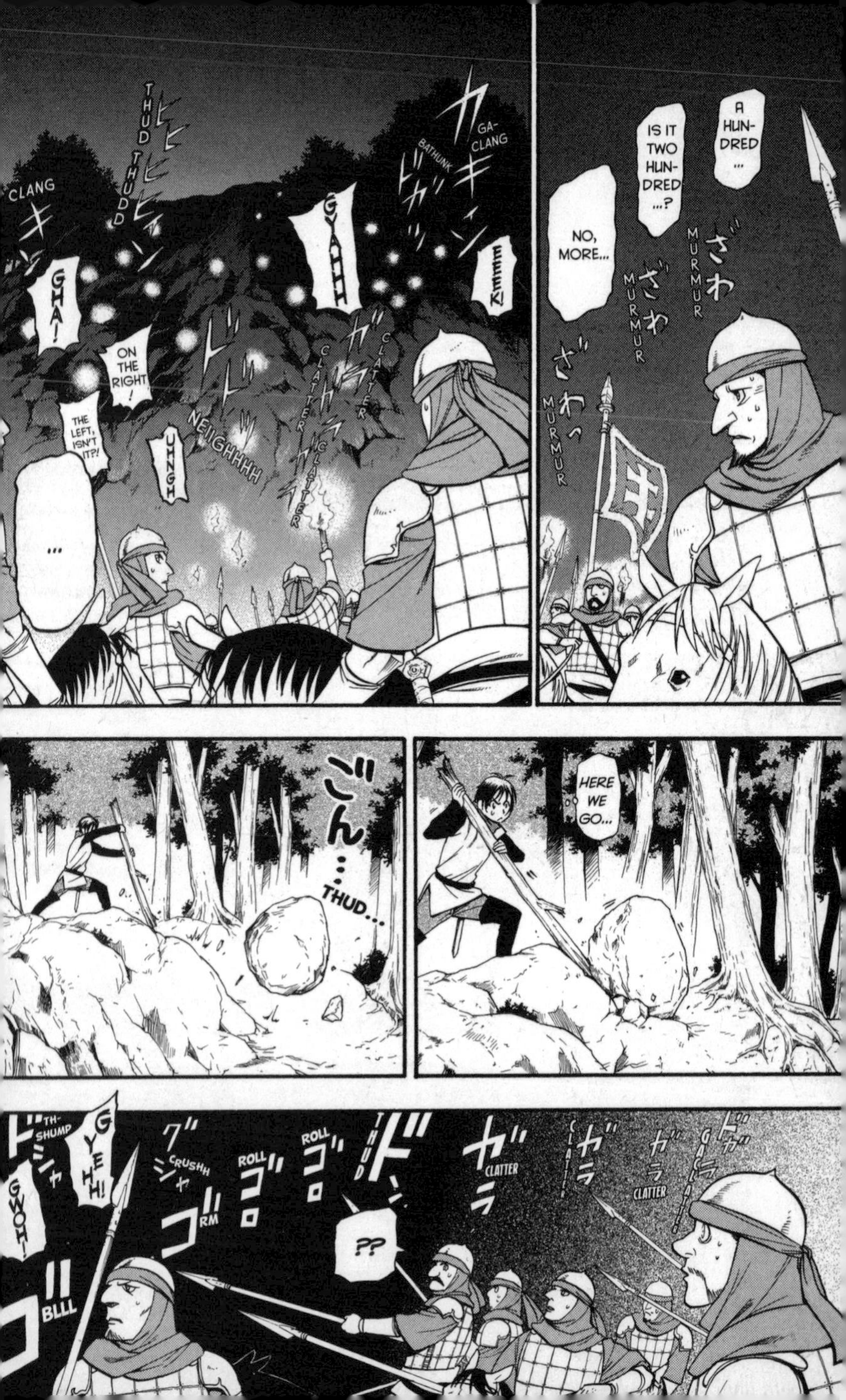
A HUNDRED...
IS IT TWO HUNDRED...?
NO, MORE...
MURMUR
MURMUR
MURMUR
MURMUR
GA-CLANG
BATHUNK
EEEEK!
GYAAAHH
CLATTER
CLATTER
CLATTER
THUD THUDD
CLANG
GHA!
ON THE RIGHT!
THE LEFT, ISN'T IT?!
NEIIGHHHH
UHNGH
...
HERE WE GO...
THUD...
CLATTER
CLATTER
CLATTER
THUD
ROLL
ROLL
RM
CRUSHH
??
TH-SHUMP
GYEHH!
GWOH!
BLLL

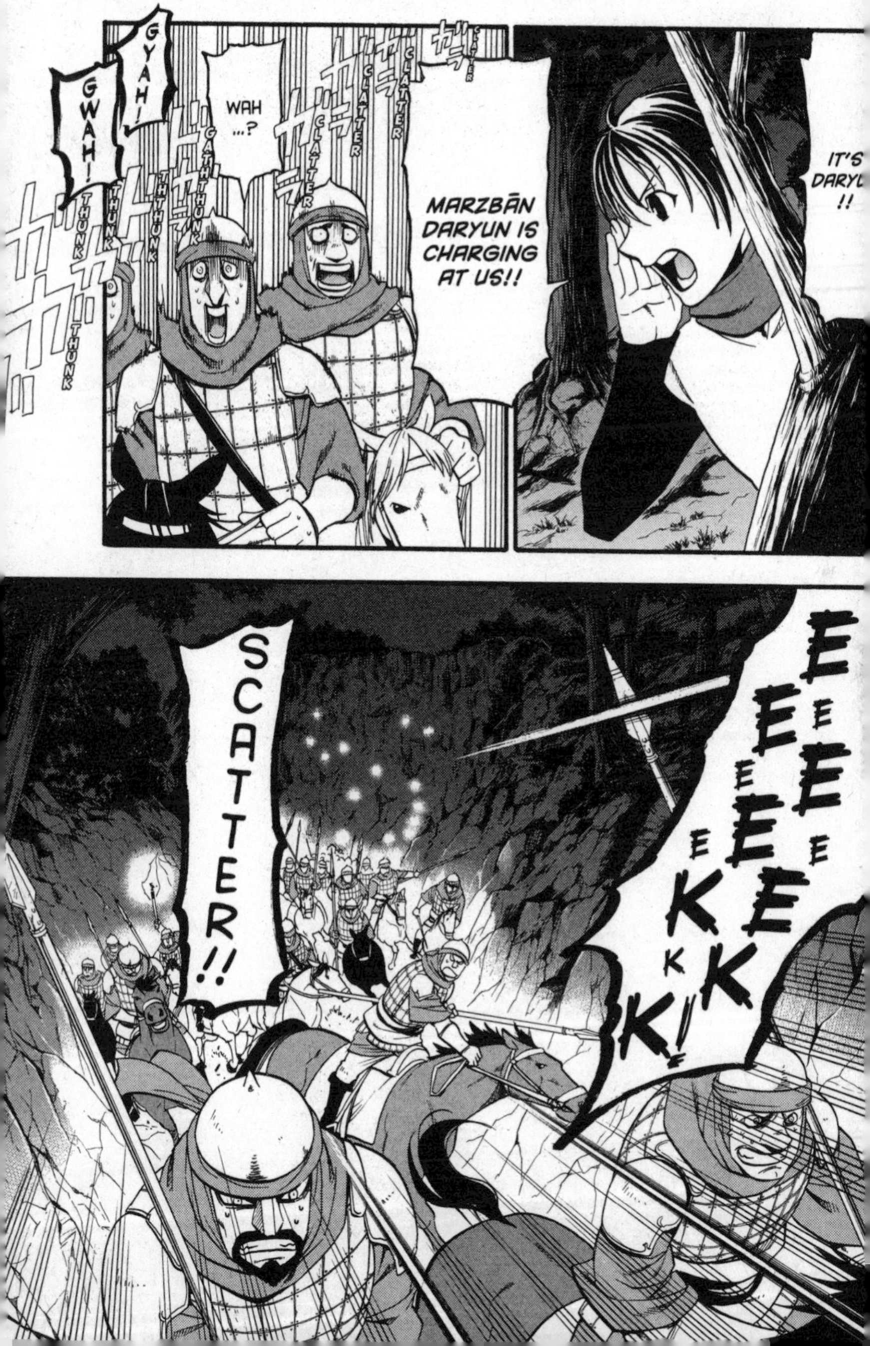
IT'S DARYU !!
CLATTER
CLATTER
CLATTER
CLATTER
MARZBĀN DARYUN IS CHARGING AT US!!
WAH ...?
GATHTHUNK
THTHUNK
GYAH!
THUNK
GWAH!
THUNK
THUNK
EEEEEEEEEKKKK!
SCATTER!!

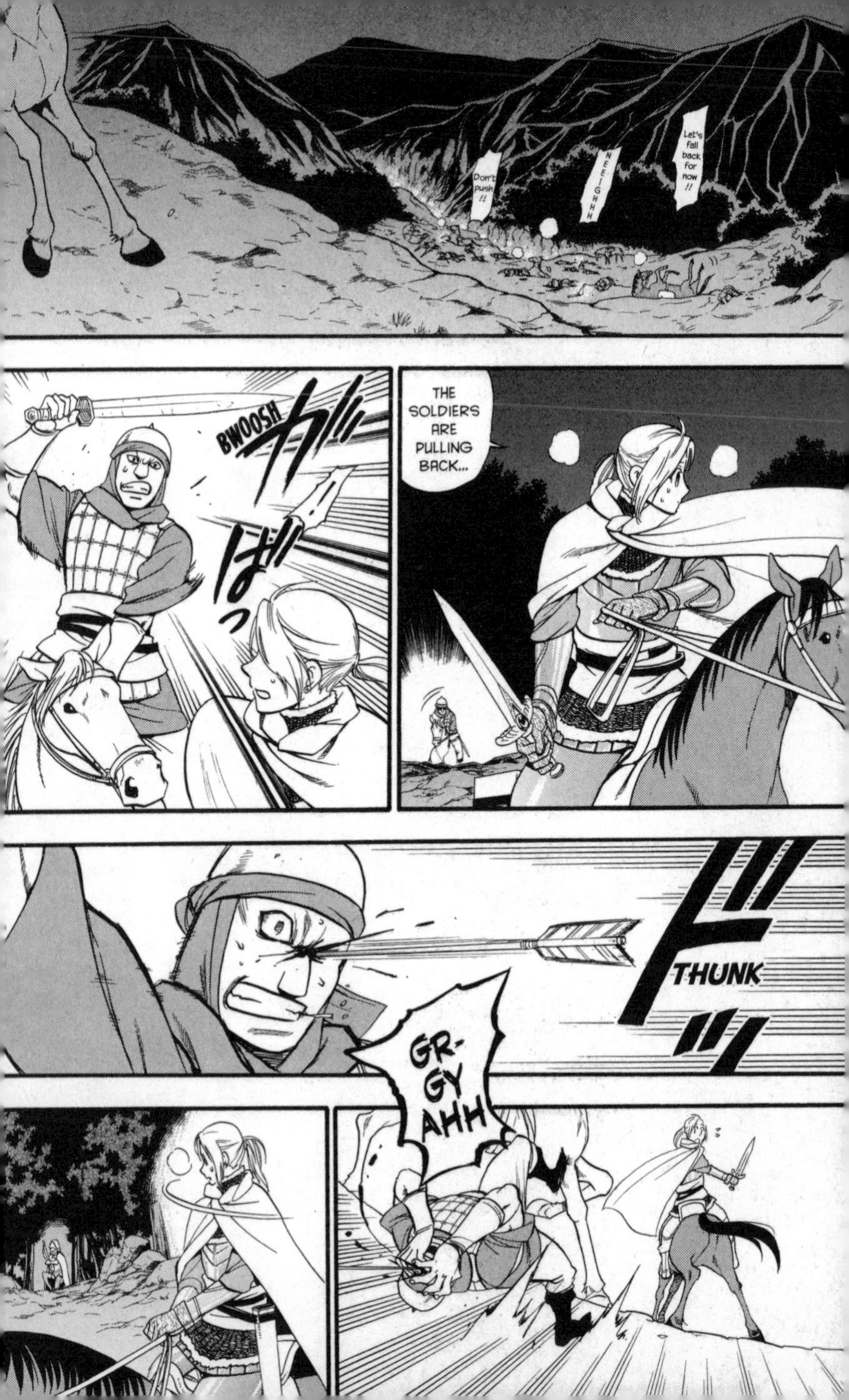
Let's fall back for now !!
NEEIGHHH
Don't push !!
THE SOLDIERS ARE PULLING BACK...
BWOOSH
THUNK
GR-GY AHH

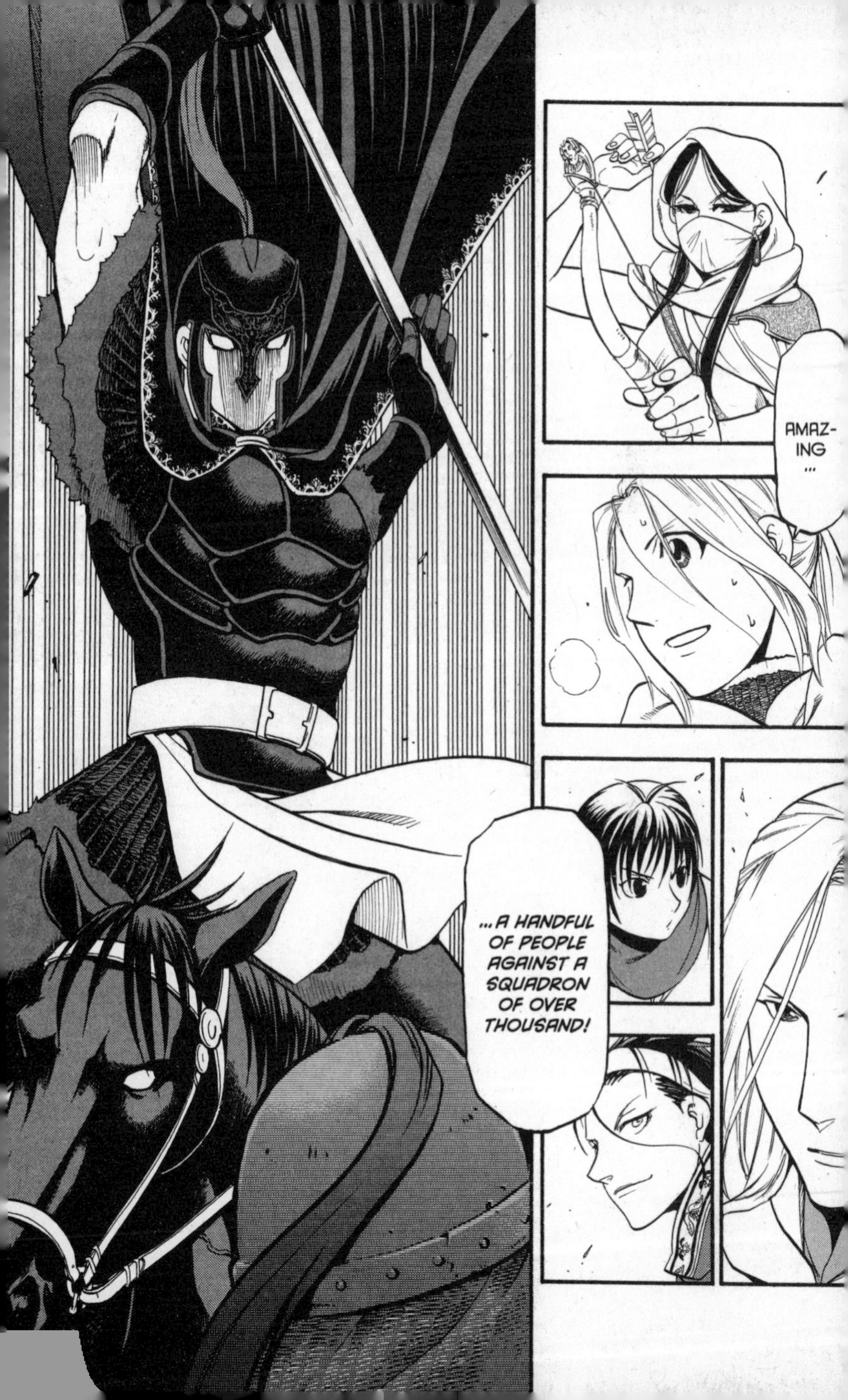
AMAZ-ING ...
...A HANDFUL OF PEOPLE AGAINST A SQUADRON OF OVER THOUSAND!

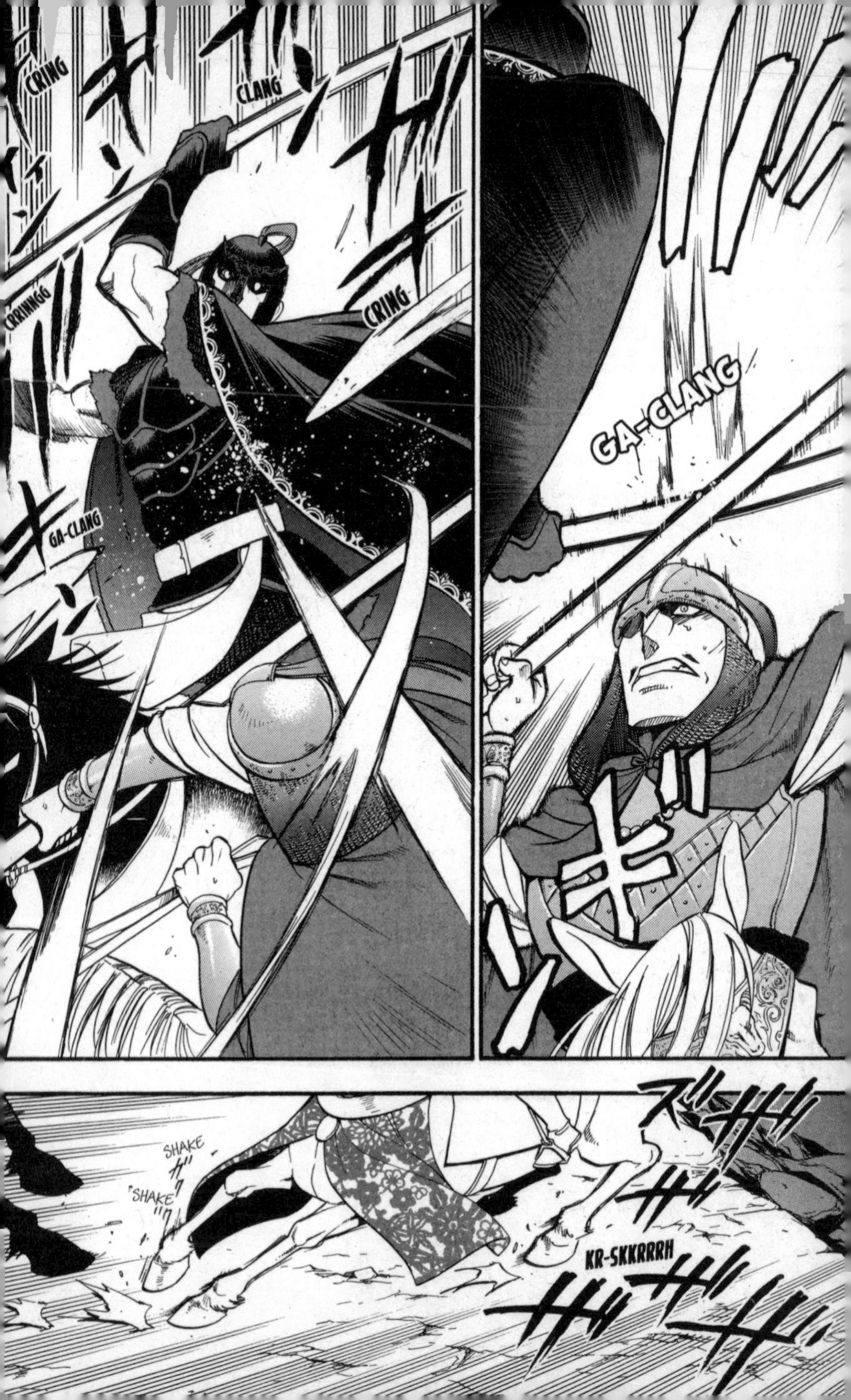
GA-CLANG
CLANG
CRING
CRING
CRRINNGG
GA-CLANG
KR-SKKRRRH
SHAKE
SHAKE

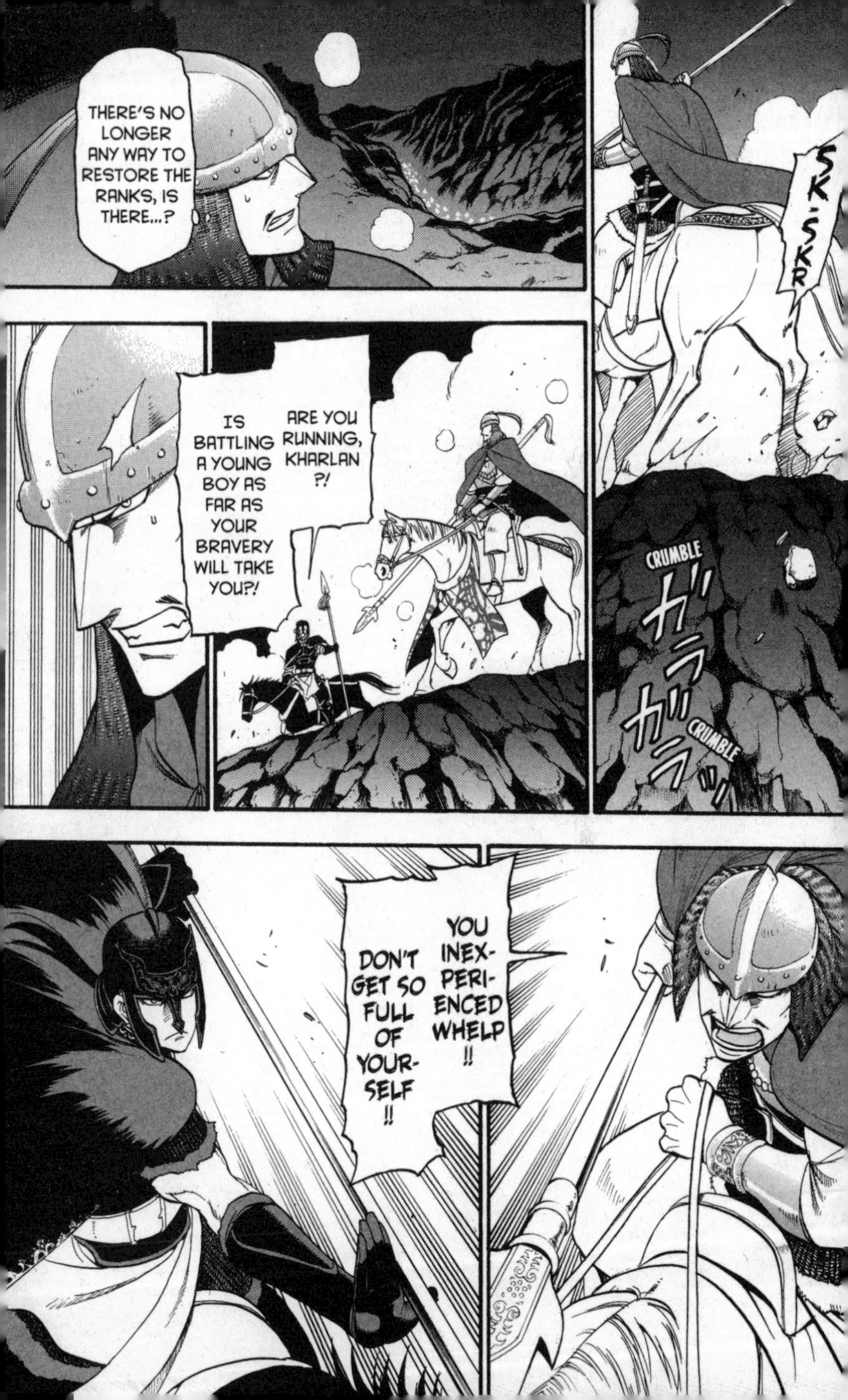
SK-SKR
CRUMBLE
ガラガラッ
CRUMBLE
THERE'S NO LONGER ANY WAY TO RESTORE THE RANKS, IS THERE...?
ARE YOU RUNNING, KHARLAN?!
IS BATTLING A YOUNG BOY AS FAR AS YOUR BRAVERY WILL TAKE YOU?!
YOU INEXPERIENCED WHELP!!
DON'T GET SO FULL OF YOURSELF!!

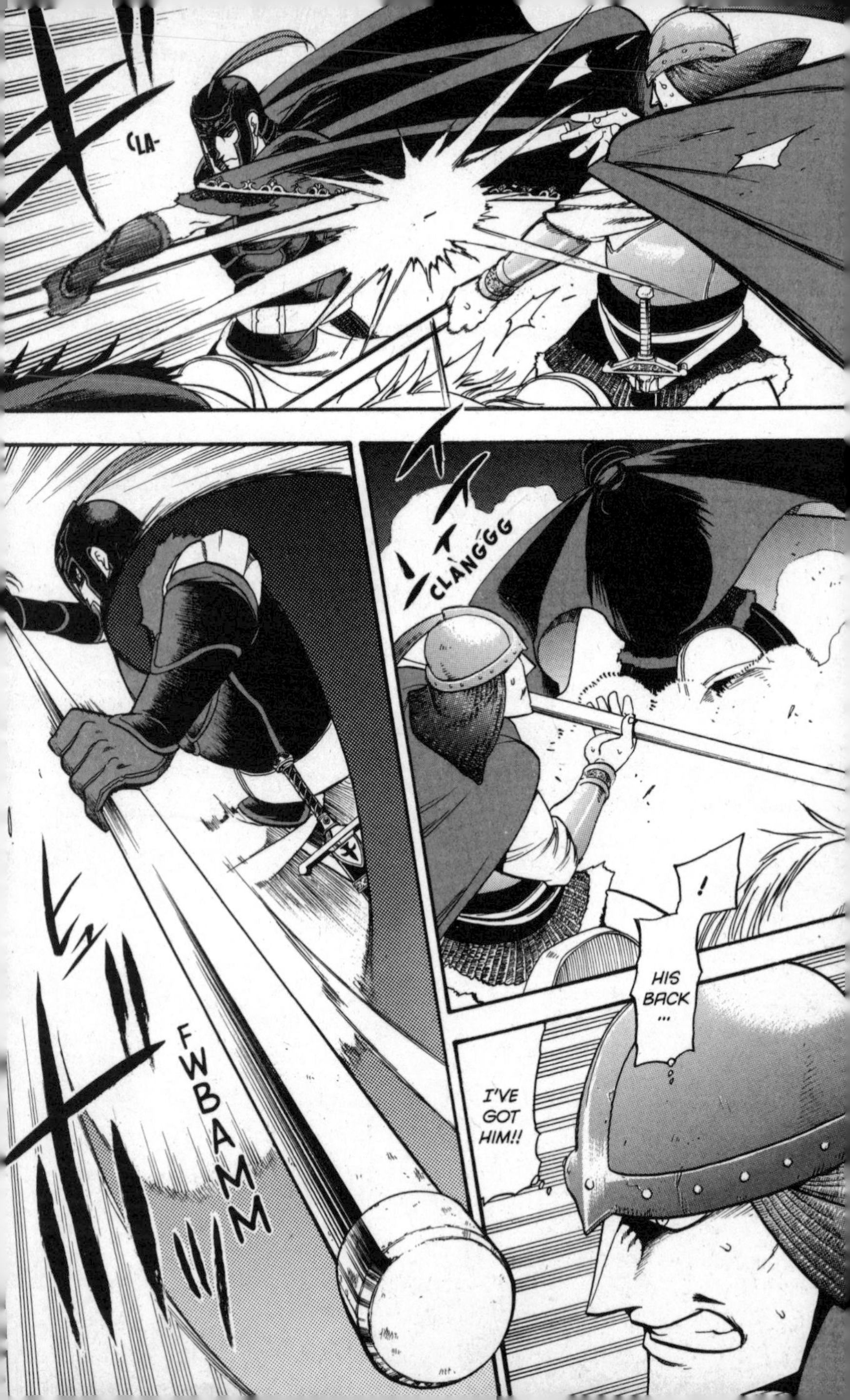
CLA-
CLANGGG
HIS BACK ...
I'VE GOT HIM!!
FWBAMM

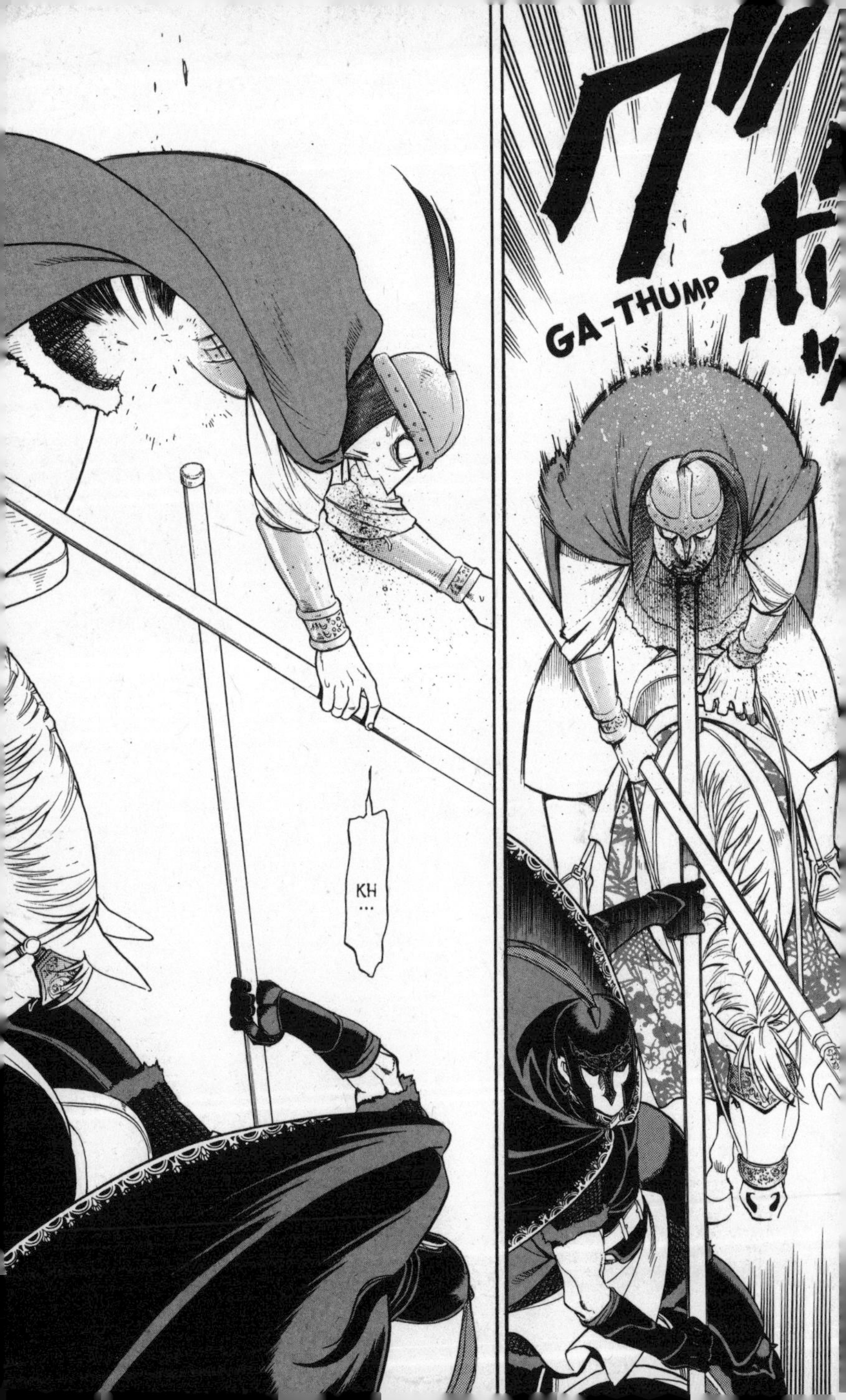
グボッ
GA-THUMP
KH...

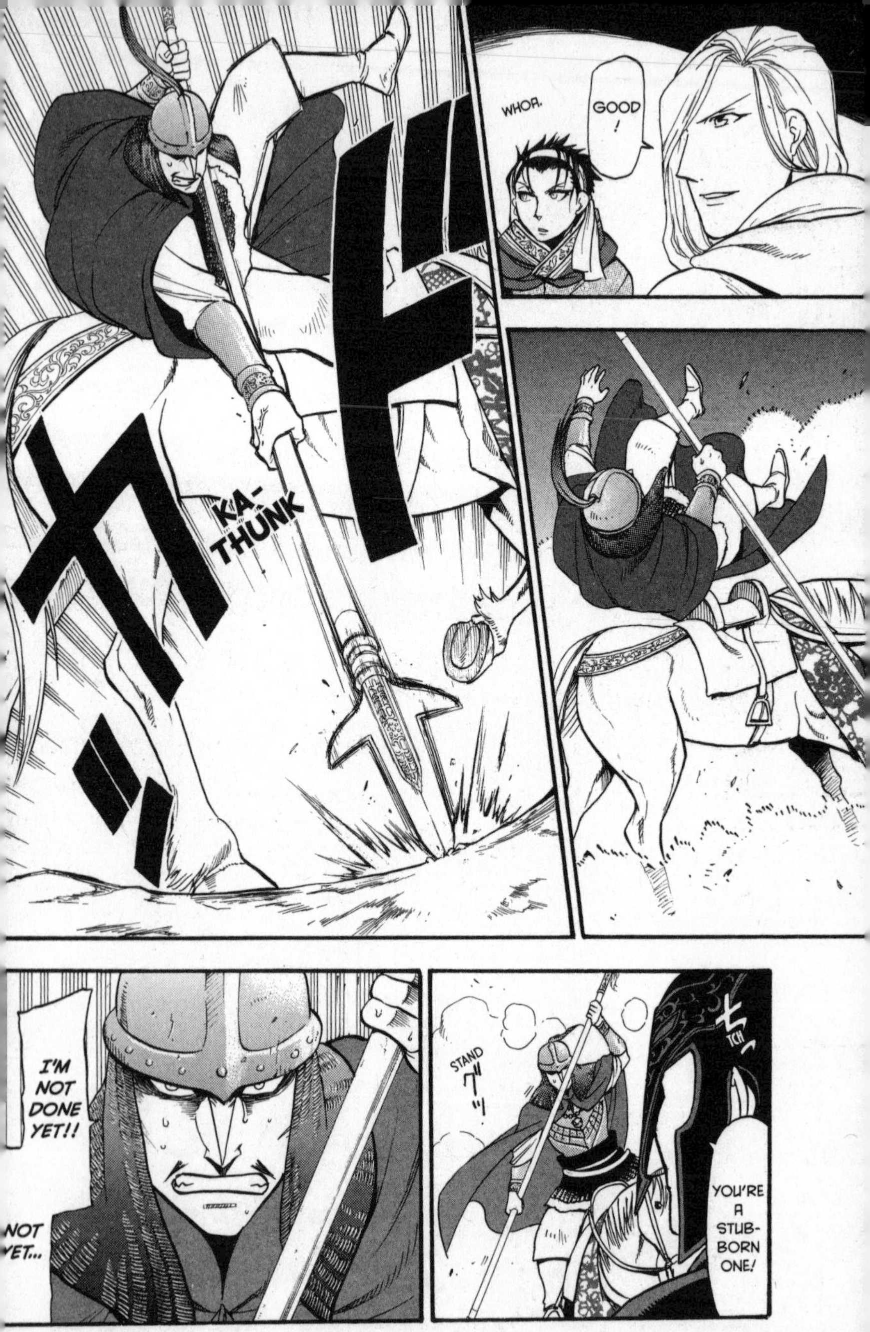
GOOD!
WHOA.
KA-THUNK
TCH
YOU'RE A STUBBORN ONE!
STAND
I'M NOT DONE YET!!
NOT YET...

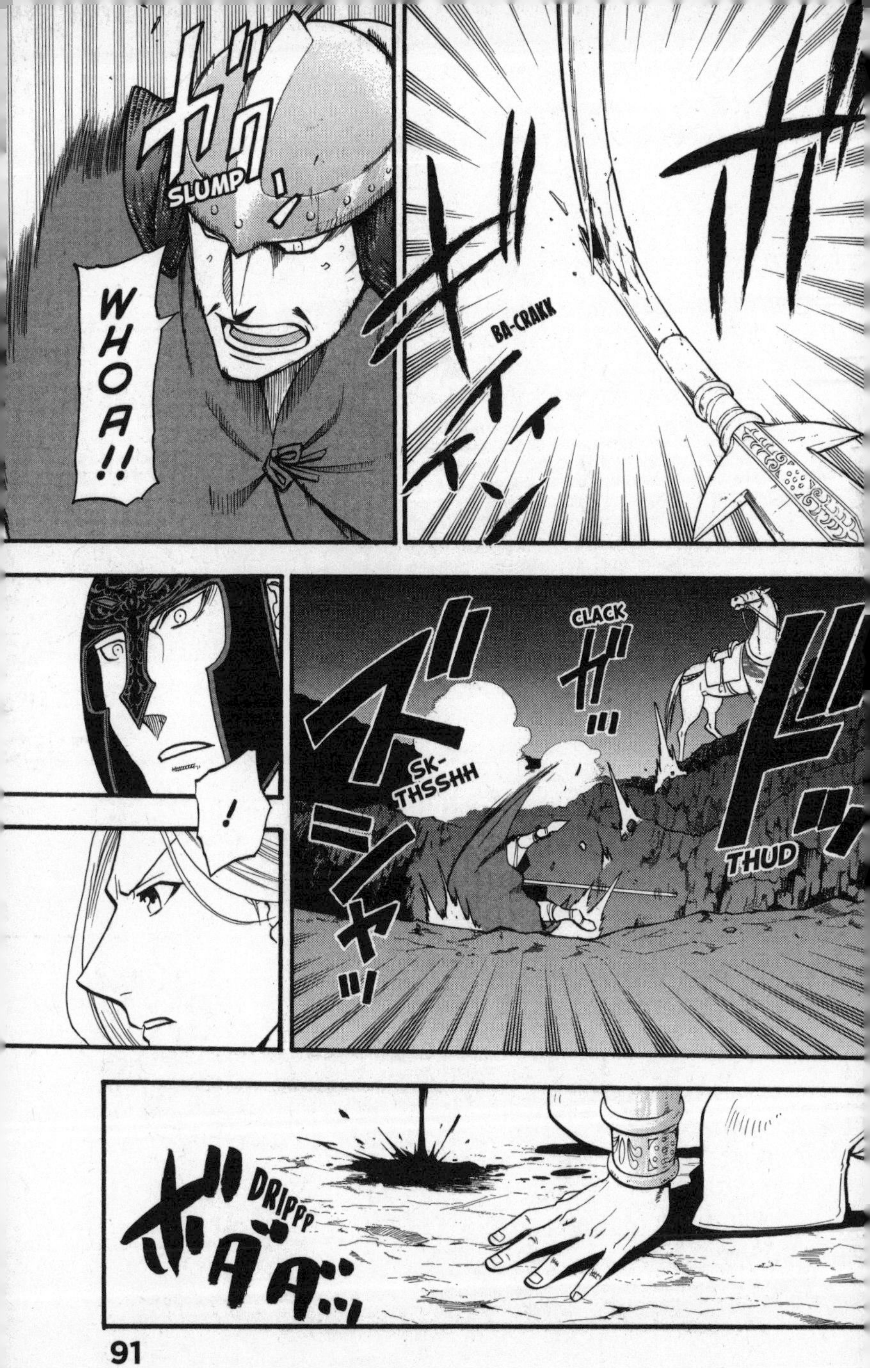

BA-CRAKK
SLUMP
WHOA!!
CLACK
SK-THSSHH
THUD
!
DRIPPP

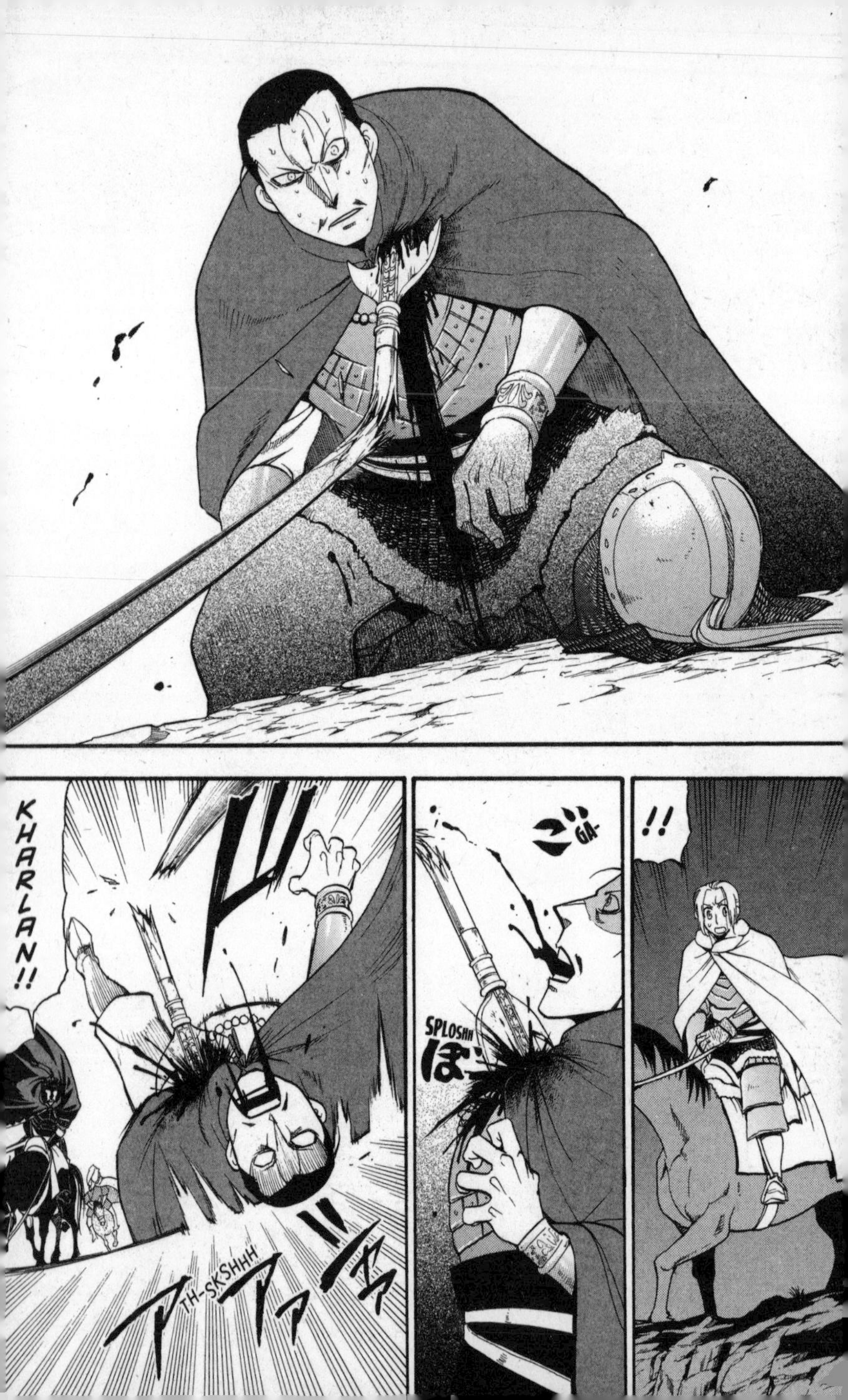
!!
GA-
SPLOSHH
KHARLAN!!
TH-SKSHHH

SPLUSH

KHARLAN.
WHERE IS
THE KING
?!

KING...
ANDRA...
GORAS...

WHEEZEEE WHEEZEEE

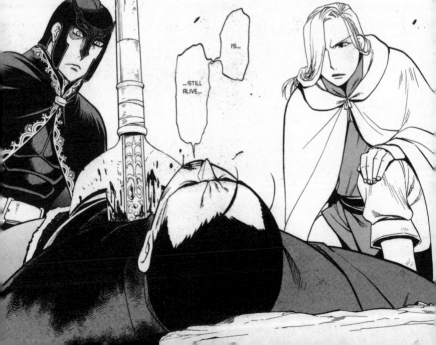

IS...

...STILL
ALIVE...

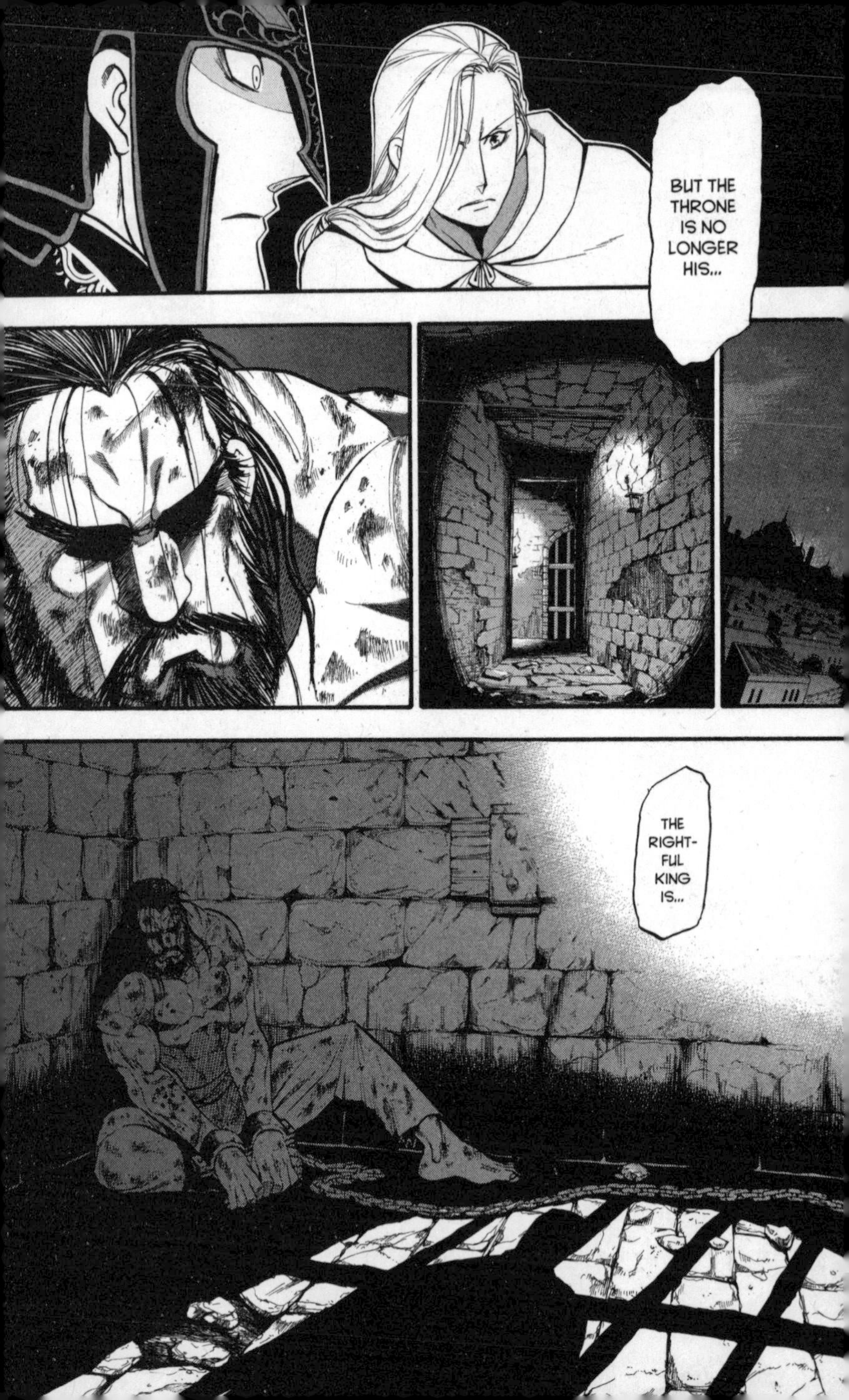
BUT THE THRONE IS NO LONGER HIS...
THE RIGHT-FUL KING IS...

Chapter Fifteen: The Rightful King

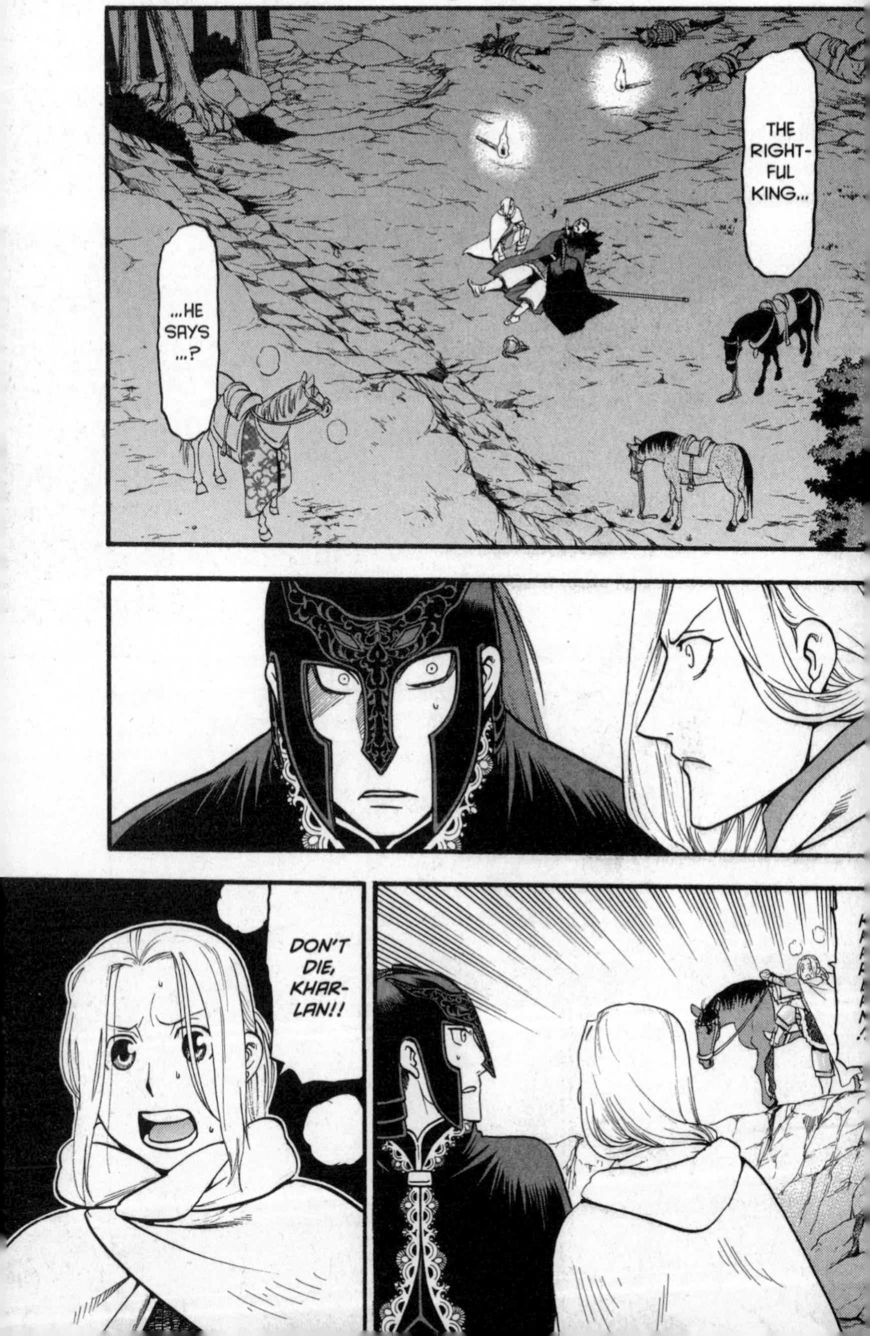
THE RIGHTFUL KING...
...HE SAYS...?
DON'T DIE, KHARLAN!!

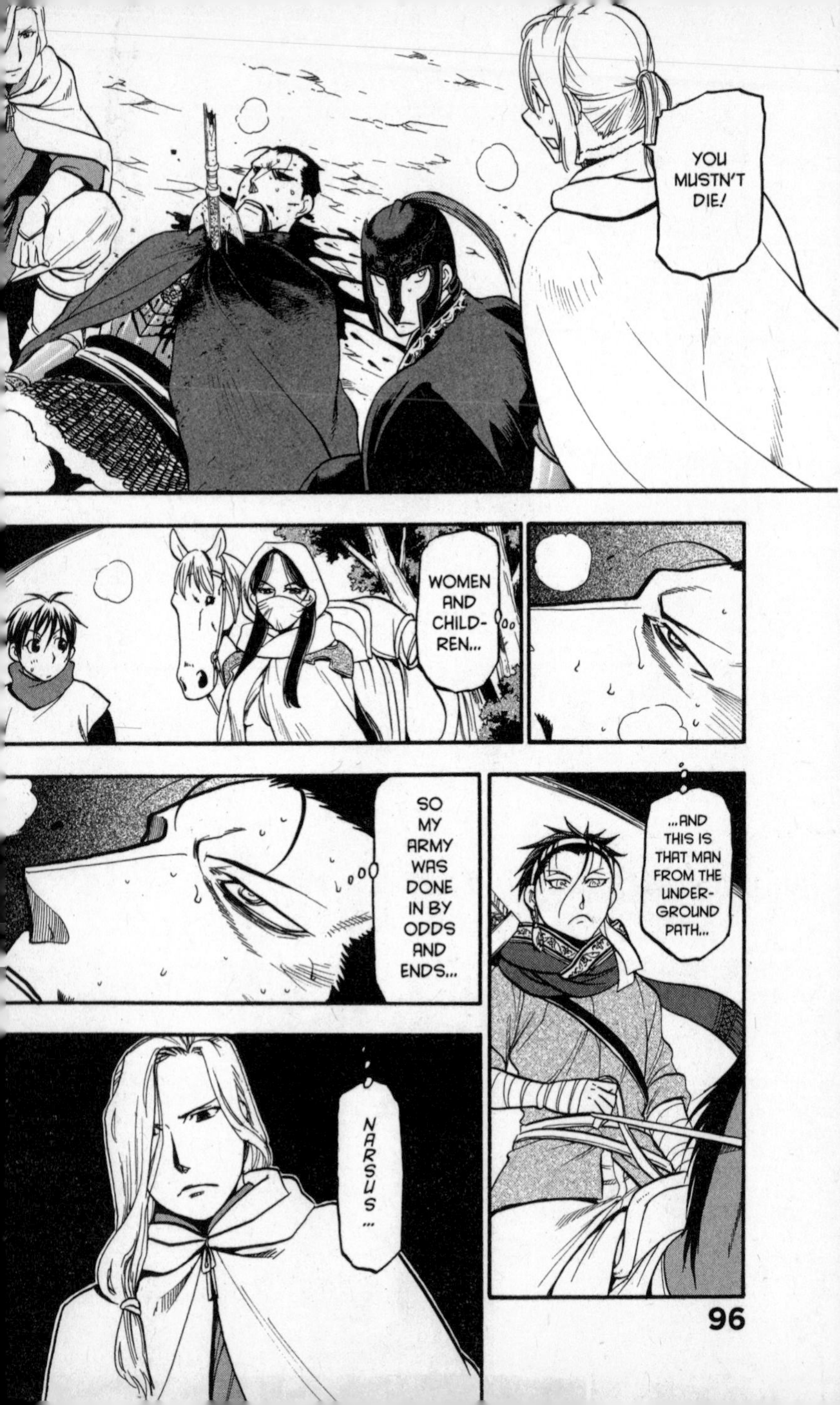
YOU MUSTN'T DIE!
WOMEN AND CHILDREN...
...AND THIS IS THAT MAN FROM THE UNDERGROUND PATH...
SO MY ARMY WAS DONE IN BY ODDS AND ENDS...
NARSUS...

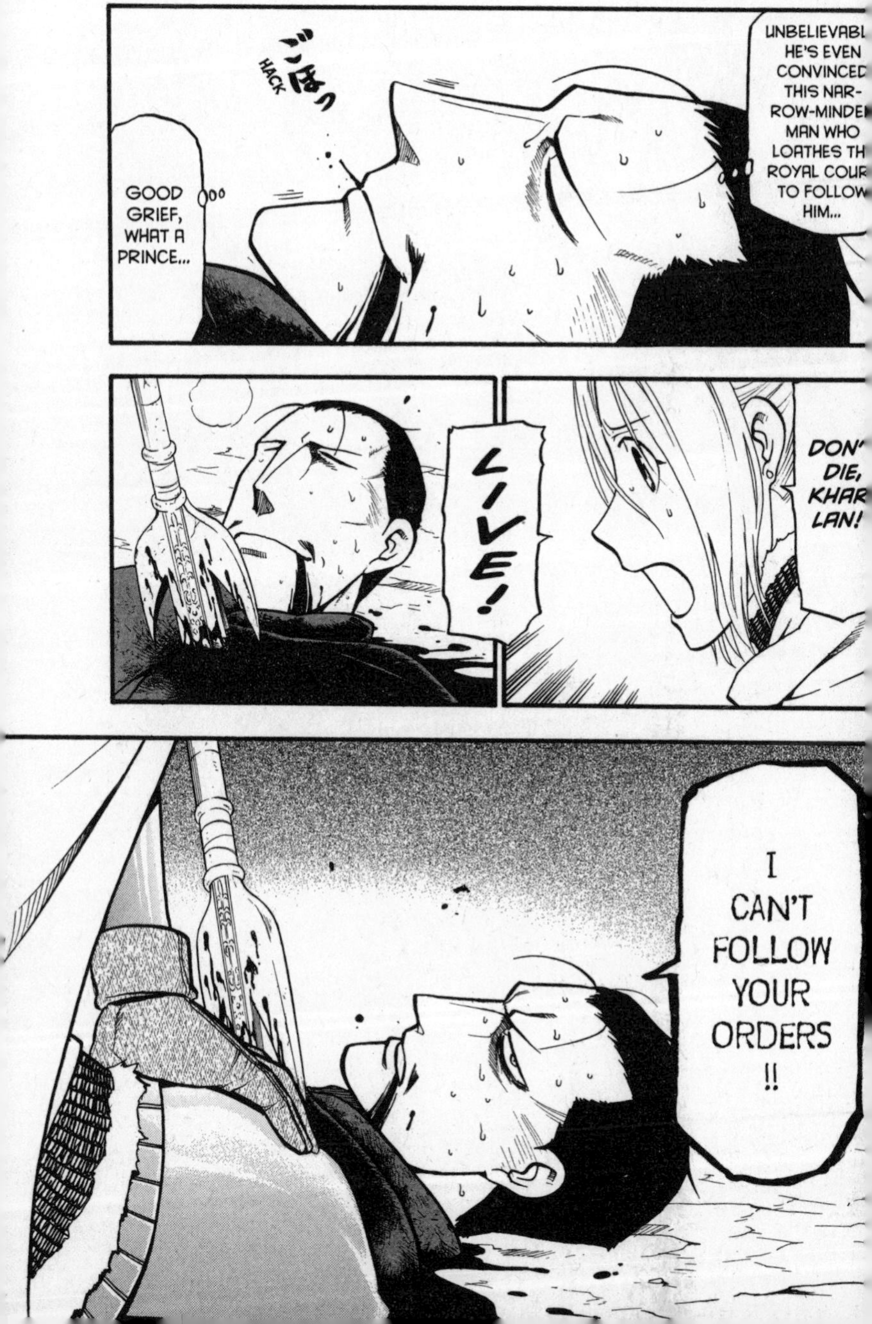
UNBELIEVABL HE'S EVEN CONVINCED THIS NAR-ROW-MINDE MAN WHO LOATHES TH ROYAL COUR TO FOLLOW HIM...
ごほっ HACK
GOOD GRIEF, WHAT A PRINCE...
DON' DIE, KHAR LAN!
LIVE!
I CAN'T FOLLOW YOUR ORDERS !!

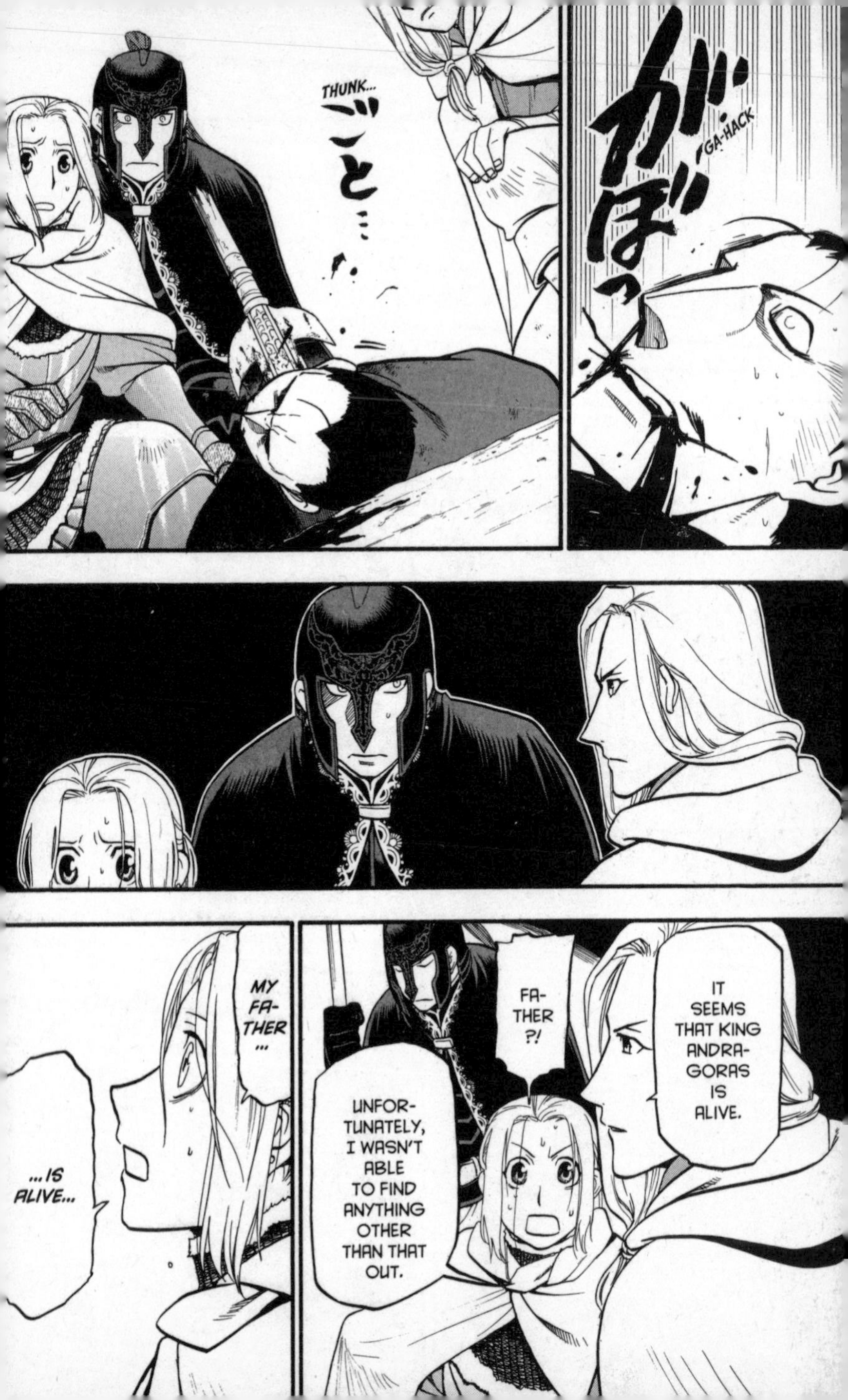
がぼっ
GA-HACK
ごとっ
THUNK...
IT SEEMS THAT KING ANDRAGORAS IS ALIVE.
FATHER?!
UNFORTUNATELY, I WASN'T ABLE TO FIND ANYTHING OTHER THAN THAT OUT.
MY FATHER...
...IS ALIVE...

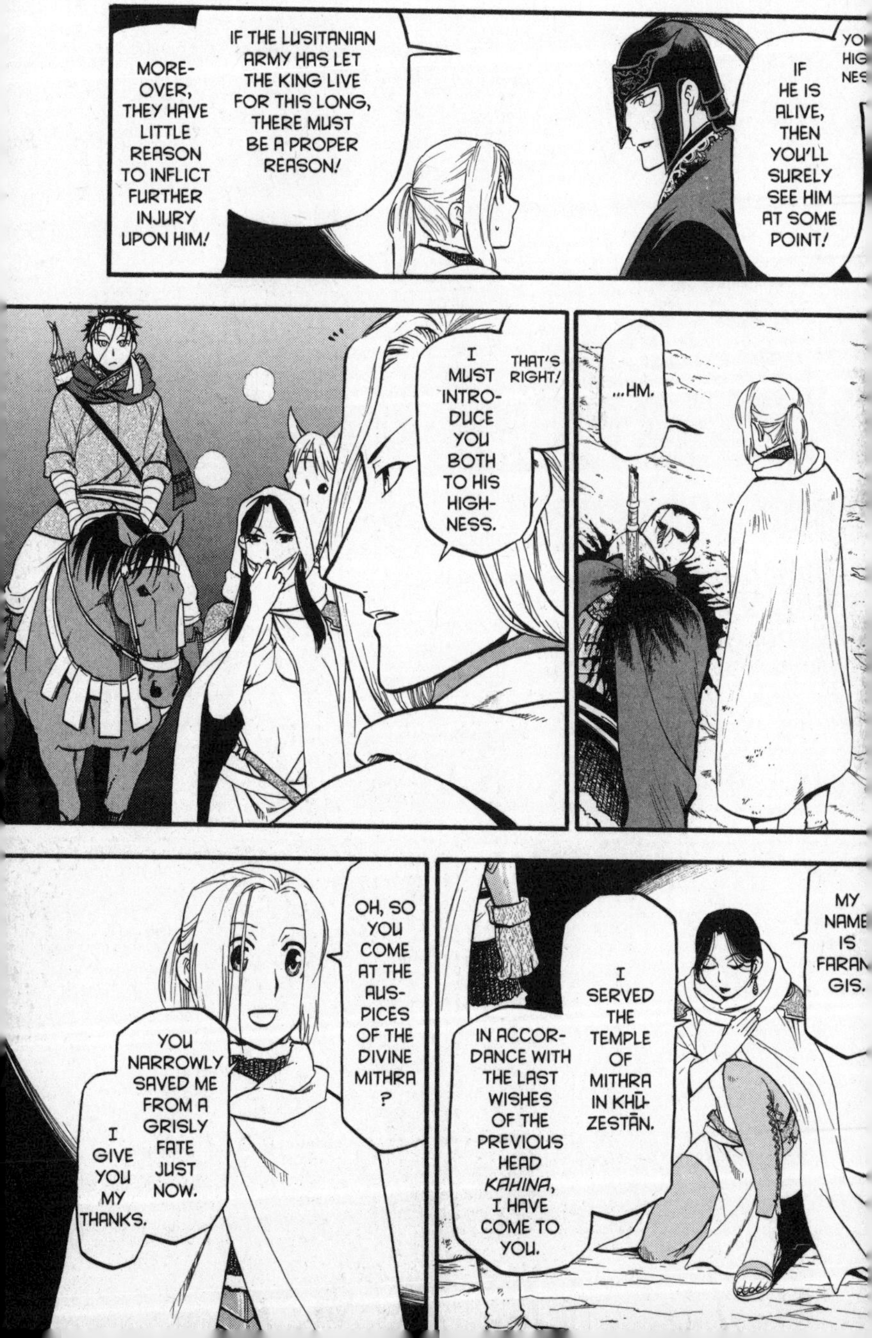
YO HIG NES
IF HE IS ALIVE, THEN YOU'LL SURELY SEE HIM AT SOME POINT!
IF THE LUSITANIAN ARMY HAS LET THE KING LIVE FOR THIS LONG, THERE MUST BE A PROPER REASON!
MORE-OVER, THEY HAVE LITTLE REASON TO INFLICT FURTHER INJURY UPON HIM!
...HM.
THAT'S RIGHT!
I MUST INTRO-DUCE YOU BOTH TO HIS HIGH-NESS.
MY NAME IS FARAN GIS.
I SERVED THE TEMPLE OF MITHRA IN KHŪ-ZESTĀN.
IN ACCOR-DANCE WITH THE LAST WISHES OF THE PREVIOUS HEAD *KAHINA*, I HAVE COME TO YOU.
OH, SO YOU COME AT THE AUS-PICES OF THE DIVINE MITHRA?
YOU NARROWLY SAVED ME FROM A GRISLY FATE JUST NOW.
I GIVE YOU MY THANKS.

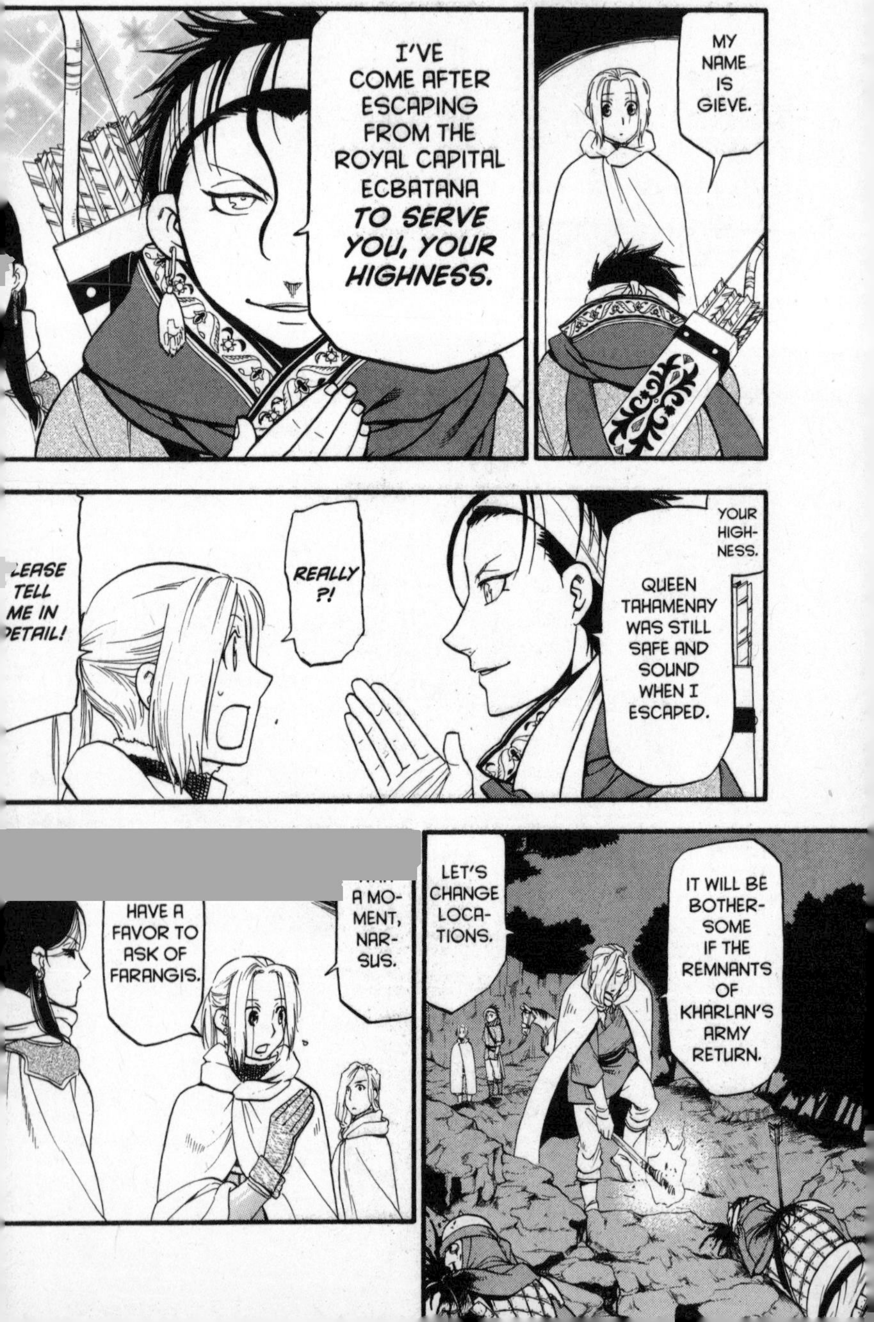
MY NAME IS GIEVE.
I'VE COME AFTER ESCAPING FROM THE ROYAL CAPITAL ECBATANA *TO SERVE YOU, YOUR HIGHNESS.*
YOUR HIGH-NESS.
QUEEN TAHAMENAY WAS STILL SAFE AND SOUND WHEN I ESCAPED.
REALLY ?!
LEASE TELL ME IN ETAIL!
IT WILL BE BOTHER-SOME IF THE REMNANTS OF KHARLAN'S ARMY RETURN.
LET'S CHANGE LOCA-TIONS.
A MO-MENT, NAR-SUS.
HAVE A FAVOR TO ASK OF FARANGIS.

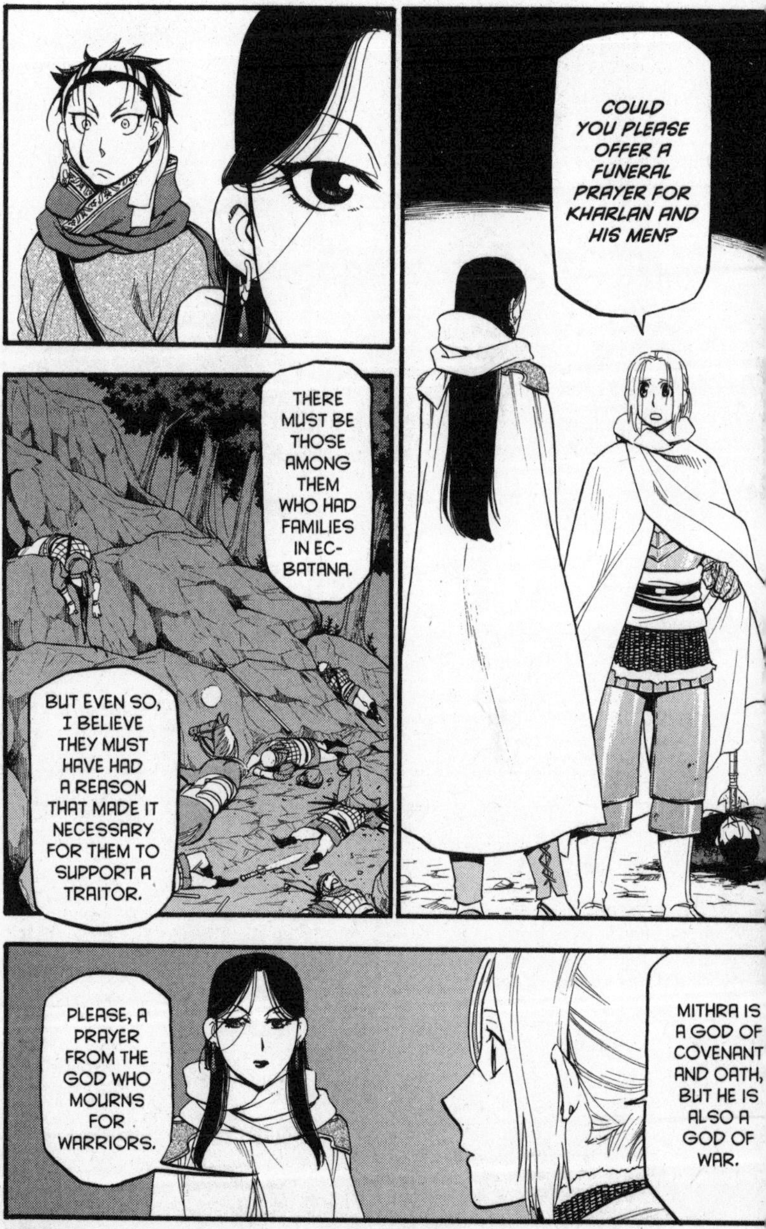
COULD YOU PLEASE OFFER A FUNERAL PRAYER FOR KHARLAN AND HIS MEN?
THERE MUST BE THOSE AMONG THEM WHO HAD FAMILIES IN EC-BATANA.
BUT EVEN SO, I BELIEVE THEY MUST HAVE HAD A REASON THAT MADE IT NECESSARY FOR THEM TO SUPPORT A TRAITOR.
MITHRA IS A GOD OF COVENANT AND OATH, BUT HE IS ALSO A GOD OF WAR.
PLEASE, A PRAYER FROM THE GOD WHO MOURNS FOR WARRIORS.

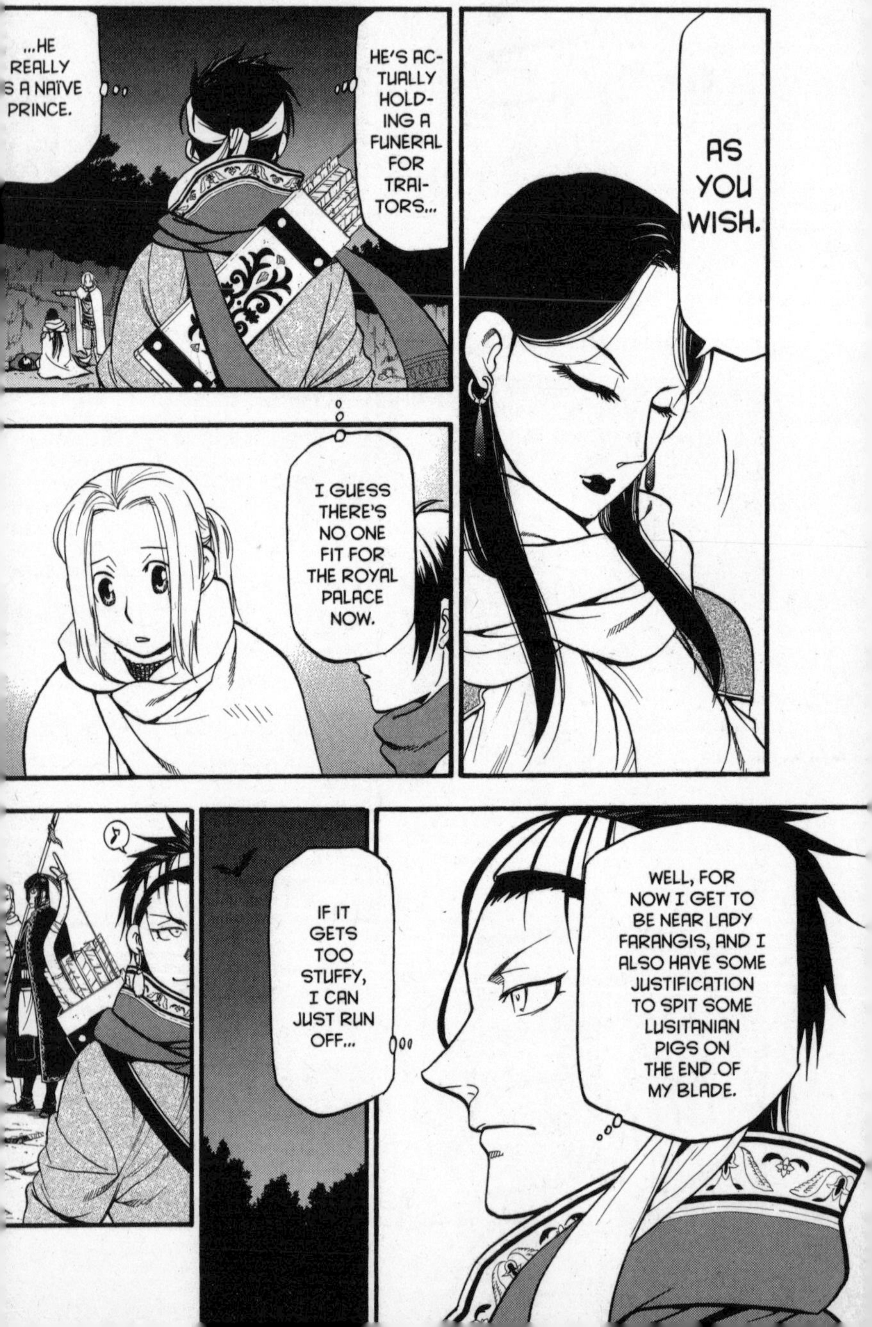
AS YOU WISH.
HE'S ACTUALLY HOLDING A FUNERAL FOR TRAITORS...
...HE REALLY S A NAÏVE PRINCE.
I GUESS THERE'S NO ONE FIT FOR THE ROYAL PALACE NOW.
WELL, FOR NOW I GET TO BE NEAR LADY FARANGIS, AND I ALSO HAVE SOME JUSTIFICATION TO SPIT SOME LUSITANIAN PIGS ON THE END OF MY BLADE.
IF IT GETS TOO STUFFY, I CAN JUST RUN OFF...
♪

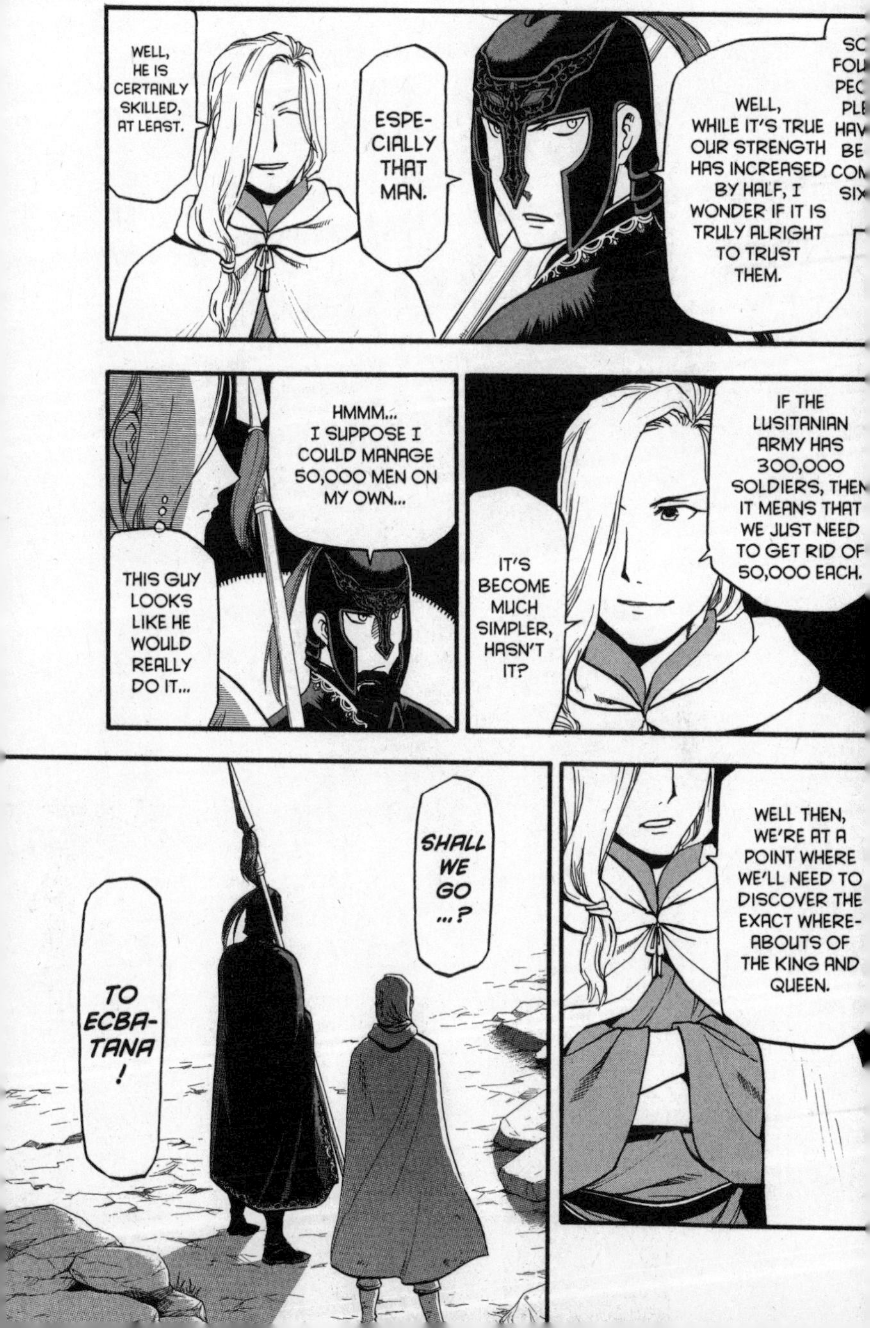
WELL, WHILE IT'S TRUE OUR STRENGTH HAS INCREASED BY HALF, I WONDER IF IT IS TRULY ALRIGHT TO TRUST THEM.
ESPECIALLY THAT MAN.
WELL, HE IS CERTAINLY SKILLED, AT LEAST.
IF THE LUSITANIAN ARMY HAS 300,000 SOLDIERS, THEN IT MEANS THAT WE JUST NEED TO GET RID OF 50,000 EACH.
IT'S BECOME MUCH SIMPLER, HASN'T IT?
HMMM... I SUPPOSE I COULD MANAGE 50,000 MEN ON MY OWN...
THIS GUY LOOKS LIKE HE WOULD REALLY DO IT...
WELL THEN, WE'RE AT A POINT WHERE WE'LL NEED TO DISCOVER THE EXACT WHEREABOUTS OF THE KING AND QUEEN.
SHALL WE GO ...?
TO ECBATANA!

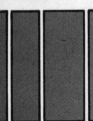

...

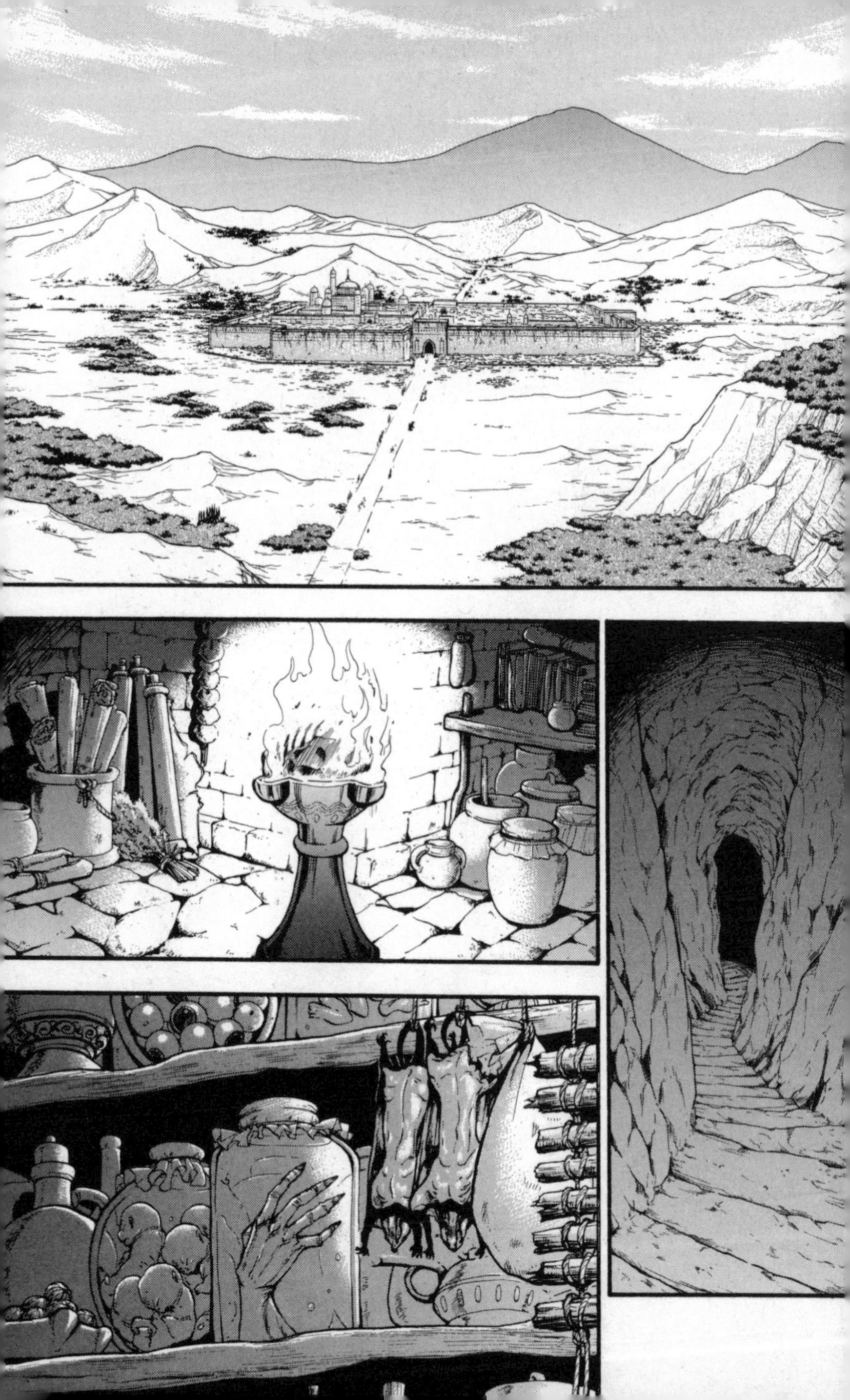

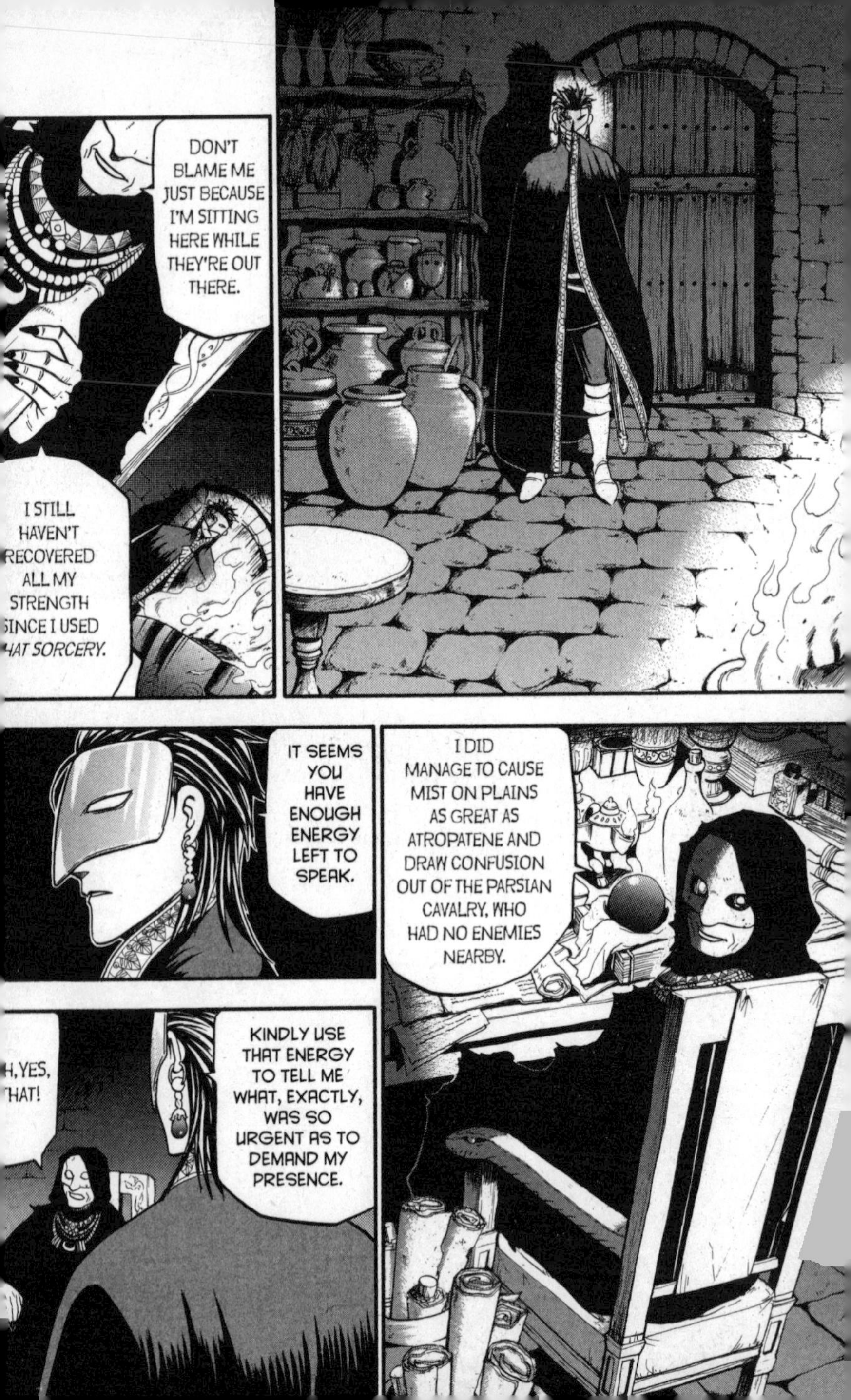
DON'T BLAME ME JUST BECAUSE I'M SITTING HERE WHILE THEY'RE OUT THERE.
I STILL HAVEN'T RECOVERED ALL MY STRENGTH SINCE I USED HAT SORCERY.
I DID MANAGE TO CAUSE MIST ON PLAINS AS GREAT AS ATROPATENE AND DRAW CONFUSION OUT OF THE PARSIAN CAVALRY, WHO HAD NO ENEMIES NEARBY.
IT SEEMS YOU HAVE ENOUGH ENERGY LEFT TO SPEAK.
KINDLY USE THAT ENERGY TO TELL ME WHAT, EXACTLY, WAS SO URGENT AS TO DEMAND MY PRESENCE.
H, YES, HAT!

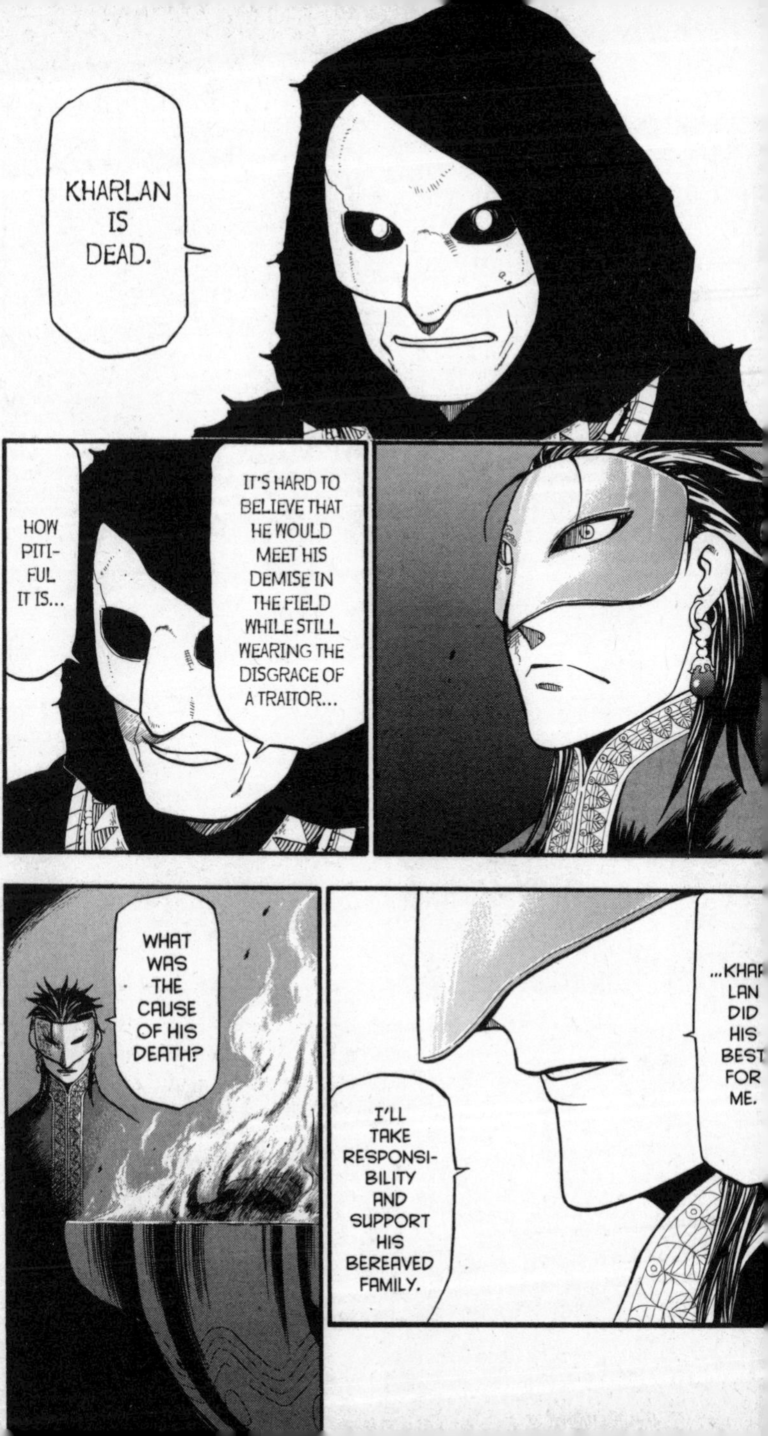
KHARLAN IS DEAD.
IT'S HARD TO BELIEVE THAT HE WOULD MEET HIS DEMISE IN THE FIELD WHILE STILL WEARING THE DISGRACE OF A TRAITOR...
HOW PITI-FUL IT IS...
...KHAR LAN DID HIS BEST FOR ME.
I'LL TAKE RESPONSI-BILITY AND SUPPORT HIS BEREAVED FAMILY.
WHAT WAS THE CAUSE OF HIS DEATH?

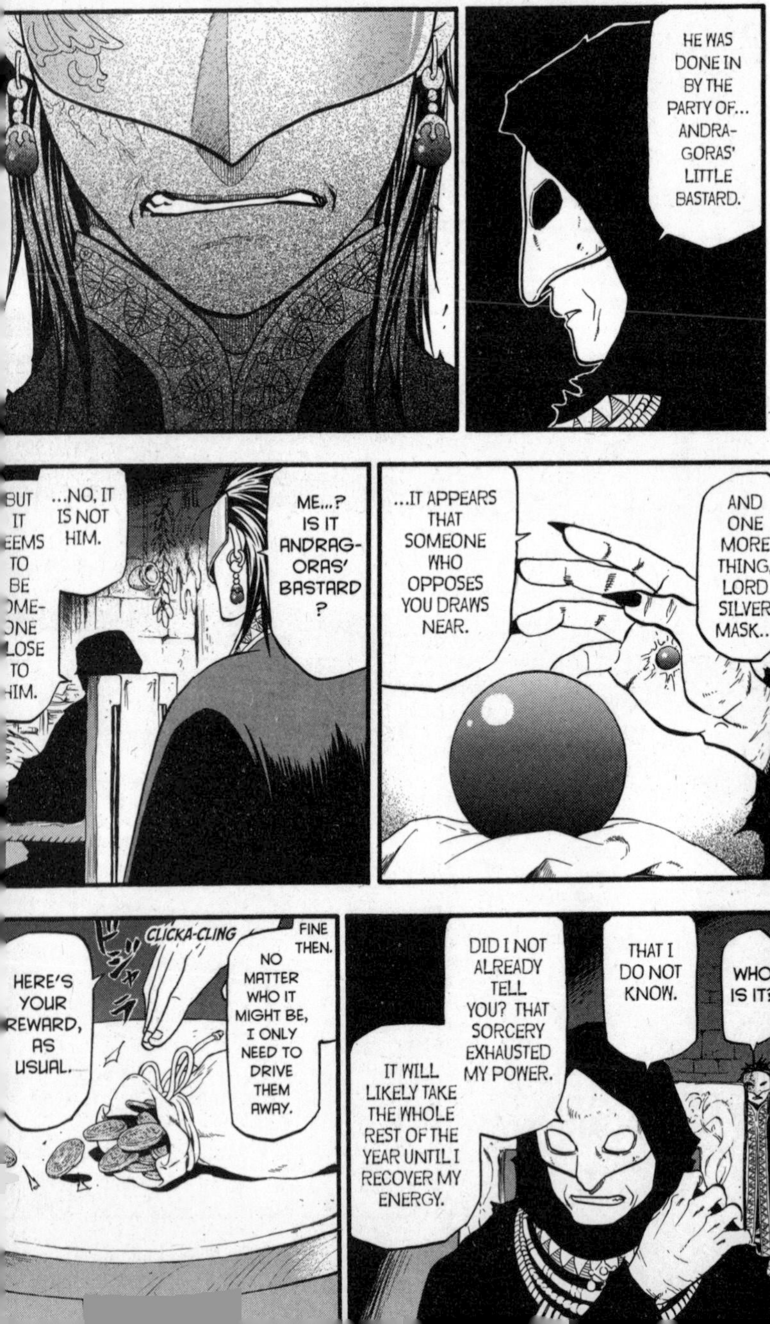
HE WAS DONE IN BY THE PARTY OF... ANDRA-GORAS' LITTLE BASTARD.
AND ONE MORE THING, LORD SILVER MASK...
...IT APPEARS THAT SOMEONE WHO OPPOSES YOU DRAWS NEAR.
ME...? IS IT ANDRAG-ORAS' BASTARD?
...NO, IT IS NOT HIM.
BUT IT EEMS TO BE OME-ONE LOSE TO HIM.
WHO IS IT?
THAT I DO NOT KNOW.
DID I NOT ALREADY TELL YOU? THAT SORCERY EXHAUSTED MY POWER.
IT WILL LIKELY TAKE THE WHOLE REST OF THE YEAR UNTIL I RECOVER MY ENERGY.
FINE THEN.
NO MATTER WHO IT MIGHT BE, I ONLY NEED TO DRIVE THEM AWAY.
CLICKA-CLING
HERE'S YOUR REWARD, AS USUAL.

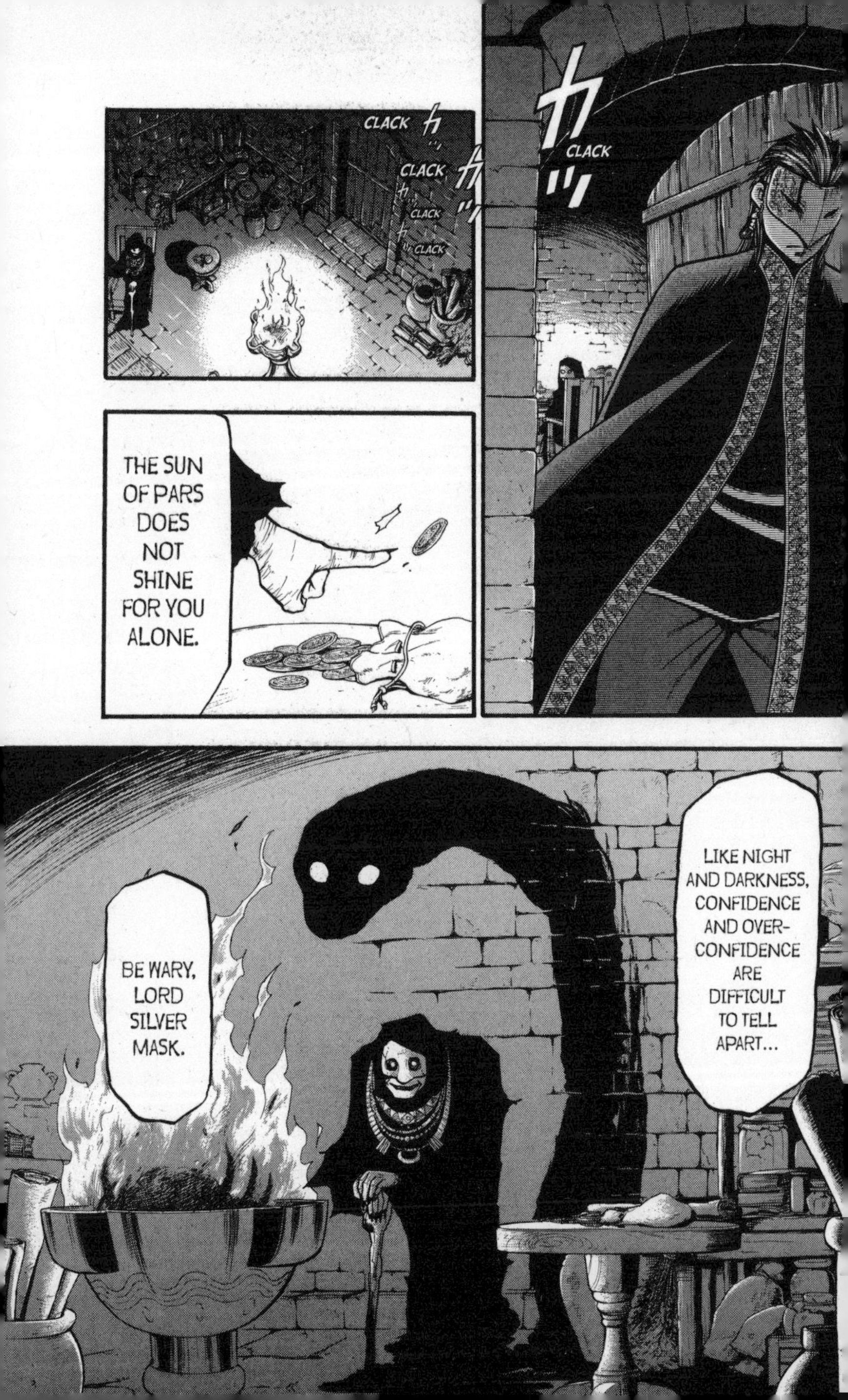
CLACK
CLACK
CLACK
CLACK
CLACK
THE SUN OF PARS DOES NOT SHINE FOR YOU ALONE.
LIKE NIGHT AND DARKNESS, CONFIDENCE AND OVER-CONFIDENCE ARE DIFFICULT TO TELL APART...
BE WARY, LORD SILVER MASK.

THE HEROIC LEGEND OF
ARSLAN

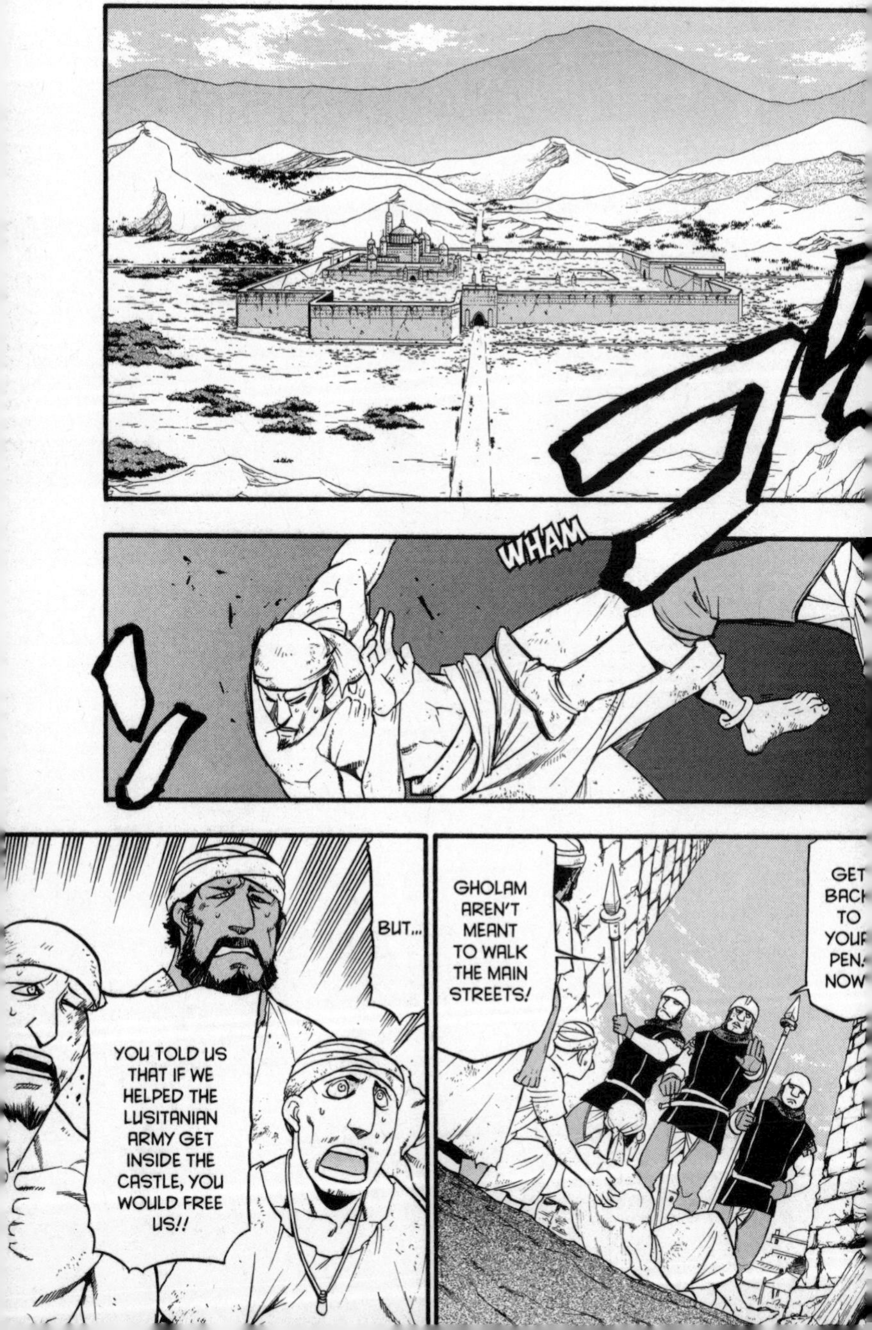
WHAM
GET BACK TO YOUR PEN. NOW
GHOLAM AREN'T MEANT TO WALK THE MAIN STREETS!
BUT...
YOU TOLD US THAT IF WE HELPED THE LUSITANIAN ARMY GET INSIDE THE CASTLE, YOU WOULD FREE US!!

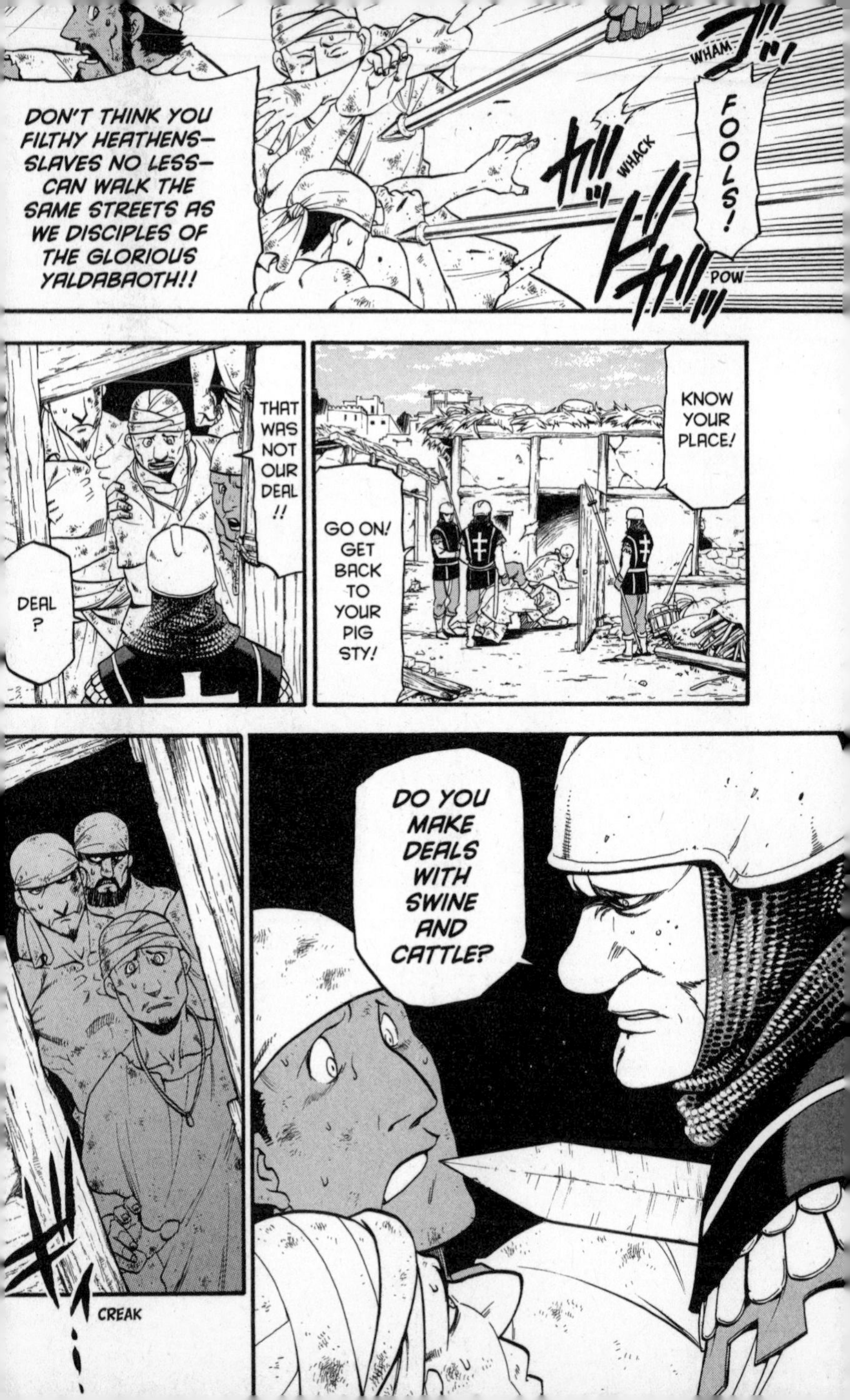
WHAM
FOOLS!
WHACK
POW
DON'T THINK YOU FILTHY HEATHENS—SLAVES NO LESS—CAN WALK THE SAME STREETS AS WE DISCIPLES OF THE GLORIOUS YALDABAOTH!!
KNOW YOUR PLACE!
GO ON! GET BACK TO YOUR PIG STY!
THAT WAS NOT OUR DEAL!!
DEAL?
DO YOU MAKE DEALS WITH SWINE AND CATTLE?
CREAK

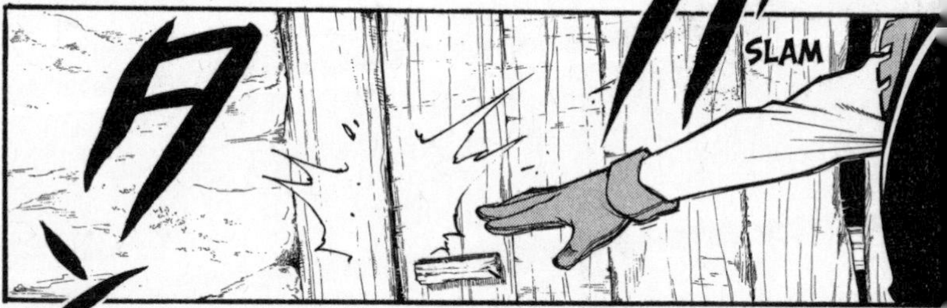
SLAM

Chapter 16: The Love of King Innocentis

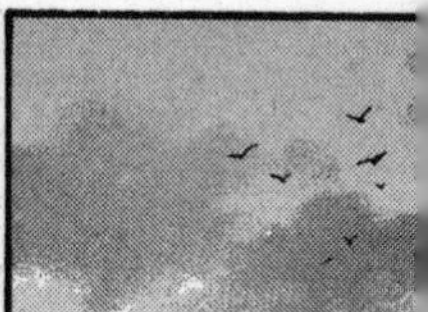

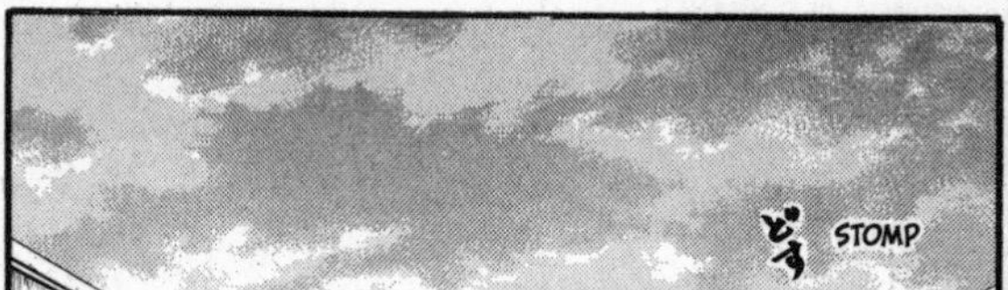
どす STOMP
どす STOMP
どす STOMP
どす STOMP
STOMP どす
STOMP どす
STOMP どす

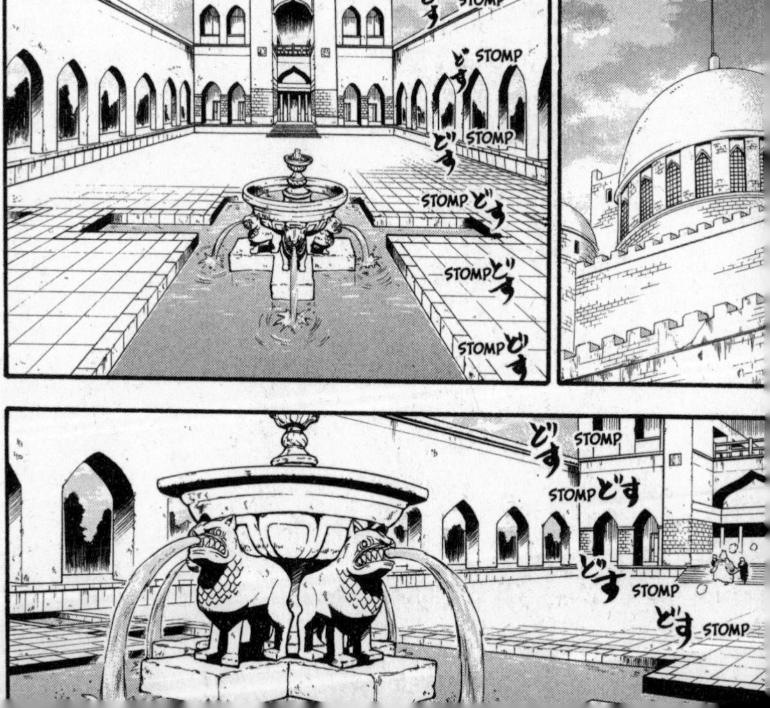
どす STOMP
STOMP どす
どす STOMP
どす STOMP

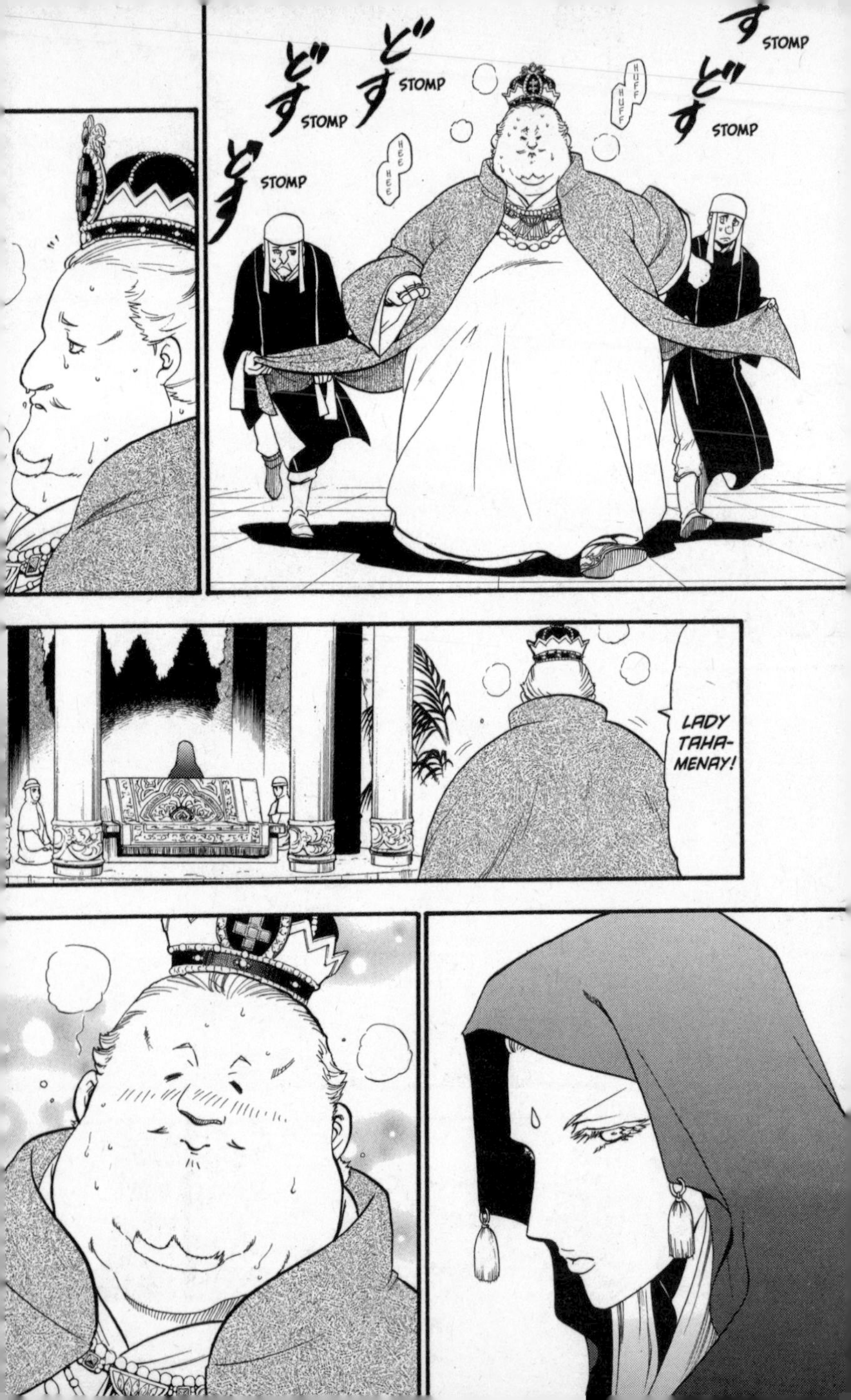

す STOMP
どす STOMP
HUFF HUFF
HEE HEE
どす STOMP
どす STOMP
ど STOMP
LADY TAHA-MENAY!

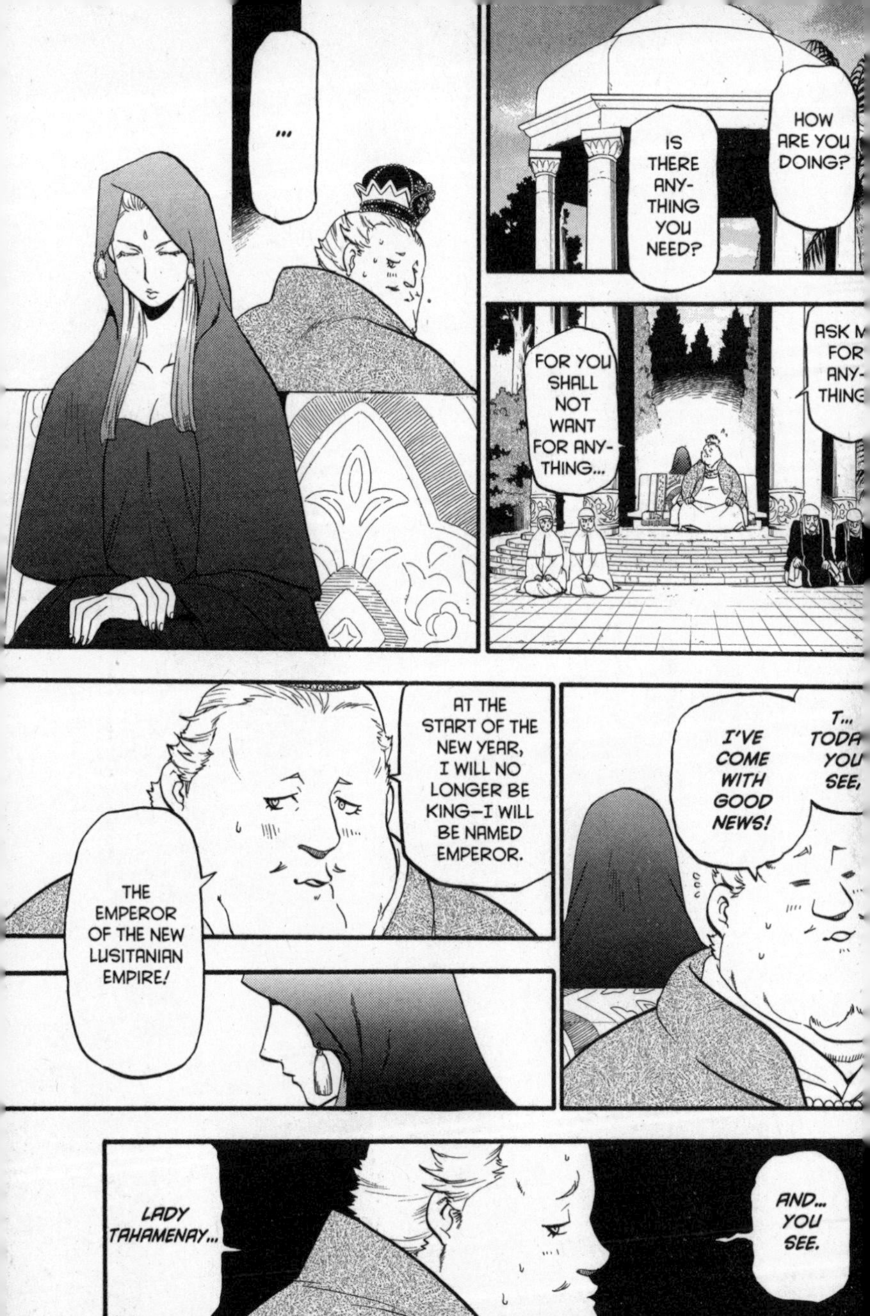
HOW ARE YOU DOING?
IS THERE ANY-THING YOU NEED?
ASK M FOR ANY-THING
FOR YOU SHALL NOT WANT FOR ANY-THING...
...
T... TODA YOU SEE,
I'VE COME WITH GOOD NEWS!
AT THE START OF THE NEW YEAR, I WILL NO LONGER BE KING—I WILL BE NAMED EMPEROR.
THE EMPEROR OF THE NEW LUSITANIAN EMPIRE!
AND... YOU SEE.
LADY TAHAMENAY...

THE PUBLIC BELIEVES AN EMPEROR NEEDS AN EMPRESS.

AND I HAPPEN TO AGREE...

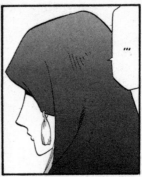

...

...?

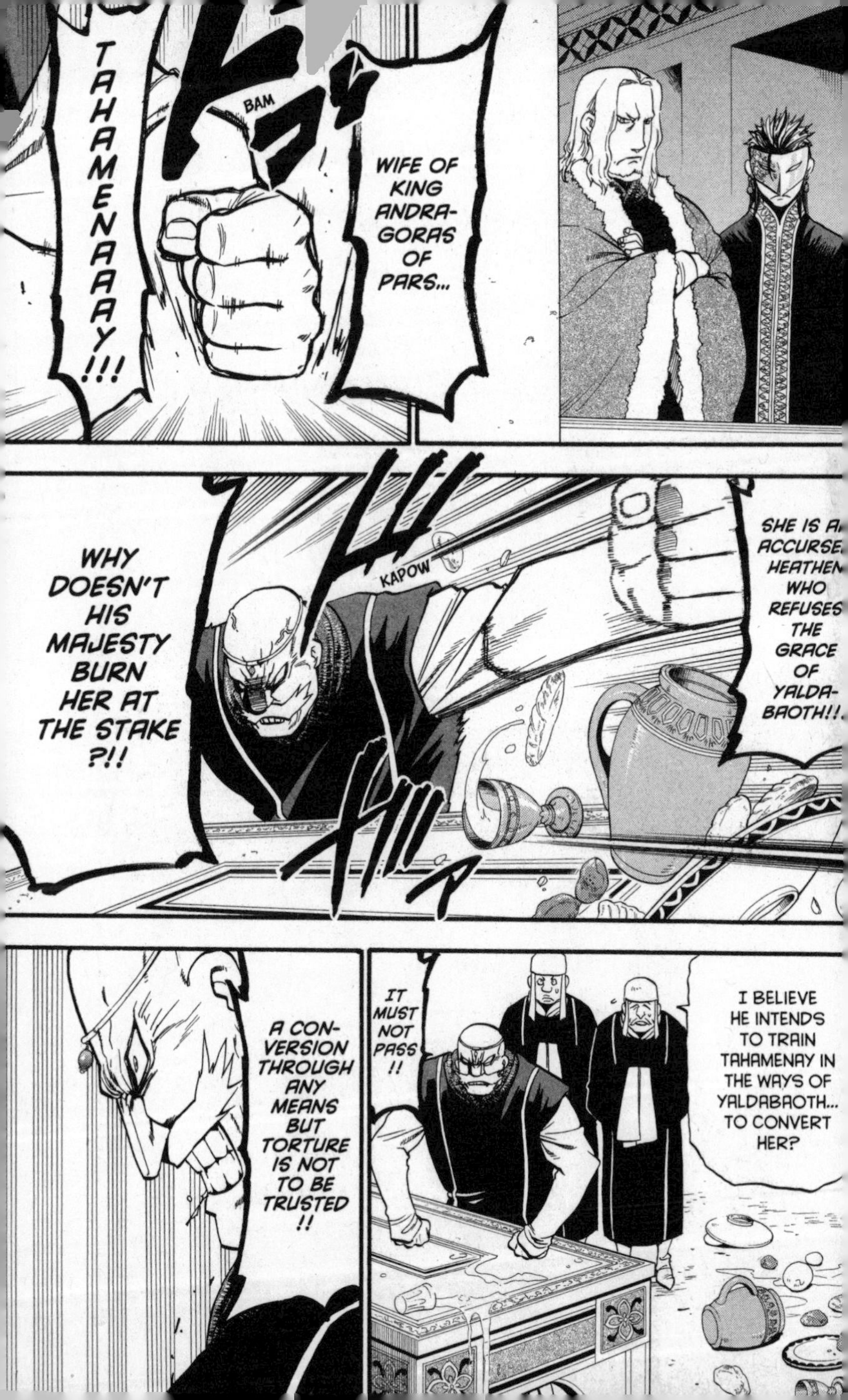

BAM
WIFE OF KING ANDRA-GORAS OF PARS...
TAHAMENAAAAY!!!
SHE IS A ACCURSE HEATHEN WHO REFUSES THE GRACE OF YALDA-BAOTH!!
KAPOW
WHY DOESN'T HIS MAJESTY BURN HER AT THE STAKE ?!!
I BELIEVE HE INTENDS TO TRAIN TAHAMENAY IN THE WAYS OF YALDABAOTH... TO CONVERT HER?
IT MUST NOT PASS !!
A CON-VERSION THROUGH ANY MEANS BUT TORTURE IS NOT TO BE TRUSTED !!

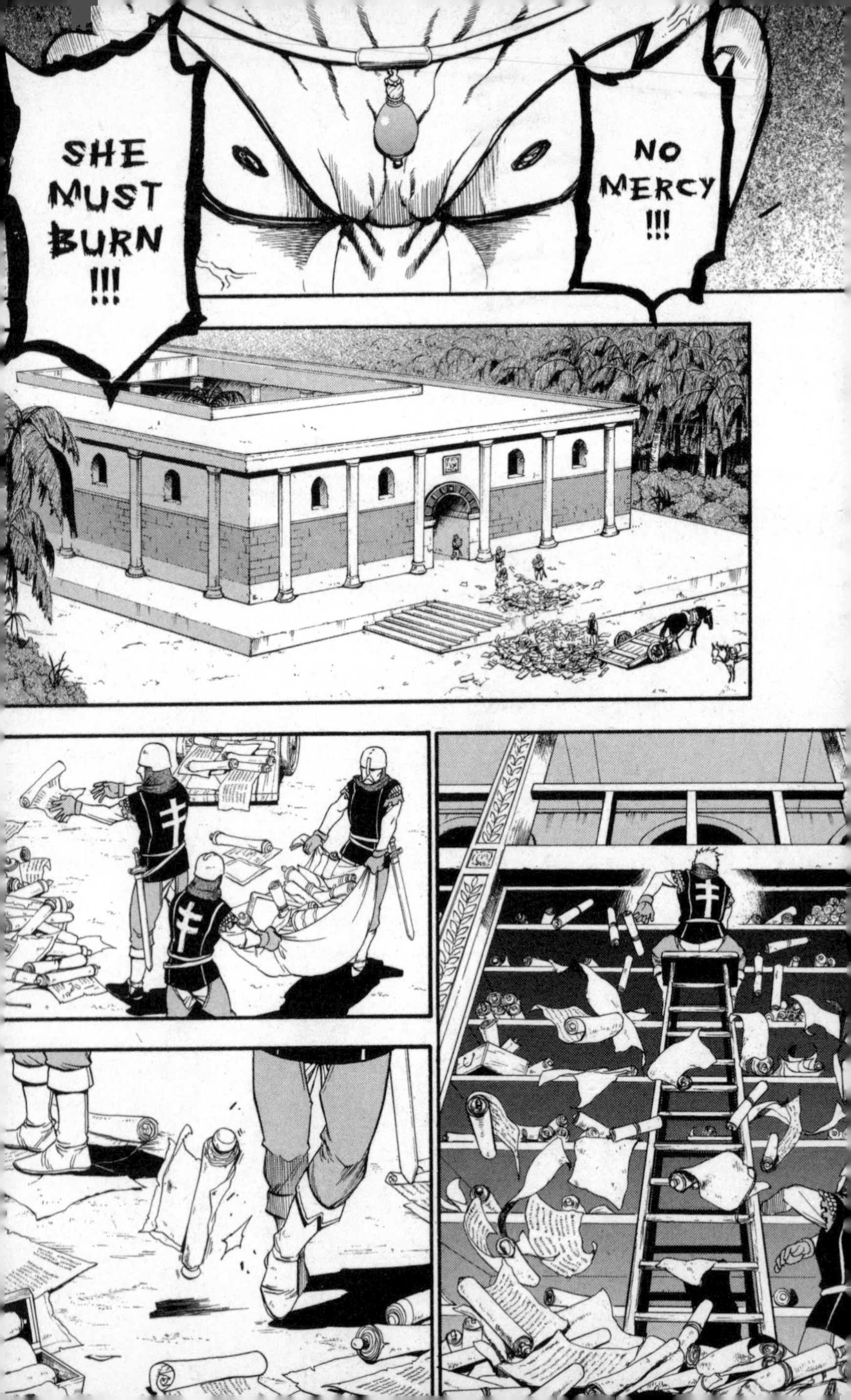
NO MERCY !!!
SHE MUST BURN !!!

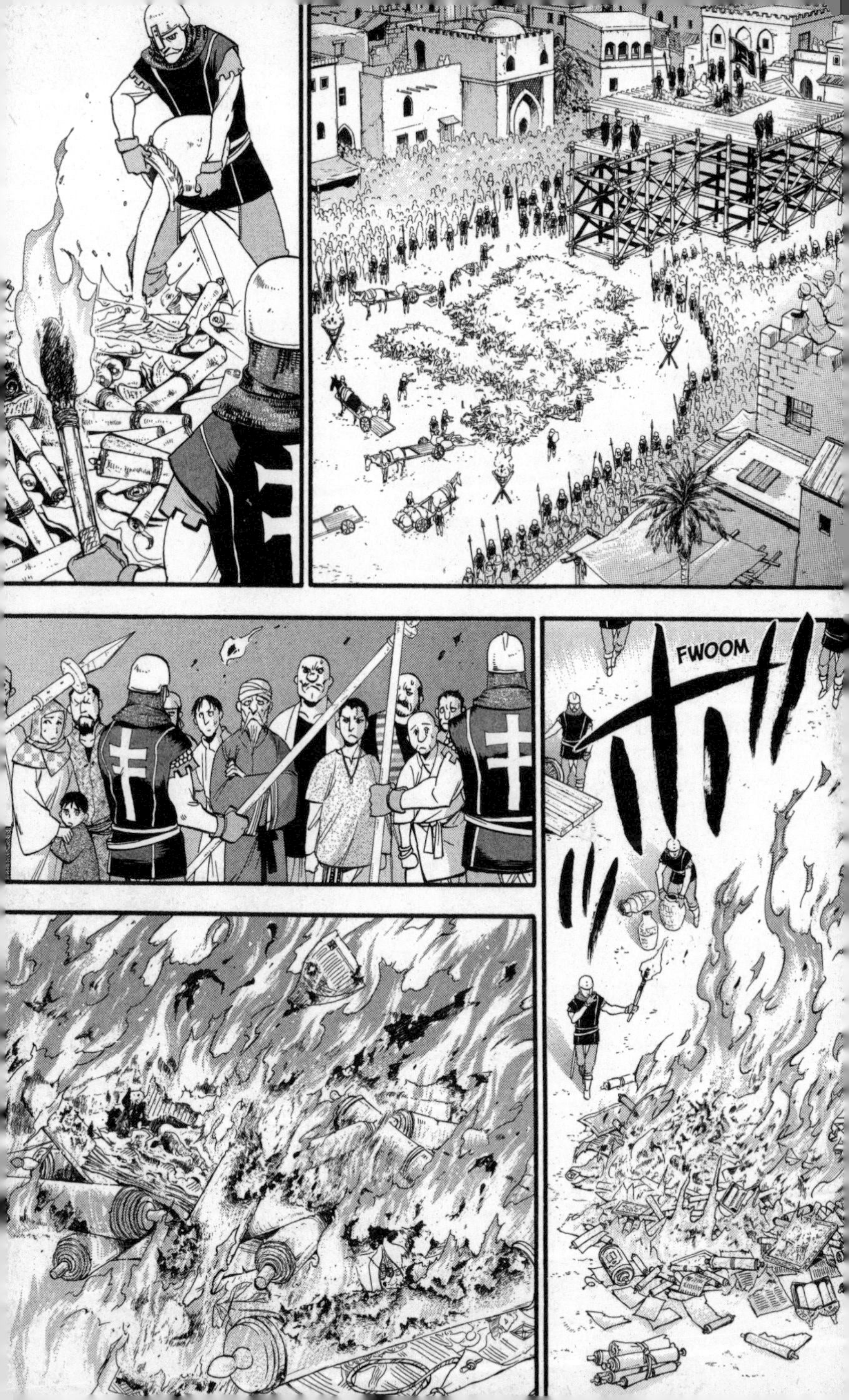
FWOOM

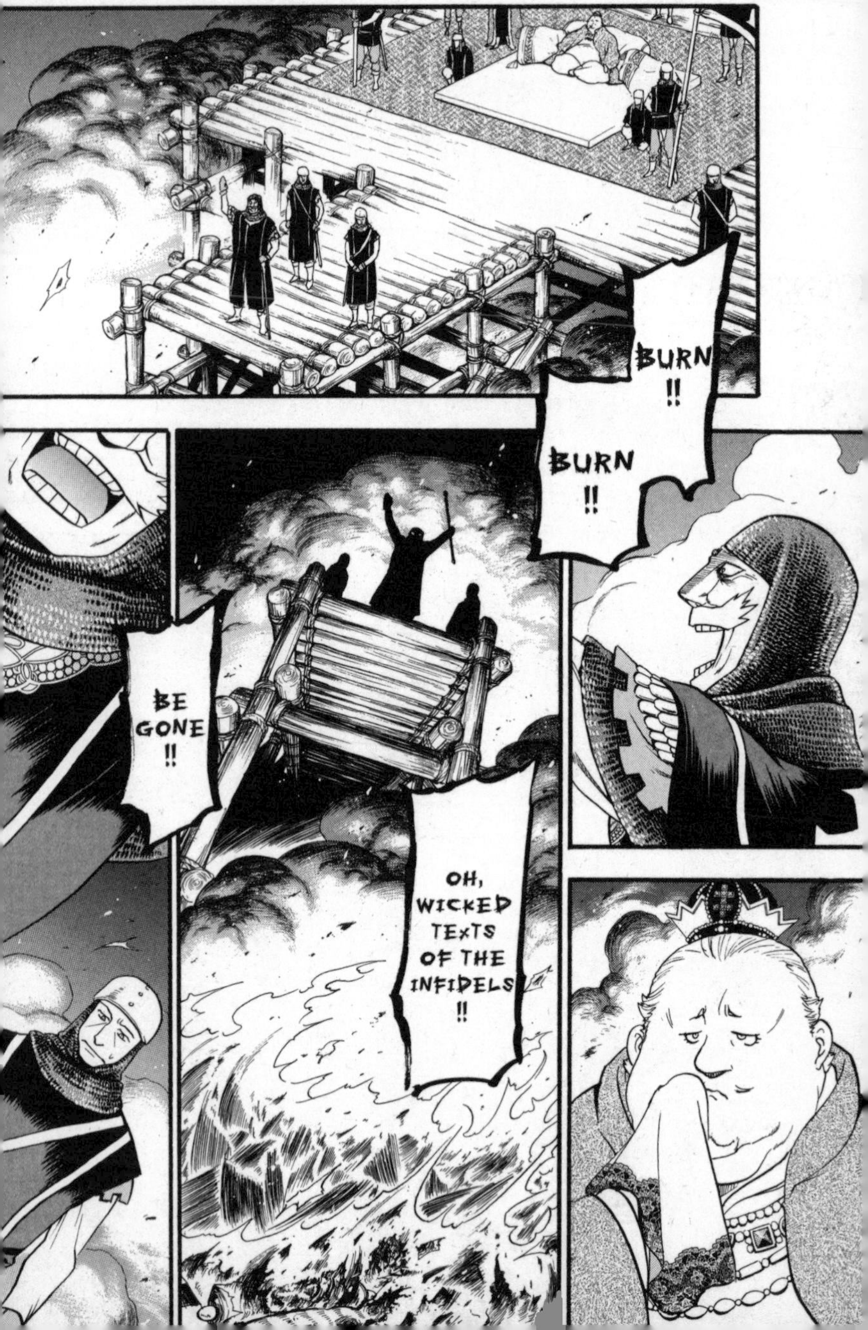
BURN !!
BURN !!
BE GONE !!
OH, WICKED TEXTS OF THE INFIDELS !!

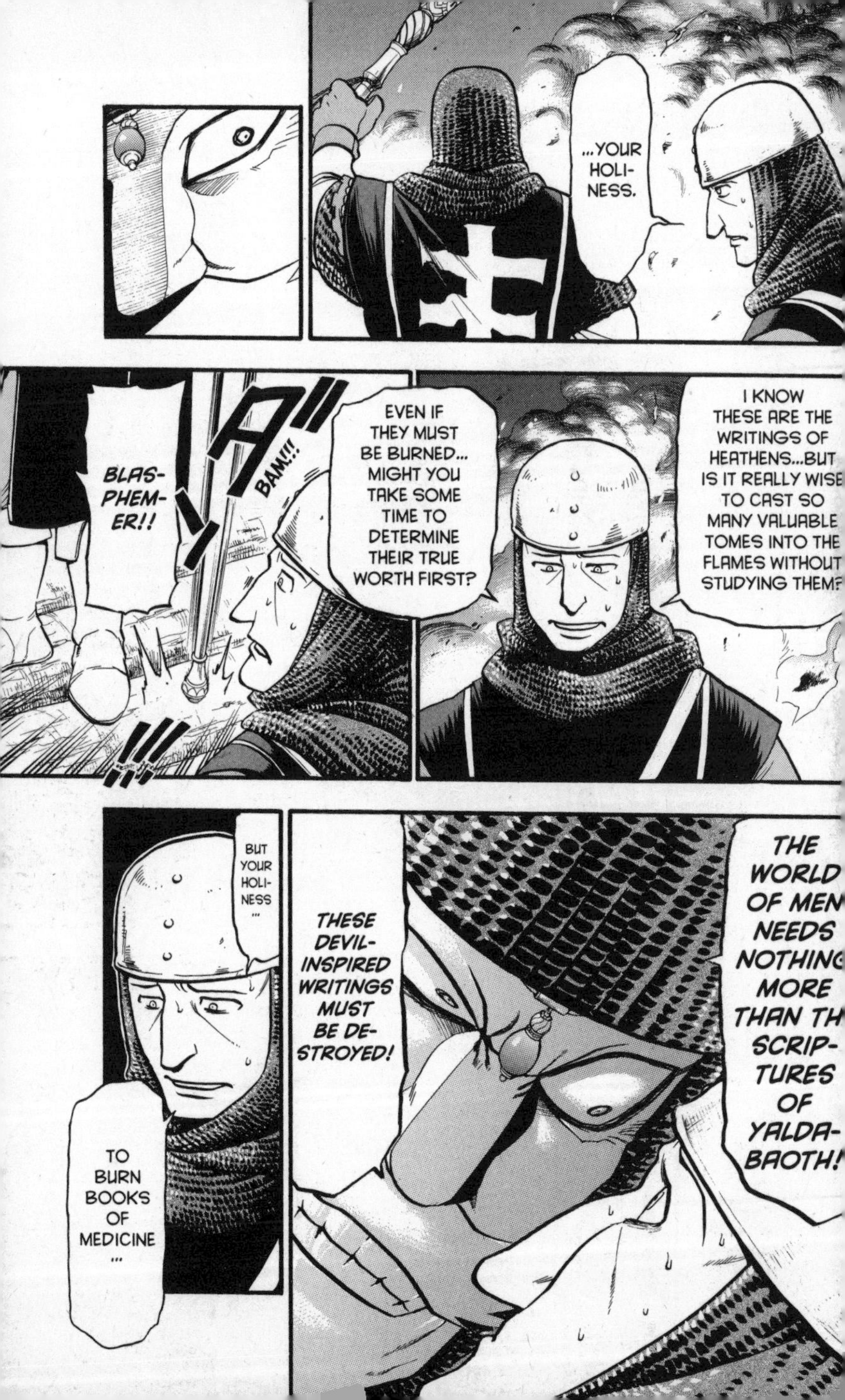
...YOUR HOLINESS.
I KNOW THESE ARE THE WRITINGS OF HEATHENS...BUT IS IT REALLY WISE TO CAST SO MANY VALUABLE TOMES INTO THE FLAMES WITHOUT STUDYING THEM?
EVEN IF THEY MUST BE BURNED... MIGHT YOU TAKE SOME TIME TO DETERMINE THEIR TRUE WORTH FIRST?
BAM!!!
BLASPHEMER!!
!!
THE WORLD OF MEN NEEDS NOTHING MORE THAN TH SCRIPTURES OF YALDABAOTH!
THESE DEVIL-INSPIRED WRITINGS MUST BE DESTROYED!
BUT YOUR HOLINESS...
TO BURN BOOKS OF MEDICINE...

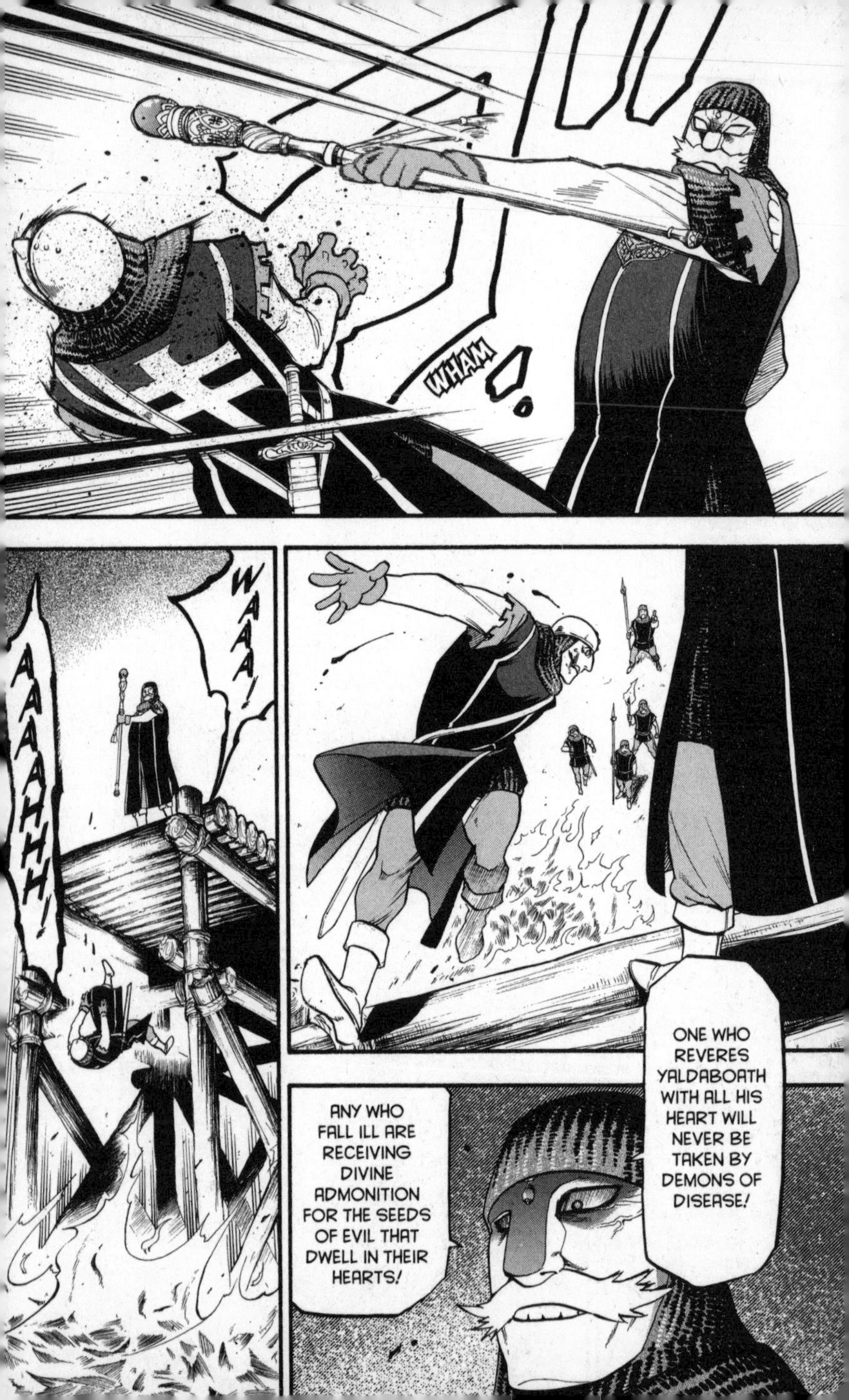
WHAM
WAAAA!
AAAAAHH!
ONE WHO REVERES YALDABOATH WITH ALL HIS HEART WILL NEVER BE TAKEN BY DEMONS OF DISEASE!
ANY WHO FALL ILL ARE RECEIVING DIVINE ADMONITION FOR THE SEEDS OF EVIL THAT DWELL IN THEIR HEARTS!

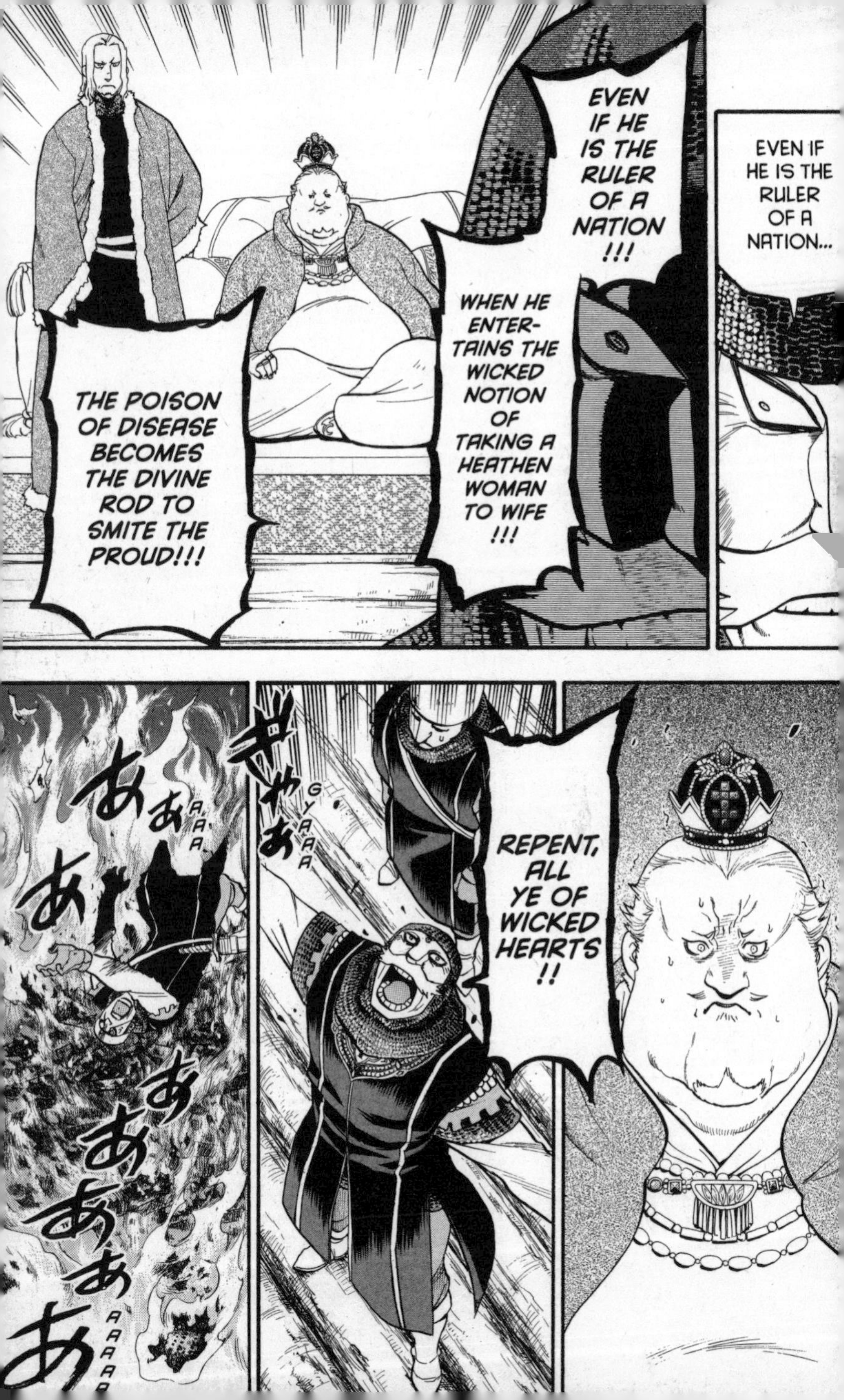
EVEN IF HE IS THE RULER OF A NATION...
EVEN IF HE IS THE RULER OF A NATION!!!
WHEN HE ENTER-TAINS THE WICKED NOTION OF TAKING A HEATHEN WOMAN TO WIFE!!!
THE POISON OF DISEASE BECOMES THE DIVINE ROD TO SMITE THE PROUD!!!
REPENT, ALL YE OF WICKED HEARTS!!
ぎゃあ GYAAA
あああ AAA
ああああ AAAAA

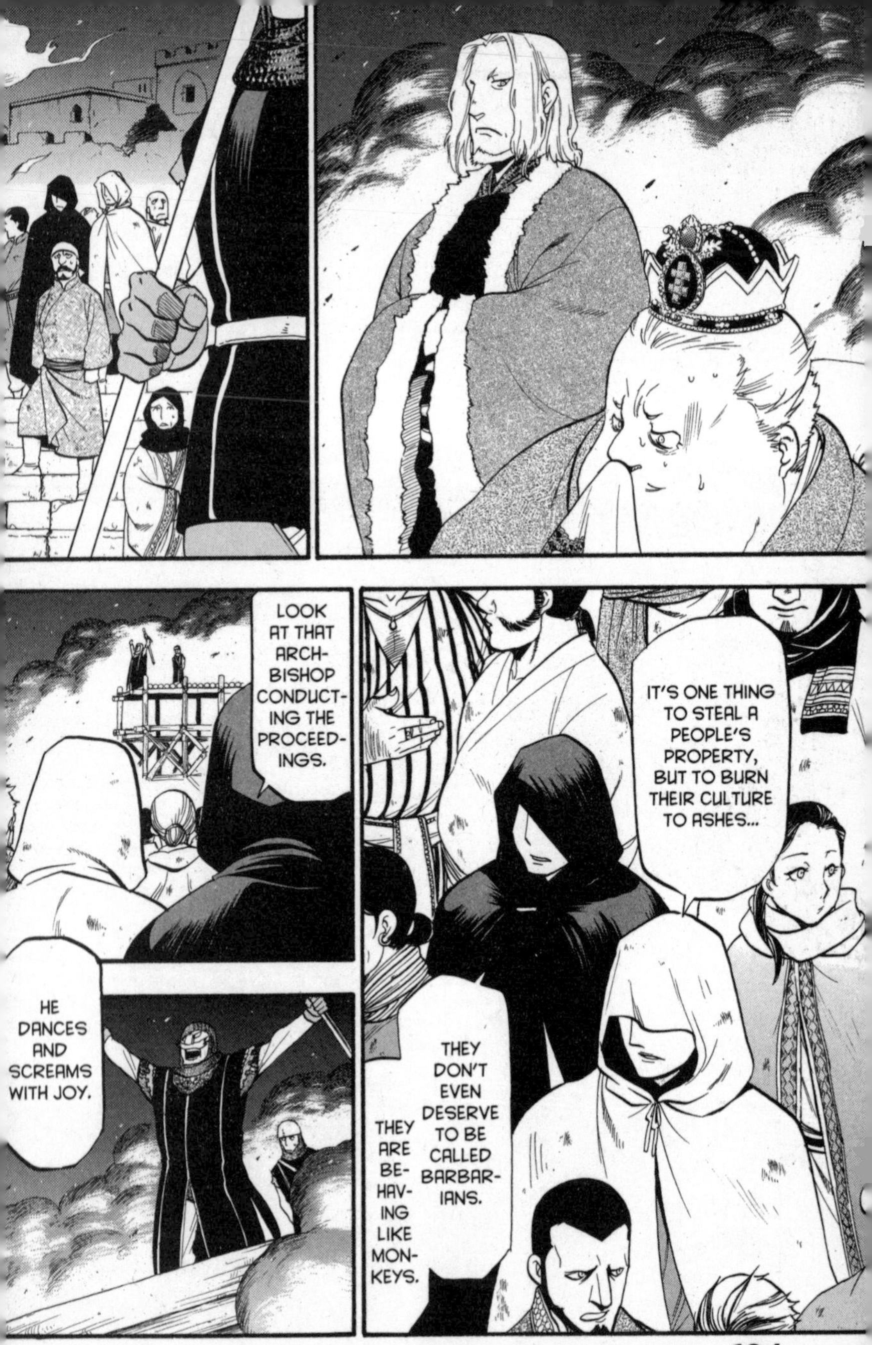
IT'S ONE THING TO STEAL A PEOPLE'S PROPERTY, BUT TO BURN THEIR CULTURE TO ASHES...
THEY DON'T EVEN DESERVE TO BE CALLED BARBARIANS.
THEY ARE BEHAVING LIKE MONKEYS.
LOOK AT THAT ARCHBISHOP CONDUCTING THE PROCEEDINGS.
HE DANCES AND SCREAMS WITH JOY.

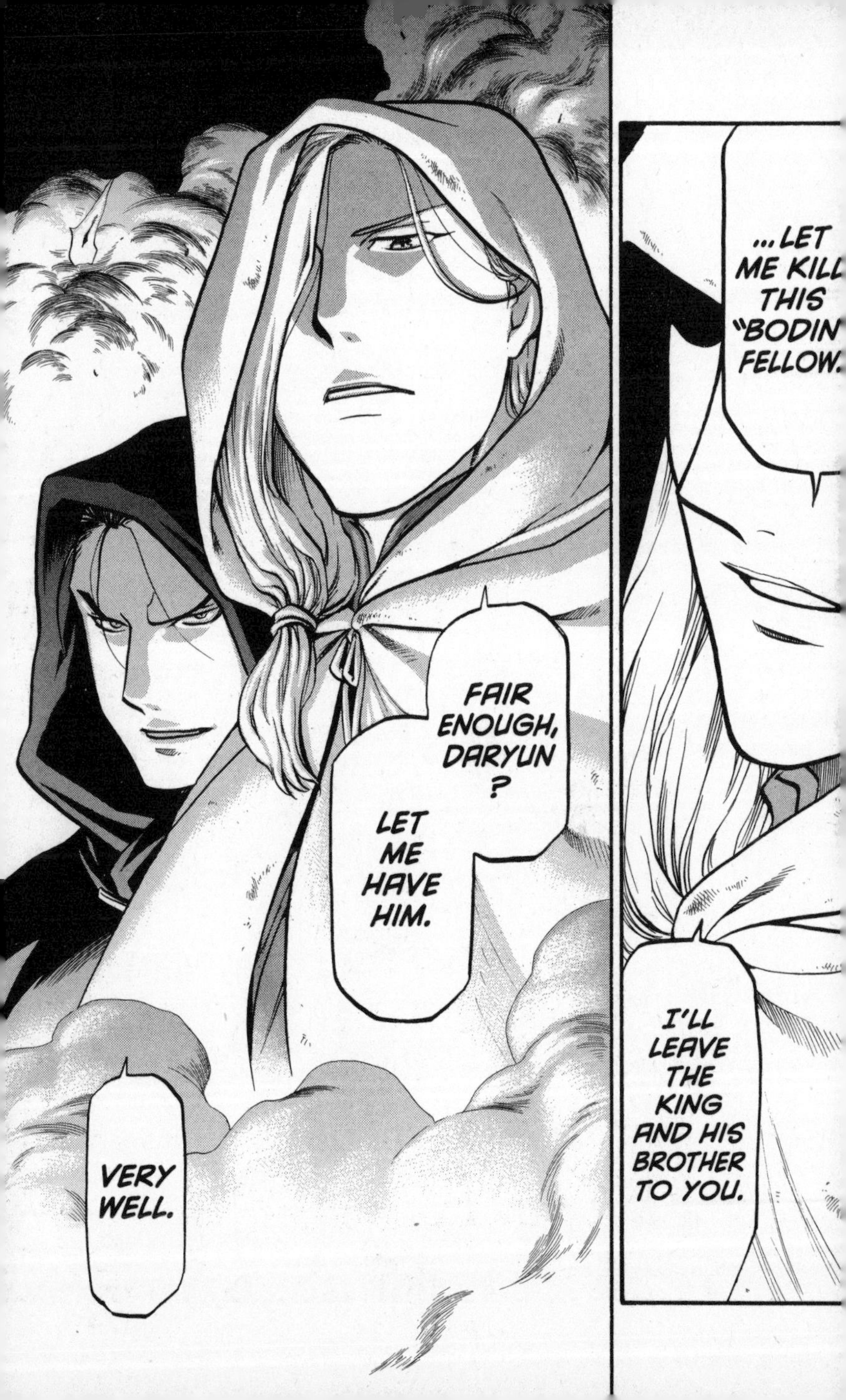
...LET ME KILL THIS "BODIN FELLOW.
I'LL LEAVE THE KING AND HIS BROTHER TO YOU.
FAIR ENOUGH, DARYUN?
LET ME HAVE HIM.
VERY WELL.

THE HEROIC LEGEND OF
ARSLAN

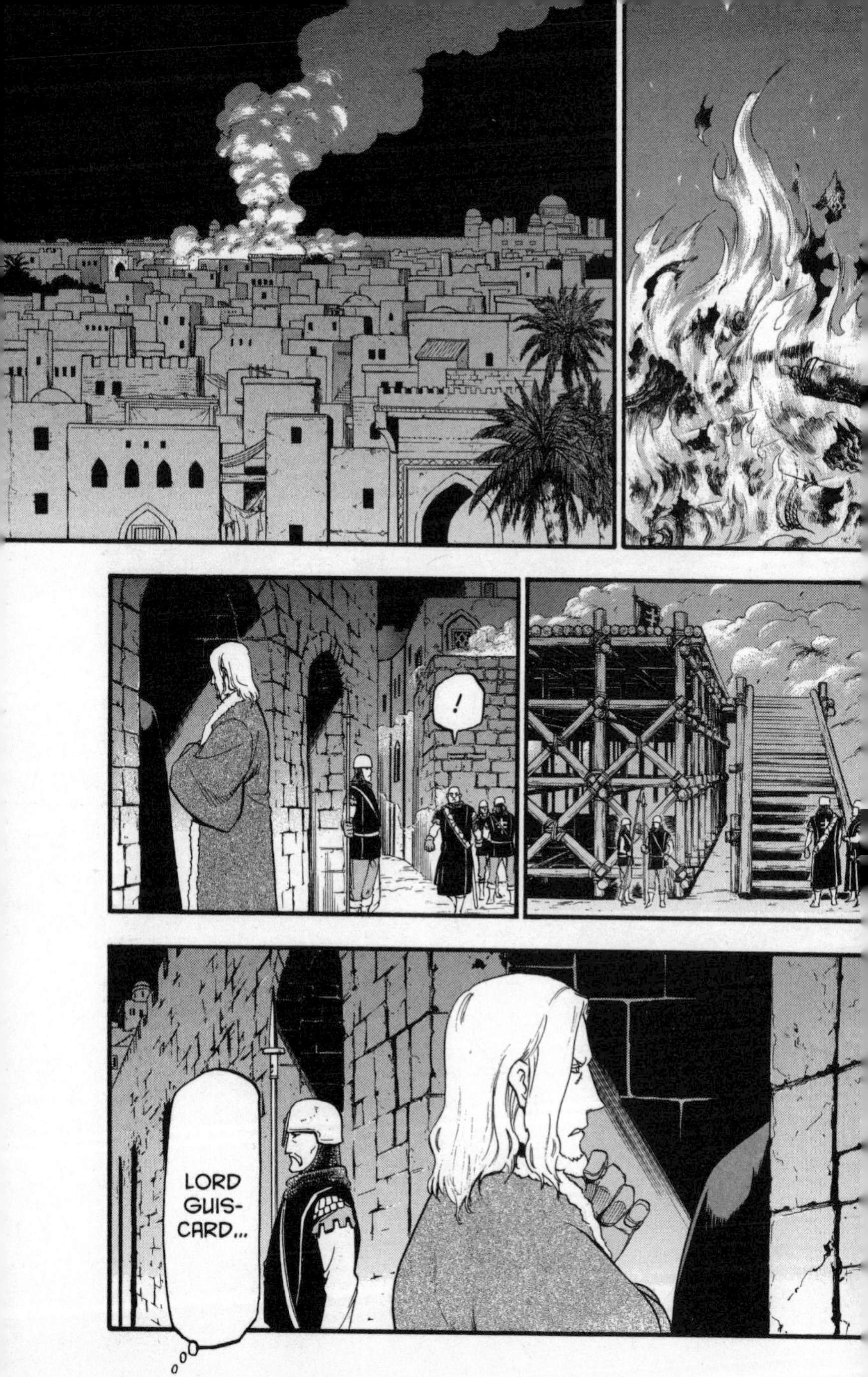
!
LORD GUIS-CARD...

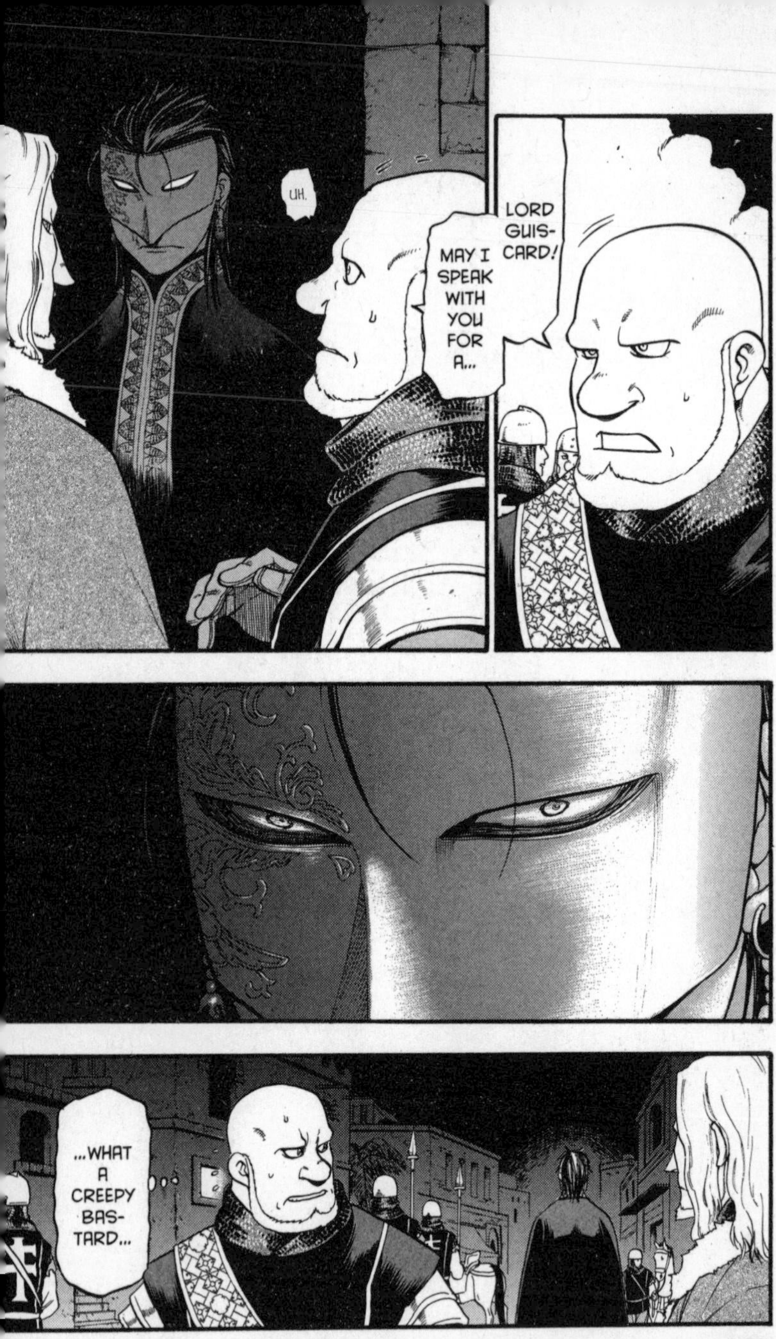
LORD GUIS-CARD!
MAY I SPEAK WITH YOU FOR A...
UH.
...WHAT A CREEPY BAS-TARD...

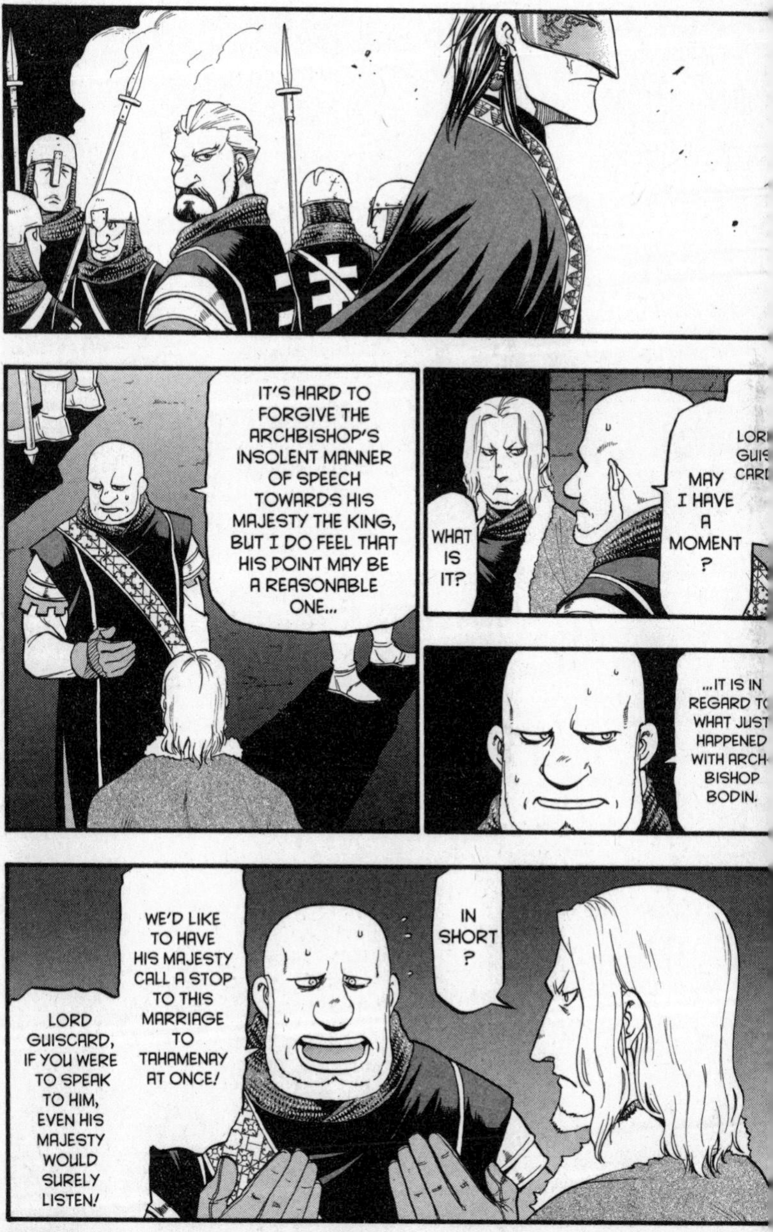
LOR GUIS CAR
MAY I HAVE A MOMENT?
WHAT IS IT?
...IT IS IN REGARD T WHAT JUST HAPPENED WITH ARCH-BISHOP BODIN.
IT'S HARD TO FORGIVE THE ARCHBISHOP'S INSOLENT MANNER OF SPEECH TOWARDS HIS MAJESTY THE KING, BUT I DO FEEL THAT HIS POINT MAY BE A REASONABLE ONE...
IN SHORT?
WE'D LIKE TO HAVE HIS MAJESTY CALL A STOP TO THIS MARRIAGE TO TAHAMENAY AT ONCE!
LORD GUISCARD, IF YOU WERE TO SPEAK TO HIM, EVEN HIS MAJESTY WOULD SURELY LISTEN!

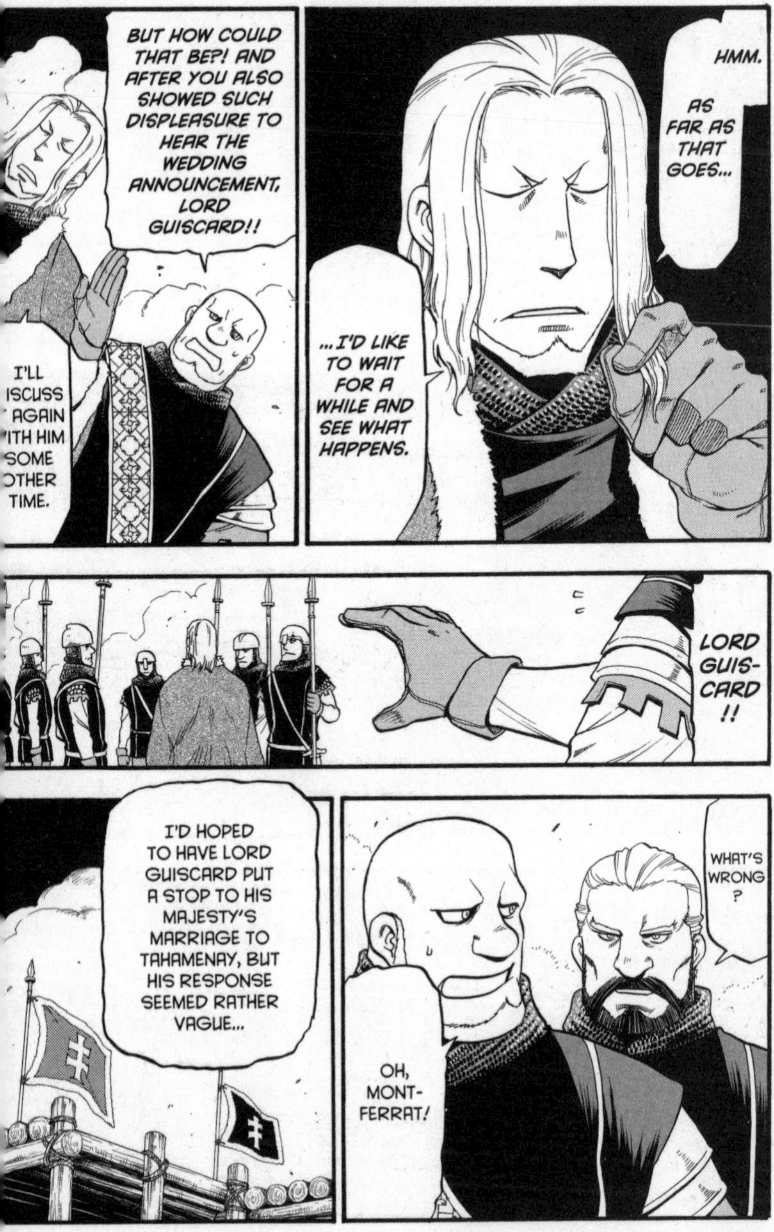
HMM.
AS FAR AS THAT GOES...
...I'D LIKE TO WAIT FOR A WHILE AND SEE WHAT HAPPENS.
BUT HOW COULD THAT BE?! AND AFTER YOU ALSO SHOWED SUCH DISPLEASURE TO HEAR THE WEDDING ANNOUNCEMENT, LORD GUISCARD!!
I'LL ISCUSS AGAIN ITH HIM SOME OTHER TIME.
LORD GUIS-CARD!!
WHAT'S WRONG?
OH, MONT-FERRAT!
I'D HOPED TO HAVE LORD GUISCARD PUT A STOP TO HIS MAJESTY'S MARRIAGE TO TAHAMENAY, BUT HIS RESPONSE SEEMED RATHER VAGUE...

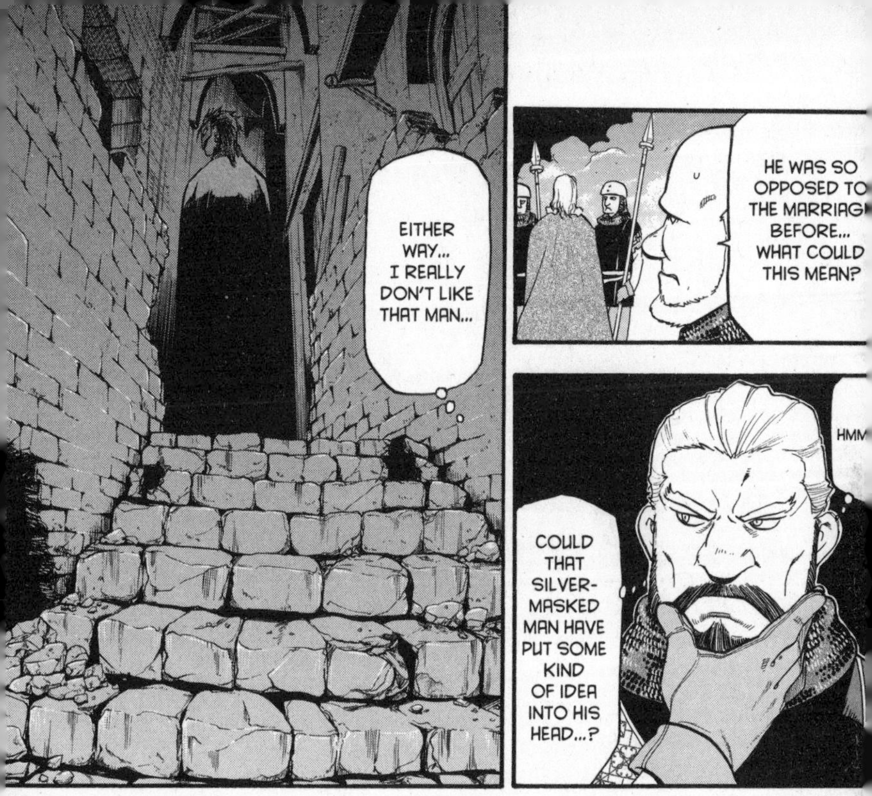
HE WAS SO OPPOSED TO THE MARRIAG BEFORE... WHAT COULD THIS MEAN?
HMM
COULD THAT SILVER-MASKED MAN HAVE PUT SOME KIND OF IDEA INTO HIS HEAD...?
EITHER WAY... I REALLY DON'T LIKE THAT MAN...

Chapter 17: Beneath the Mask

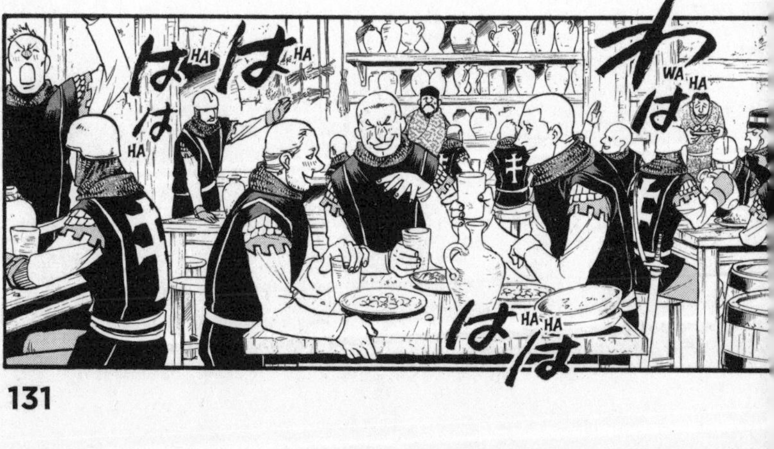
わは
WA HA
はは
HA HA
ははは
HA HA
HA

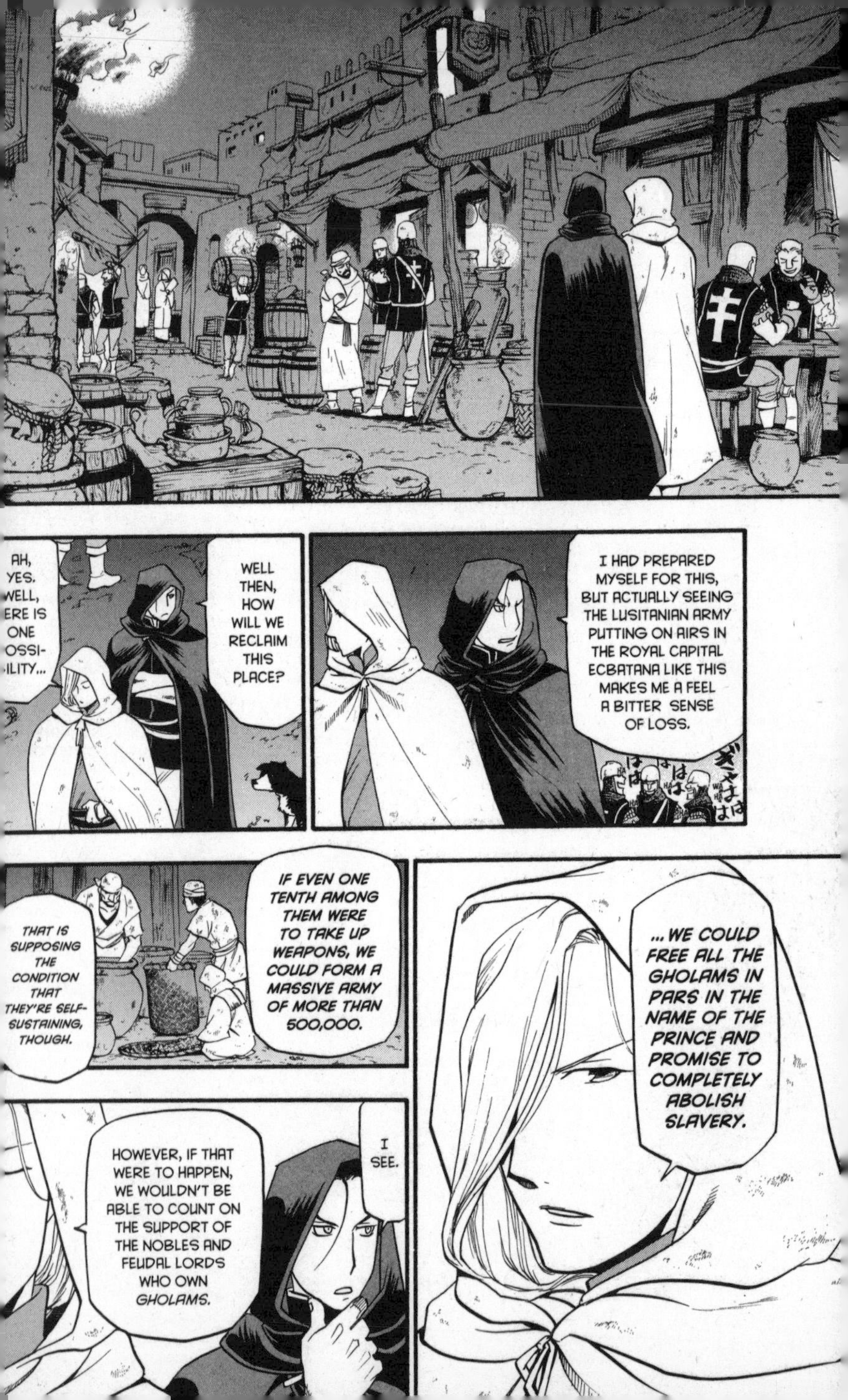
I HAD PREPARED MYSELF FOR THIS, BUT ACTUALLY SEEING THE LUSITANIAN ARMY PUTTING ON AIRS IN THE ROYAL CAPITAL ECBATANA LIKE THIS MAKES ME A FEEL A BITTER SENSE OF LOSS.
WELL THEN, HOW WILL WE RECLAIM THIS PLACE?
AH, YES. WELL, ERE IS ONE OSSI- ILITY...
...WE COULD FREE ALL THE GHOLAMS IN PARS IN THE NAME OF THE PRINCE AND PROMISE TO COMPLETELY ABOLISH SLAVERY.
IF EVEN ONE TENTH AMONG THEM WERE TO TAKE UP WEAPONS, WE COULD FORM A MASSIVE ARMY OF MORE THAN 500,000.
THAT IS SUPPOSING THE CONDITION THAT THEY'RE SELF-SUSTAINING, THOUGH.
I SEE.
HOWEVER, IF THAT WERE TO HAPPEN, WE WOULDN'T BE ABLE TO COUNT ON THE SUPPORT OF THE NOBLES AND FEUDAL LORDS WHO OWN GHOLAMS.

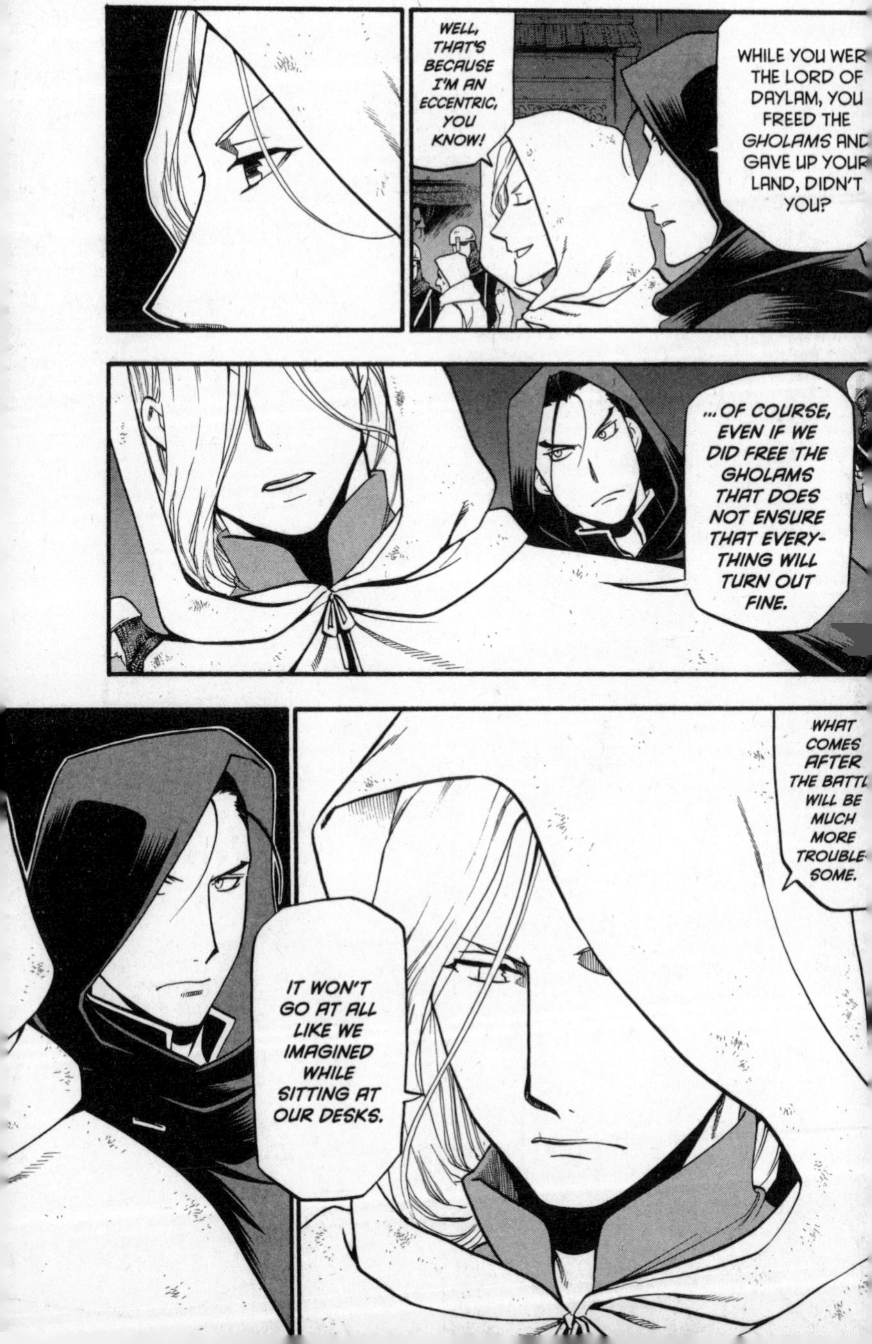
WHILE YOU WER THE LORD OF DAYLAM, YOU FREED THE GHOLAMS AND GAVE UP YOUR LAND, DIDN'T YOU?
WELL, THAT'S BECAUSE I'M AN ECCENTRIC, YOU KNOW!
...OF COURSE, EVEN IF WE DID FREE THE GHOLAMS THAT DOES NOT ENSURE THAT EVERY-THING WILL TURN OUT FINE.
WHAT COMES AFTER THE BATTL WILL BE MUCH MORE TROUBLE-SOME.
IT WON'T GO AT ALL LIKE WE IMAGINED WHILE SITTING AT OUR DESKS.

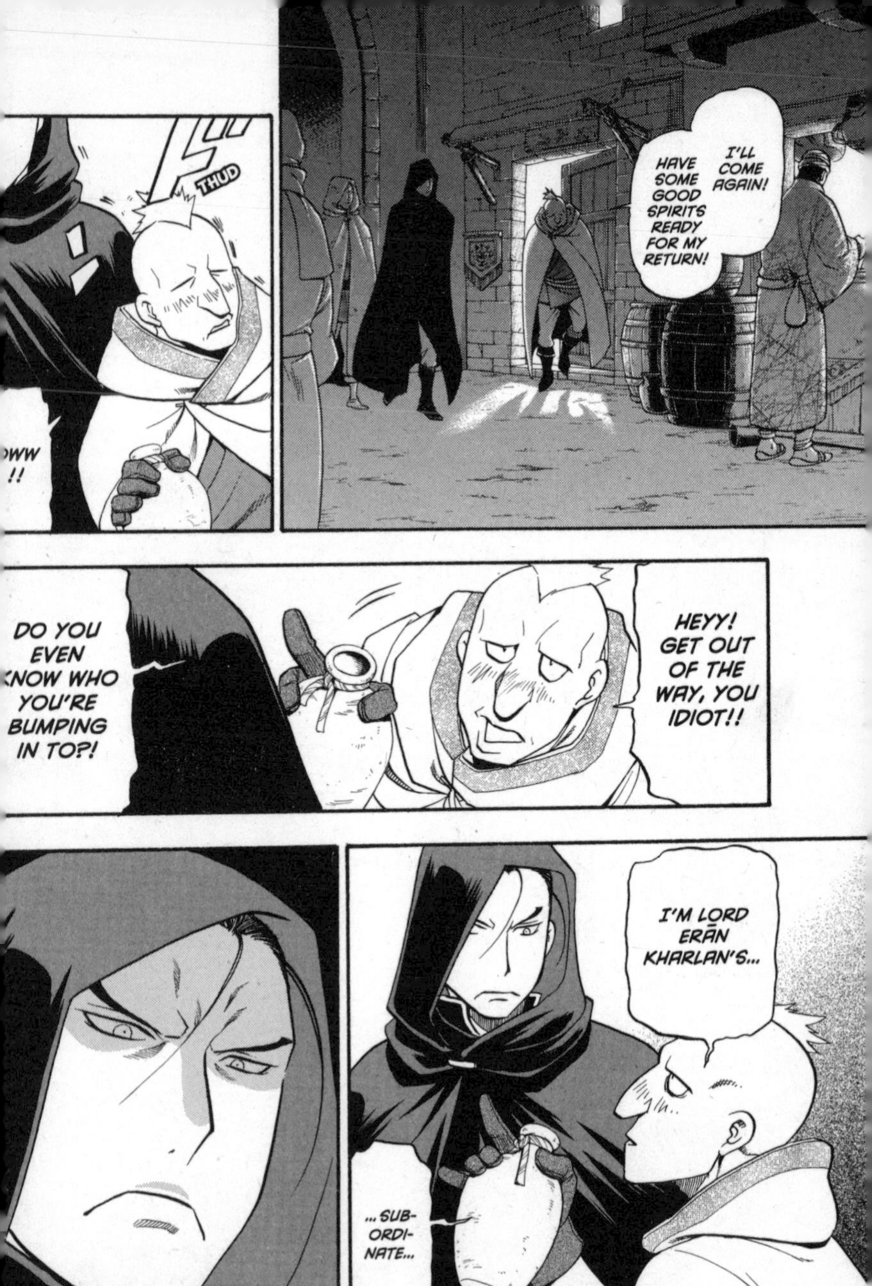
I'LL COME AGAIN! HAVE SOME GOOD SPIRITS READY FOR MY RETURN!
THUD
OWW !!
HEYY! GET OUT OF THE WAY, YOU IDIOT!!
DO YOU EVEN NOW WHO YOU'RE BUMPING IN TO?!
I'M LORD ERĀN KHARLAN'S...
...SUB-ORDI-NATE...

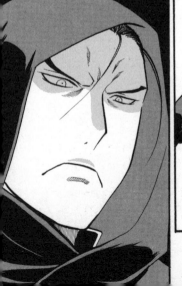

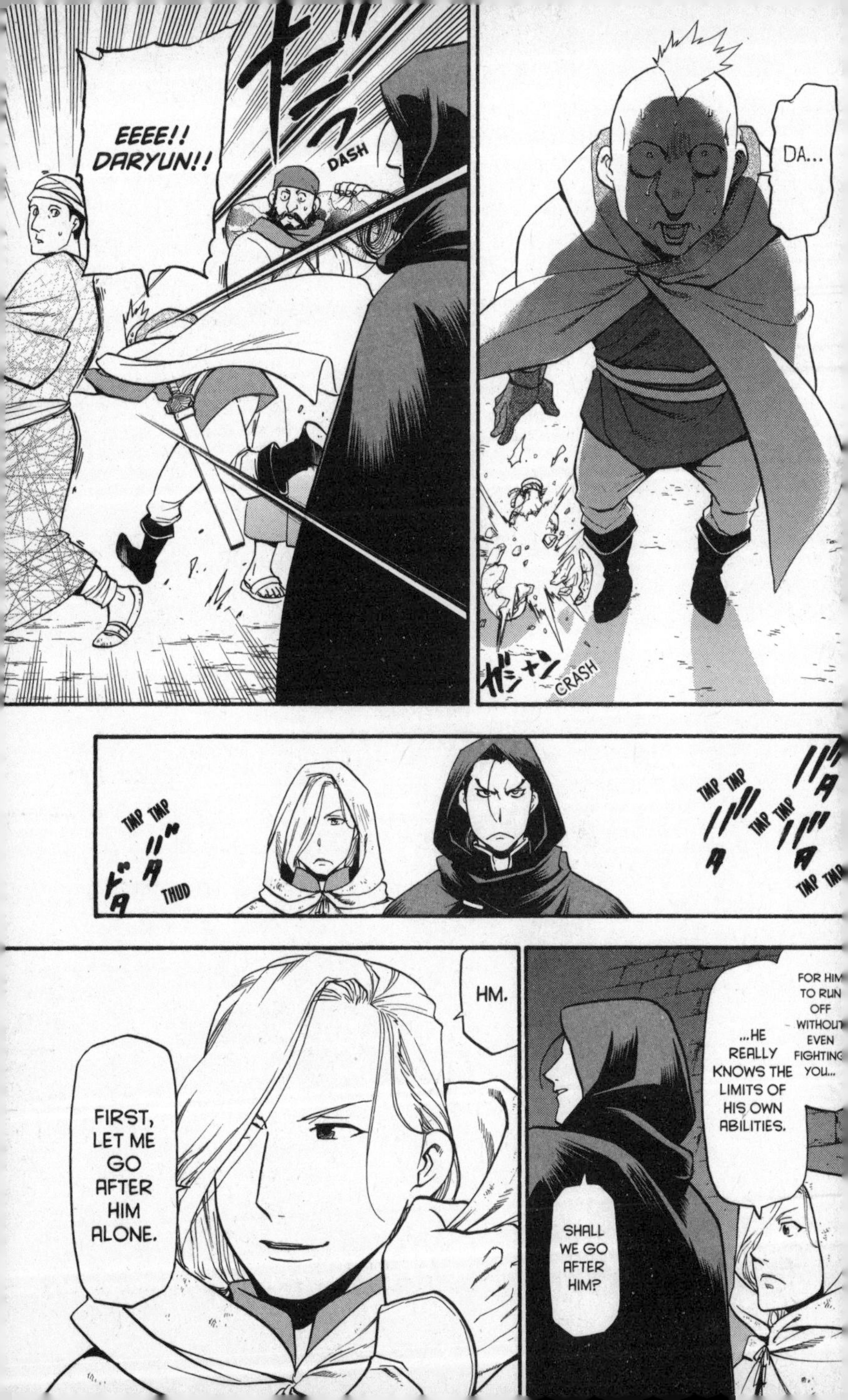
DA...
CRASH
EEEE!! DARYUN!!
DASH
TMP TMP
TMP TMP
TMP TMP
TMP TMP
THUD
FOR HIM TO RUN OFF WITHOUT EVEN FIGHTING YOU...
...HE REALLY KNOWS THE LIMITS OF HIS OWN ABILITIES.
SHALL WE GO AFTER HIM?
HM.
FIRST, LET ME GO AFTER HIM ALONE.

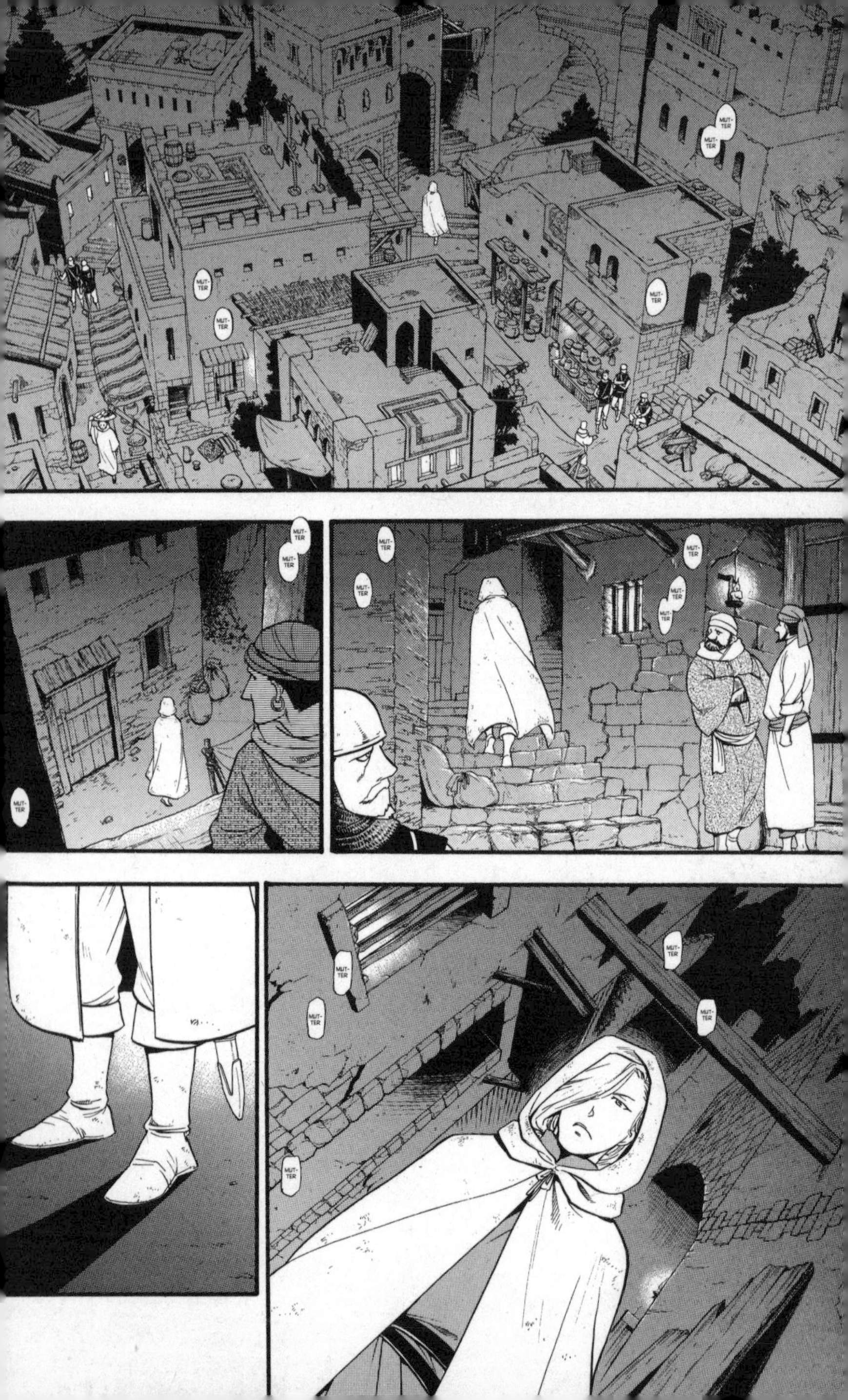
MUT-TER
MUT-TER
MUT-TER
MUT-TER
MUT-TER
MUT-TER
MUT-TER
MUT-TER
MUT-TER
MUT-TER
MUT-TER
MUT-TER
MUT-TER
MUT-TER
MUT-TER
MUT-TER
MUT-TER
MUT-TER

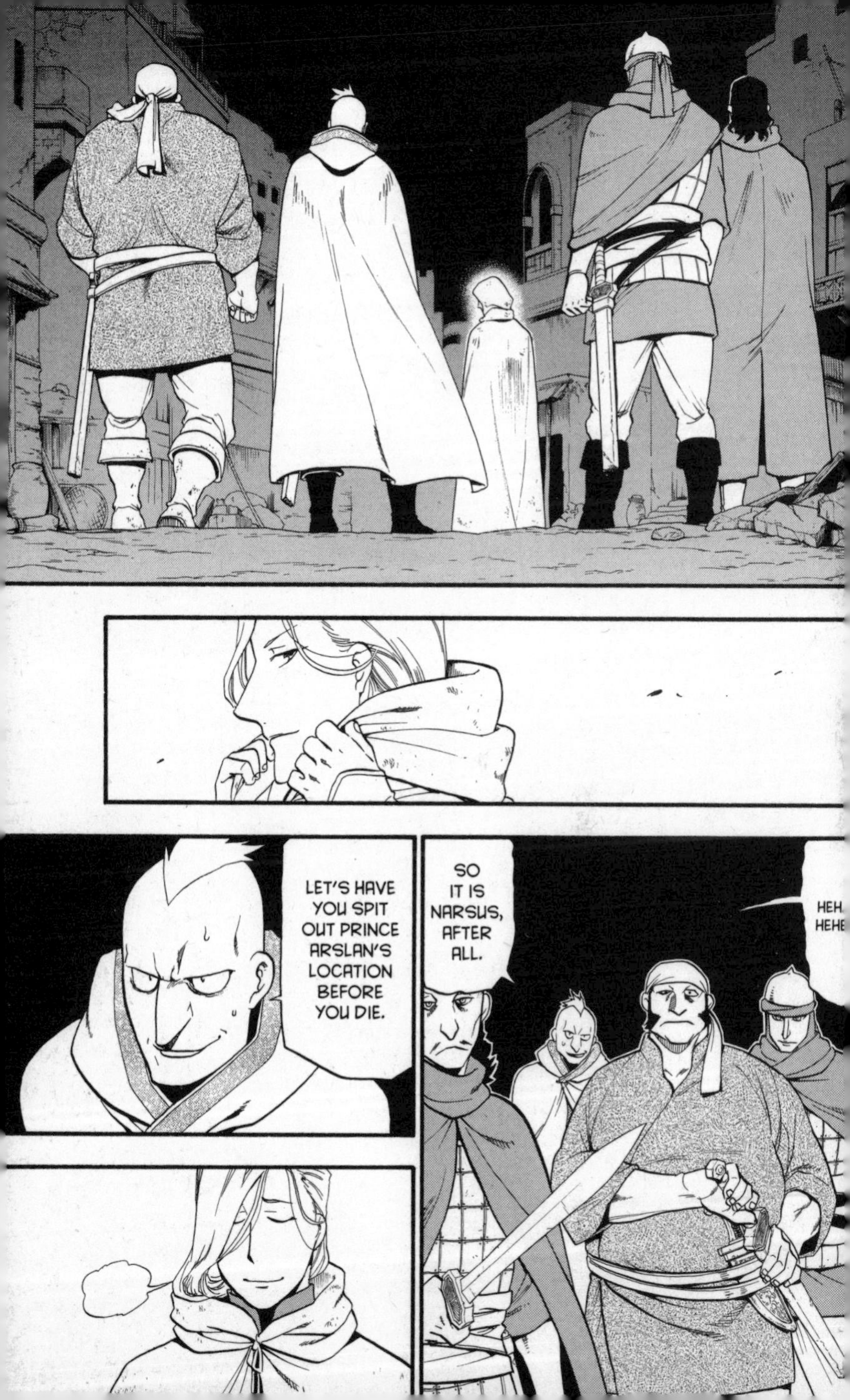
HEH. HEHE
SO IT IS NARSUS, AFTER ALL.
LET'S HAVE YOU SPIT OUT PRINCE ARSLAN'S LOCATION BEFORE YOU DIE.

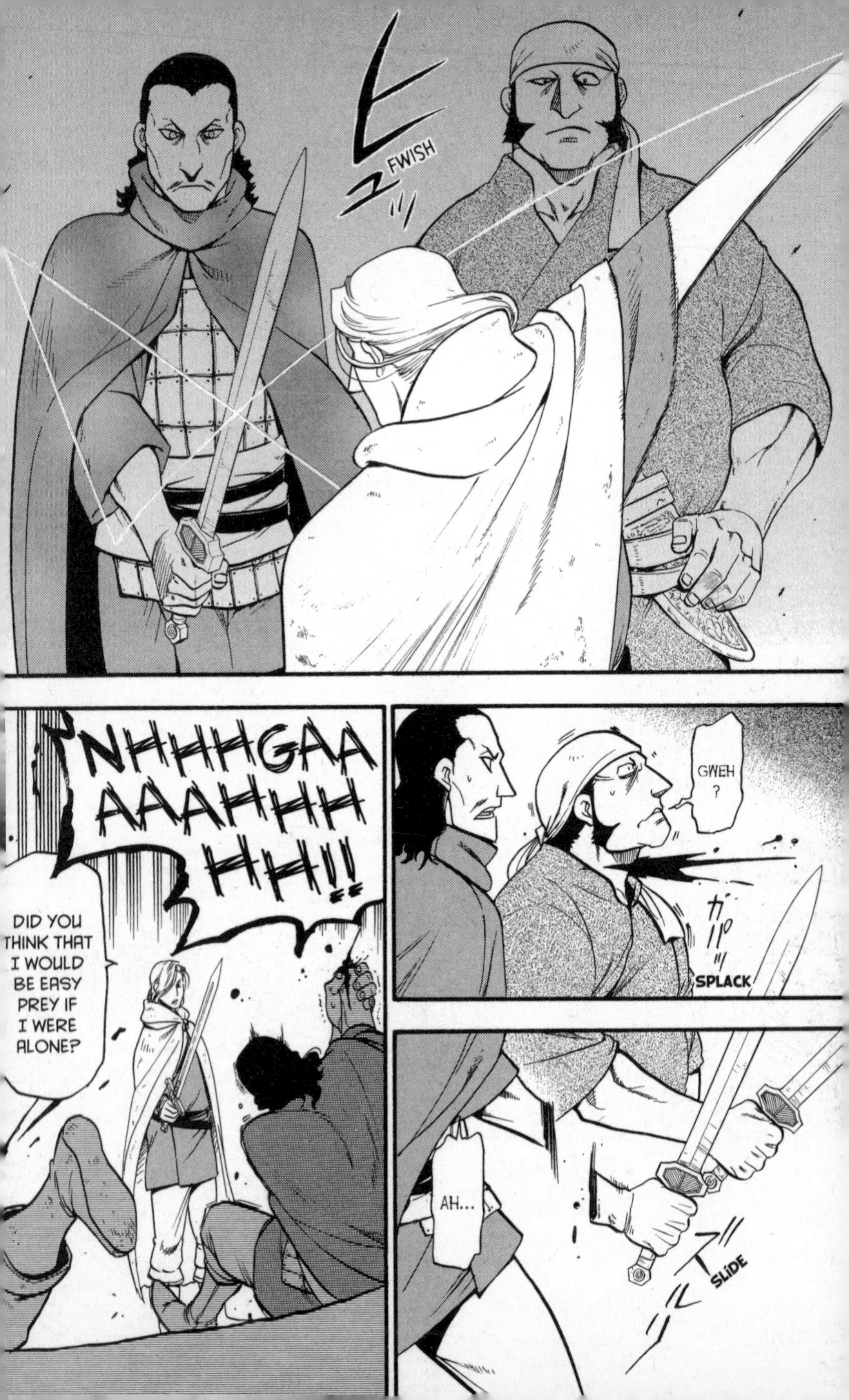
FWISH
GWEH ?
SPLACK
AH...
SLIDE
NHHGAA AAAHHH HH!!
DID YOU THINK THAT I WOULD BE EASY PREY IF I WERE ALONE?

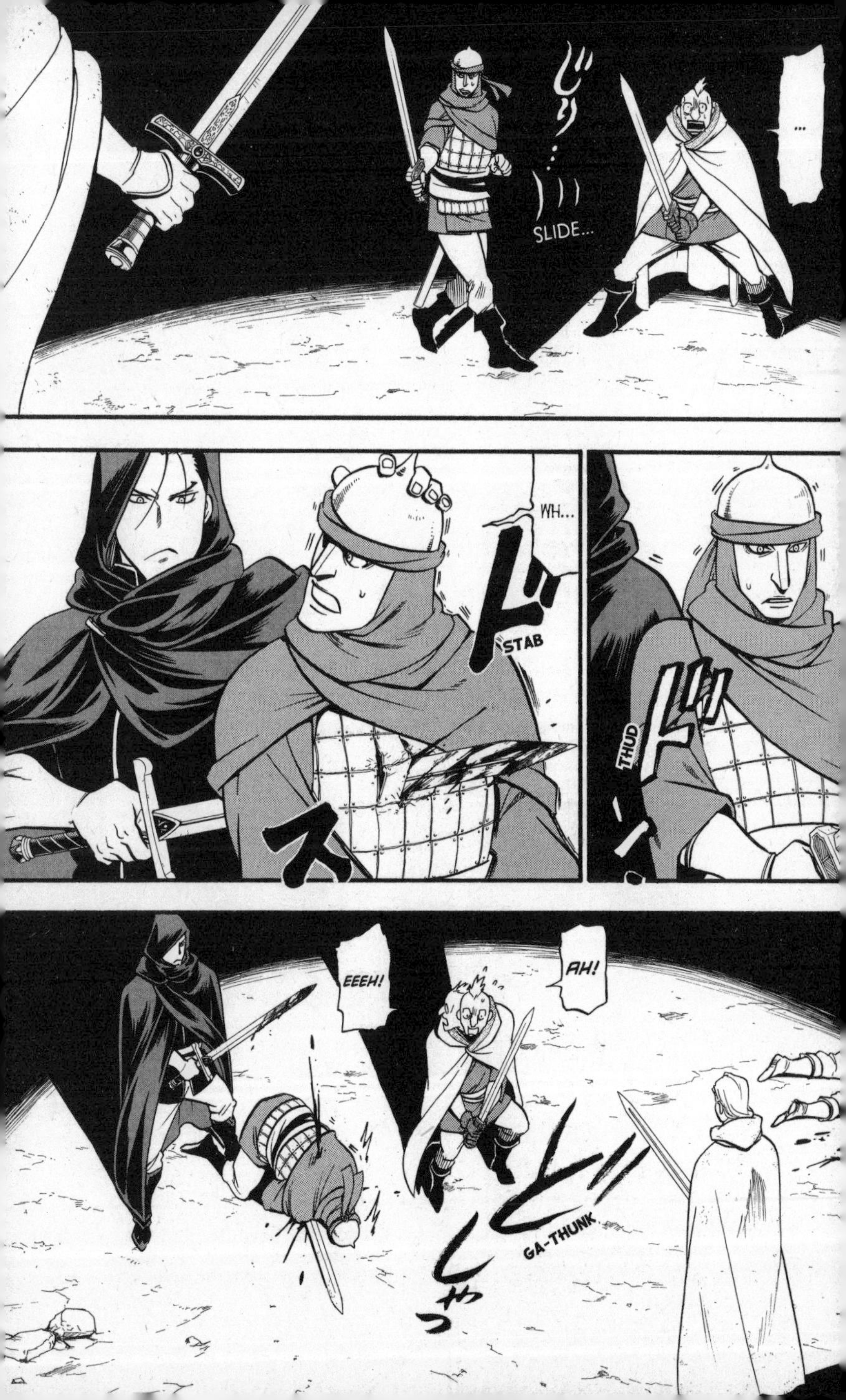
...
SLIDE...
THUD
WH...
STAB
AH!
EEEH!
GA-THUNK

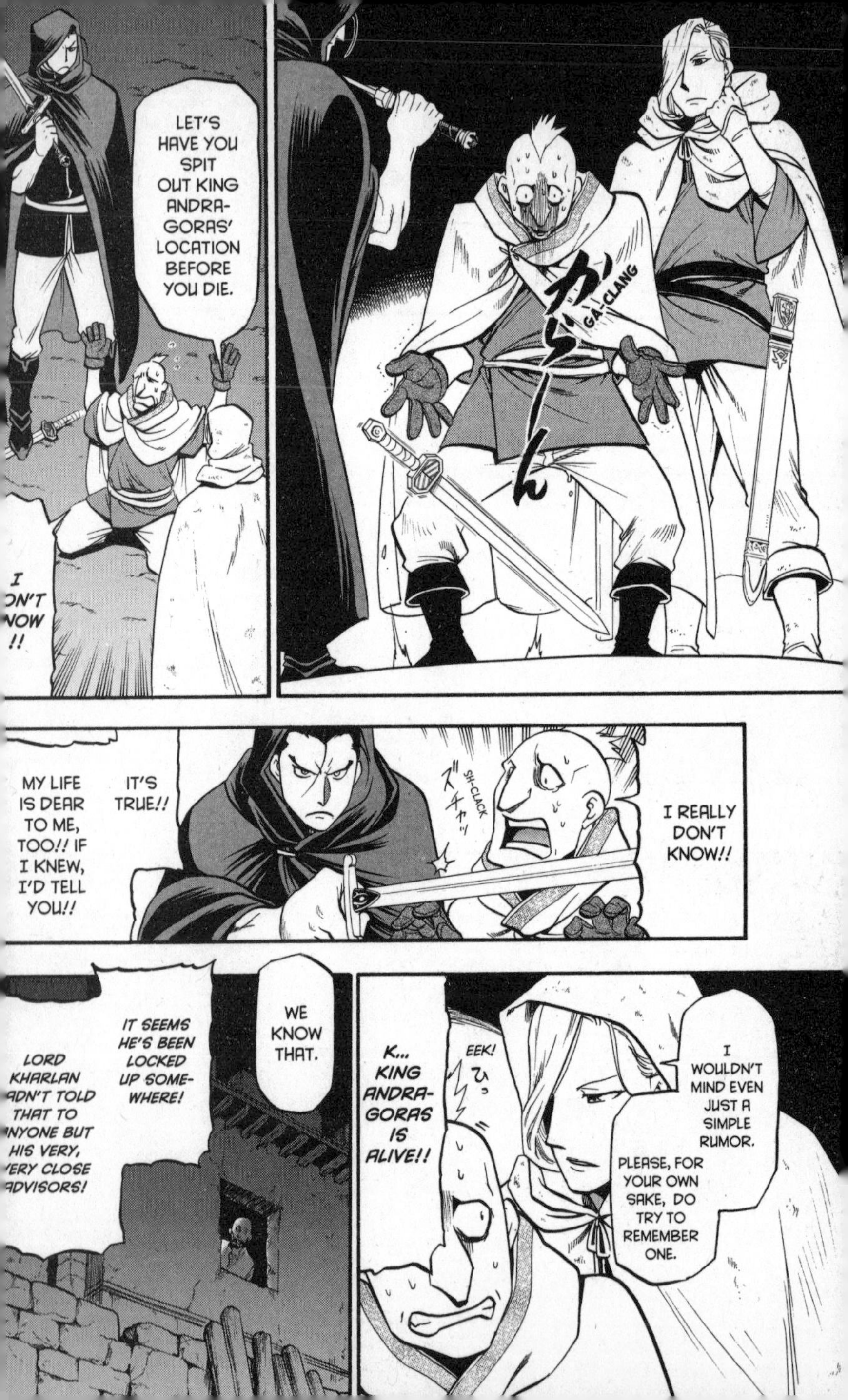
がらーん
GA-CLANG
LET'S HAVE YOU SPIT OUT KING ANDRAGORAS' LOCATION BEFORE YOU DIE.
I ON'T NOW !!
I REALLY DON'T KNOW!!
ズチャッ
SH-CLACK
IT'S TRUE!!
MY LIFE IS DEAR TO ME, TOO!! IF I KNEW, I'D TELL YOU!!
I WOULDN'T MIND EVEN JUST A SIMPLE RUMOR.
PLEASE, FOR YOUR OWN SAKE, DO TRY TO REMEMBER ONE.
EEK!
ひっ
K... KING ANDRAGORAS IS ALIVE!!
WE KNOW THAT.
IT SEEMS HE'S BEEN LOCKED UP SOMEWHERE!
LORD KHARLAN ADN'T TOLD THAT TO NYONE BUT HIS VERY, ERY CLOSE ADVISORS!

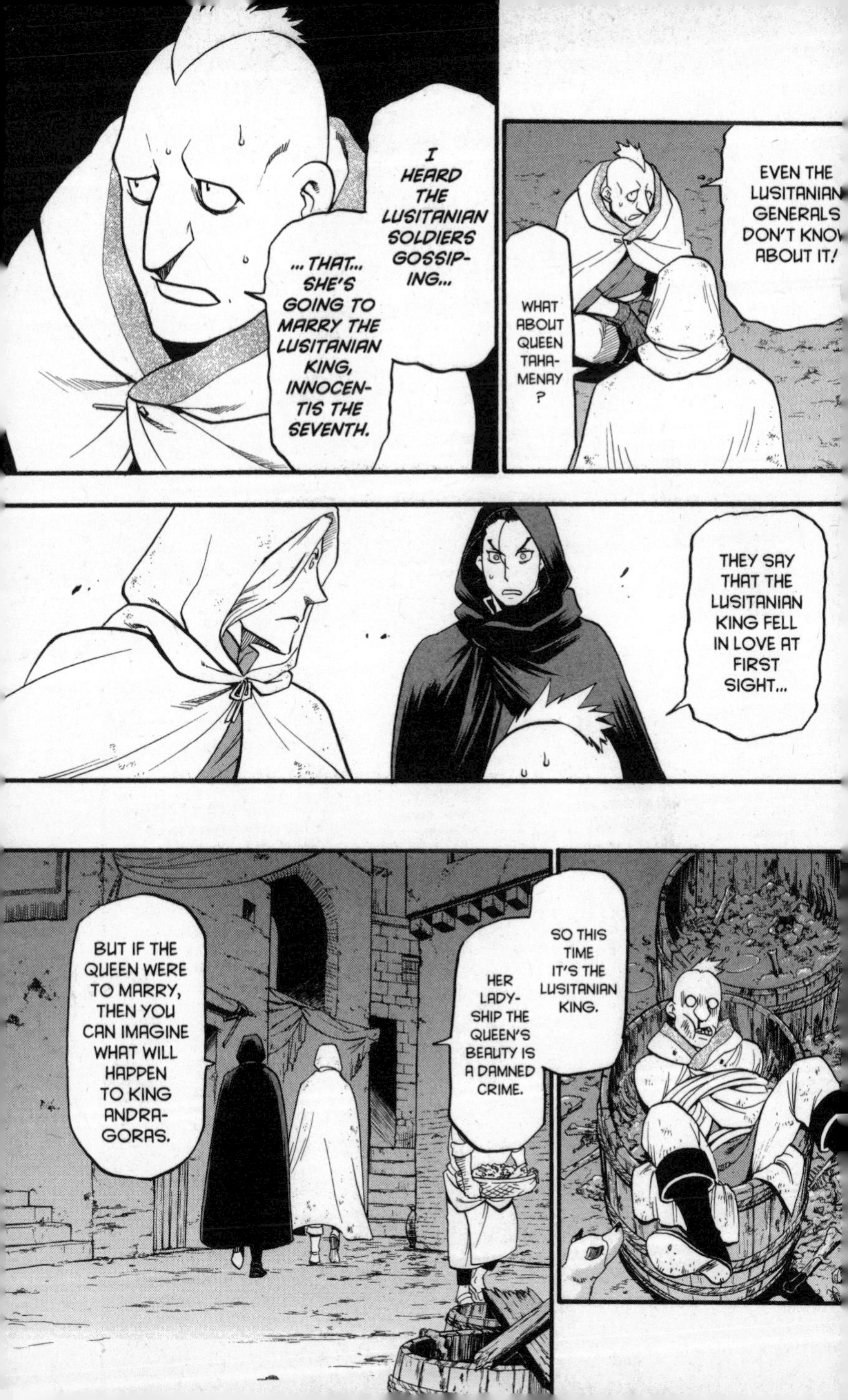
EVEN THE LUSITANIAN GENERALS DON'T KNOW ABOUT IT!
WHAT ABOUT QUEEN TAHAMENAY?
I HEARD THE LUSITANIAN SOLDIERS GOSSIPING...
...THAT... SHE'S GOING TO MARRY THE LUSITANIAN KING, INNOCENTIS THE SEVENTH.
THEY SAY THAT THE LUSITANIAN KING FELL IN LOVE AT FIRST SIGHT...
SO THIS TIME IT'S THE LUSITANIAN KING.
HER LADYSHIP THE QUEEN'S BEAUTY IS A DAMNED CRIME.
BUT IF THE QUEEN WERE TO MARRY, THEN YOU CAN IMAGINE WHAT WILL HAPPEN TO KING ANDRAGORAS.

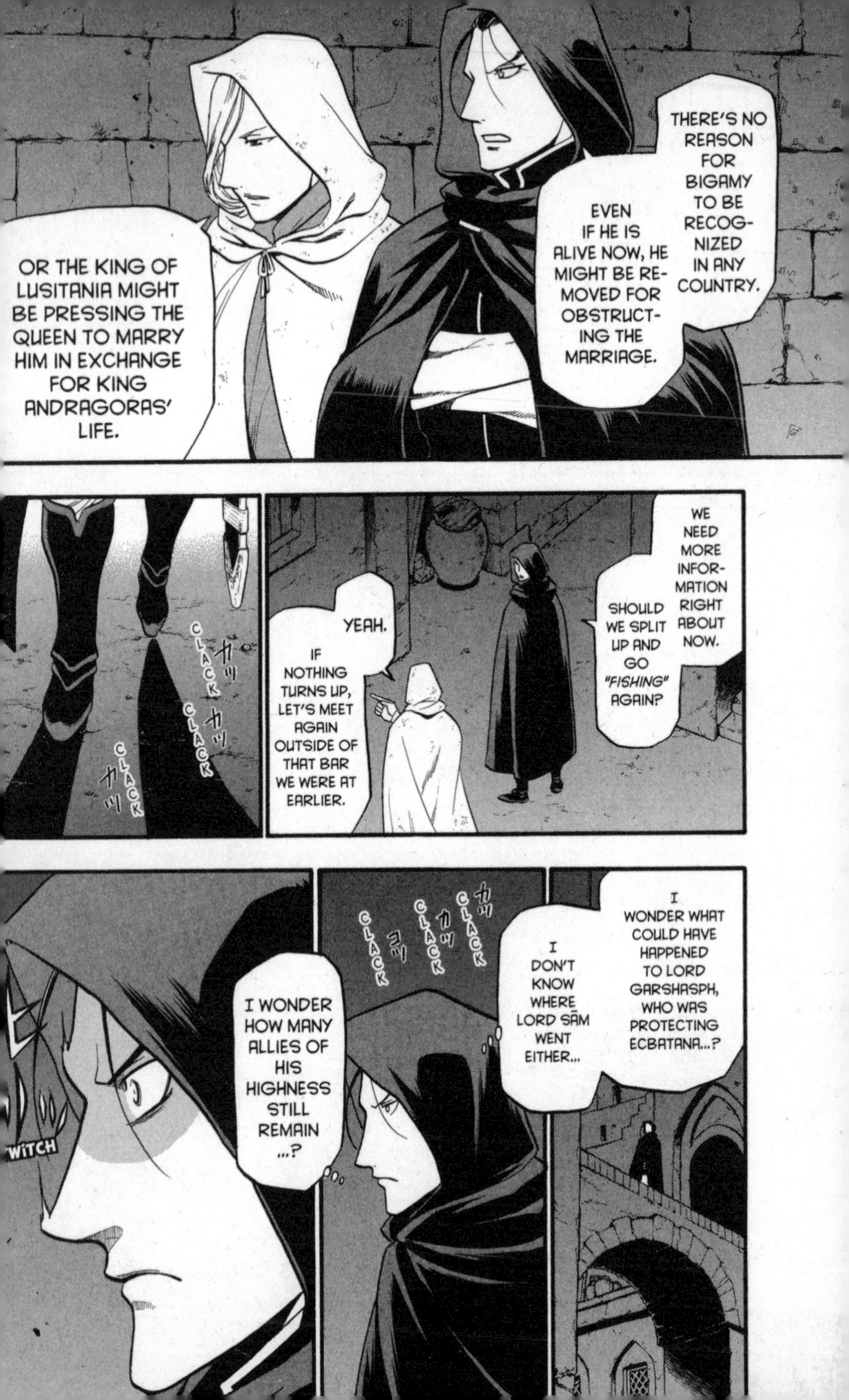
THERE'S NO REASON FOR BIGAMY TO BE RECOG-NIZED IN ANY COUNTRY.
EVEN IF HE IS ALIVE NOW, HE MIGHT BE RE-MOVED FOR OBSTRUCT-ING THE MARRIAGE.
OR THE KING OF LUSITANIA MIGHT BE PRESSING THE QUEEN TO MARRY HIM IN EXCHANGE FOR KING ANDRAGORAS' LIFE.
WE NEED MORE INFOR-MATION RIGHT ABOUT NOW.
SHOULD WE SPLIT UP AND GO "FISHING" AGAIN?
YEAH.
IF NOTHING TURNS UP, LET'S MEET AGAIN OUTSIDE OF THAT BAR WE WERE AT EARLIER.
CLACK カッ
CLACK カッ
CLACK カッ
I WONDER WHAT COULD HAVE HAPPENED TO LORD GARSHASPH, WHO WAS PROTECTING ECBATANA...?
I DON'T KNOW WHERE LORD SĀM WENT EITHER...
CLACK カッ
CLACK カッ
CLACK コッ
I WONDER HOW MANY ALLIES OF HIS HIGHNESS STILL REMAIN ...?
WITCH

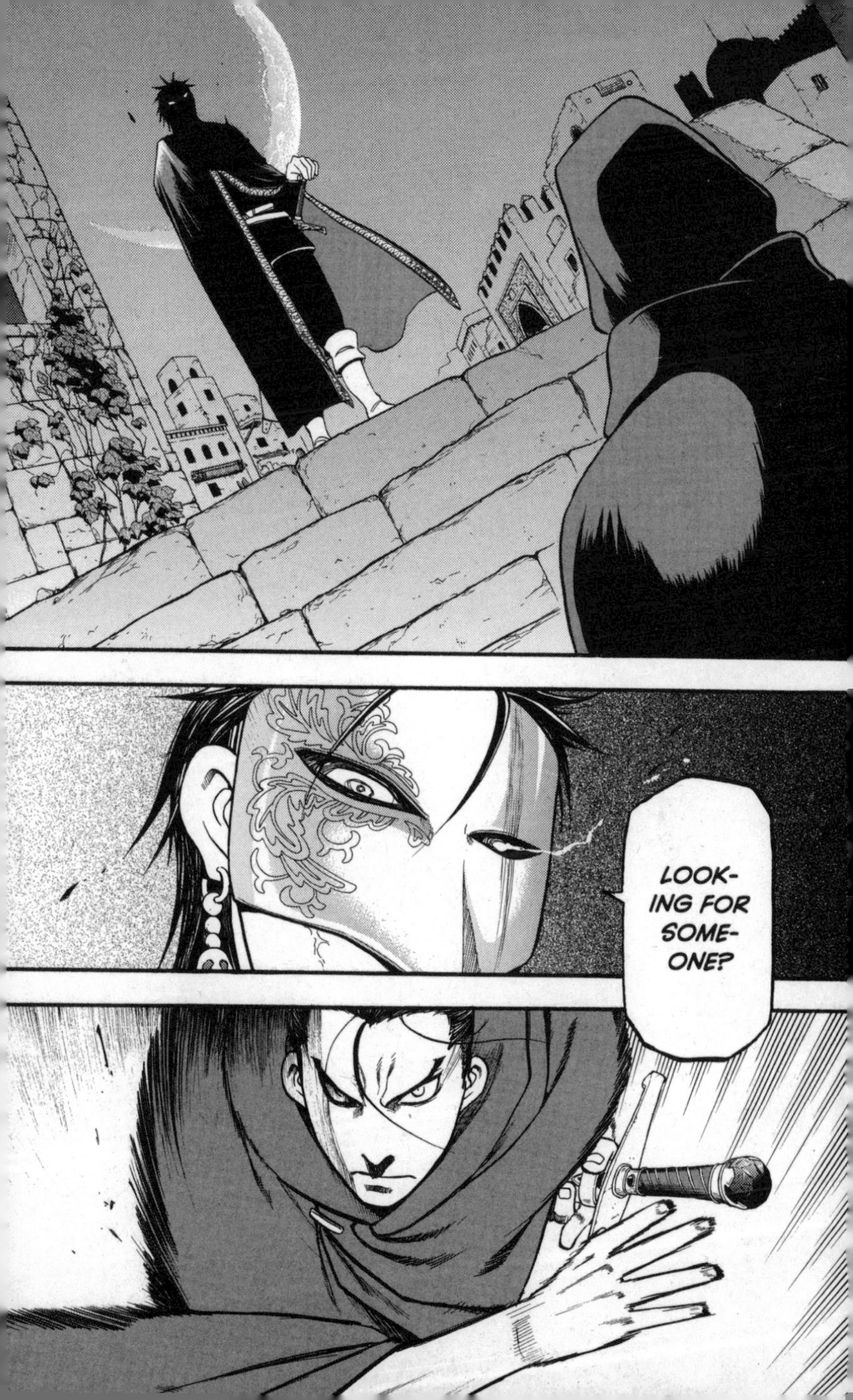
LOOK-
ING FOR
SOME-
ONE?

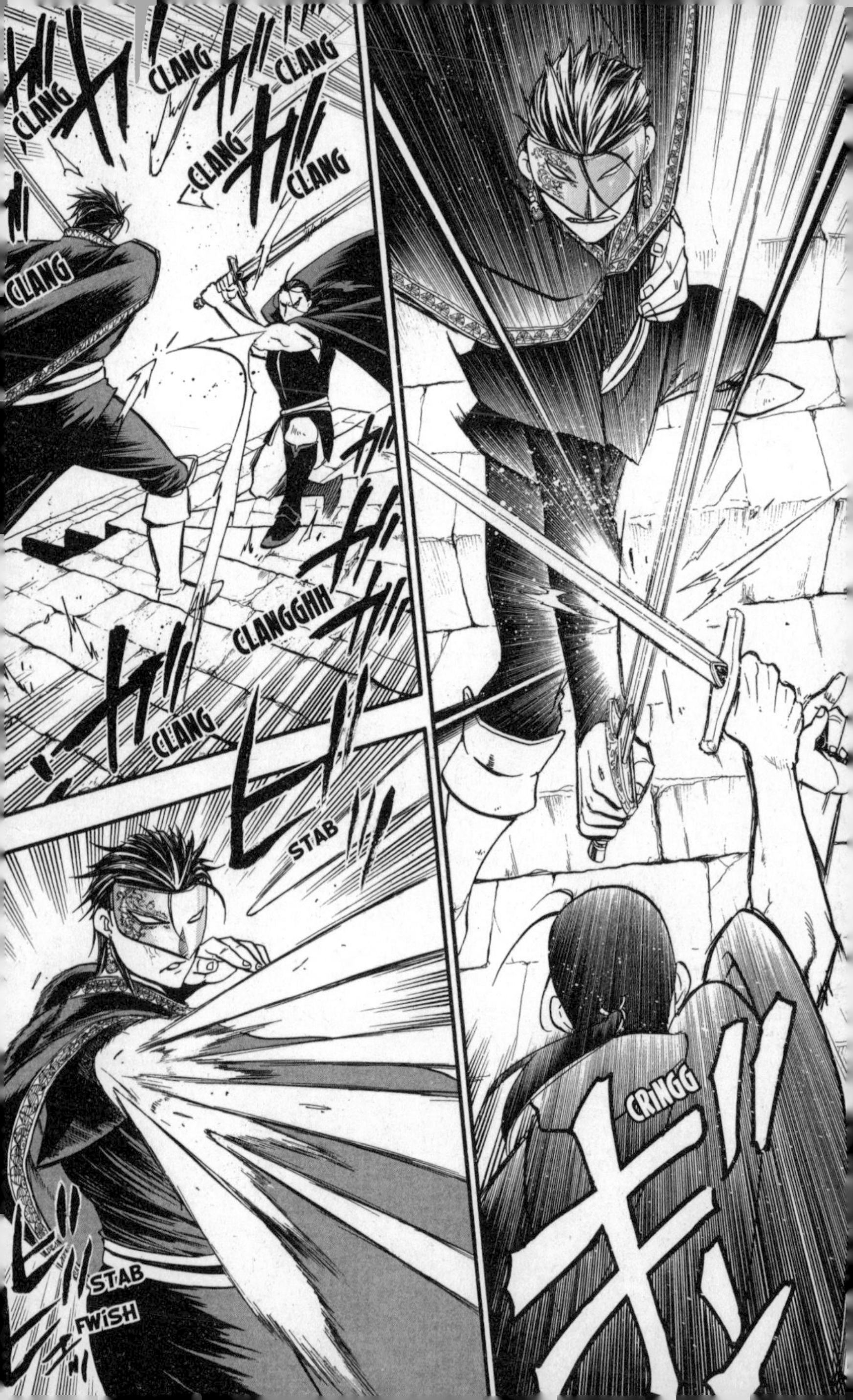
CLANG
CLANG
CLANG
CLANG
CLANG
CLANG
CLANGGHH
CLANG
STAB
CRINGG
STAB
FWISH

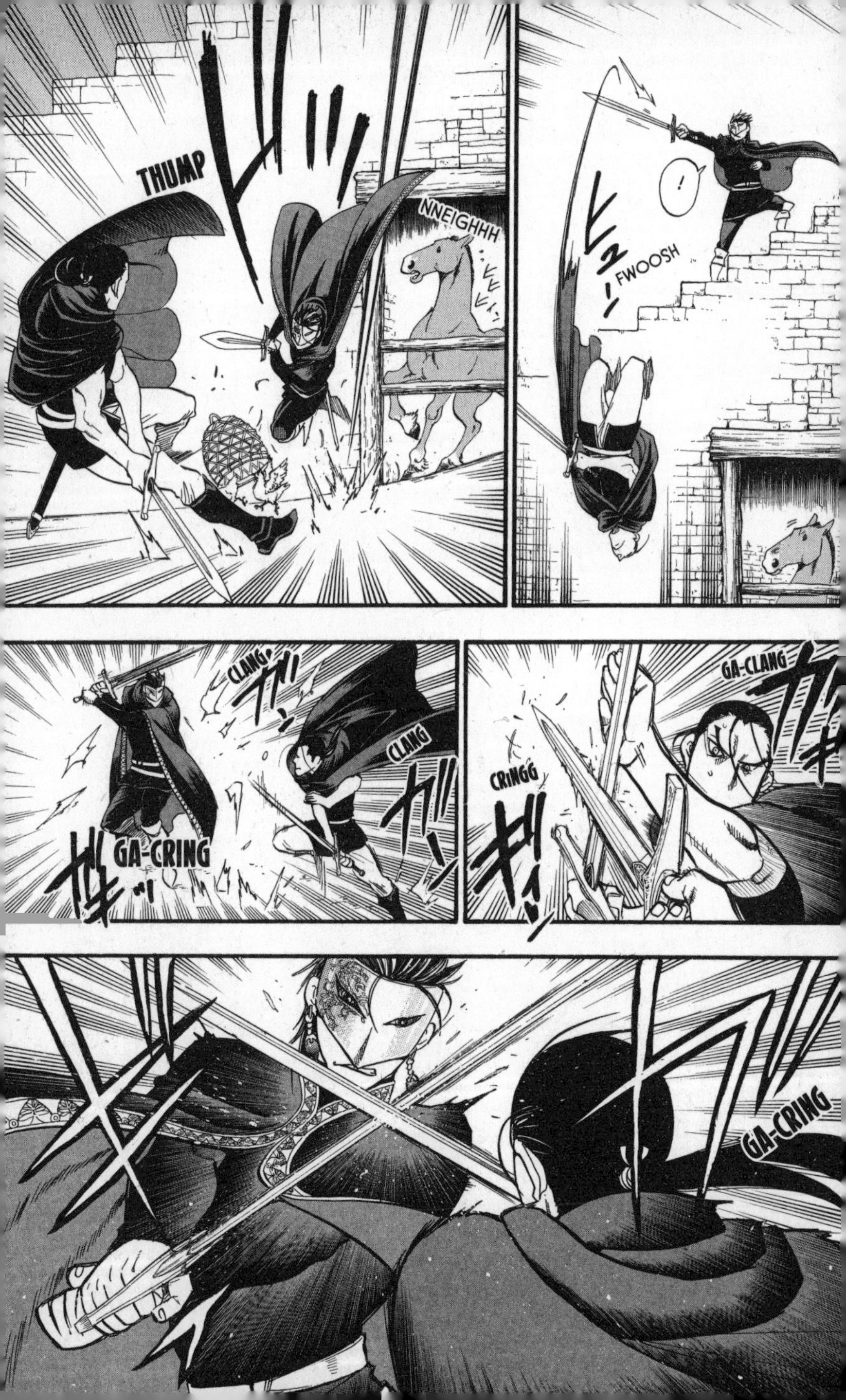
!
FWOOSH
NNEIGHHH
THUMP
GA-CLANG
CRINGG
CLANG
CLANG
GA-CRING
GA-CRING

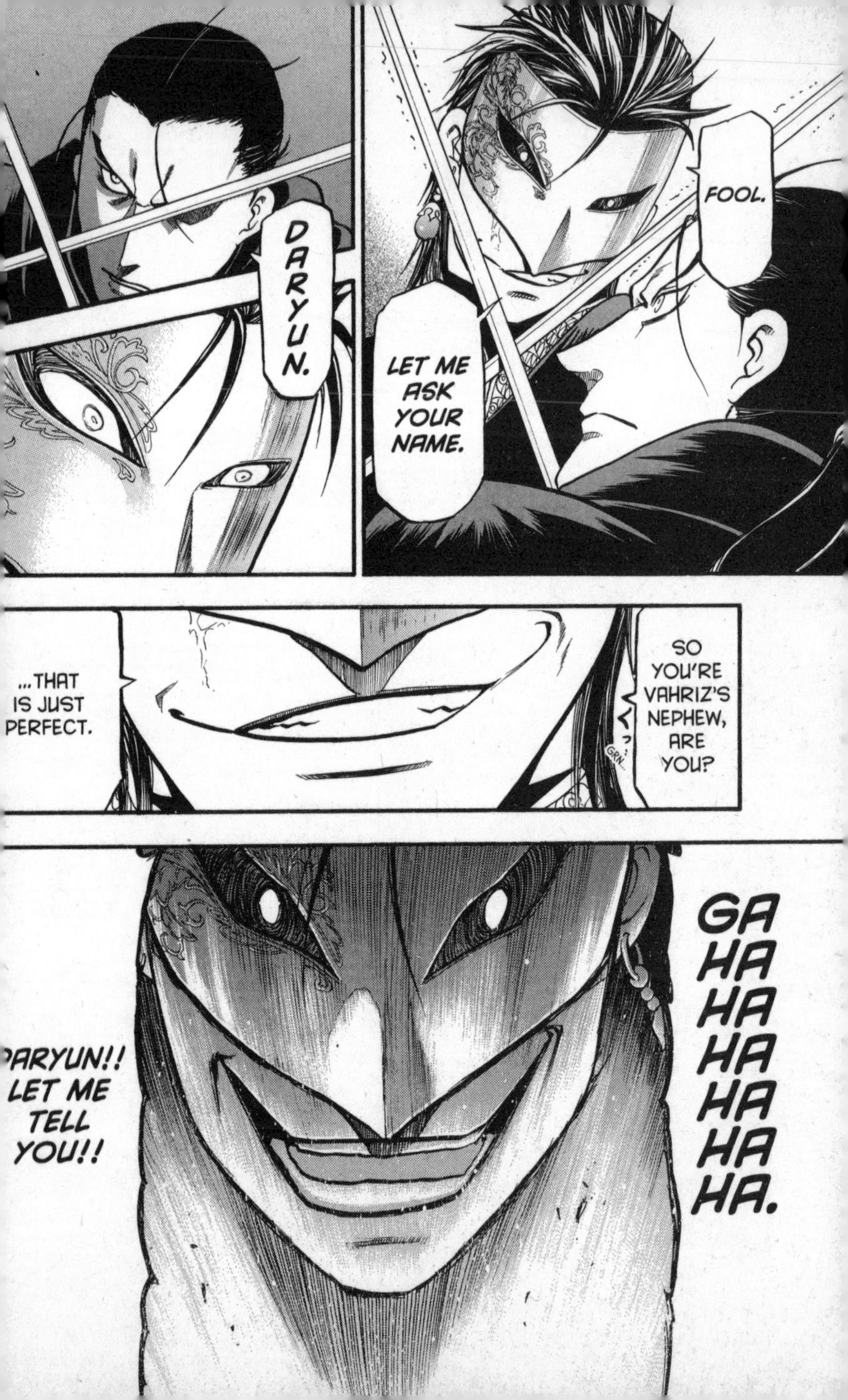
FOOL.
LET ME ASK YOUR NAME.
DARYUN.
SO YOU'RE VAHRIZ'S NEPHEW, ARE YOU?
GRN...
...THAT IS JUST PERFECT.
GAHAHAHAHAHAHAHA.
ARYUN!! LET ME TELL YOU!!

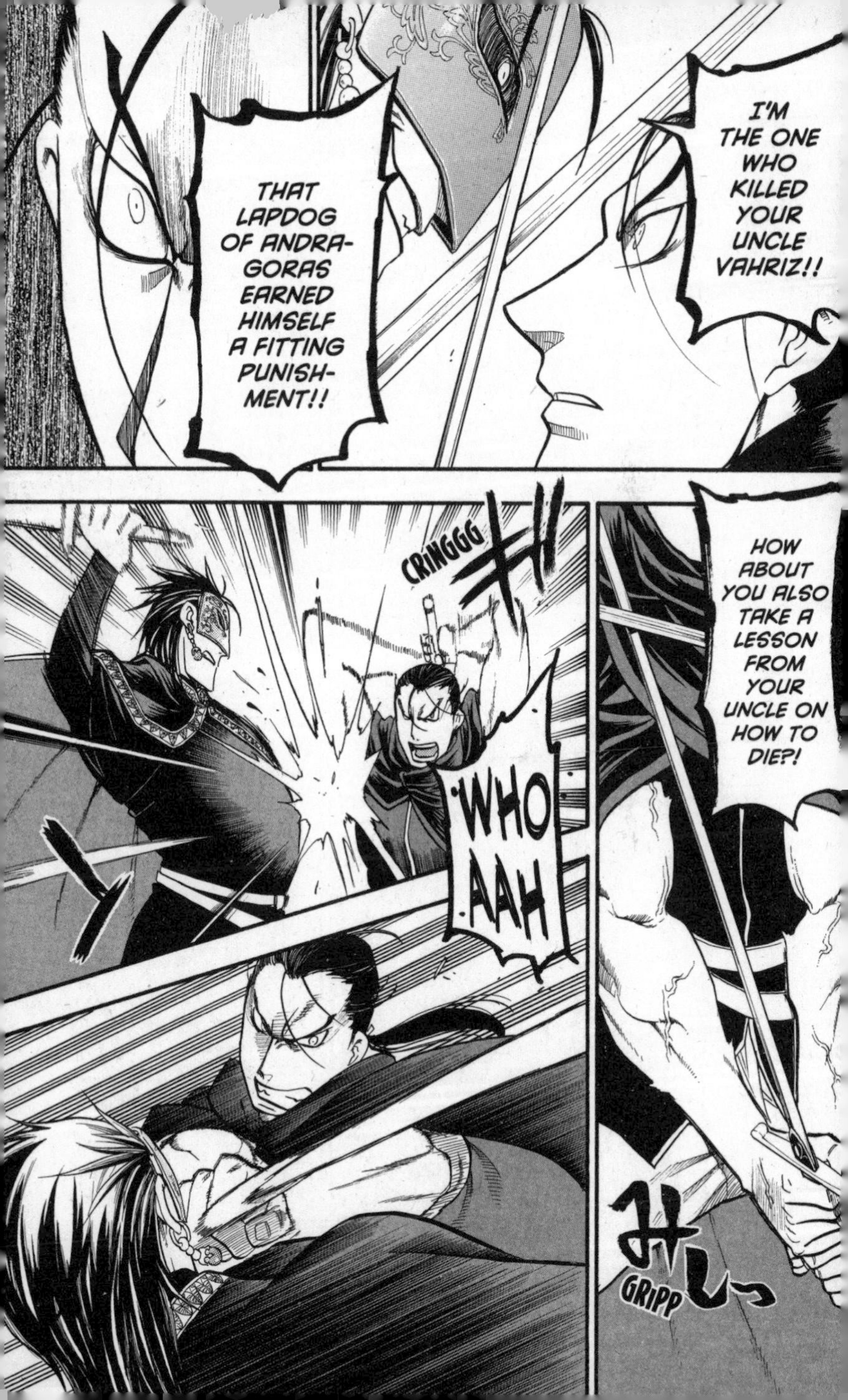
I'M THE ONE WHO KILLED YOUR UNCLE VAHRIZ!!
THAT LAPDOG OF ANDRAGORAS EARNED HIMSELF A FITTING PUNISHMENT!!
HOW ABOUT YOU ALSO TAKE A LESSON FROM YOUR UNCLE ON HOW TO DIE?!
GRIPP
CRINGGG
WHOAAH

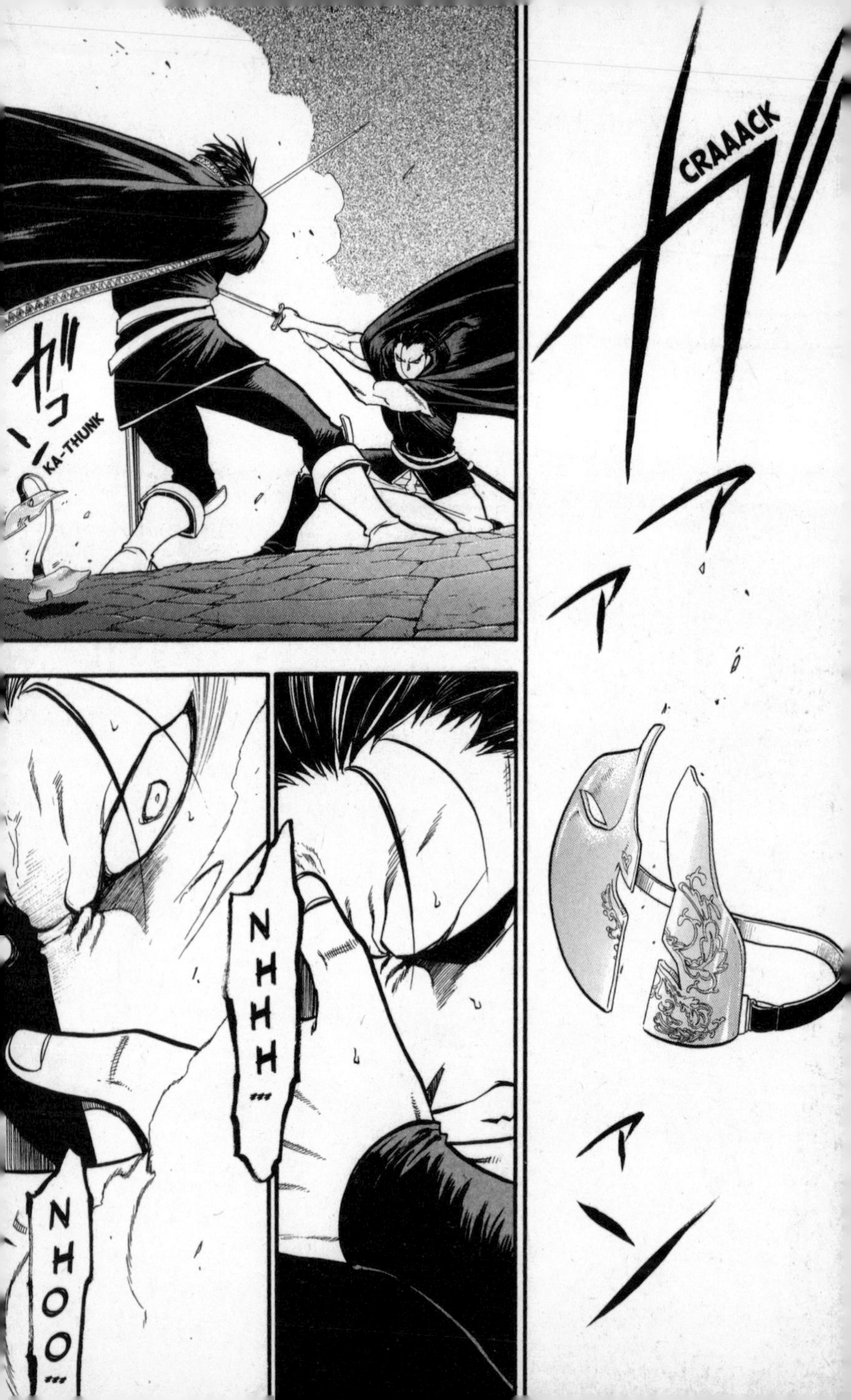
CRAAACK
KA-THUNK
NHHH...
NHOO...

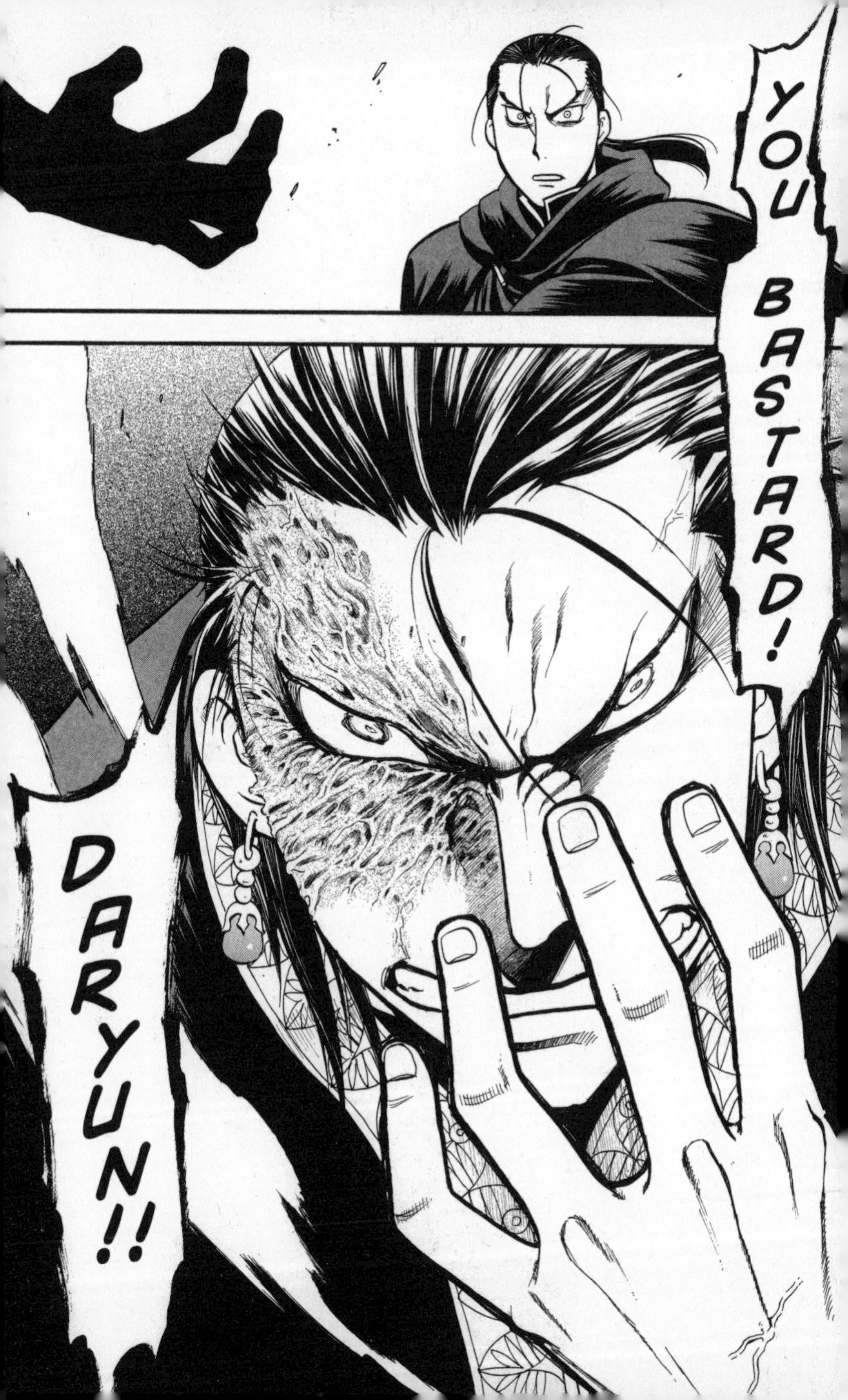
YOU BASTARD!
DARYUN!!

THE HEROIC LEGEND OF
ARSLAN

Chapter 18: Reunion by the Shore

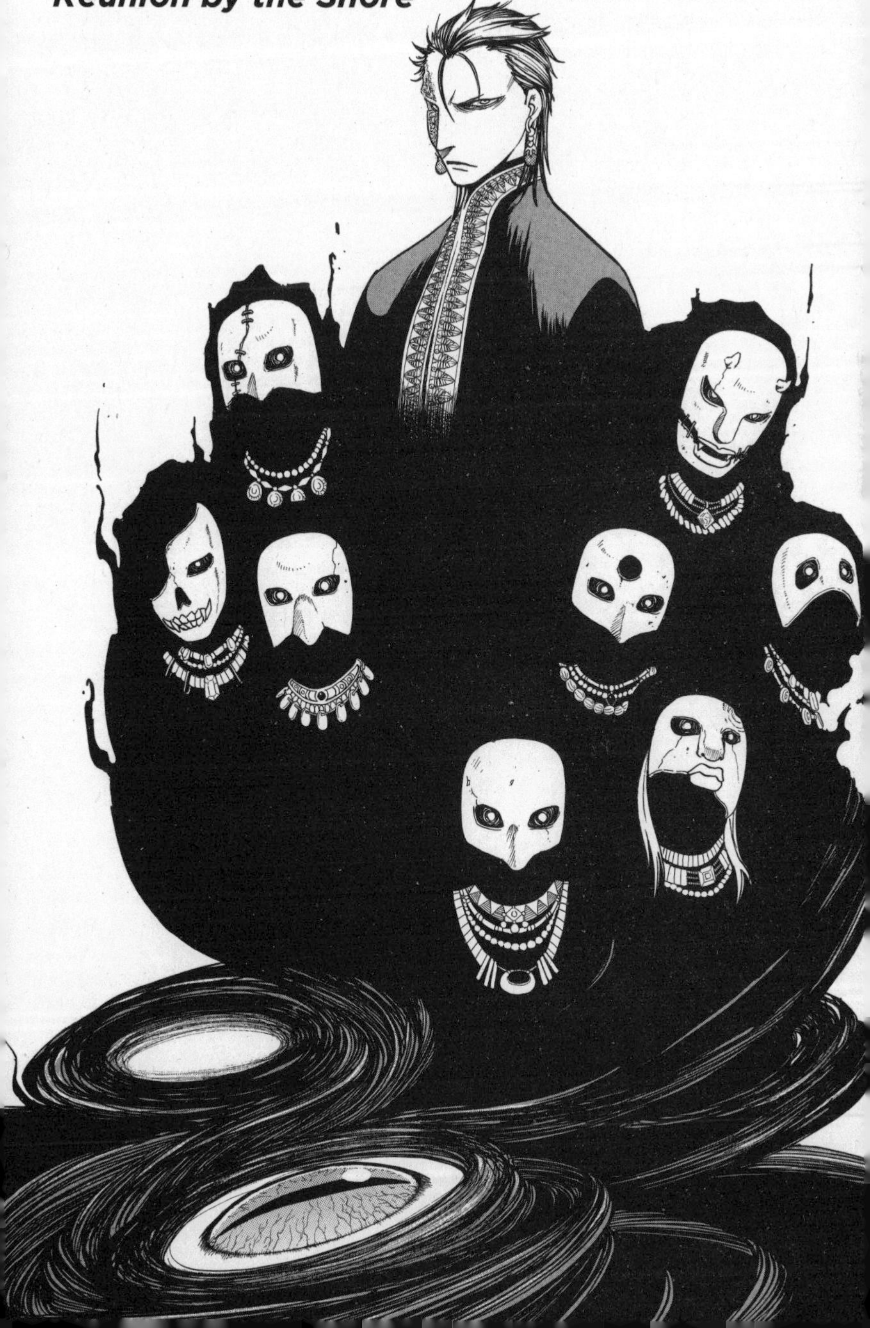

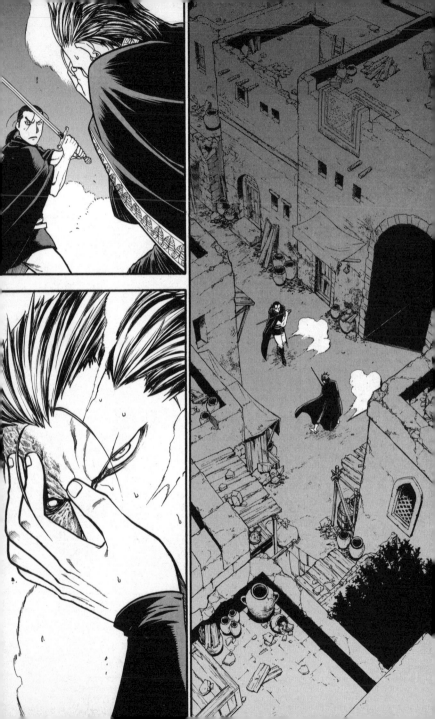

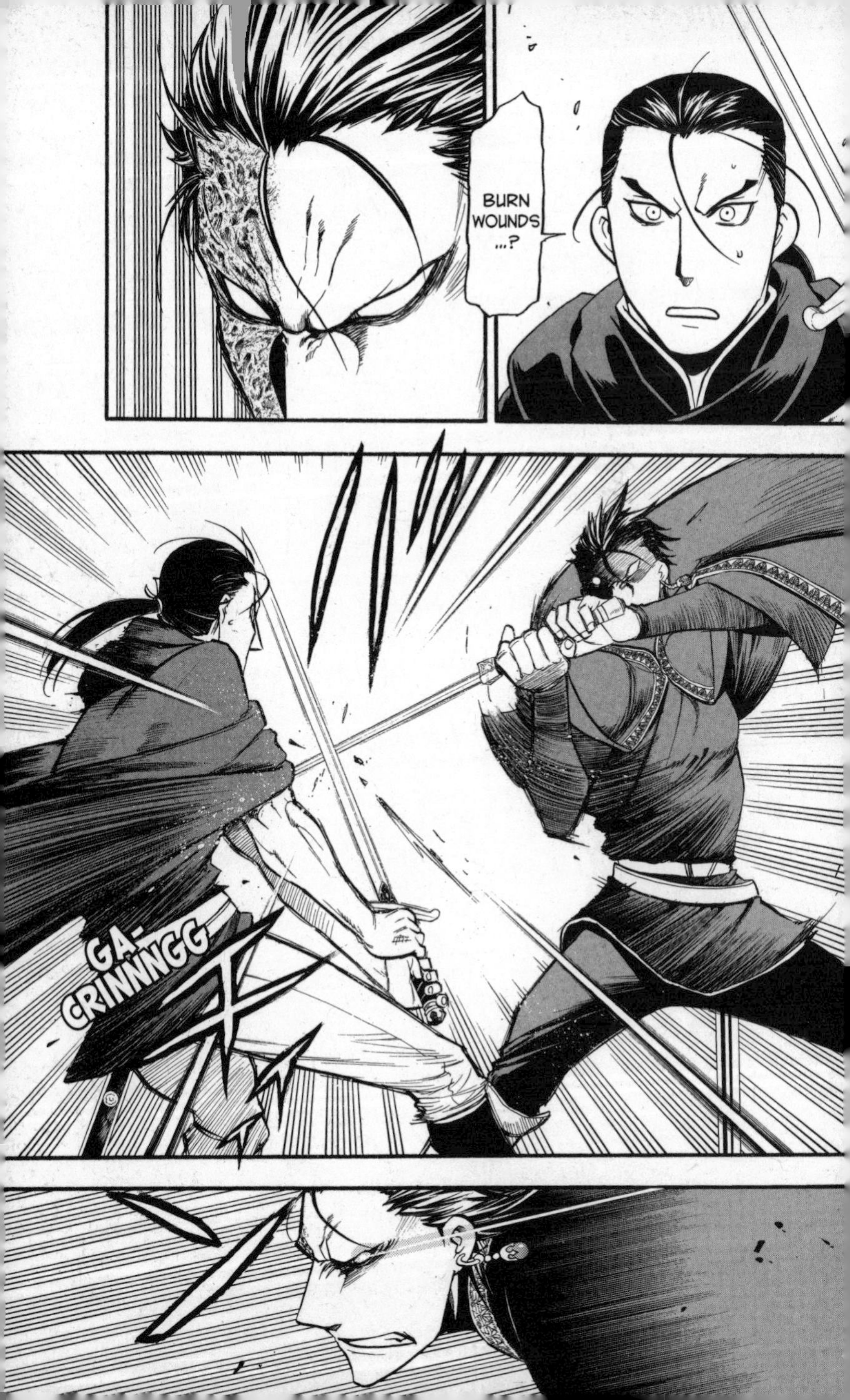
BURN WOUNDS ...?
GA-CRINNNGG

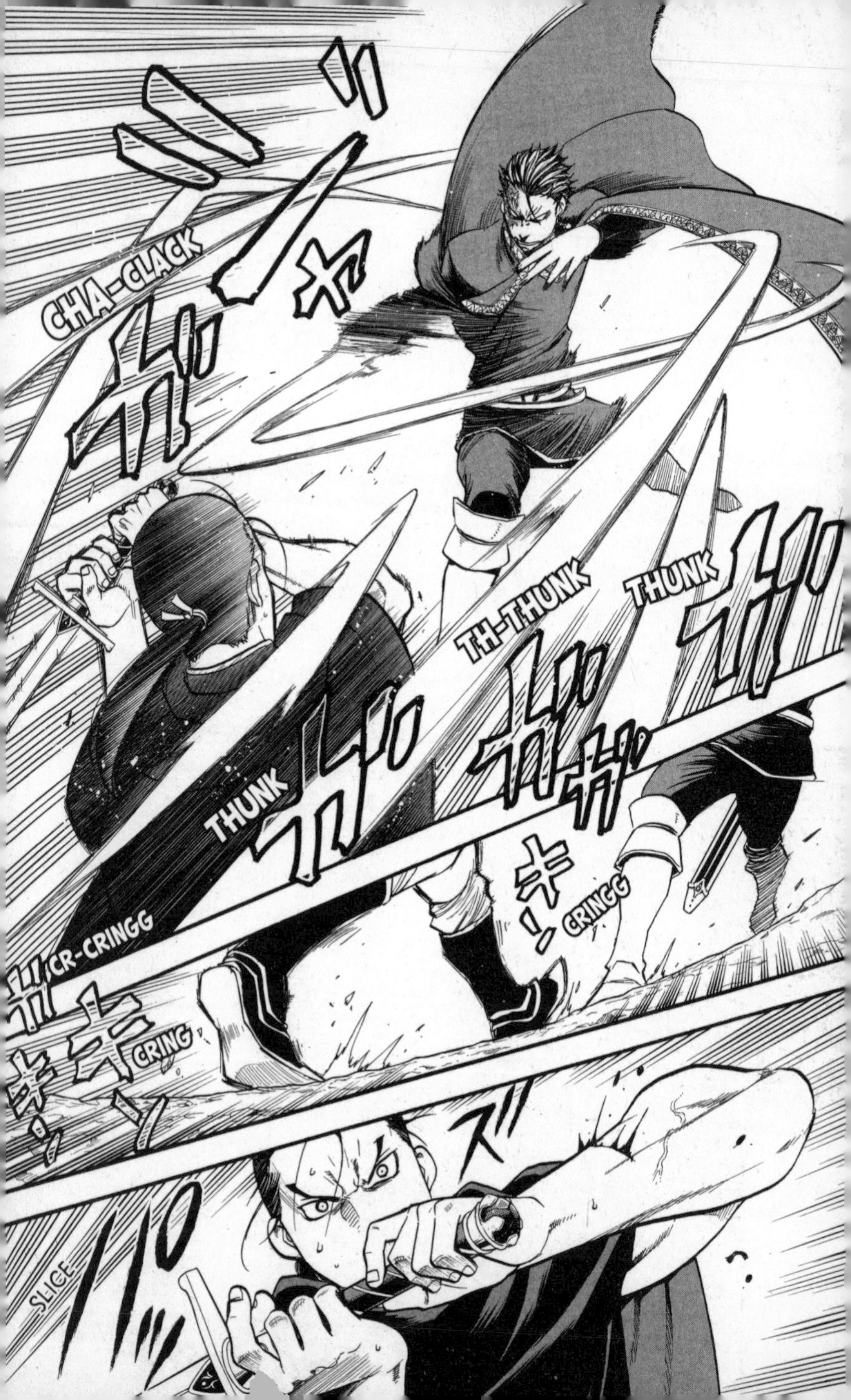
CHA-CLACK
THUNK
TH-THUNK
THUNK
CRINGG
CR-CRINGG
CRING
SLICE

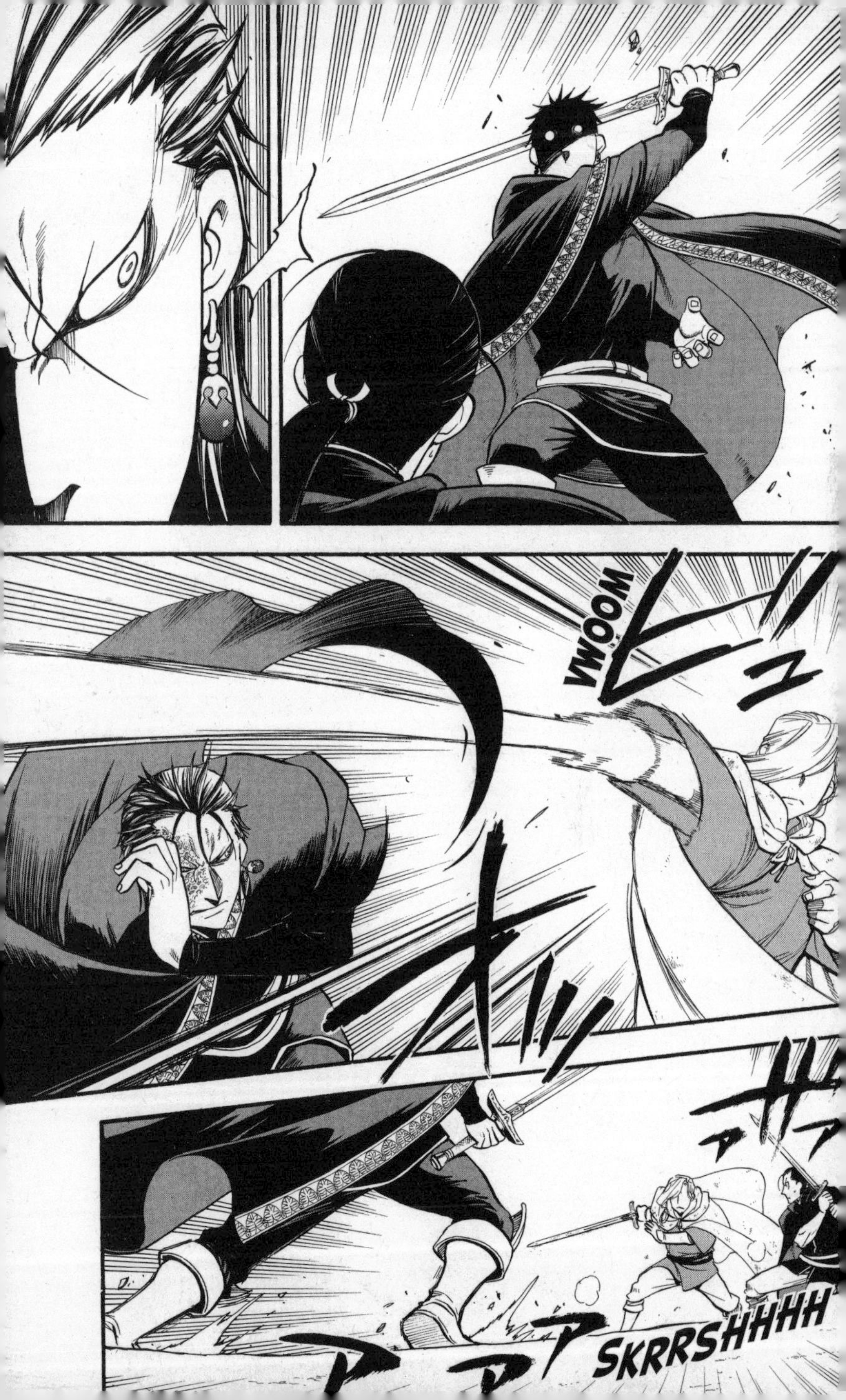
VWOOM
SKRRSHHHH

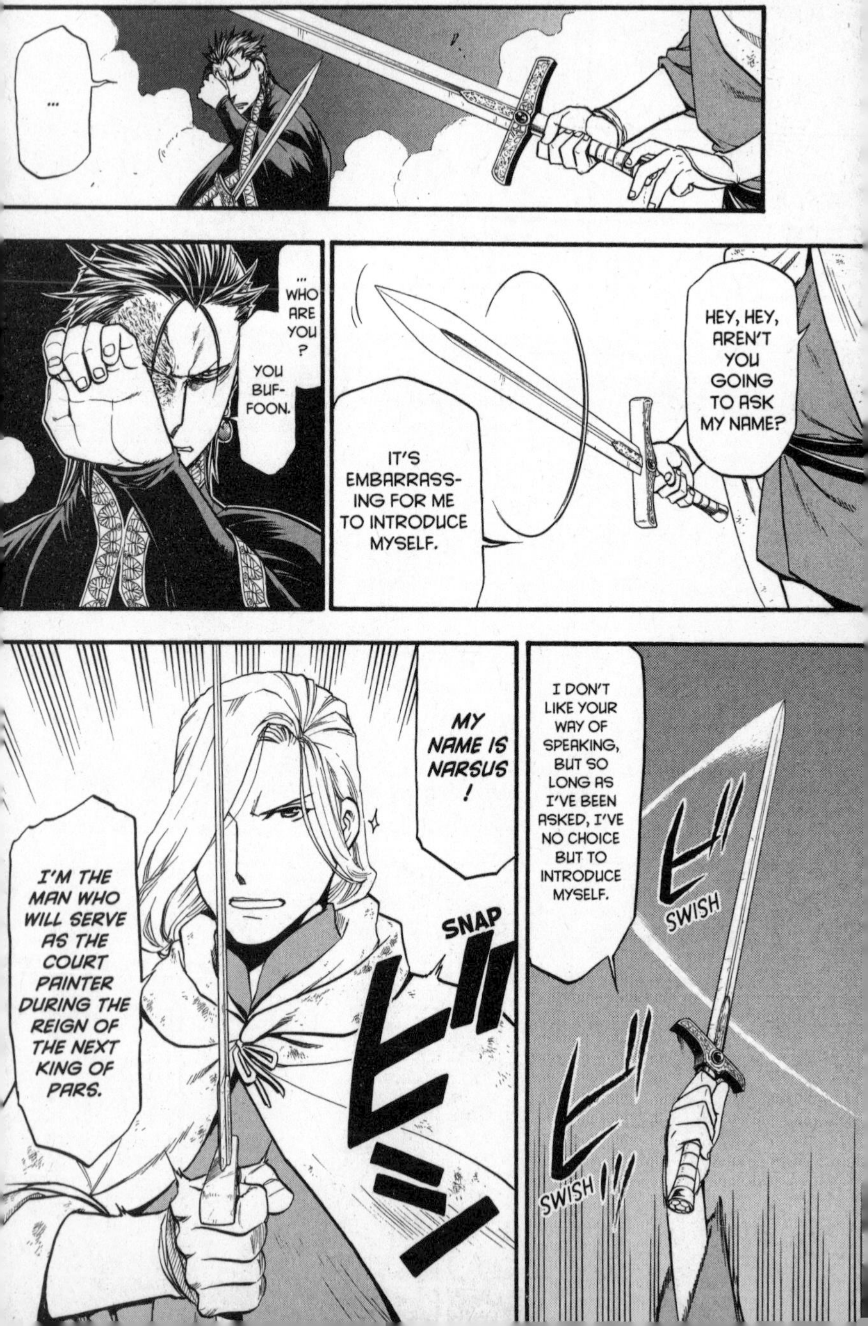
...
HEY, HEY, AREN'T YOU GOING TO ASK MY NAME?
IT'S EMBARRASSING FOR ME TO INTRODUCE MYSELF.
... WHO ARE YOU?
YOU BUFFOON.
I DON'T LIKE YOUR WAY OF SPEAKING, BUT SO LONG AS I'VE BEEN ASKED, I'VE NO CHOICE BUT TO INTRODUCE MYSELF.
SWISH
SWISH
MY NAME IS NARSUS!
SNAP
I'M THE MAN WHO WILL SERVE AS THE COURT PAINTER DURING THE REIGN OF THE NEXT KING OF PARS.

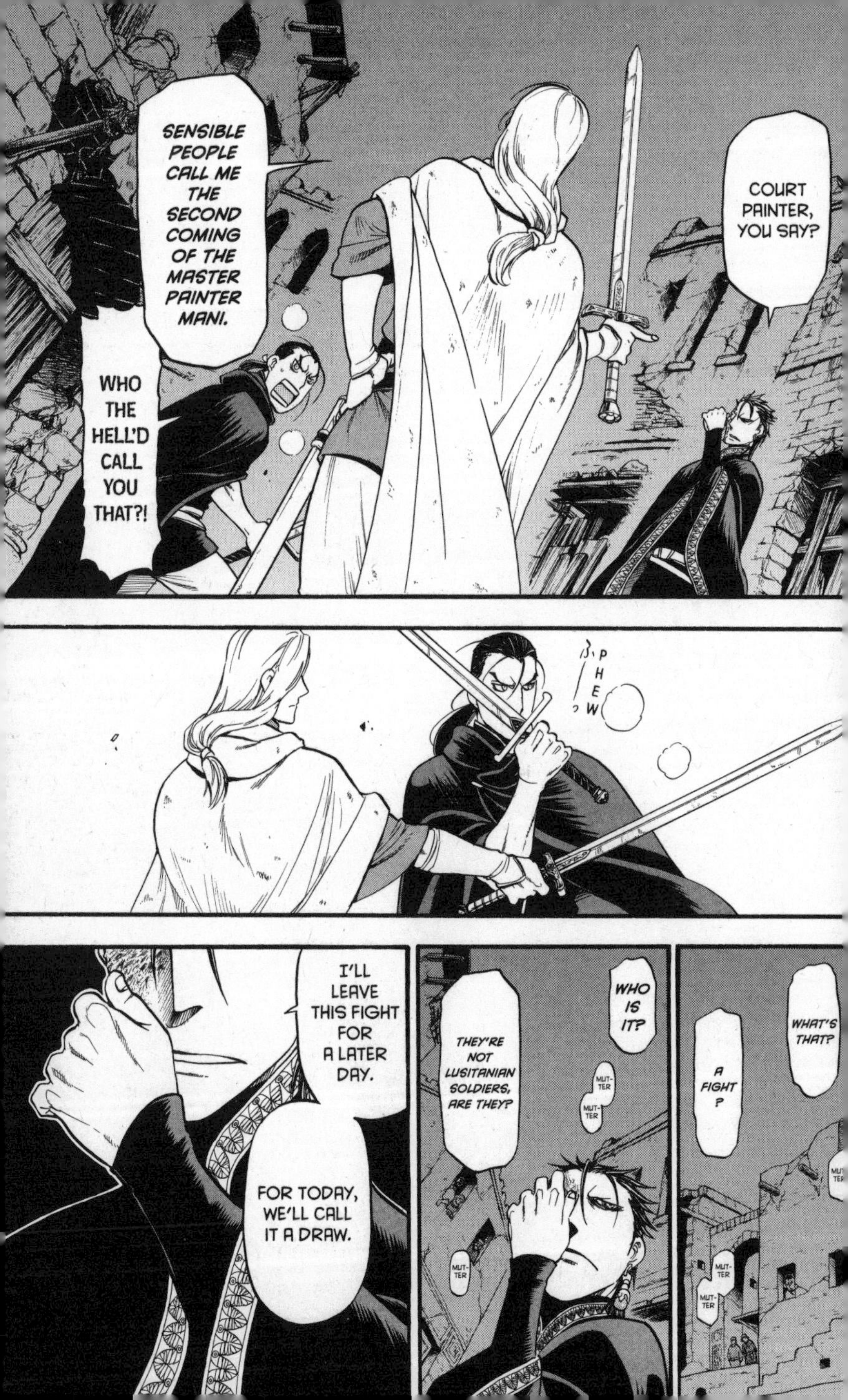
COURT PAINTER, YOU SAY?
SENSIBLE PEOPLE CALL ME THE SECOND COMING OF THE MASTER PAINTER MANI.
WHO THE HELL'D CALL YOU THAT?!
PHEW
WHAT'S THAT?
A FIGHT?
MUTTER
MUTTER
MUTTER
WHO IS IT?
THEY'RE NOT LUSITANIAN SOLDIERS, ARE THEY?
MUTTER
MUTTER
MUTTER
I'LL LEAVE THIS FIGHT FOR A LATER DAY.
FOR TODAY, WE'LL CALL IT A DRAW.

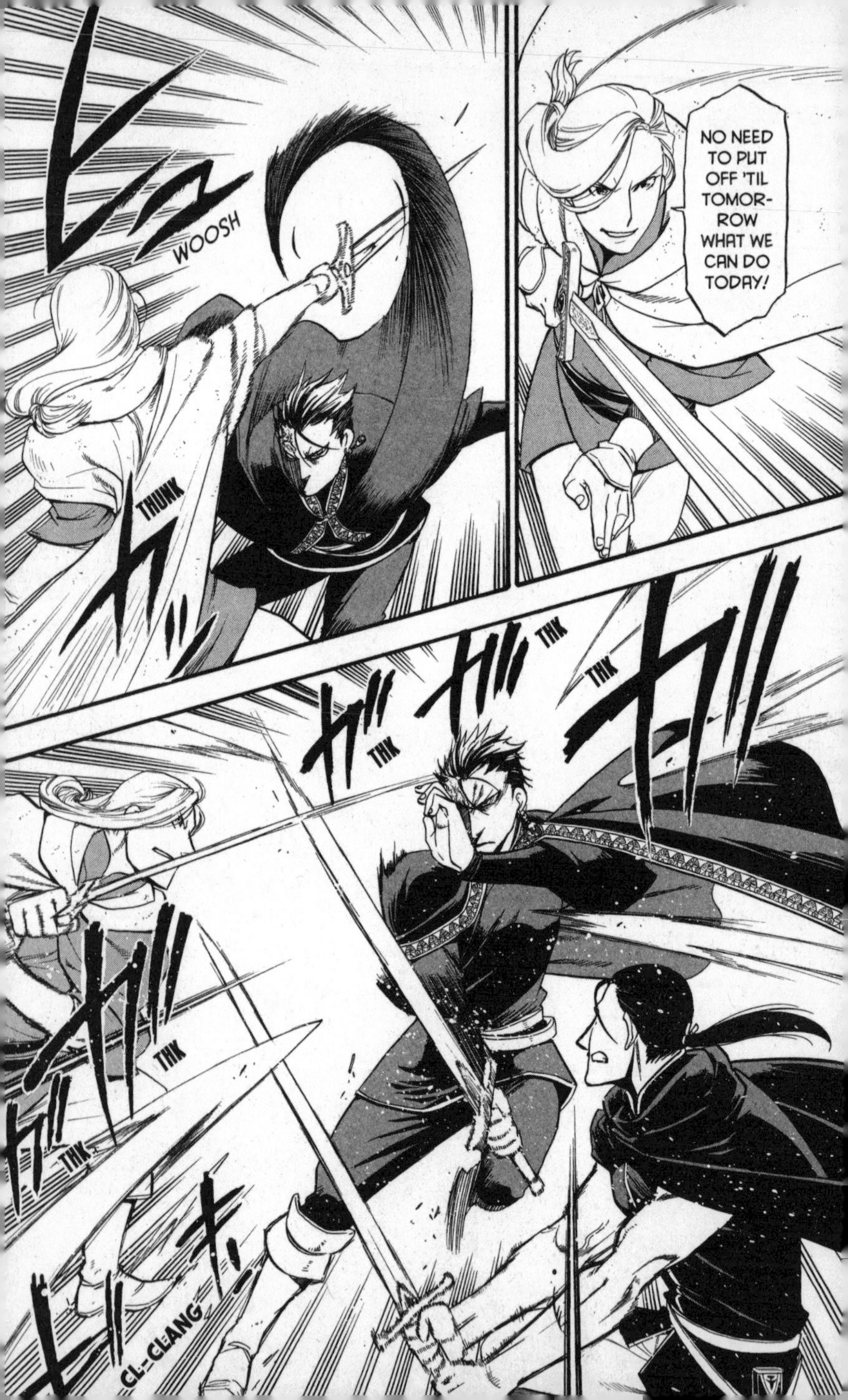
NO NEED TO PUT OFF 'TIL TOMOR-ROW WHAT WE CAN DO TODAY!
WOOSH
THUNK
THK
THK
THK
THK
THK
CL-CLANG

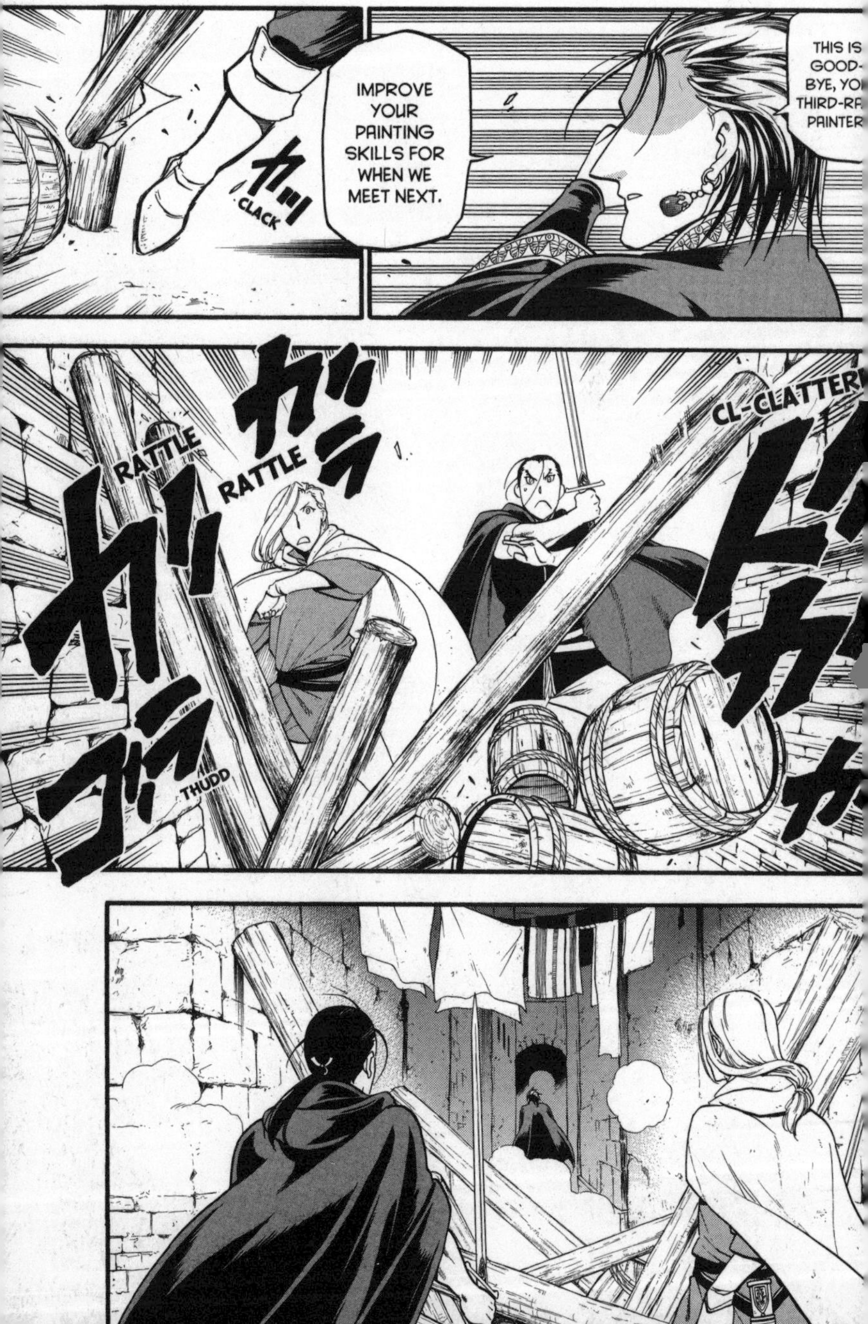
THIS IS GOOD-BYE, YO THIRD-RA PAINTER
IMPROVE YOUR PAINTING SKILLS FOR WHEN WE MEET NEXT.
CLACK
CL-CLATTER
RATTLE
RATTLE
THUDD

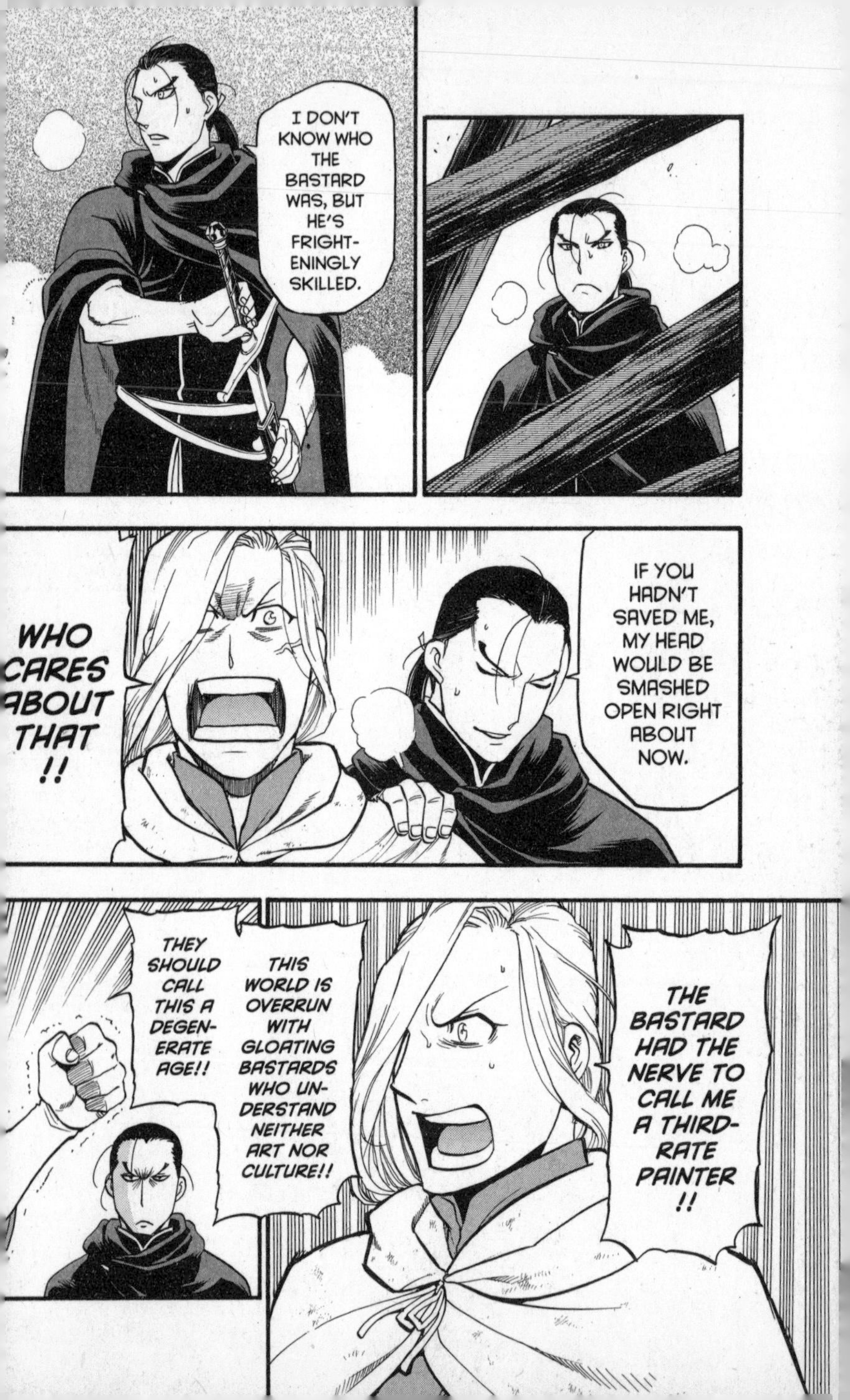
I DON'T KNOW WHO THE BASTARD WAS, BUT HE'S FRIGHTENINGLY SKILLED.
IF YOU HADN'T SAVED ME, MY HEAD WOULD BE SMASHED OPEN RIGHT ABOUT NOW.
WHO CARES ABOUT THAT!!
THE BASTARD HAD THE NERVE TO CALL ME A THIRD-RATE PAINTER!!
THIS WORLD IS OVERRUN WITH GLOATING BASTARDS WHO UNDERSTAND NEITHER ART NOR CULTURE!!
THEY SHOULD CALL THIS A DEGENERATE AGE!!

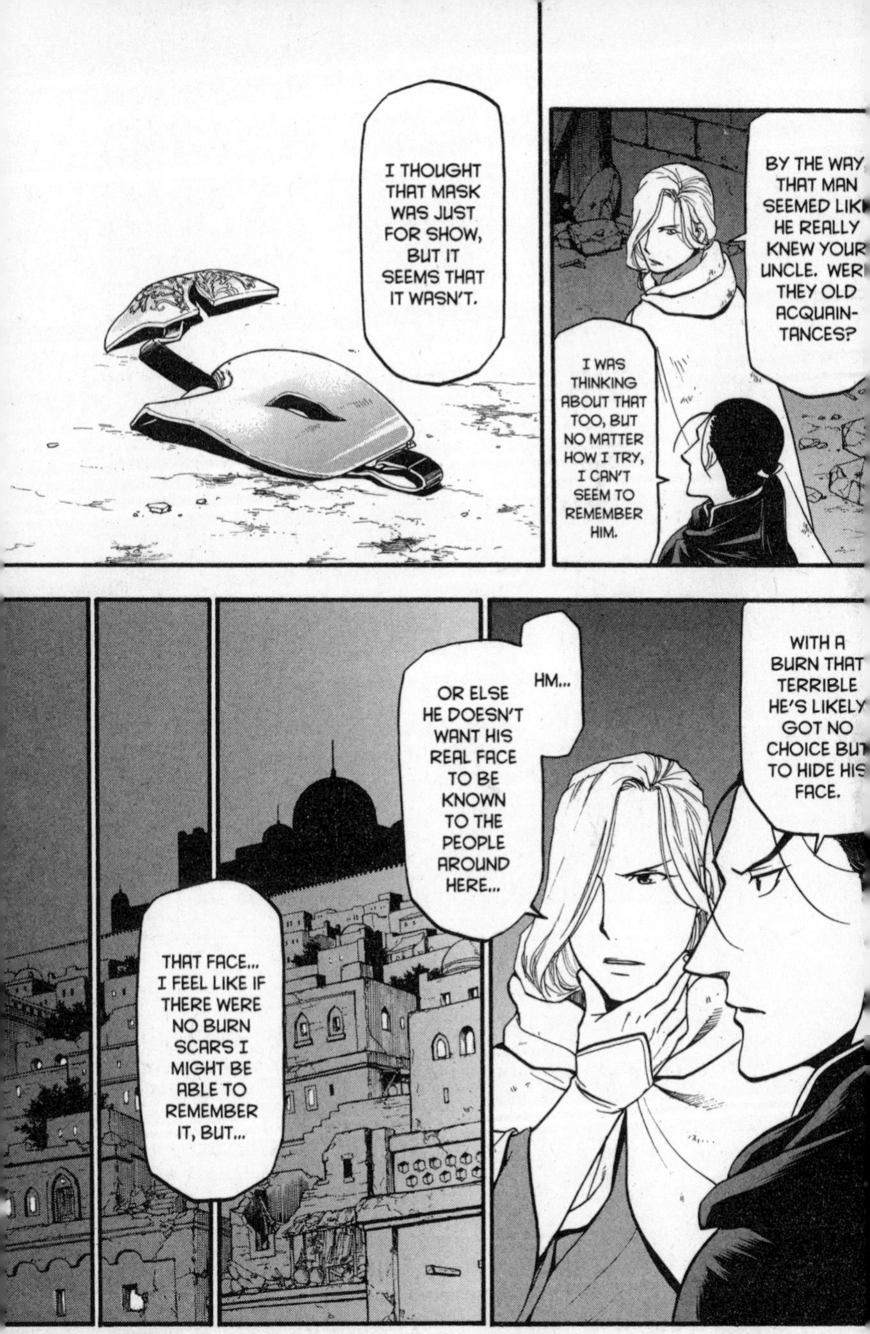
BY THE WAY, THAT MAN SEEMED LIKE HE REALLY KNEW YOUR UNCLE. WERE THEY OLD ACQUAINTANCES?
I WAS THINKING ABOUT THAT TOO, BUT NO MATTER HOW I TRY, I CAN'T SEEM TO REMEMBER HIM.
I THOUGHT THAT MASK WAS JUST FOR SHOW, BUT IT SEEMS THAT IT WASN'T.
WITH A BURN THAT TERRIBLE HE'S LIKELY GOT NO CHOICE BUT TO HIDE HIS FACE.
HM...
OR ELSE HE DOESN'T WANT HIS REAL FACE TO BE KNOWN TO THE PEOPLE AROUND HERE...
THAT FACE... I FEEL LIKE IF THERE WERE NO BURN SCARS I MIGHT BE ABLE TO REMEMBER IT, BUT...

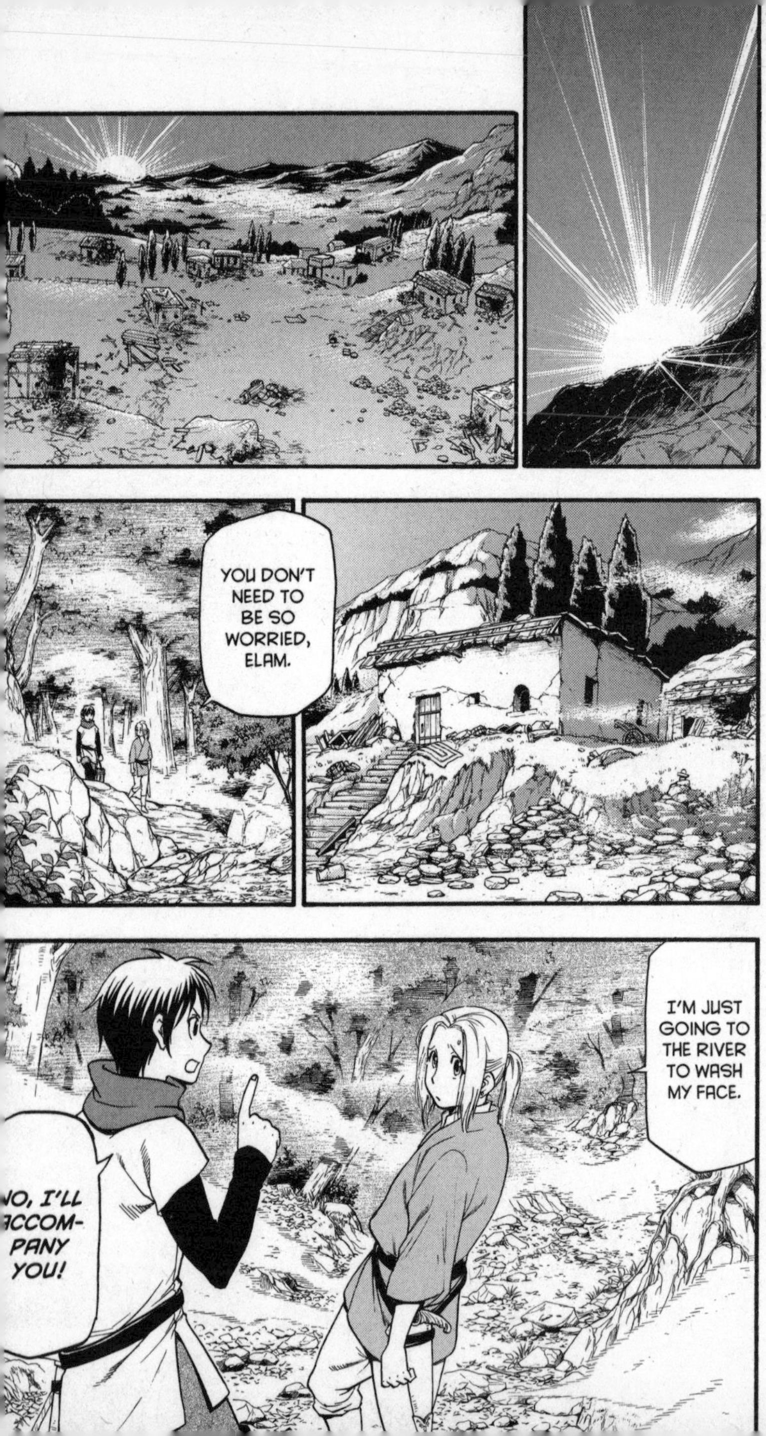
YOU DON'T NEED TO BE SO WORRIED, ELAM.
I'M JUST GOING TO THE RIVER TO WASH MY FACE.
NO, I'LL ACCOMPANY YOU!

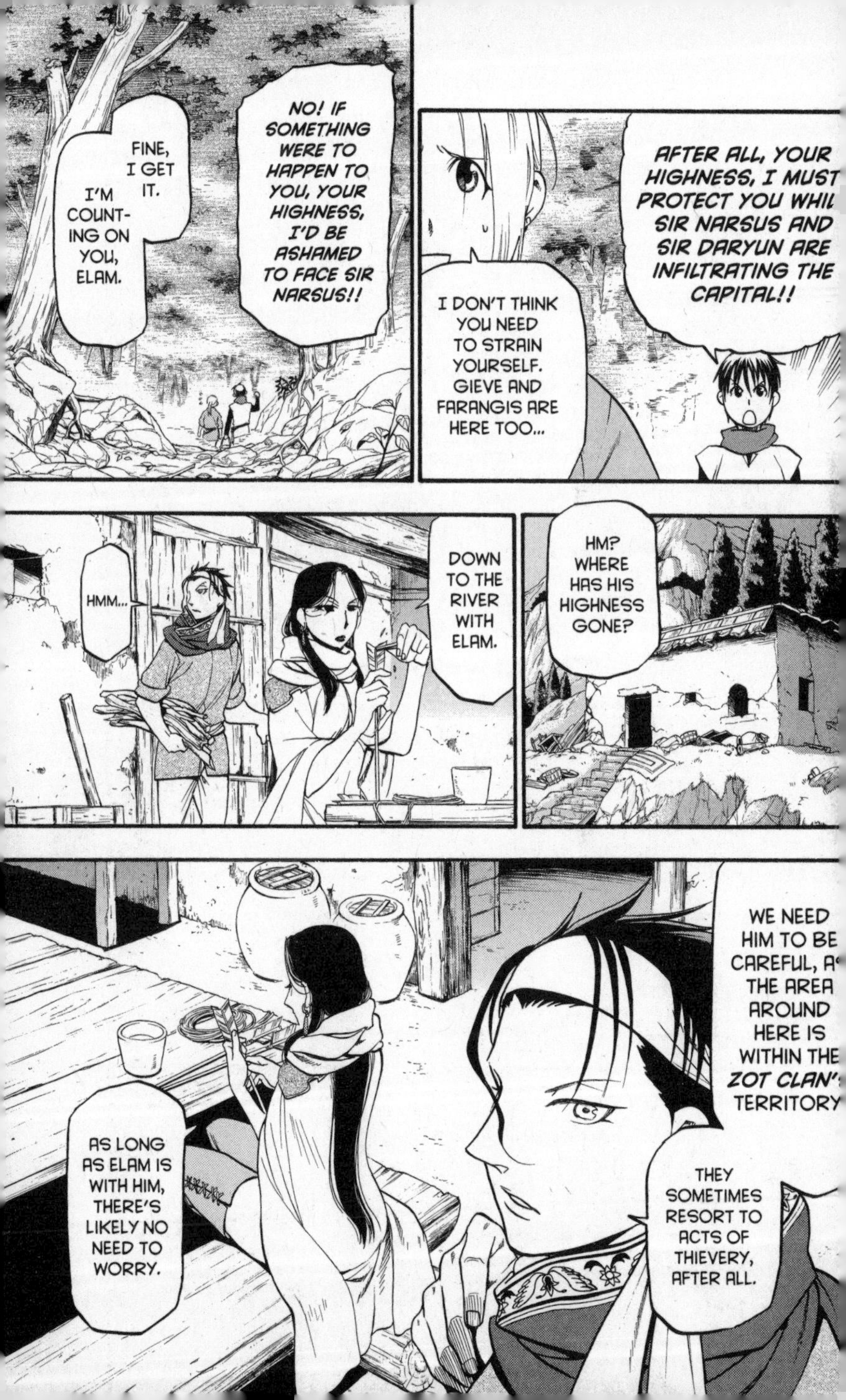

AFTER ALL, YOUR HIGHNESS, I MUST PROTECT YOU WHIL SIR NARSUS AND SIR DARYUN ARE INFILTRATING THE CAPITAL!!
I DON'T THINK YOU NEED TO STRAIN YOURSELF. GIEVE AND FARANGIS ARE HERE TOO...
NO! IF SOMETHING WERE TO HAPPEN TO YOU, YOUR HIGHNESS, I'D BE ASHAMED TO FACE SIR NARSUS!!
FINE, I GET IT.
I'M COUNTING ON YOU, ELAM.
HM? WHERE HAS HIS HIGHNESS GONE?
DOWN TO THE RIVER WITH ELAM.
HMM...
WE NEED HIM TO BE CAREFUL, A THE AREA AROUND HERE IS WITHIN THE ZOT CLAN' TERRITORY
THEY SOMETIMES RESORT TO ACTS OF THIEVERY, AFTER ALL.
AS LONG AS ELAM IS WITH HIM, THERE'S LIKELY NO NEED TO WORRY.

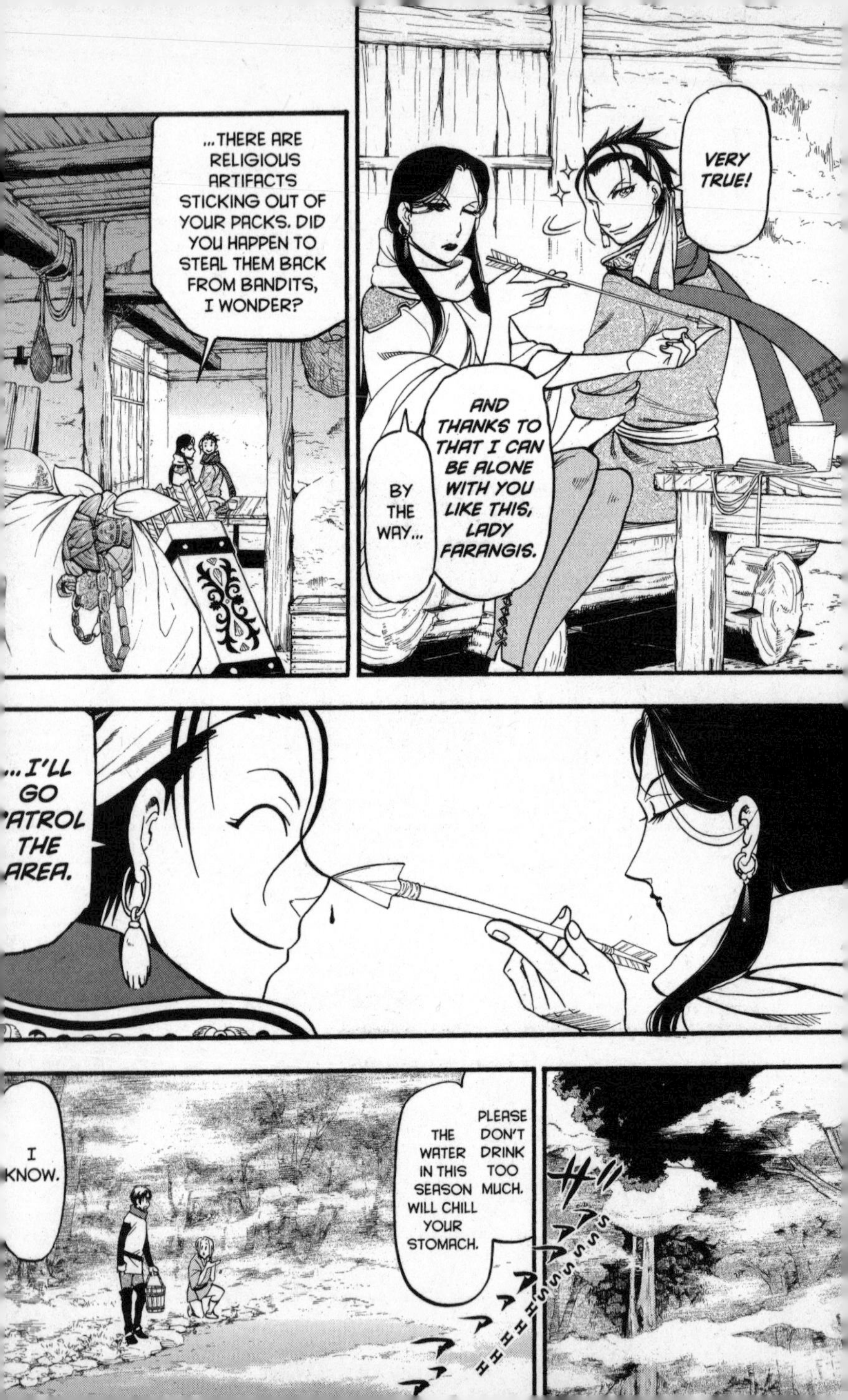
VERY TRUE!
AND THANKS TO THAT I CAN BE ALONE WITH YOU LIKE THIS, LADY FARANGIS.
BY THE WAY...
...THERE ARE RELIGIOUS ARTIFACTS STICKING OUT OF YOUR PACKS. DID YOU HAPPEN TO STEAL THEM BACK FROM BANDITS, I WONDER?
...I'LL GO
THE AREA.
PLEASE DON'T DRINK TOO MUCH.
THE WATER IN THIS SEASON WILL CHILL YOUR STOMACH.
I KNOW.

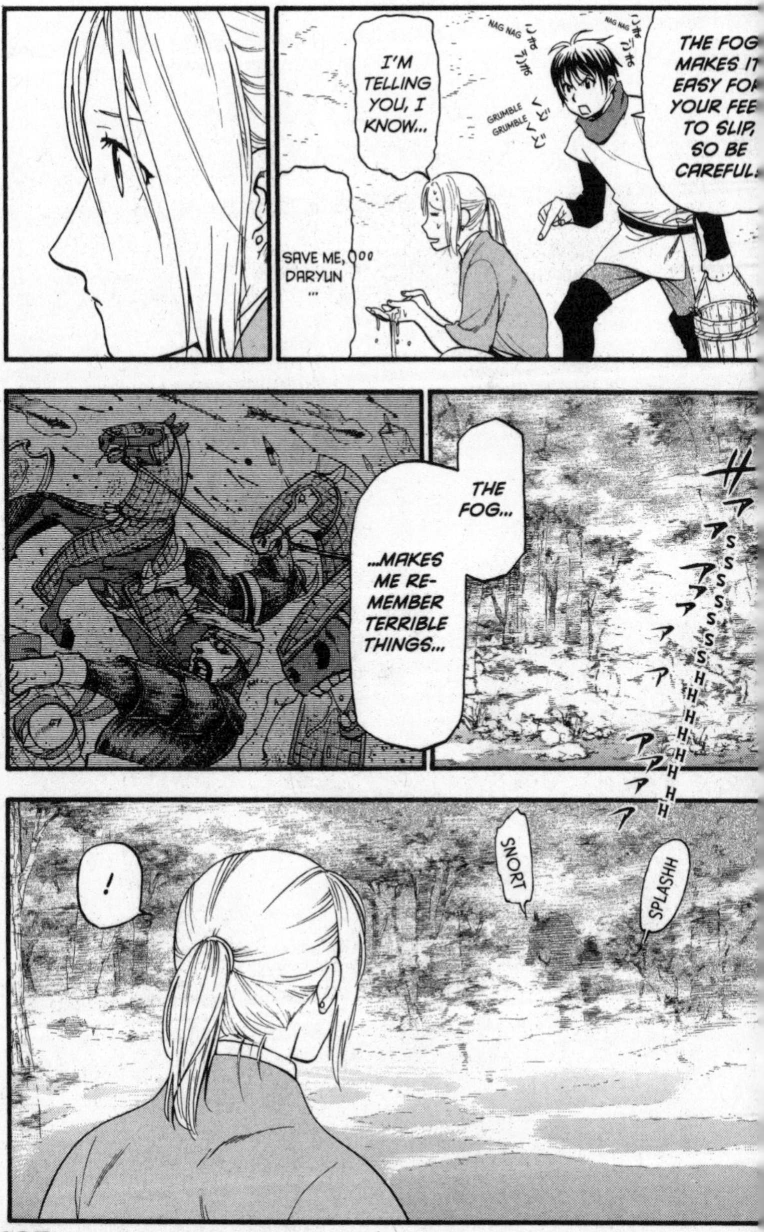
THE FOG MAKES IT EASY FOR YOUR FEE TO SLIP, SO BE CAREFUL.
NAG NAG
こまごま
NAG NAG
こまごま
GRUMBLE GRUMBLE
くどくど
I'M TELLING YOU, I KNOW...
SAVE ME, DARYUN...
ザァァァァァァァァ
SSSSSSHHHHHHHH
THE FOG...
...MAKES ME RE-MEMBER TERRIBLE THINGS...
SPLASHH
SNORT
!

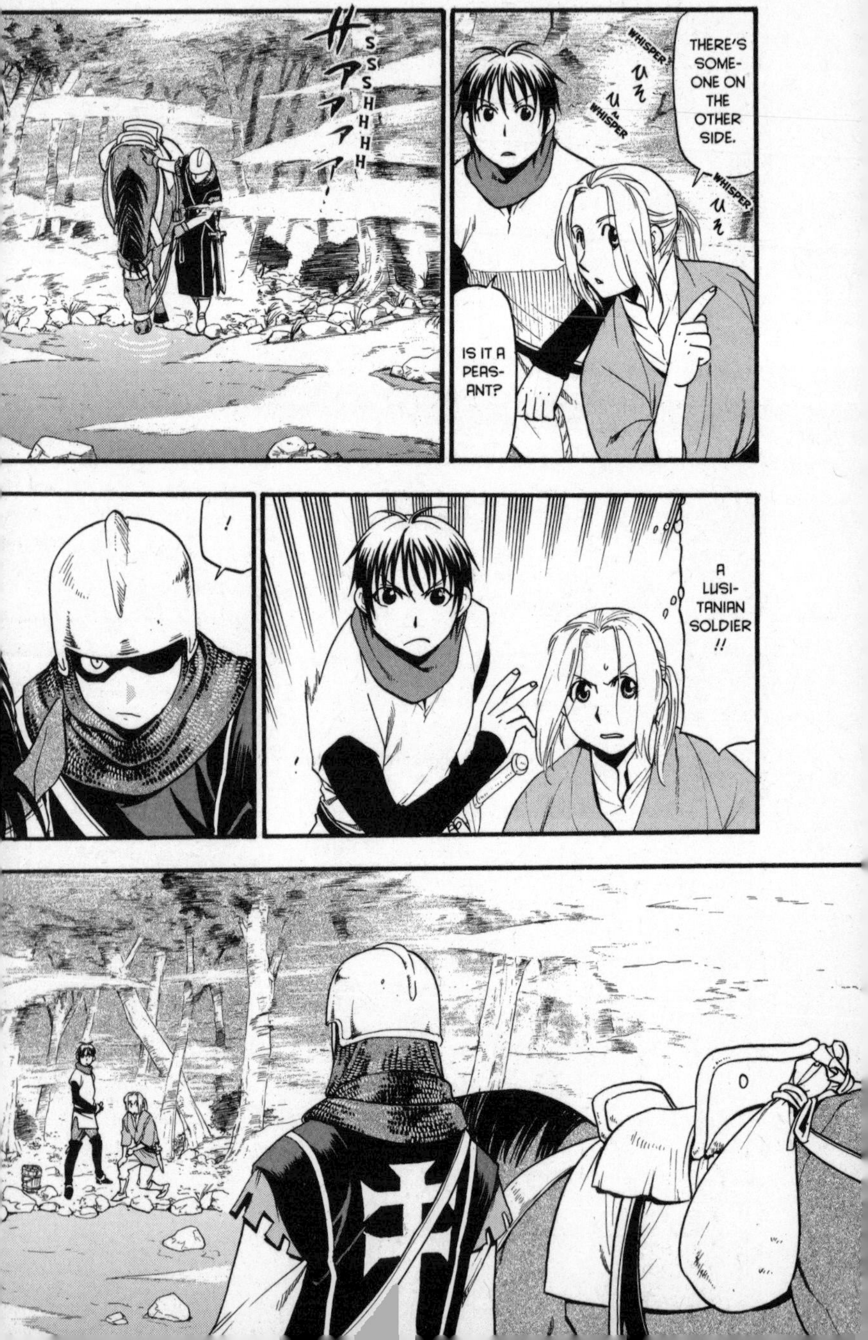
THERE'S SOME-ONE ON THE OTHER SIDE.
WHISPER ひそ
WHISPER ひそ
WHISPER ひそ
IS IT A PEAS-ANT?
ザァァァ…
SSHHHH
A LUSI-TANIAN SOLDIER !!
!

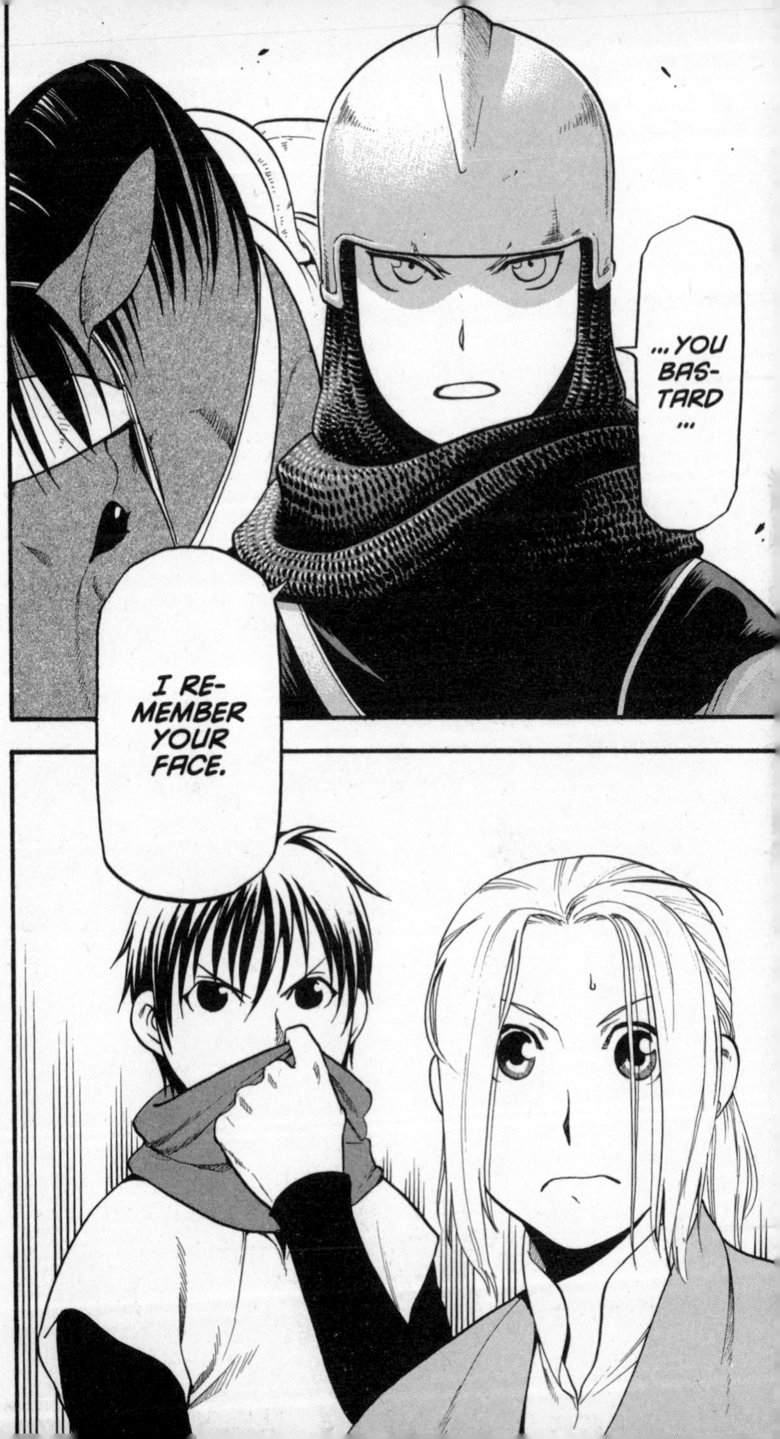
...YOU BAS- TARD ...
I RE- MEMBER YOUR FACE.

The Heroic Legend of
ARSLAN

Chapter 19: The Second Prince

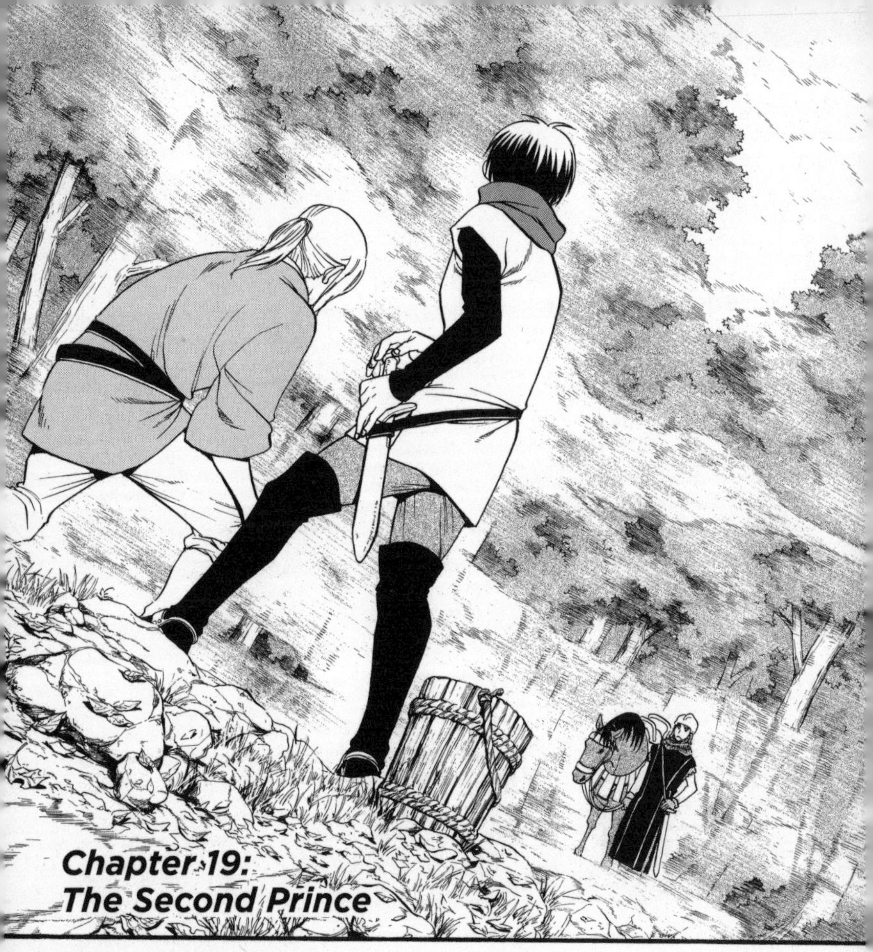

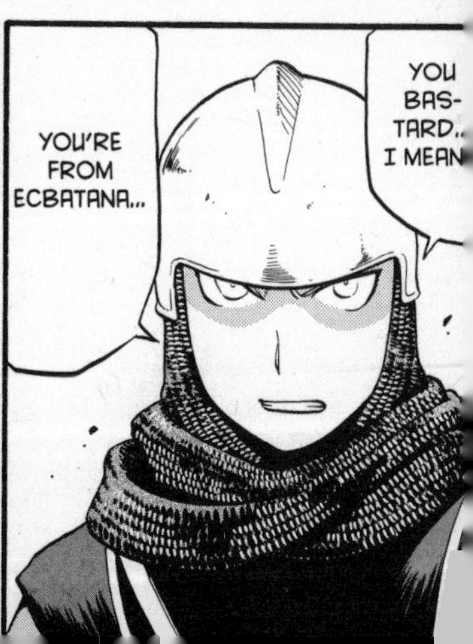
YOU BAS-TARD.. I MEAN
YOU'RE FROM ECBATANA...

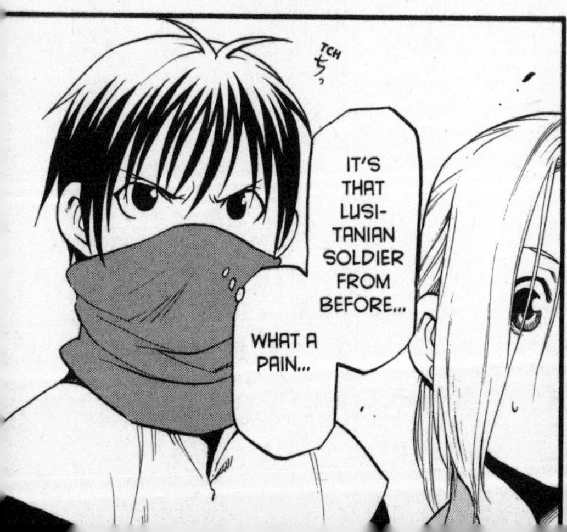
TCH
IT'S THAT LUSI-TANIAN SOLDIER FROM BEFORE...
WHAT A PAIN...

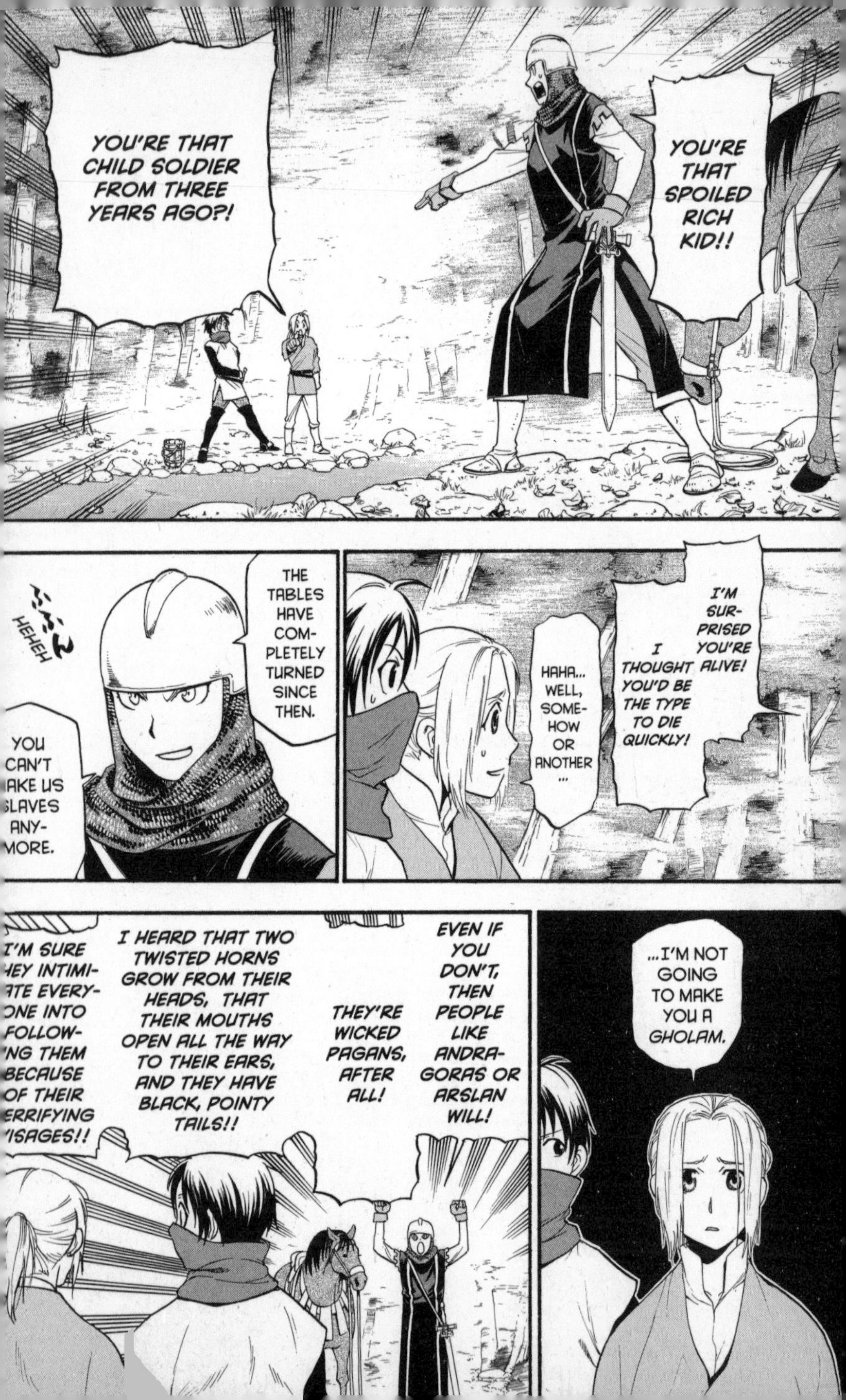
YOU'RE THAT SPOILED RICH KID!!
YOU'RE THAT CHILD SOLDIER FROM THREE YEARS AGO?!
I'M SURPRISED YOU'RE ALIVE!
I THOUGHT YOU'D BE THE TYPE TO DIE QUICKLY!
HAHA... WELL, SOMEHOW OR ANOTHER...
THE TABLES HAVE COMPLETELY TURNED SINCE THEN.
ふふん HEHEH
YOU CAN'T AKE US LAVES ANYMORE.
...I'M NOT GOING TO MAKE YOU A GHOLAM.
EVEN IF YOU DON'T, THEN PEOPLE LIKE ANDRAGORAS OR ARSLAN WILL!
THEY'RE WICKED PAGANS, AFTER ALL!
I HEARD THAT TWO TWISTED HORNS GROW FROM THEIR HEADS, THAT THEIR MOUTHS OPEN ALL THE WAY TO THEIR EARS, AND THEY HAVE BLACK, POINTY TAILS!!
I'M SURE HEY INTIMI-ATE EVERYONE INTO FOLLOW-NG THEM BECAUSE OF THEIR ERRIFYING ISAGES!!

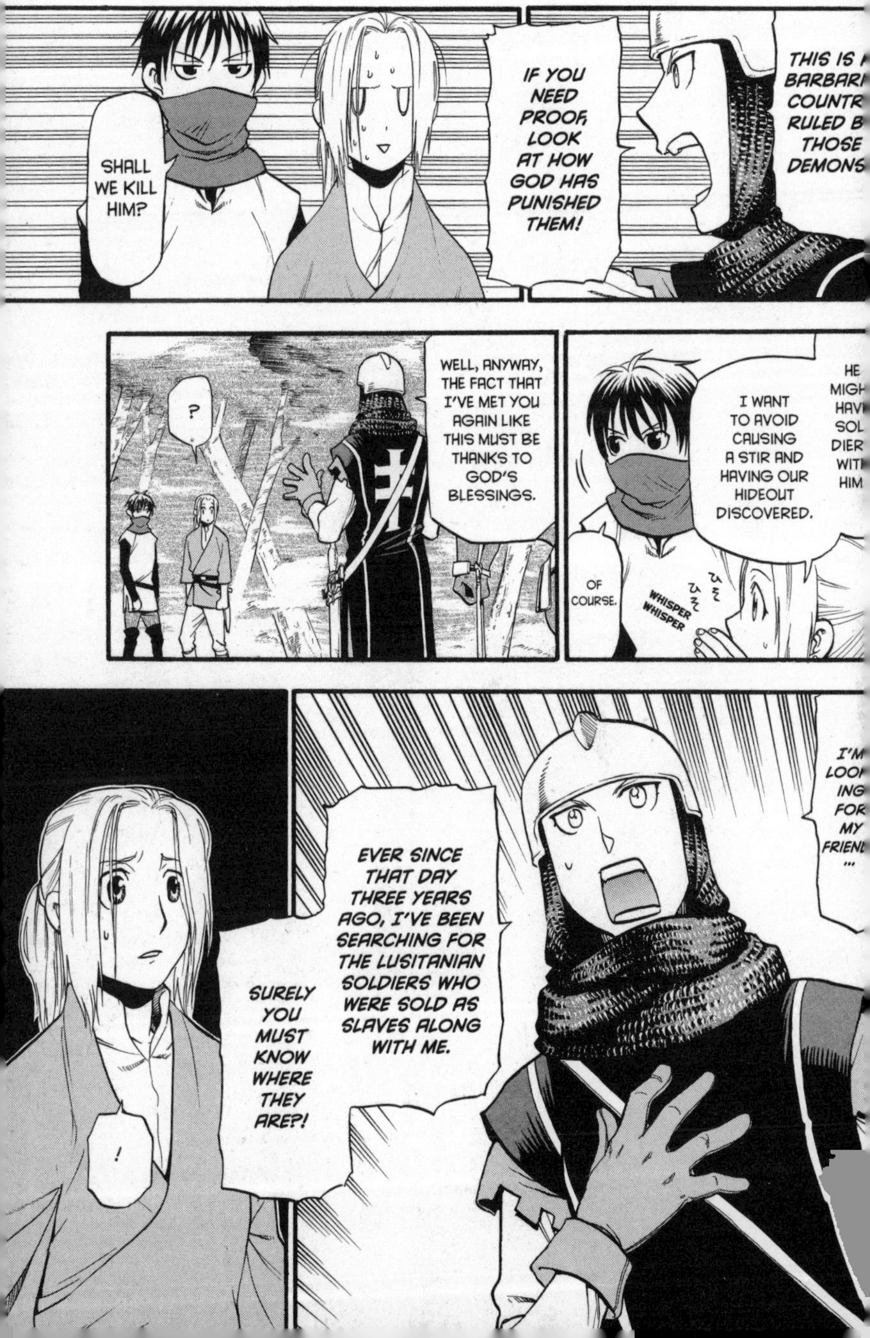
THIS IS BARBARI COUNTR RULED B THOSE DEMONS
IF YOU NEED PROOF, LOOK AT HOW GOD HAS PUNISHED THEM!
SHALL WE KILL HIM?
HE MIGH HAV SOL DIER WIT HIM
I WANT TO AVOID CAUSING A STIR AND HAVING OUR HIDEOUT DISCOVERED.
ひそ ひそ
WHISPER WHISPER
OF COURSE.
WELL, ANYWAY, THE FACT THAT I'VE MET YOU AGAIN LIKE THIS MUST BE THANKS TO GOD'S BLESSINGS.
?
I'M LOOK ING FOR MY FRIEND ...
EVER SINCE THAT DAY THREE YEARS AGO, I'VE BEEN SEARCHING FOR THE LUSITANIAN SOLDIERS WHO WERE SOLD AS SLAVES ALONG WITH ME.
SURELY YOU MUST KNOW WHERE THEY ARE?!
!

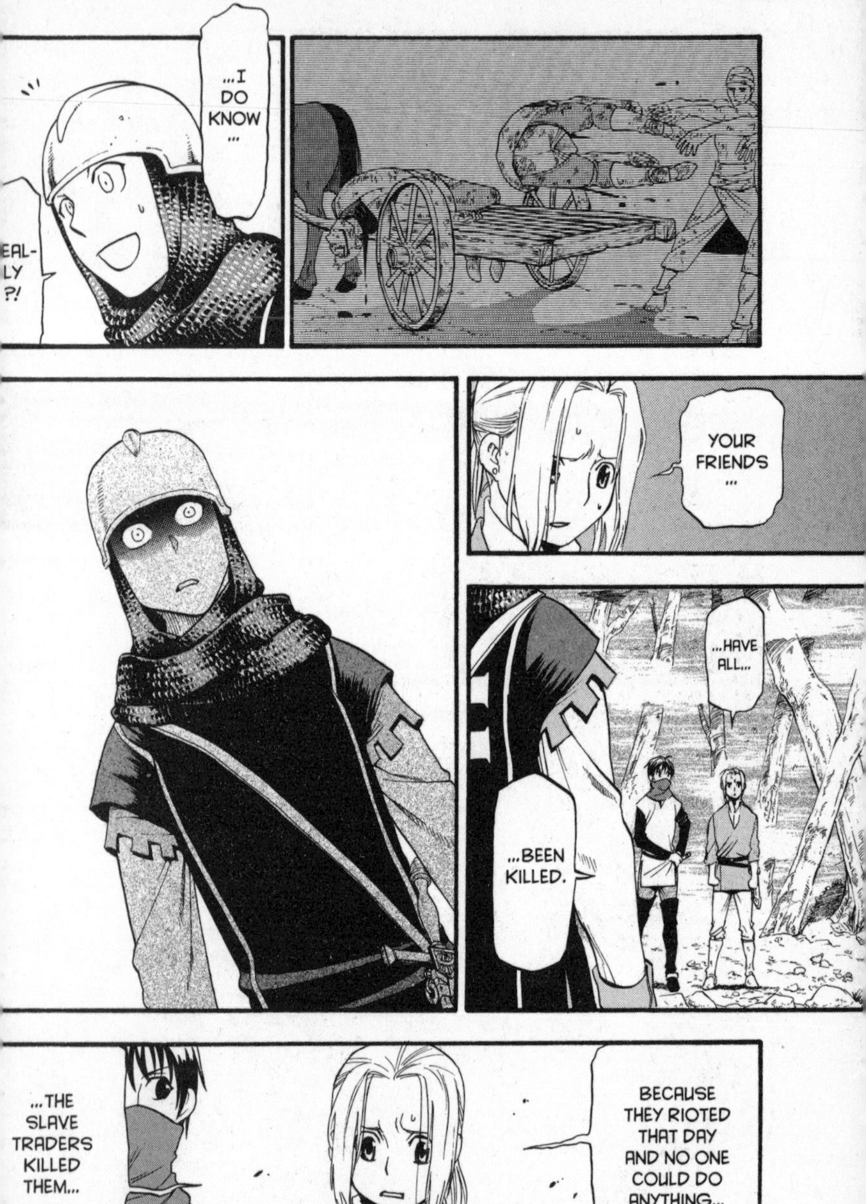
...I DO KNOW...
EAL-LY?!
YOUR FRIENDS...
...HAVE ALL...
...BEEN KILLED.
BECAUSE THEY RIOTED THAT DAY AND NO ONE COULD DO ANYTHING...
...THE SLAVE TRADERS KILLED THEM...

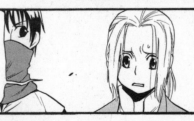

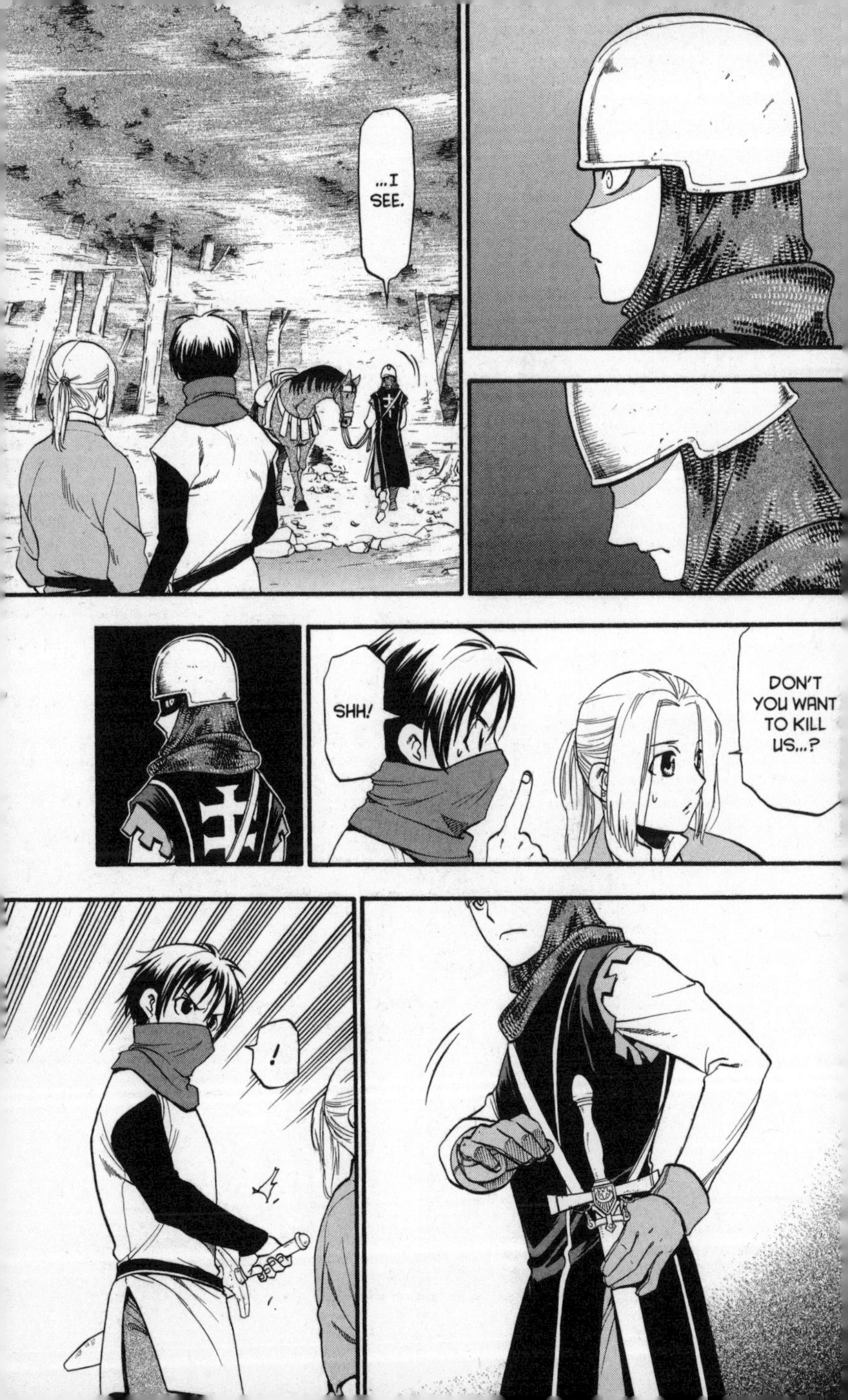
...I SEE.
DON'T YOU WANT TO KILL US...?
SHH!
!

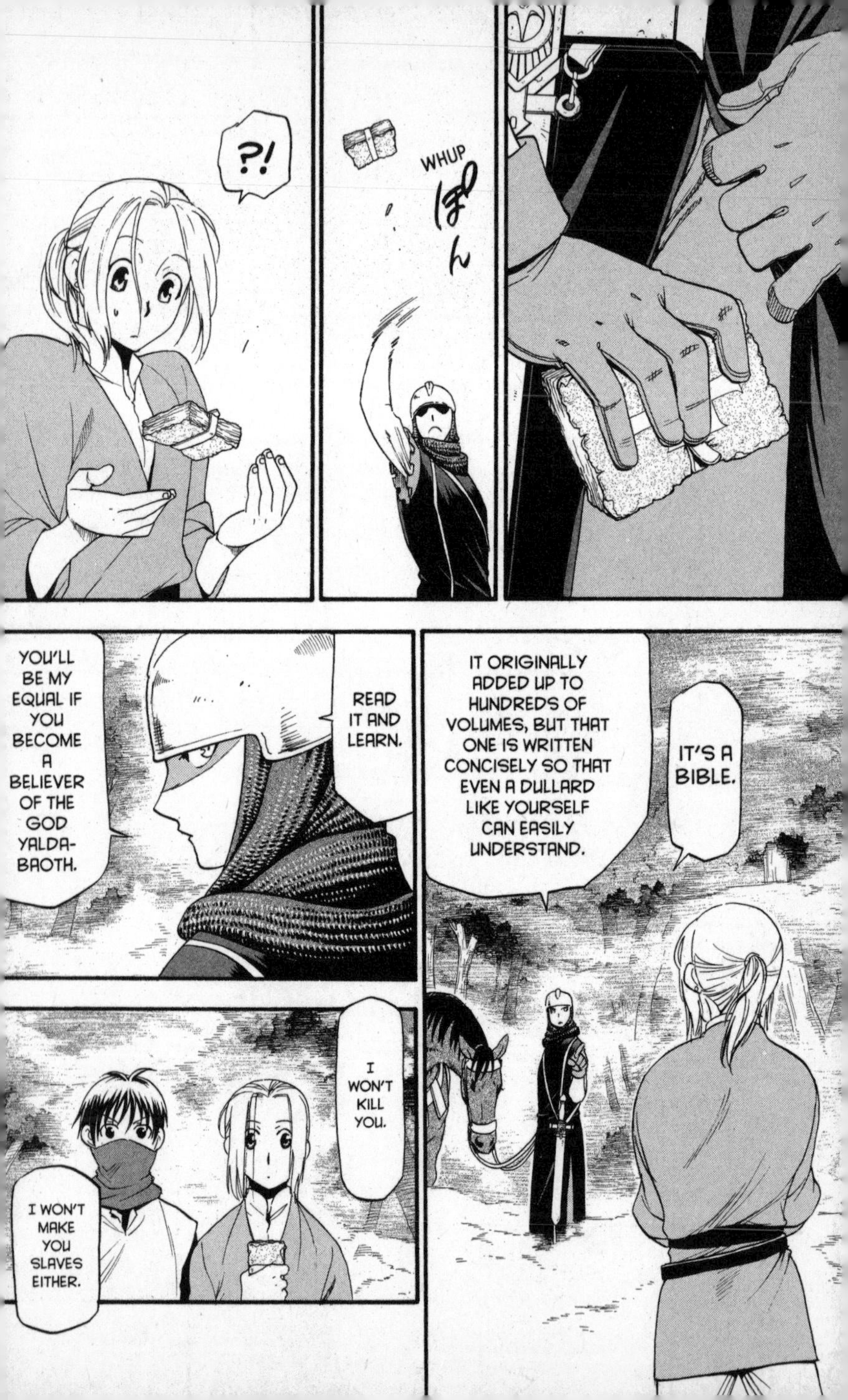
WHUP
ぽん
?!
IT'S A BIBLE.
IT ORIGINALLY ADDED UP TO HUNDREDS OF VOLUMES, BUT THAT ONE IS WRITTEN CONCISELY SO THAT EVEN A DULLARD LIKE YOURSELF CAN EASILY UNDERSTAND.
READ IT AND LEARN.
YOU'LL BE MY EQUAL IF YOU BECOME A BELIEVER OF THE GOD YALDA-BAOTH.
I WON'T KILL YOU.
I WON'T MAKE YOU SLAVES EITHER.

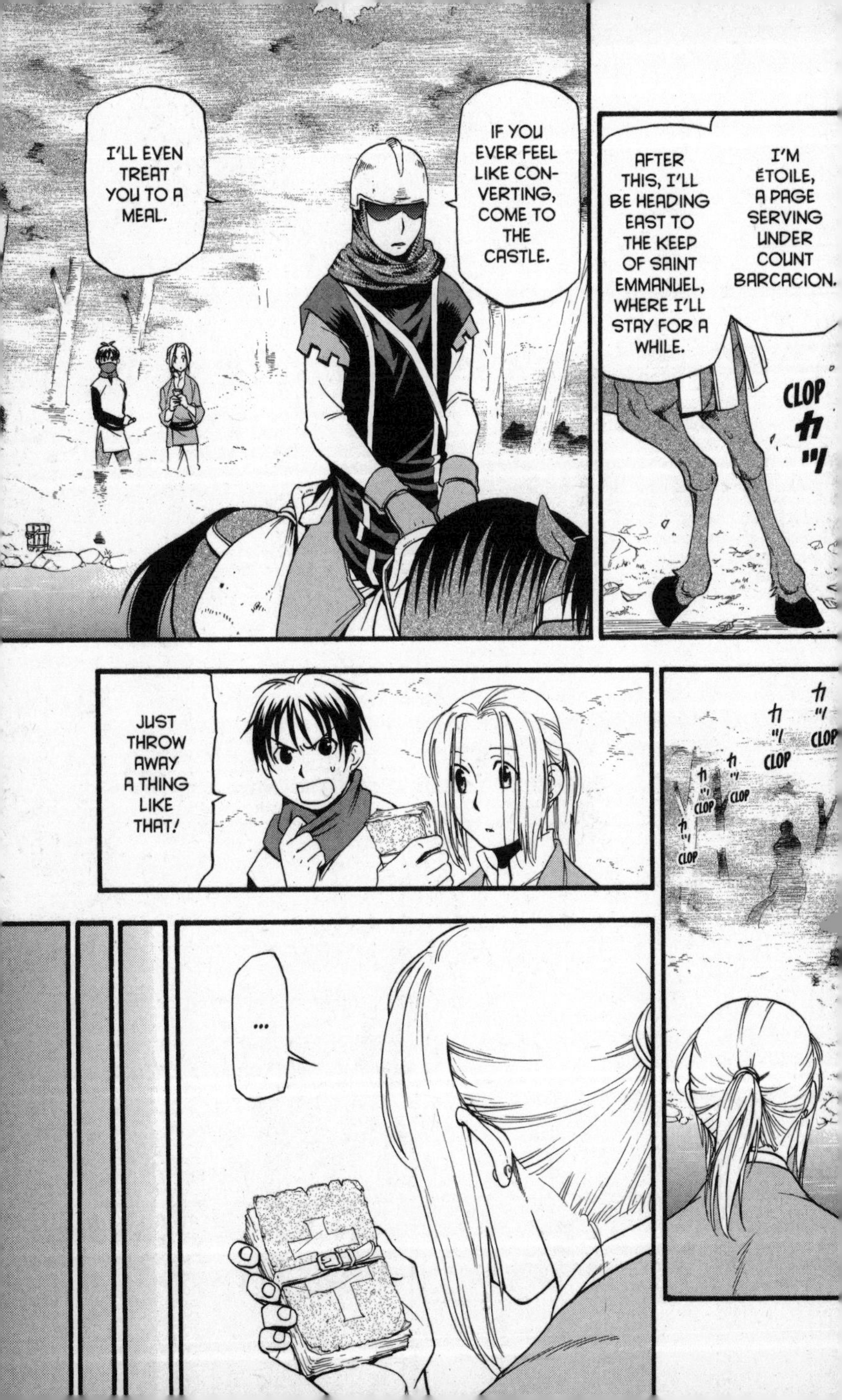
I'M ÉTOILE, A PAGE SERVING UNDER COUNT BARCACION.
AFTER THIS, I'LL BE HEADING EAST TO THE KEEP OF SAINT EMMANUEL, WHERE I'LL STAY FOR A WHILE.
CLOP カッ
IF YOU EVER FEEL LIKE CON-VERTING, COME TO THE CASTLE.
I'LL EVEN TREAT YOU TO A MEAL.
カッ CLOP
カッ CLOP
カッ CLOP
カッ CLOP
カッ CLOP
カッ CLOP
JUST THROW AWAY A THING LIKE THAT!
...

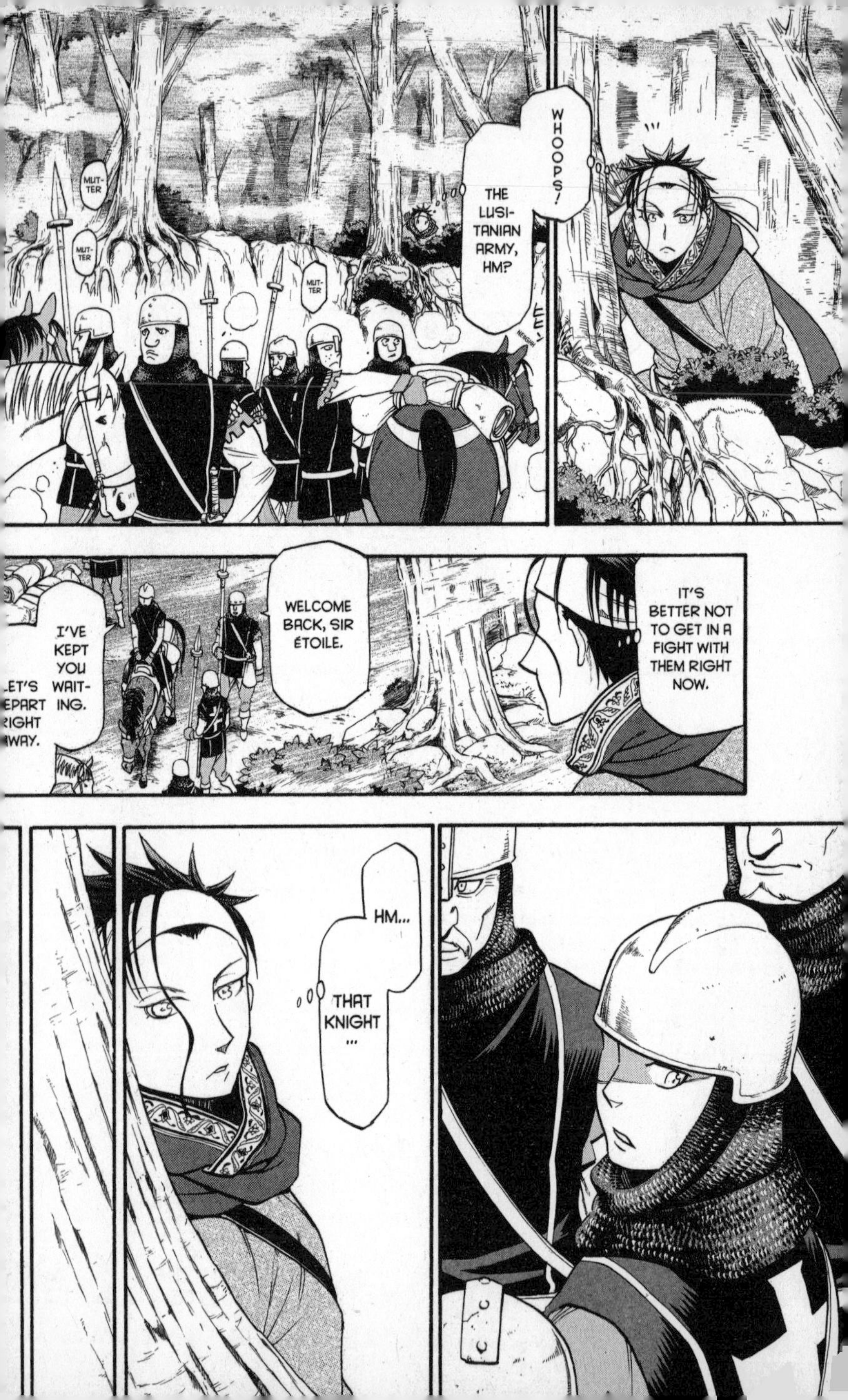
WHOOPS!
THE LUSITANIAN ARMY, HM?
NEIGH
MUTTER
MUTTER
MUTTER
IT'S BETTER NOT TO GET IN A FIGHT WITH THEM RIGHT NOW.
WELCOME BACK, SIR ÉTOILE.
I'VE KEPT YOU WAITING.
LET'S EPART RIGHT WAY.
HM...
THAT KNIGHT...

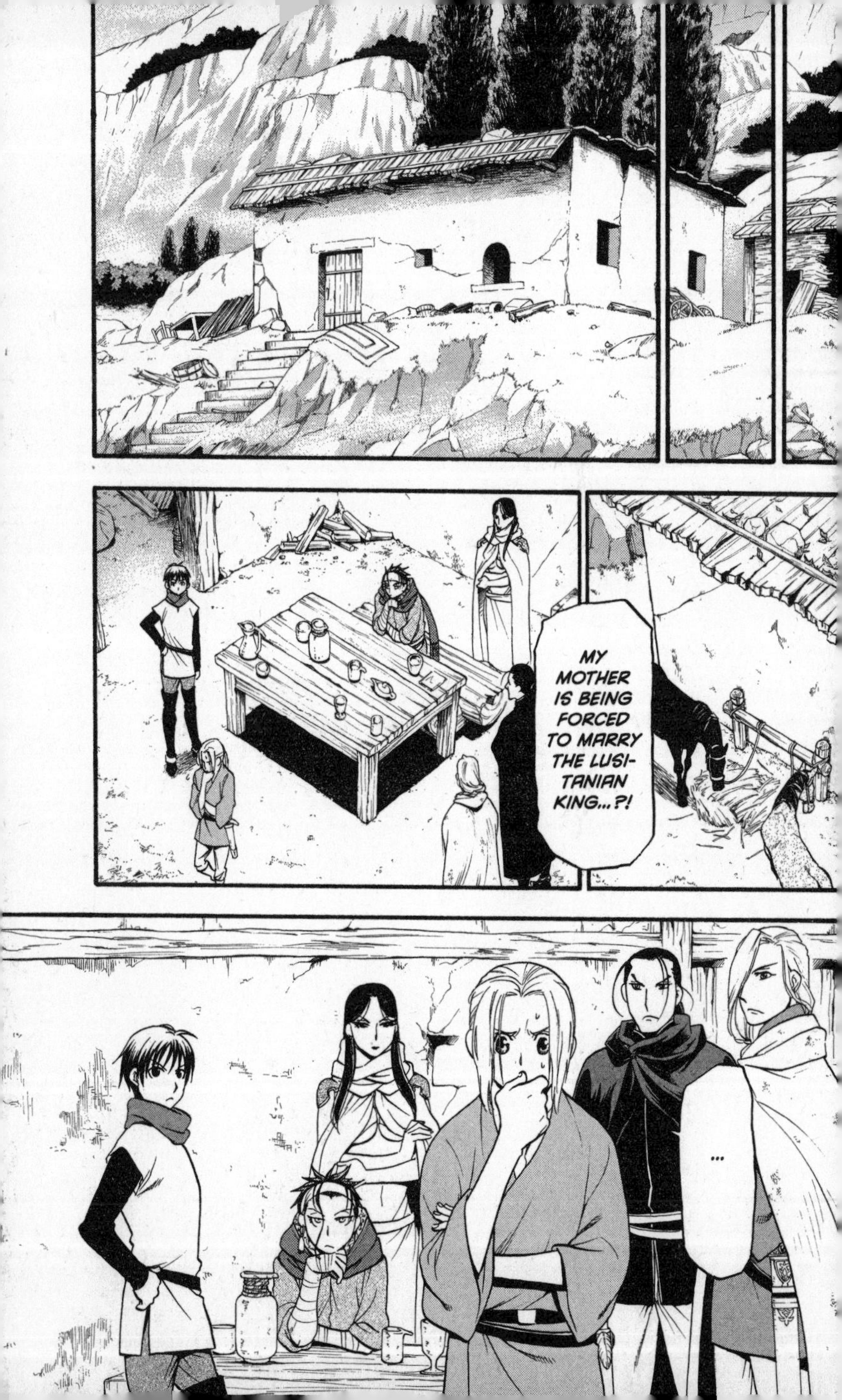
MY MOTHER IS BEING FORCED TO MARRY THE LUSI-TANIAN KING...?!
...

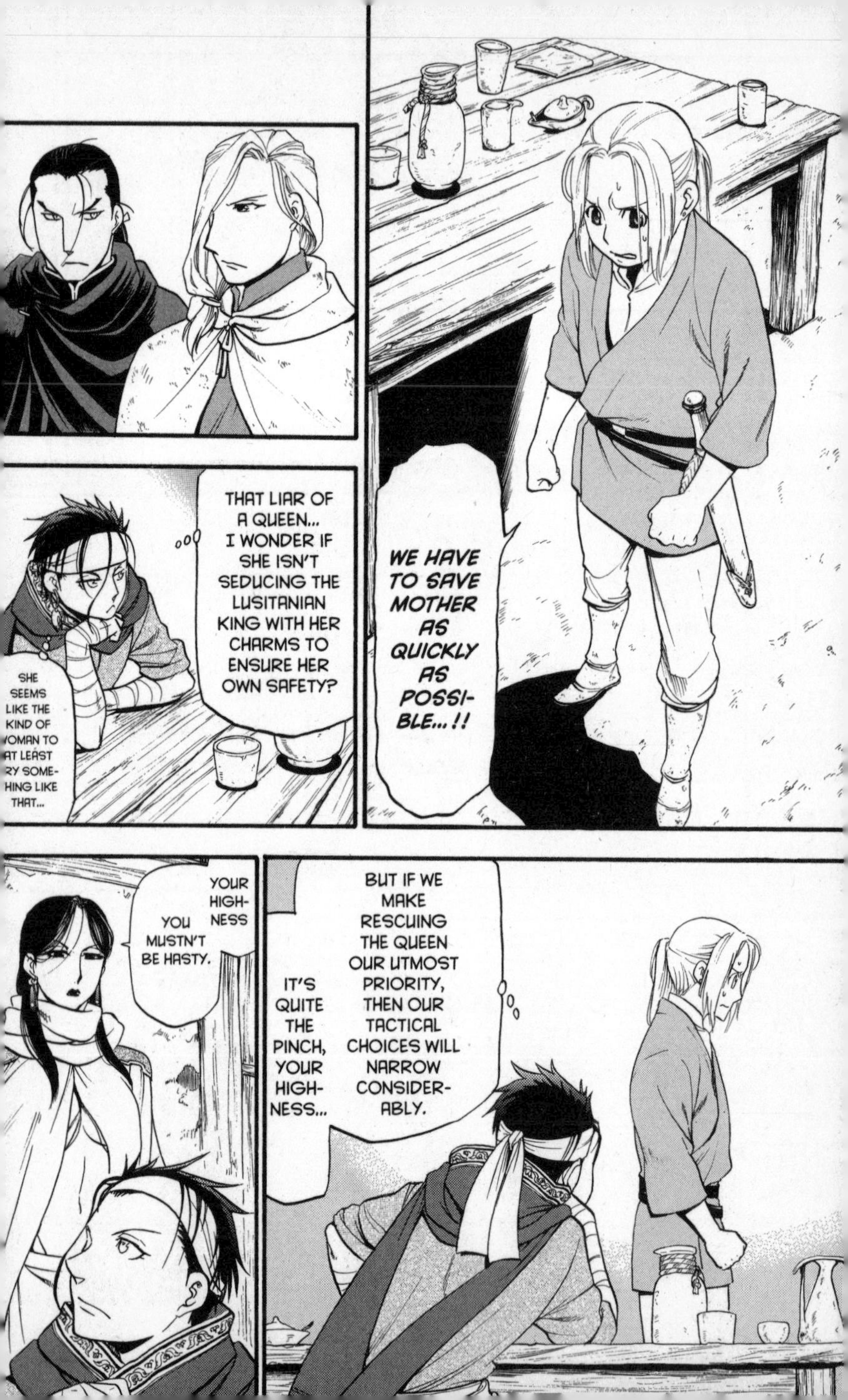
WE HAVE TO SAVE MOTHER AS QUICKLY AS POSSIBLE...!!
THAT LIAR OF A QUEEN... I WONDER IF SHE ISN'T SEDUCING THE LUSITANIAN KING WITH HER CHARMS TO ENSURE HER OWN SAFETY?
SHE SEEMS LIKE THE KIND OF OMAN TO AT LEAST RY SOME- HING LIKE THAT...
BUT IF WE MAKE RESCUING THE QUEEN OUR UTMOST PRIORITY, THEN OUR TACTICAL CHOICES WILL NARROW CONSIDERABLY.
IT'S QUITE THE PINCH, YOUR HIGHNESS...
YOUR HIGHNESS
YOU MUSTN'T BE HASTY.

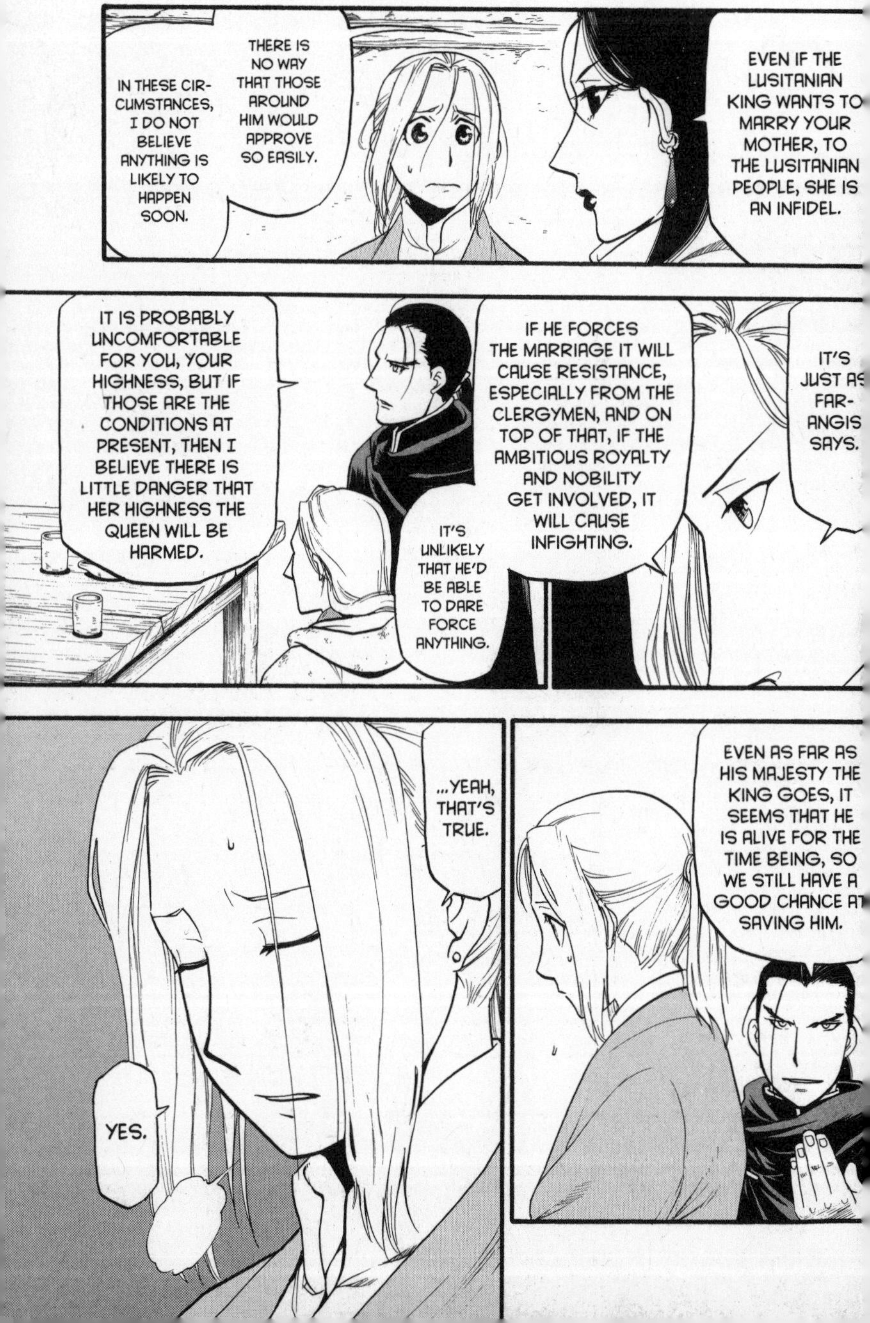
EVEN IF THE LUSITANIAN KING WANTS TO MARRY YOUR MOTHER, TO THE LUSITANIAN PEOPLE, SHE IS AN INFIDEL.
THERE IS NO WAY THAT THOSE AROUND HIM WOULD APPROVE SO EASILY.
IN THESE CIR-CUMSTANCES, I DO NOT BELIEVE ANYTHING IS LIKELY TO HAPPEN SOON.
IT'S JUST AS FAR-ANGIS SAYS.
IF HE FORCES THE MARRIAGE IT WILL CAUSE RESISTANCE, ESPECIALLY FROM THE CLERGYMEN, AND ON TOP OF THAT, IF THE AMBITIOUS ROYALTY AND NOBILITY GET INVOLVED, IT WILL CAUSE INFIGHTING.
IT'S UNLIKELY THAT HE'D BE ABLE TO DARE FORCE ANYTHING.
IT IS PROBABLY UNCOMFORTABLE FOR YOU, YOUR HIGHNESS, BUT IF THOSE ARE THE CONDITIONS AT PRESENT, THEN I BELIEVE THERE IS LITTLE DANGER THAT HER HIGHNESS THE QUEEN WILL BE HARMED.
EVEN AS FAR AS HIS MAJESTY THE KING GOES, IT SEEMS THAT HE IS ALIVE FOR THE TIME BEING, SO WE STILL HAVE A GOOD CHANCE AT SAVING HIM.
...YEAH, THAT'S TRUE.
YES.

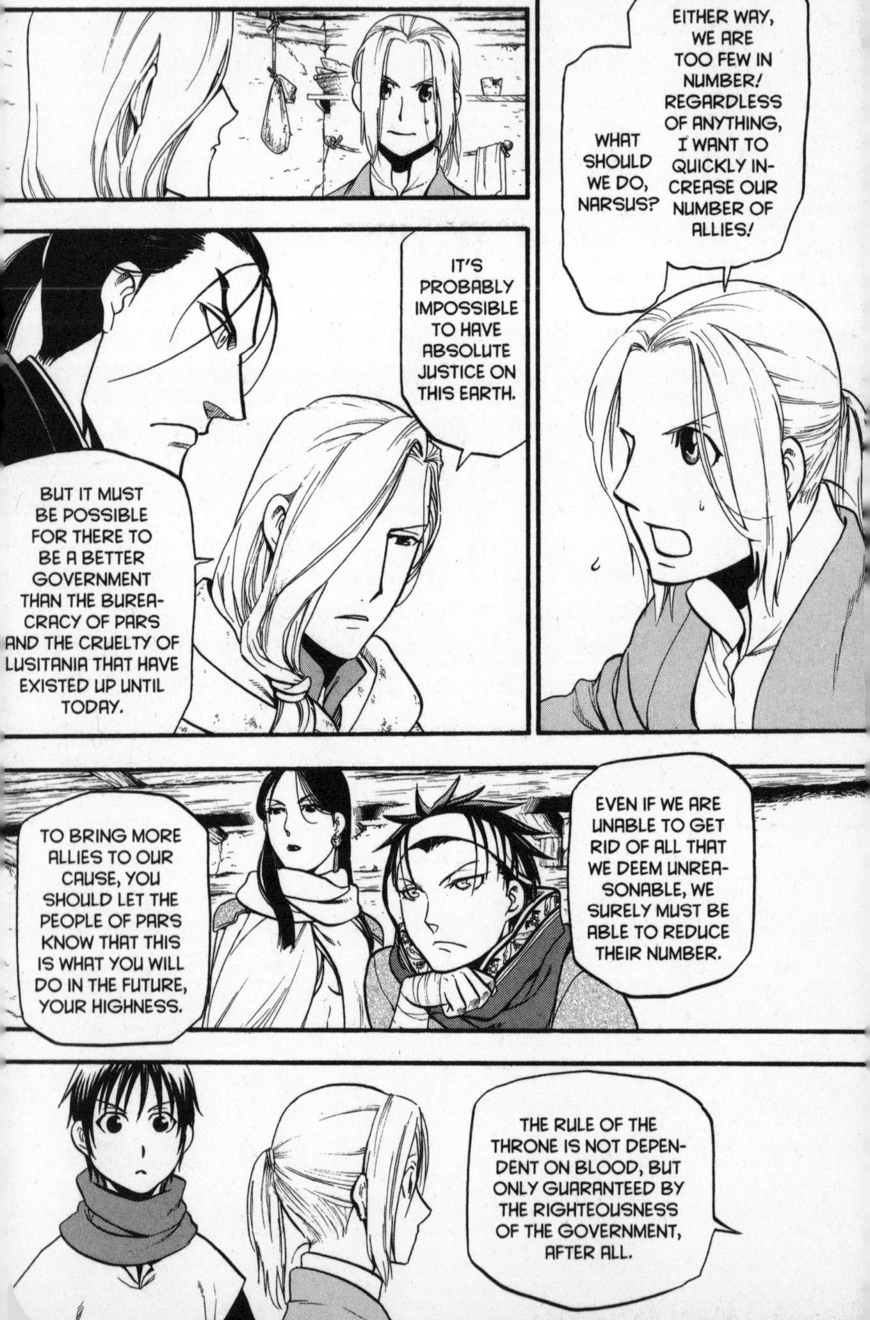
EITHER WAY, WE ARE TOO FEW IN NUMBER! REGARDLESS OF ANYTHING, I WANT TO QUICKLY INCREASE OUR NUMBER OF ALLIES!
WHAT SHOULD WE DO, NARSUS?
IT'S PROBABLY IMPOSSIBLE TO HAVE ABSOLUTE JUSTICE ON THIS EARTH.
BUT IT MUST BE POSSIBLE FOR THERE TO BE A BETTER GOVERNMENT THAN THE BUREACRACY OF PARS AND THE CRUELTY OF LUSITANIA THAT HAVE EXISTED UP UNTIL TODAY.
EVEN IF WE ARE UNABLE TO GET RID OF ALL THAT WE DEEM UNREASONABLE, WE SURELY MUST BE ABLE TO REDUCE THEIR NUMBER.
TO BRING MORE ALLIES TO OUR CAUSE, YOU SHOULD LET THE PEOPLE OF PARS KNOW THAT THIS IS WHAT YOU WILL DO IN THE FUTURE, YOUR HIGHNESS.
THE RULE OF THE THRONE IS NOT DEPENDENT ON BLOOD, BUT ONLY GUARANTEED BY THE RIGHTEOUSNESS OF THE GOVERNMENT, AFTER ALL.

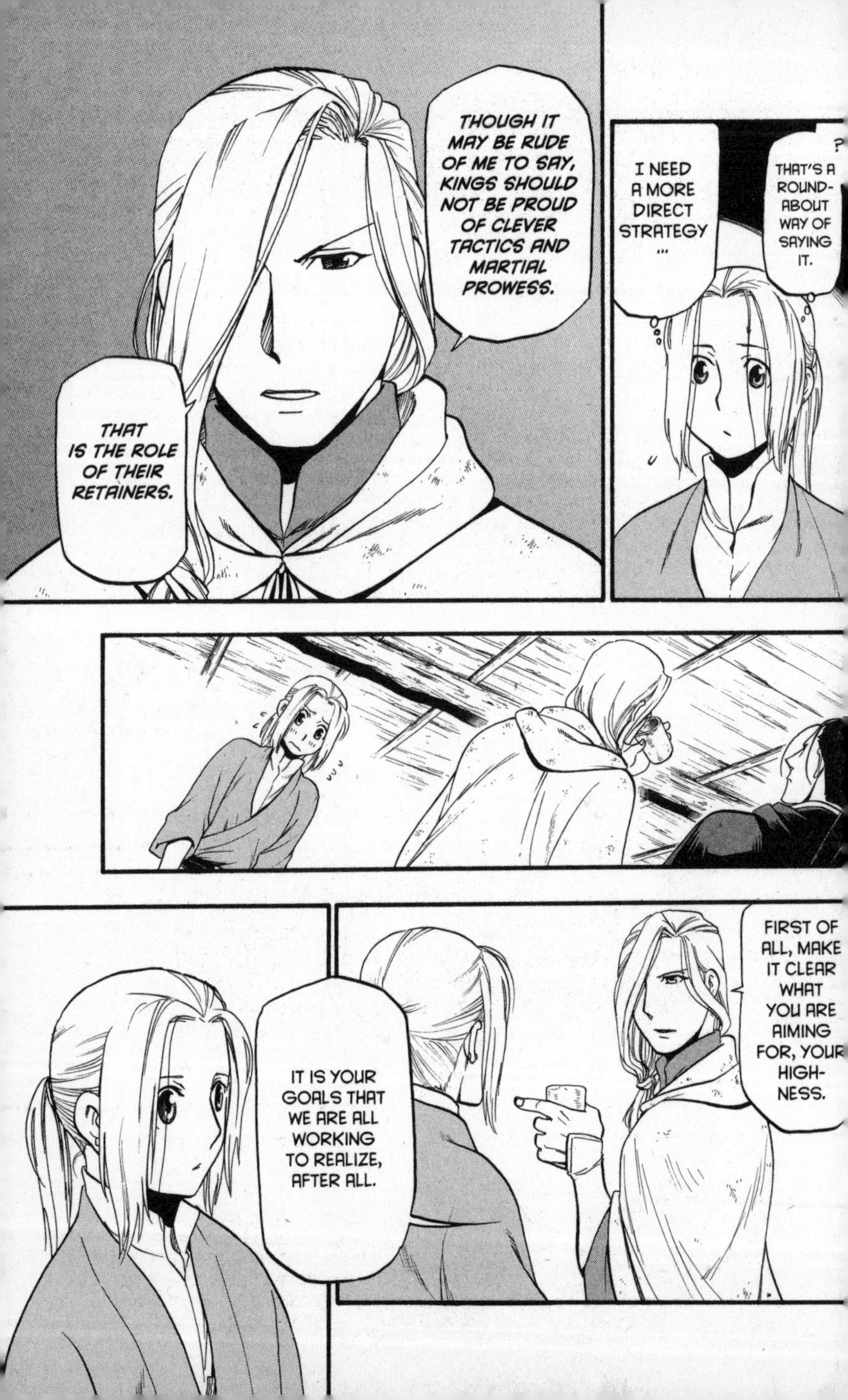
?
THAT'S A ROUND-ABOUT WAY OF SAYING IT.
I NEED A MORE DIRECT STRATEGY ...
THOUGH IT MAY BE RUDE OF ME TO SAY, KINGS SHOULD NOT BE PROUD OF CLEVER TACTICS AND MARTIAL PROWESS.
THAT IS THE ROLE OF THEIR RETAINERS.
FIRST OF ALL, MAKE IT CLEAR WHAT YOU ARE AIMING FOR, YOUR HIGH-NESS.
IT IS YOUR GOALS THAT WE ARE ALL WORKING TO REALIZE, AFTER ALL.

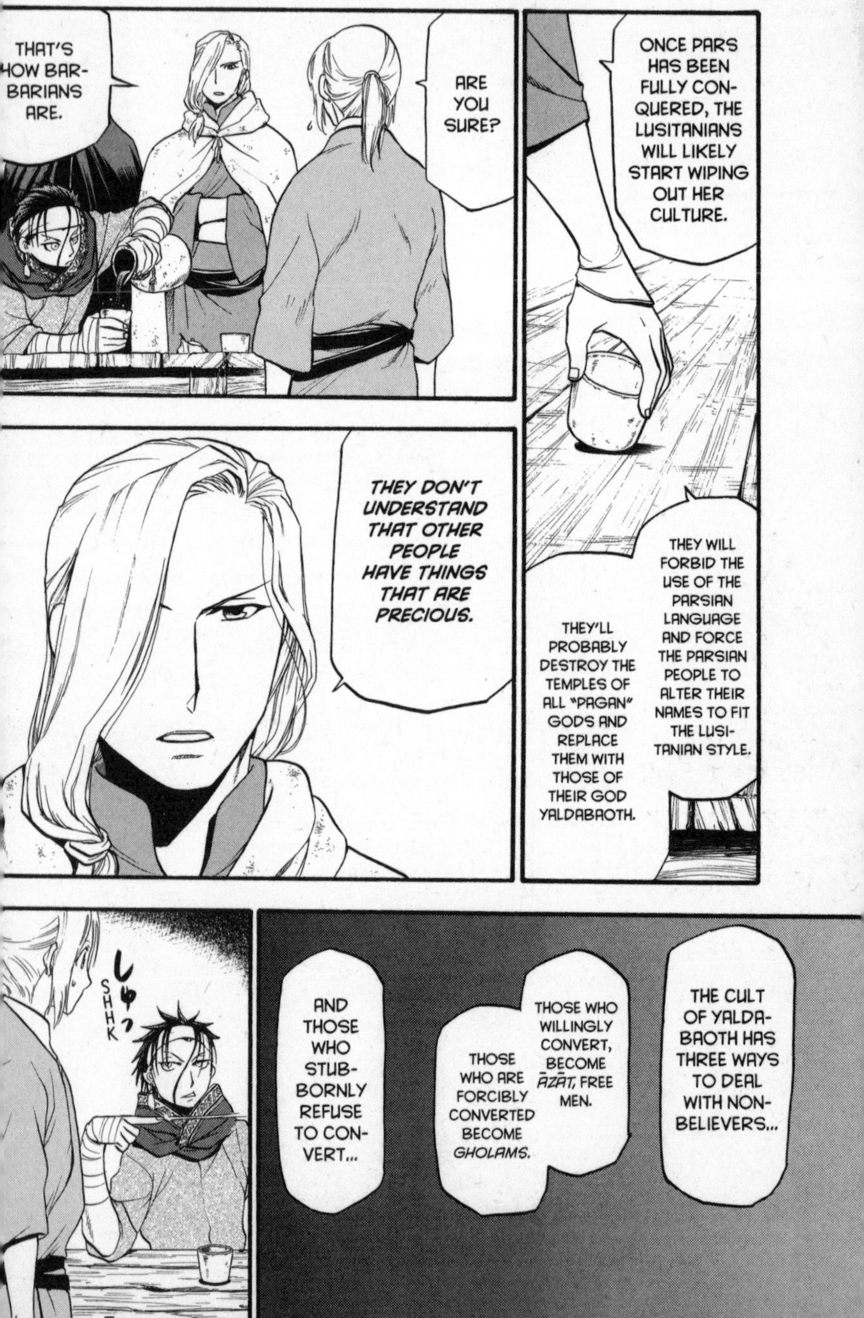
ONCE PARS HAS BEEN FULLY CONQUERED, THE LUSITANIANS WILL LIKELY START WIPING OUT HER CULTURE.
THEY WILL FORBID THE USE OF THE PARSIAN LANGUAGE AND FORCE THE PARSIAN PEOPLE TO ALTER THEIR NAMES TO FIT THE LUSITANIAN STYLE.
THEY'LL PROBABLY DESTROY THE TEMPLES OF ALL "PAGAN" GODS AND REPLACE THEM WITH THOSE OF THEIR GOD YALDABAOTH.
ARE YOU SURE?
THAT'S HOW BARBARIANS ARE.
THEY DON'T UNDERSTAND THAT OTHER PEOPLE HAVE THINGS THAT ARE PRECIOUS.
THE CULT OF YALDABAOTH HAS THREE WAYS TO DEAL WITH NON-BELIEVERS...
THOSE WHO WILLINGLY CONVERT, BECOME ĀZĀT, FREE MEN.
THOSE WHO ARE FORCIBLY CONVERTED BECOME GHOLAMS.
AND THOSE WHO STUBBORNLY REFUSE TO CONVERT...
しゅっ
SHHK

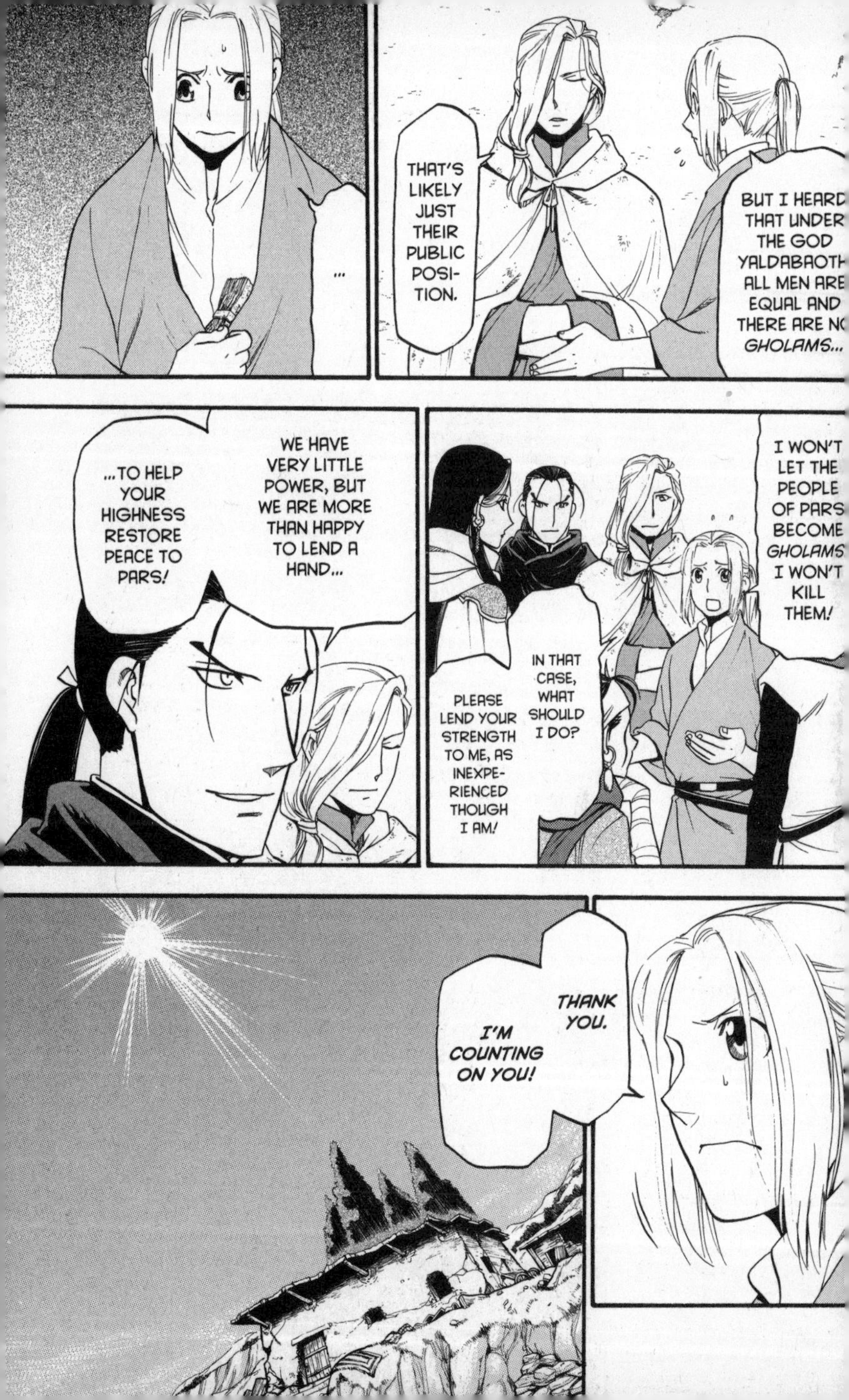
BUT I HEARD THAT UNDER THE GOD YALDABAOTH ALL MEN ARE EQUAL AND THERE ARE NO *GHOLAMS*...
THAT'S LIKELY JUST THEIR PUBLIC POSITION.
...
I WON'T LET THE PEOPLE OF PARS BECOME *GHOLAMS*. I WON'T KILL THEM!
IN THAT CASE, WHAT SHOULD I DO?
PLEASE LEND YOUR STRENGTH TO ME, AS INEXPERIENCED THOUGH I AM!
WE HAVE VERY LITTLE POWER, BUT WE ARE MORE THAN HAPPY TO LEND A HAND...
...TO HELP YOUR HIGHNESS RESTORE PEACE TO PARS!
THANK YOU.
I'M COUNTING ON YOU!

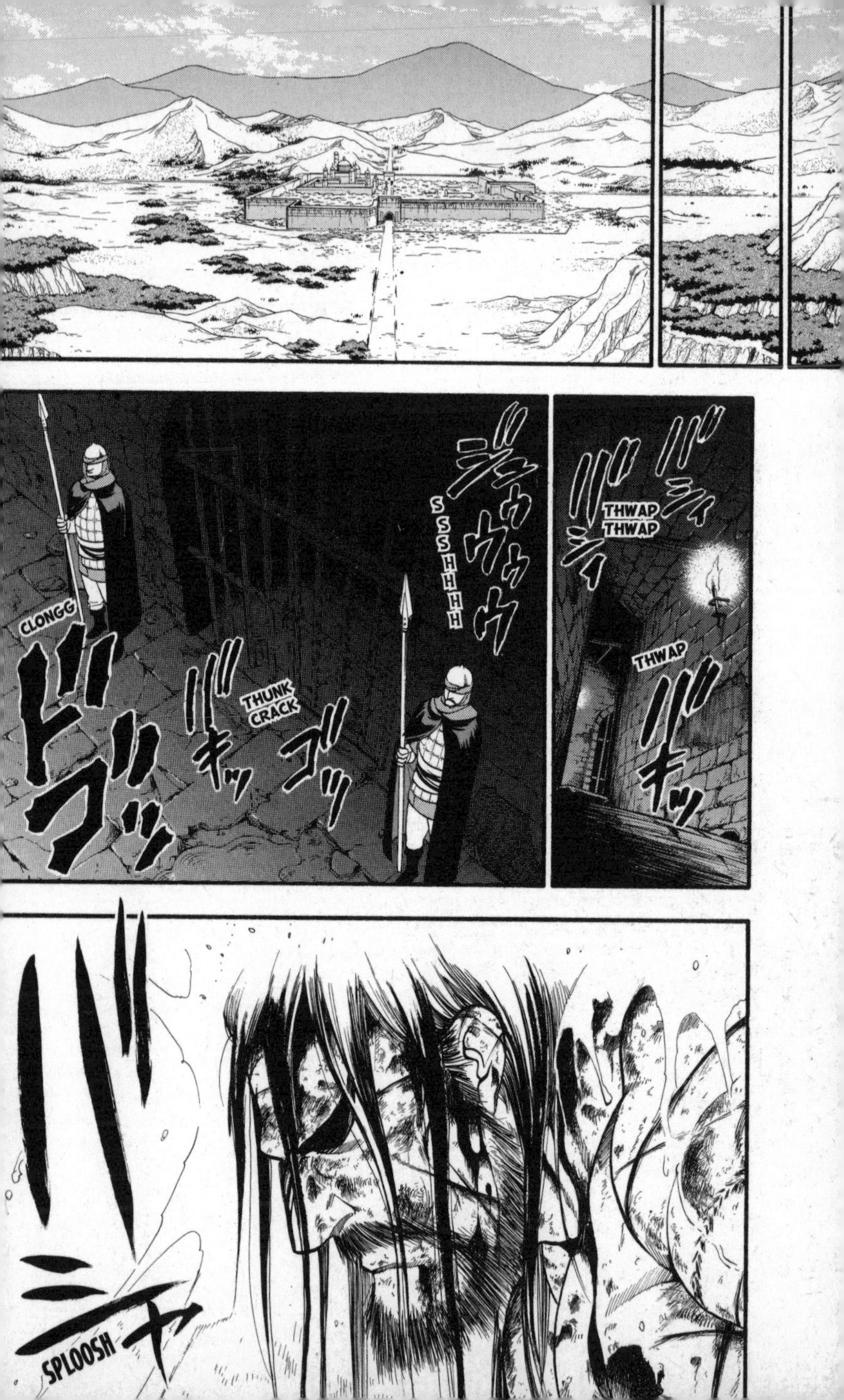
THWAP THWAP
THWAP
SSSHHHH
THUNK CRACK
CLONGG
SPLOOSH

TREAT HIM.

YES, SIR.

カツーーン KA-CLACK
カツーーン KA-CLACK
カツーーン KA-CLACK
カツーーン KA-CLACK

カツーーン KA-CLACK
カツーーン KA-CLACK
カツーーン KA-CLACK
カツーーン KA-CLACK

カツーーン KA-CLACK
カツーーン KA-CLACK
カツーーン KA-CLACK
カツーーン KA-CLACK

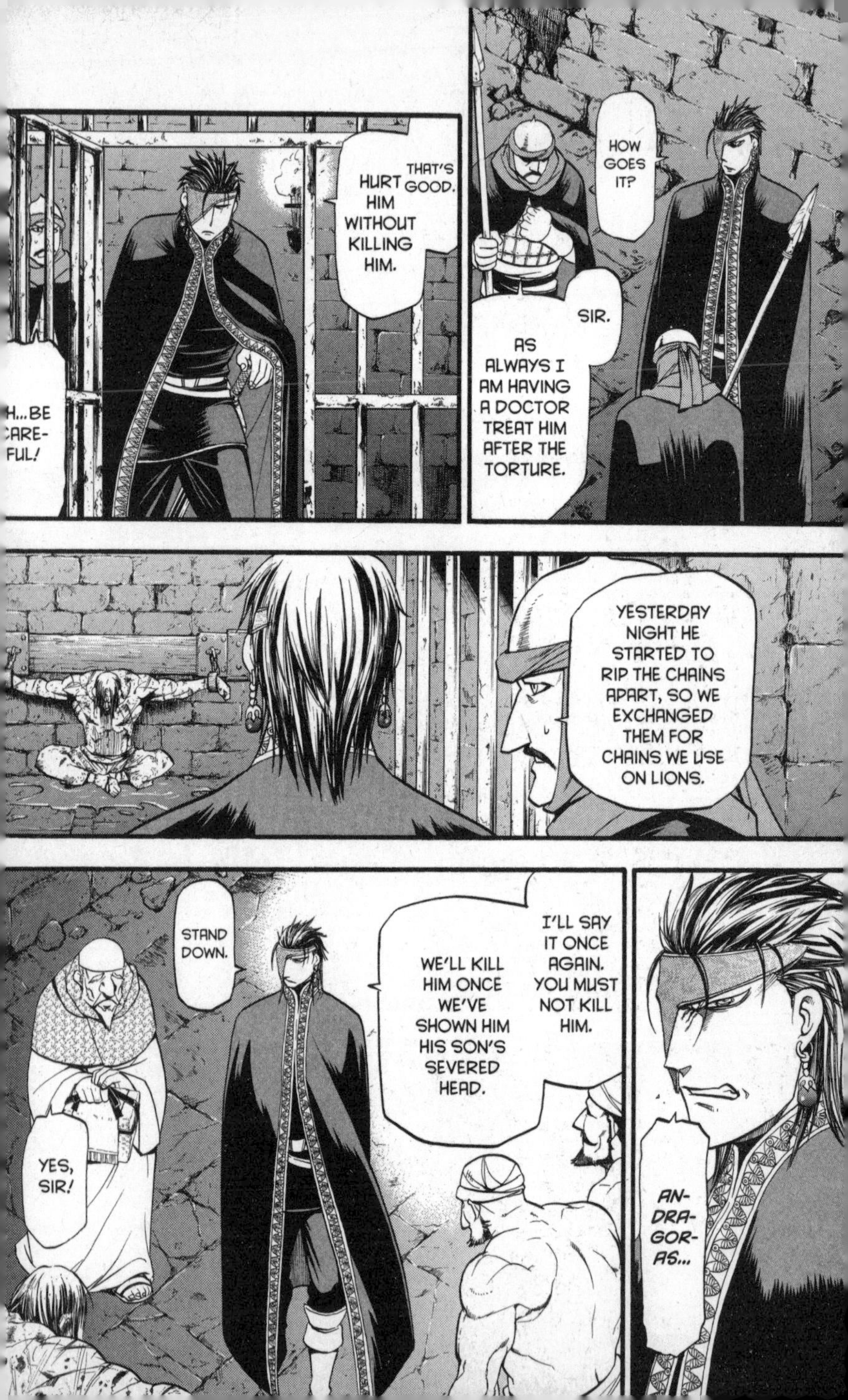
HOW GOES IT?
SIR.
AS ALWAYS I AM HAVING A DOCTOR TREAT HIM AFTER THE TORTURE.
THAT'S GOOD.
HURT HIM WITHOUT KILLING HIM.
H...BE CAREFUL!
YESTERDAY NIGHT HE STARTED TO RIP THE CHAINS APART, SO WE EXCHANGED THEM FOR CHAINS WE USE ON LIONS.
AN-DRA-GOR-AS...
I'LL SAY IT ONCE AGAIN. YOU MUST NOT KILL HIM.
WE'LL KILL HIM ONCE WE'VE SHOWN HIM HIS SON'S SEVERED HEAD.
STAND DOWN.
YES, SIR!

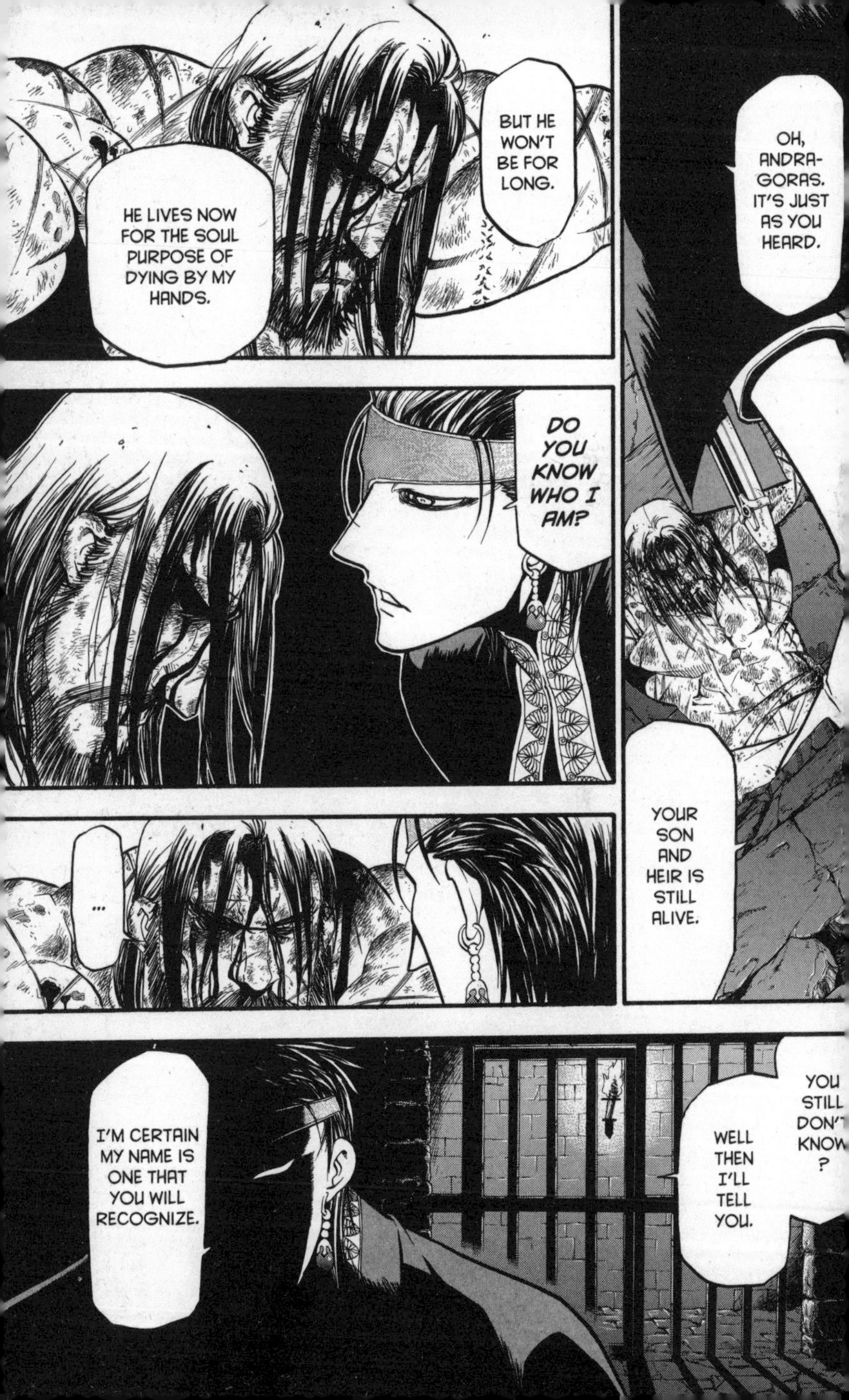
OH, ANDRAGORAS. IT'S JUST AS YOU HEARD.
YOUR SON AND HEIR IS STILL ALIVE.
BUT HE WON'T BE FOR LONG.
HE LIVES NOW FOR THE SOUL PURPOSE OF DYING BY MY HANDS.
DO YOU KNOW WHO I AM?
...
YOU STILL DON'T KNOW?
WELL THEN I'LL TELL YOU.
I'M CERTAIN MY NAME IS ONE THAT YOU WILL RECOGNIZE.

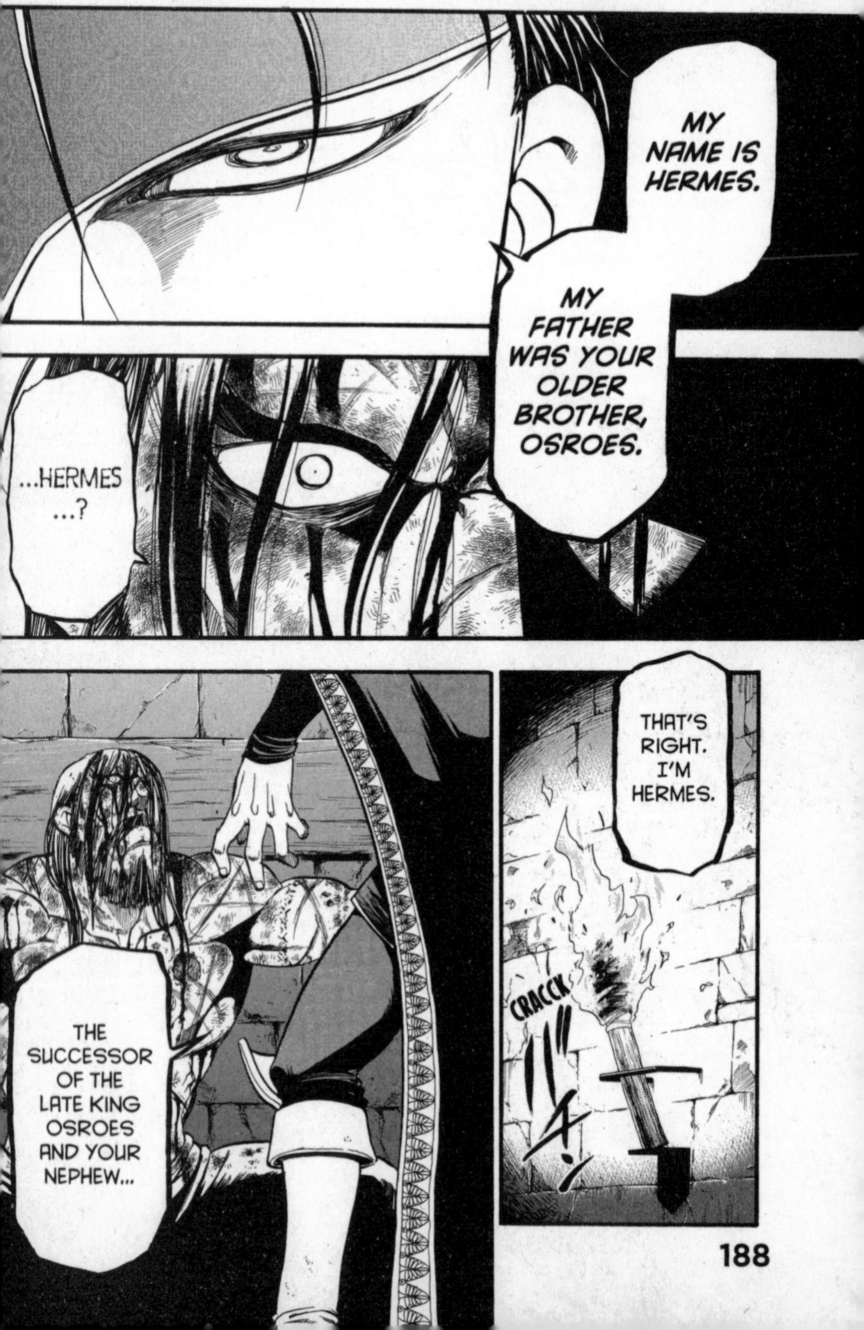
MY NAME IS HERMES.
MY FATHER WAS YOUR OLDER BROTHER, OSROES.
...HERMES ...?
THAT'S RIGHT. I'M HERMES.
CRACCK
THE SUCCESSOR OF THE LATE KING OSROES AND YOUR NEPHEW...

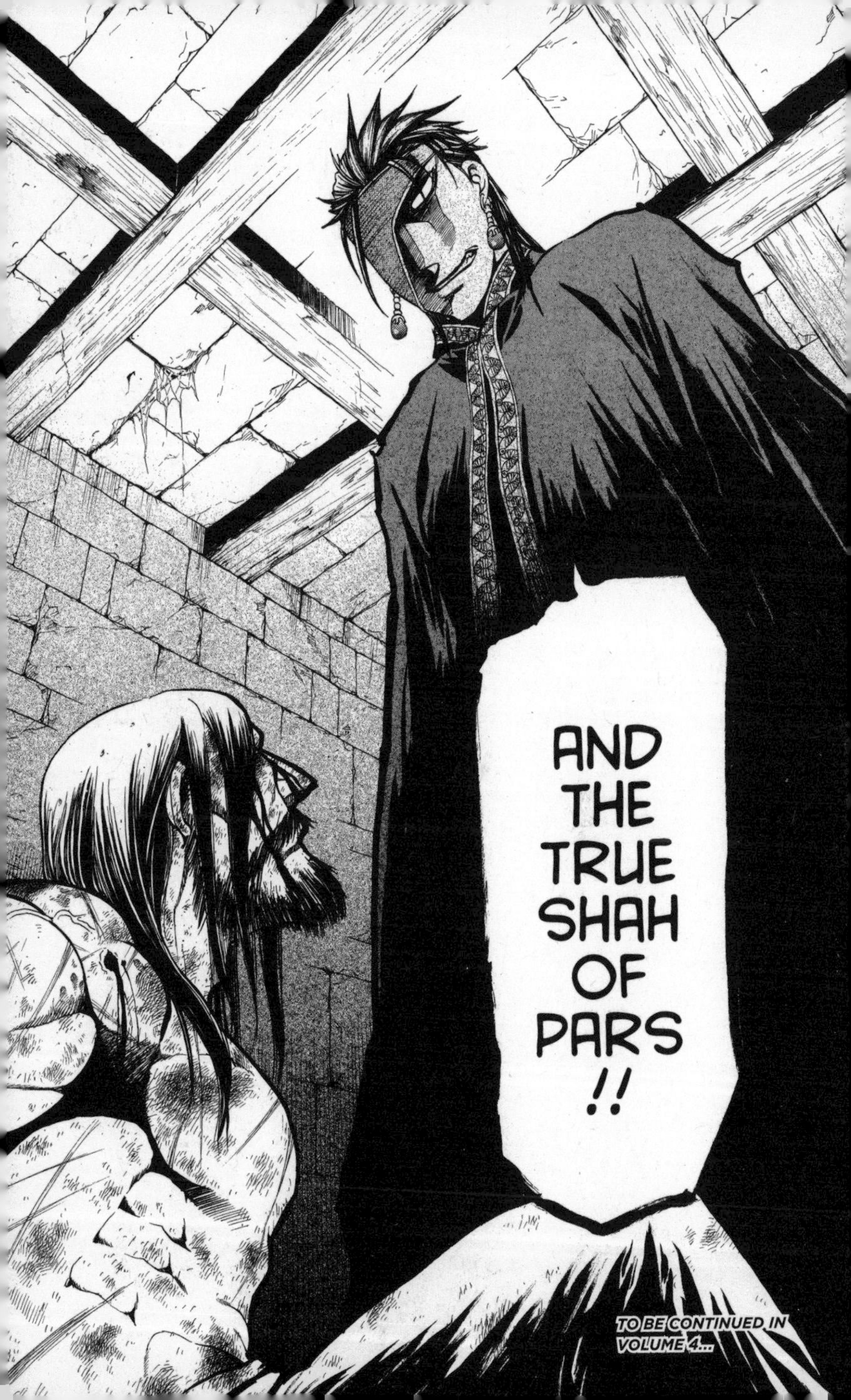
AND THE TRUE SHAH OF PARS!!
TO BE CONTINUED IN VOLUME 4...

- BONUS SKETCHES -

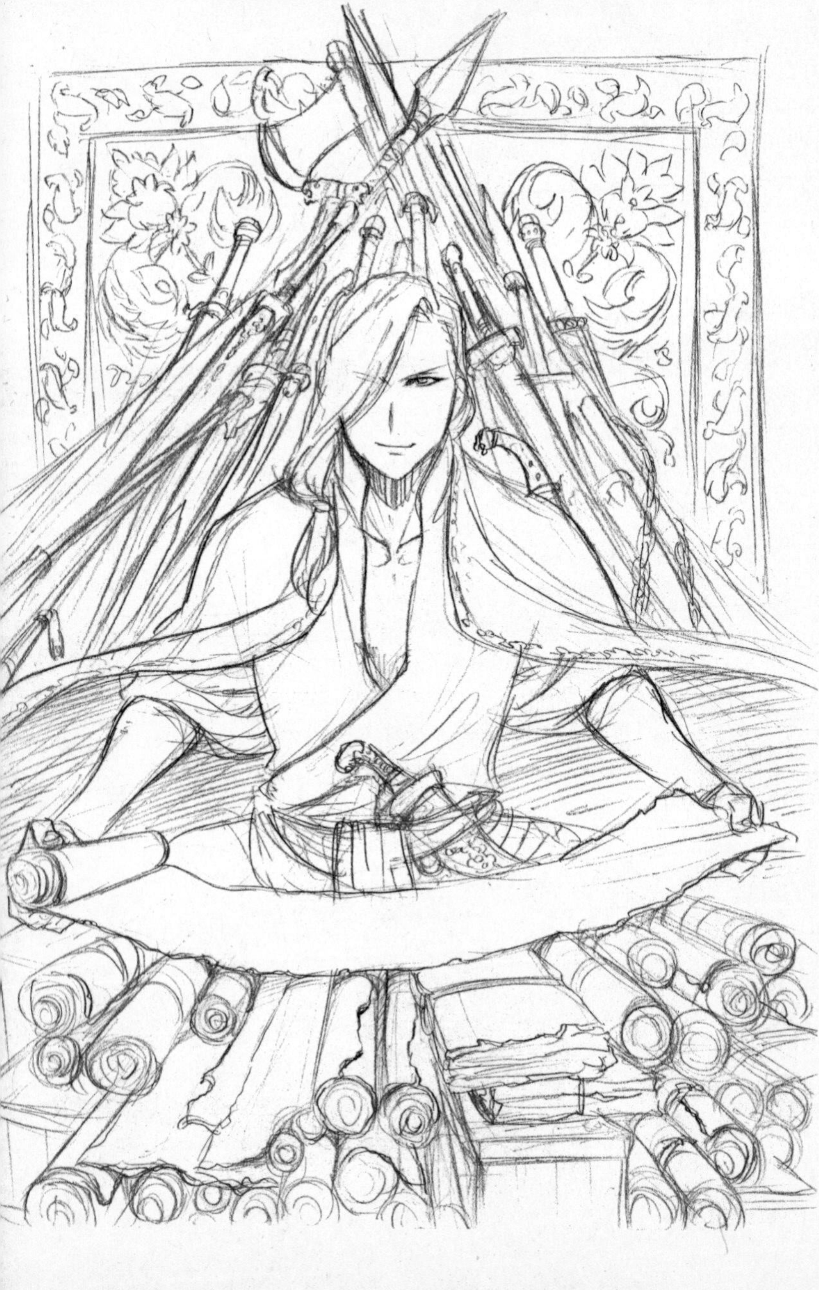

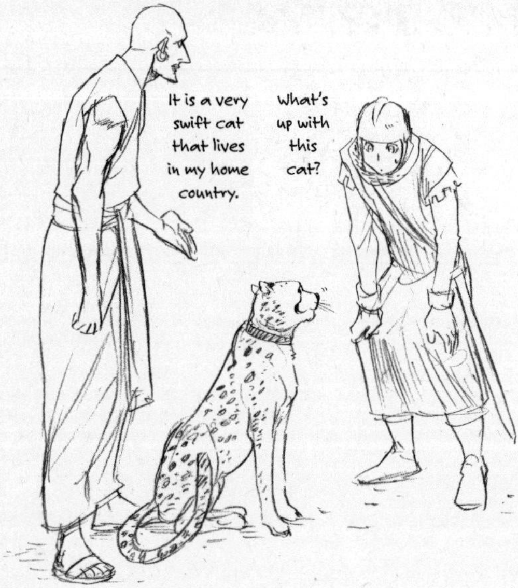
What's up with this cat?
It is a very swift cat that lives in my home country.

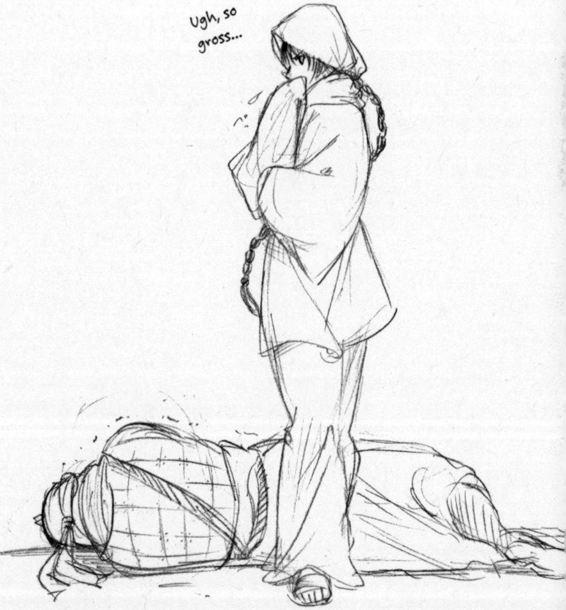
Ugh, so gross...

Tanaka, Yoshiki, 1952-
The heroic legend of
Arslan. 3 /
2015.
33305249479472
sa   05/11/21

The Heroic Legend of Arslan volume 3 is a work of fiction. Names, characters, places, and incidents are the products of the author's imagination or are used fictitiously. Any resemblance to actual events, locales, or persons, living or dead, is entirely coincidental.

A Kodansha Comics Trade Paperback Original.

The Heroic Legend of Arslan volume 3 copyright © 2015 Hiromu Arakawa & Yoshiki Tanaka
English translation copyright © 2015 Hiromu Arakawa & Yoshiki Tanaka

All rights reserved.

Published in the United States by Kodansha Comics, an imprint of Kodansha USA Publishing, LLC, New York.

Publication rights for this English edition arranged through Kodansha Ltd., Tokyo.

First published in Japan in 2015 by Kodansha Ltd., Tokyo, as *Arslan Senki* volume 3.

ISBN 978-1-61262-974-2

Printed in the United States of America.

www.kodanshacomics.com

9 8 7 6 5 4 3 2 1

Translator: Lindsey Akashi
Lettering: Erika Terriquez, Scott Brown, & April Brown
Editing: Ajani Oloye